Praise for *PHILIP & ELIZABETH*, 2004

GYLES BRANDRETH:

'The writer who got closest to the human truth about our long-serving senior royals' Libby Purves, *THE TIMES*

'*Philip & Elizabeth* boldly goes where other royal biographers have previously feared to tread . . . The book is exceptionally hard to put down' Humphrey Carpenter, *SUNDAY TIMES*

'Probably the most revealing portrait ever of the Queen' Marian Finucane, *RTE*

'The most insightful portrait of Prince Philip written to date' Robert Lacey, *SUNDAY TIMES*

'Wonderfully entertaining . . . impressive . . . compelling' John-Paul Flintoff, *FINANCIAL TIMES*

'Thoroughly entertaining . . . Filled with insights . . . He has had enviable access and he has used it well' Penny Junor, *DAILY TELEGRAPH*

'Cheeky, gossipy, often highly amusing . . . A most engagingly intimate volume' Peter Mackay, *EVENING STANDARD*

'A joy . . . thoughtful . . . outrageous . . . sympathetic, wholly original, often hilarious, occasionally profound and unfailingly interesting . . . I came away with the strong feeling that I had glimpsed the Queen and Prince Philip for the first time as they really are' Craig Brown, *MAIL ON SUNDAY*

'*Philip & Elizabeth* is a unique biography. It is a powerful and revealing portrait of a remarkable partnership, told with authority and insight, and illustrated with photographs from the couple's collections' Ingrid Seward, *MAJESTY*

Elizabeth

An intimate portrait

GYLES BRANDRETH

MICHAEL JOSEPH

PENGUIN MICHAEL JOSEPH

UK | USA | Canada | Ireland | Australia
India | New Zealand | South Africa

Penguin Michael Joseph is part of the Penguin Random House group of companies
whose addresses can be found at global.penguinrandomhouse.com

Penguin
Random House
UK

First published 2022

005

Copyright © Gyles Brandreth, 2022

The moral right of the author has been asserted

Set in Garamond MT

Typeset by Couper Street Type Co.

Printed in Great Britain by Clays Ltd, Elcograf S.p.A.

The authorized representative in the EEA is Penguin Random House Ireland,
Morrison Chambers, 32 Nassau Street, Dublin D02 YH68

A CIP catalogue record for this book is available from the British Library

HARDBACK ISBN: 978-0-241-58258-9
PAPERBACK ISBN: 978-0-241-63796-8

www.greenpenguin.co.uk

CONTENTS

PROLOGUE

September 2022

It is Tuesday 6 September 2022, seventy years and seven months – 25,780 days – since Elizabeth II became Queen.

I am sitting in the Royal Library at Windsor Castle – in the Elizabeth I gallery, the third of the three remarkable rooms that make up the library and house its many treasures, from Henry VIII's Bible to the First Folio of Shakespeare's plays that King Charles I read – and annotated – as he awaited his execution in January 1649.

As I begin this book, my account of Elizabeth II, planned for publication after her death, this beautiful library seems a fitting place to contemplate the mystery of monarchy and its peculiar and undiminished hold on the public imagination. For more than a thousand years, in Britain, our kings and queens have been central to our island story and, curiously, now, in the twenty-first century, when the sovereign is no longer an executive monarch and has no real 'power' to speak of, around the world there continues to be a fascination with the British royal family. Britain was once the centre of a global empire. No longer. Ours is only the twenty-first most populated country in the world with the sixth largest economy, but every survey shows that our monarch remains the most famous head of state on earth. Elizabeth II is a global figure – the longest-serving sovereign in our history and, at home and abroad, arguably the best-loved and most respected.

Windsor Castle is the oldest and largest inhabited castle in the world, originally built by William the Conqueror in the eleventh century, following the Norman invasion of England in 1066. It has been used by kings and queens since the time of Henry I, who reigned from 1100 to 1135. Elizabeth II often claimed it as her 'favourite' home.

This morning, to my right, through the window, in the late summer sunshine, beneath the castle ramparts, I can see two guardsmen marching between their sentry boxes in the courtyard below. To my left, on the table immediately in front of me, sits a small French Psalter – a little book of psalms – that belonged to Elizabeth I when she was a teenage girl, in the 1540s, before she became Queen. I have been leafing through it (with permission) and marvelling at the poem the young princess inscribed at the back of the book and signed 'Elizabeth' in a clear and elegant hand. With her brother Edward (the future Edward VI), Elizabeth (also a child of Henry VIII) was taught to write in the fine Italic script which had been developed during the early Renaissance period.

In 1547 the young Princess Elizabeth sent a painted portrait of herself to her brother, Edward, accompanied by a letter in which she described the portrait as 'the outward shadow of the body' and expressed a wish that her 'inward mind' could be more often in her brother's presence.

As I sit here, I realise that is my challenge with this book: to try to present to you the 'inward mind' of Elizabeth I's successor, Elizabeth II. You know the 'outward shadow': you know what our Queen looks like. Living so long, no one in the history of the world has been painted from life more often or been photographed more frequently than Elizabeth II. She has been depicted on stage and screen, in plays, in films, in television series, as a waxwork, as a puppet, even as an avatar. But what is she really like? Who is Elizabeth II? What is the nature of her 'inward mind'?

The Queen herself is not here today. She is at Balmoral – on duty, as ever. As I sit here at Windsor (at the invitation of HRH The Duchess of Cornwall, who will be the Queen Consort by the time you read this), Her Majesty is in the Drawing Room at Balmoral Castle in Aberdeenshire – her other 'favourite' home, a place with 'a special atmosphere all its own' she used to say, a royal residence since 1852 when Prince Albert bought the estate for Queen Victoria as a Scottish royal retreat.

Today, Victoria's great-great-granddaughter, Elizabeth II, wearing a tartan skirt and a lavender blouse and matching cardigan, carrying a favourite handbag on her left arm, steadying herself on one of her late husband's walking sticks, is awaiting the arrival of Boris Johnson MP, her fourteenth prime minister. He has come, with his wife Carrie, to tender his resignation to his sovereign. Shortly afterwards, Her Majesty is due to receive Liz Truss MP and her husband, Hugh O'Leary. Ms Truss, the Queen's fifteenth prime minister, another Elizabeth, was born in 1975. Sir Winston Churchill, her first, was born in 1874. From Churchill to Truss, from Truman to Trump, from Idi Amin to Vladimir Putin, the Queen has met them all. The broadcaster James Naughtie told me that once, when she was asked to name the person she had met in her life who she considered the most remarkable, she named Nelson Mandela, because, she explained, he had emerged from twenty-seven years of imprisonment 'without rancour'.

The Queen is a committed Christian who told me she repeated the Lord's Prayer on a daily basis – as my father used to do, saying his prayers on his knees at his bedside every night, as people of that generation did. 'Sometimes,' said the Queen, 'it's all you need':

3

Our Father, who art in heaven, hallowed be thy name; thy
kingdom come; thy will be done; on earth as it is in heaven.
Give us this day our daily bread. And forgive us our
trespasses, as we forgive those who trespass against us.
And lead us not into temptation; but deliver us from evil.
For thine is the kingdom, the power and the glory, for ever
and ever. Amen.

Elizabeth II believes in the power of prayer and in the
importance of forgiveness. She is a woman without rancour.
Her husband told me that her greatest quality was 'tolerance'.
'She is infinitely tolerant,' the Duke of Edinburgh said, 'and
forgiving.' Famously, in 2012, in an historic encounter at
Belfast's Lyric Theatre, the Queen shook hands with Martin
McGuinness, then Northern Ireland's Deputy First Minister,
but formerly an Irish Republican Army commander. She lost
a close relative, Lord Mountbatten of Burma, her husband's
uncle, to an IRA bomb in 1979.

The Queen believes, too, in the reality of redemption. She
looks for the good in people, not the bad. Here in the Royal
Library, across from where I am sitting, I can see a display of
the ribbons of the Order of the Garter, the order of chivalry
founded by Edward III in 1348, the most senior order of
knighthood in the British honours system, outranked in precedence only by the Victoria Cross and the George Cross. The
Order's motto is *Honi soit qui mal y pense* – 'Shame on him who
thinks evil of it'.

Elizabeth I's Psalter was given to the future Elizabeth II
as a wedding present in 1947. She cherished it and was, she
said, 'particularly struck' by the thought expressed in the short
verse the young princess inscribed at the back of the little
book four hundred years ago:

No crooked leg, no bleared eye,
No part deformed out of kind,
Nor yet so ugly half can be
As is the inward suspicious mind.

Honi soit qui mal y pense.

*

It is now 7 September – Elizabeth I's birthday, as it happens
– and I am back in London thinking about this book: my
attempt at a personal portrait of Elizabeth II. Every newspaper is carrying pictures of the Queen at Balmoral yesterday.
She appears old, yes, she is ninety-six, and frail – there is a
dark bruise mark on the back of her right hand – but she
looks alert and very much alive. She is smiling, looking over
the tops of her spectacles at the camera. There is a definite,
mischievous twinkle in her eye.

That said, suddenly, here in London, rumour is rife. It is
late in the afternoon and I have just had a call from my son-
in-law (a former Coldstream Guards officer) to say that he is
at the Cavalry and Guards Club in Piccadilly where groups are
gathering to discuss the detail of Operation London Bridge
– the codename for the action-plan that comes into being
the moment the sovereign dies. A newspaper editor has just
called my agent to ask what we've heard. What is happening?
The Queen was in good form twenty-four hours ago – and
busy, presenting her outgoing Communications Secretary with
an honour as well as spending time with her fourteenth and
fifteenth prime ministers and their partners. Boris Johnson
reported that she was in fine fettle, full of 'characteristic
humour and wisdom'.

Clive Cox, one of Her Majesty's favourite racehorse trainers, got a call from her at ten o'clock yesterday morning. She wanted to chat to him about the prospects for her two-year-old, Love Affairs, who was running in the two o'clock at Goodwood. 'We talked about the filly,' he said, 'how the race might pan out, how another horse of hers was doing in my stable, and about a couple of other things. She was sharp as a tack.'

Yesterday, clearly, she was very much alive. The royal family was not expecting this. Prince Charles has spent the day doing good works in Lanarkshire. Tonight, he is hosting a dinner at Dumfries House in Ayreshire. Edward and Sophie, the Earl and Countess of Wessex, are at events across Lancashire. Princess Anne, the Princess Royal, is visiting the Isle of Skye and the Isle of Ramsay. It's business as usual – except, it seems, it isn't.

*

Thursday 8 September 2022. Elizabeth II is dead. Rumour swirled all morning. At 12:32 p.m. Buckingham Palace issued a statement saying the Queen's doctors were concerned for her health and, though she was 'comfortable', recommended she remain under medical supervision while family members were informed. The Queen's helicopter left Windsor Castle at 6:48 a.m. to collect Prince Charles from Dumfries House where he had spent the night. He reached Balmoral at 10:27 a.m. Camilla had spent the night at Birkhall on the Balmoral Estate and was driven by car to join him. The Princess Royal was already there – at her mother's side to the end. Andrew and Edward, the Queen's younger sons, and Sophie, Edward's wife, and Prince William and Prince Harry were reported to be on their way. There was confusion about whether or not

Harry's wife, Meghan, would go up to Scotland with him. When it became clear that Catherine was not going because she would be collecting her children from school, it emerged that Meghan was not going, either.

Andrew, Edward and Sophie, and Prince William arrived at Aberdeen airport in an RAF executive jet at 3:50 p.m. and William drove the four of them to Balmoral, forty-five miles away. They arrived at 5:06 p.m. The Queen was already dead. The formal announcement of her death came from Buckingham Palace at 6:30 p.m. while Prince Harry was still in the air. His flight from Luton airport to Aberdeen was delayed. He was the last of the family to arrive at Balmoral, and the first to leave.

I have spent the evening in different BBC studios contributing to the coverage of the Queen's death – alongside every royal correspondent, royal biographer, commentator and relevant public figure you can imagine. We all tried to say the right things, many with a catch in our voices and tears in our eyes. I thought Nicholas Soames, grandson of Sir Winston, and Stephen Cottrell, the Archbishop of York, were particularly good – one emphasising the Queen's ability to take the long view, 'having met everybody and seen it all', and the other underlining the centrality of her faith to her life and explaining that her personal modesty and 'lack of self' came from her consciousness that, while she was a queen to whom others bowed and curtsied, she would 'always bend the knee to one greater than any, Almighty God.'

Travelling to the studio in the early evening I saw a double rainbow in the sky above Buckingham Palace. And I found out from a friend in the racing world that the Queen's horse, Love Affairs, comfortably won the two o'clock at Goodwood on Tuesday: 'led field centre, made all, ridden and stayed on gamely final furlong, unchallenged.'

Friday 9 September 2022. I am writing this in my notebook standing outside the gates of Buckingham Palace. It is early in the morning, cold and damp, but already there are hundreds of people here – soon there will be thousands. They are people of all ages from many countries: some have brought flowers and flags and home-made condolence cards. There are parents who have brought children here and, interestingly, more young people and middle-aged people than, as I had expected, people of my vintage. And though there are so many here, crowding around the gates and beginning to fill the Mall, it is very quiet. Some people are crying. Several have said to me, 'I can't believe she's gone, she's been part of my life for as long as I can remember.' Some mention their love and admiration for her: all mention their respect.

Later.

In parliament today, the new prime minister and former prime ministers, and politicians of every stripe, are paying tribute to the Queen – 'Elizabeth the Great', as Boris Johnson describes her in probably the most eloquent speech of the day. President Macron of France is eloquent, too – speaking in English of his and his country's deep admiration and affection for the Queen, who visited France often, who spoke French well and who, when she was young, had got to know the great General de Gaulle, who led the Free French from London during the Second World War. The leaders of the world are united in their praise for Queen Elizabeth II. Even Vladimir Putin has put in a good word for her.

Social media is swamped with pictures and tributes. Alongside my favourite photograph of her, taken by Cecil Beaton when she was a girl in the 1940s, I posted my own:

Driven by duty, sustained by faith, made happy by her love for her dogs & horses. A remarkable human being, kind, considerate, consistent, instinctively generous & forgiving. She was the best & brought out the best in others. A wonderful example to us all. May she rest in peace.

Later still.

Back in a BBC studio I took part in a programme about the succession, alongside Tony Blair (an admirer of Prince Charles) and the actor David Oyelowo (a grateful beneficiary of the Prince's Trust), whose family came originally from Nigeria, and who Charles saw play the title role in Shakespeare's *Henry VI* – one of the new King's favourite plays. The Prince once asked me, 'How on earth did Shakespeare manage it? I *am* Prince of Wales. Shakespeare wasn't, but he knew exactly what it's like. *Exactly*. How did he do it?'

We all agreed that the new King's speech this evening – his first televised broadcast as sovereign – was pitch-perfect: his praise of his mother and of her example, his renewal of her vow of lifelong service, his commitment to the principles of constitutional monarchy, his announcement that he is today making William Prince of Wales, and his expression of his 'love for Harry and Meghan as they continue to build their lives overseas.'

He spoke from the Blue Drawing Room at Buckingham Palace, a room sometimes used by the Queen for her Christmas messages. To one side of him there was a framed photograph of his mother, to the other, in a small vase at the base of which were three little corgis, a posy of sweet peas and rosemary – 'There's rosemary, that's for remembrance,' as Ophelia says in *Hamlet*. There was another quotation from *Hamlet* at the end of the King's speech, too: 'And to my darling Mama, as you begin your last great journey to join my dear late Papa, I want simply to say this: thank you. Thank you for your love and devotion to our family and to the family of nations you have served so diligently all these years. May "flights of Angels sing thee to thy rest".'

Watching the King's speech, I smiled and thought, 'We're going to get more Shakespeare and fewer horses during this reign.' More seriously, I also thought the new King rose to the occasion completely.

*

Saturday 10 September 2022. It's official. At 10:00 a.m. this morning at St James's Palace, in a form of ceremony dating back centuries, and to a fanfare of trumpets, Charles III was proclaimed King at a meeting of the Accession Council of privy counsellors. The new King, with Camilla, his Queen Consort, and his heir, William, the new Prince of Wales, at his side, swore, with the help of God, to dedicate 'what remains to me of my life' to 'carrying out the heavy task that has been laid upon me.'

He will do it well. I know him and admire him – and like him. He is a good man with a good heart. Sometimes in the past he seemed to walk about with an invisible rain cloud hovering over his head. Not so now. He is equal to this moment and you can see it straight away – in his bearing, in his tone of voice, in his turn of phrase. He will be a fine king and will fulfil his destiny in his own way – which inevitably, because of her example and the length of her reign, will be largely her way. Elizabeth II casts a long shadow.

That is why I am writing this. I want to understand this remarkable woman; I want to know what made her the extraordinary person she was.

I was born in 1948 – the same year as Charles III. The Queen has been part of my life for as long as I can remember. I know that I first became aware of the idea of 'death' when the Queen's grandmother, Queen Mary, died in March 1953. I had just turned five and my parents did their best to explain the newspaper headlines to me. I remember the Coronation in June 1953, sitting on my father's shoulders, somewhere along the Mall, trying to watch the procession through a toy periscope made of cardboard and tin mirrors. Like so many families in Britain, we got our first television set to watch the Coronation. (We didn't buy the television: we hired it by the month from a company called Radio Rentals.)

I first became aware of the Duke of Edinburgh when I was a small boy in the 1950s because my mother supported the charity the Queen's father, then the Duke of York, had founded in the 1920s and that the Duke of Edinburgh became President of in 1948: the National Playing Fields Association. Every year my mother bought the NPFA calendar, and it hung on a cupboard door in the kitchen. She used it to record family appointments – swimming lessons, outings, visits to the dentist – so we consulted it every day. Each month the calendar featured a different photograph of the Queen's handsome young husband – playing cricket or polo, kicking a football around a playground or racing in a yacht off the Isle of Wight.

I remember seeing lots in the newspapers in the 1950s about the Queen's sister, Princess Margaret, and her 'friend', Peter Townsend. I don't think I understood quite what the fuss was about. I certainly understood later that when the Queen's sister married the photographer Antony Armstrong-Jones in 1960, it meant we got a day off school. Later still, I got to know Tony Snowdon quite well. He was a brilliant photographer and a great charmer: I would not have wanted to be married to him, but for several years we were proper friends.

My parents talked a good deal about the royals. Among their best friends were Mary and John Paice (my godfather), and their son, Peter Paice, happened to be 'Guardian', or Head Boy, at Gordonstoun when Prince Charles arrived at the school in 1962, so we heard at first-hand about how the young prince was settling in – or, rather, wasn't. My father was a solicitor, legal adviser to the Automobile Association, of which the Duke of Edinburgh was President. Occasionally, when the Duke was alleged to have driven his car too fast or parked it where he shouldn't, my father would be summoned to Buckingham Palace to meet with the Duke and his private secretary. Once, my father took me to the Palace with him. I don't remember much about it, beyond the distinctive scrunching sound our feet made as we walked across the gravel from the right-hand gates of the Palace to what's known as the Privy Purse door.

I first met the Queen on 2 May 1968, when I was a student at Oxford and she came to visit the university debating society, the Oxford Union. When she'd gone, I reprimanded William Waldegrave (the Union President, now Baron Waldegrave of North Hill and Provost of Eton) for not carrying Her Majesty's umbrella for her as he escorted her across the court-yard in the rain. He told me, 'The Queen insists on holding her own umbrella – always. If someone else holds it, the rain trickles down her neck.'

Years later, I asked the Queen if she remembered that Oxford visit. She did, she said, because Harold Macmillan (her third prime minister) was the University Chancellor at the time, and she recalled giving him a lift back to London in the royal train at the end of the day. She remembered the wonderful stories Macmillan told. Recently (on 12 July 2022 – I can be precise about dates because I keep a diary), Susan

Hussey told me she remembered that visit to Oxford, too. She was one of William Waldegrave's older sisters and was 'in waiting' to the Queen that day. Now Baroness Hussey of North Bradley GCVO (she married Marmaduke Hussey, later chairman of the Board of Governors of the BBC, when she was nineteen), she served as a Woman of the Bedchamber to Her Majesty over many years. From her 'boss', she received the Royal Household Long and Faithful Service medal (a civil decoration established by Queen Victoria) with 30-, 40-, 50- and 60-year bars. She is a godmother to Prince William and accompanied the Queen to Prince Philip's funeral in 2021. She is also the mother-in-law of Sir Francis Brooke, baronet and racing man and the Queen's representative at Ascot, and grandmother to Olivia Brooke, who happened to be the production assistant looking after me and Dame Sheila Hancock (and treating us like royalty!) when we made two television series together on England's canals in 2020 and 2021.

I have been lucky to know these people – and, over the years, other ladies-in-waiting to the Queen, courtiers and private secretaries, personal friends and members of her staff – but, in my experience, the closer they were to Her Majesty the more discreet they were. Knowing and talking with them will, I hope, have informed this portrait, and made it more intimate, but none of them is guilty of betraying any confidences.

I first met Prince Philip in the 1970s, when he was in his fifties and I was in my twenties, and I became involved in the work of the National Playing Fields Association. It is a good cause (protecting and enhancing recreational space, sports fields and playgrounds), if a touch unglamorous. Prince Philip, as a young Duke of Edinburgh, took on the presidency of NPFA (now known as Fields in Trust) in 1948, soon after he married Princess Elizabeth. It was the first national charity in which he became involved. He remained its president until the week of his ninety-second birthday in June 2013, when he handed over the reins to his grandson, Prince William. The Duke was unwell on hand-over day (13 June), but the Queen came with Prince William and Catherine. (I was there, too, of course, introducing the proceedings – and making notes. 'People who write books ought to be shut up,' said King George V. Perhaps he was right.)

As the President of the NPFA Prince Philip was impressive: informed, committed, personally involved. He took the responsibilities of his office seriously. He was an effective fund-raiser. 'The fund-raising never stops!' he used to sigh. He was an intelligent and persuasive leader, with an unnerving eye for detail (and for flannel and flimflam), who was at his best when given a problem to solve, a difficult meeting to chair, an internal row requiring resolution. He liked to be given something specific to do. He welcomed detail. I accompanied him to the opening of a youth centre on Merseyside. His debriefing note to me was devoted to how best to relocate the lavatories and showers so as to maximise the space available for the sports facilities. 'Yes,' he said, 'I am practical. I like to help make things work.' He wanted to make a difference where others, often, only make a noise. He wasn't one for honeyed words and empty gestures. He did not give his wife bunches of flowers or cards inscribed with sentimental messages: he gave her pieces of jewellery he had designed and made himself.

I liked his style. I admired his achievement. Until this week I thought he was irreplaceable. I was wrong. Seeing King Charles III and his Queen Consort travelling to the four corners of the United Kingdom this week, watching them together every step of the way through the difficult, tense and crowded days since the Queen died, I see my old boss (and hero) reborn – in Camilla.

If we regard the remarkable reign of Elizabeth II as a success (and I imagine you are reading this book because you do), the joint author of that success was Prince Philip. A quarter of a century from now, when people look back on Charles III's reign, if it proves to work out as sure-footedly as it has begun, the co-author of that success will be Camilla – the Prince of Wales's wife of seventeen years, his 'non-negotiable' partner, whose value to him and whose worth as a person were both so clearly recognised by Elizabeth II that in her Platinum Jubilee message the Queen declared her 'sincere wish' that her daughter-in-law become Queen Consort. Elizabeth II was a wise woman. She knew what she was doing and, as ever, she got it right.

Famously, the Queen described Prince Philip as her 'strength and stay'. That's exactly what Camilla is to Charles. She is fundamental to the architecture of his life. She is his good companion and best friend and, now that his children have left home (one has even left the country), she is the only person in the entire world with whom he can be completely free and open. He could confide in his grandmother (and did absolutely) and in his mother (the soul of discretion), but they are both gone now. Camilla is his strength and stay, the ally who knows him better than anyone and, now that he's King, the only person who can still treat him as an equal.

I have watched them at close quarters – at Highgrove (before they were married and since), at Clarence House, at Buckingham Palace. He adores her, clearly. In small-talk, he mentions 'my darling wife' in almost every sentence. She looks at him with a kindly eye, amused and aware of his foibles. When he gets tetchy (because the pen doesn't work, as it didn't when he was signing a document at Hillsborough Castle in County Down this week, or the inkwell is in the wrong place, as it was at the meeting of the Accession Council in St James's Palace on Saturday) she soothes him, putting out a hand and kneading him gently in the small of his back. When he is running late or talking too much, she tugs discreetly at the back of his jacket – sometimes quite vigorously.

Like Prince Philip, Camilla has accepted her destiny. She did not seek it. She has never wanted a place centre stage. Prince Philip always knew he was the support act not the star attraction. In more than seventy years as the Queen's consort, he never over-reached himself. He always made sure he walked one step behind Her Majesty. Watch closely and you will see Camilla does exactly the same.

In July 2022, not two months before the Queen's death, along with the actress Dame Joanna Lumley, I hosted a happy lunch to mark Camilla's 75th birthday. The guests were all friends and admirers, theatrical knights and dames, sports personalities and Chelsea Pensioners, Twiggy, Michael Palin and Andrew Lloyd-Webber – the usual suspects. The Duchess of Cornwall (as she then was) made a speech worthy of the Duke of Edinburgh. She talked about the year she was born, 1947, adding, 'by the way, a vintage year for claret'. It was also, she told us, 'the year when the first of the Ealing Comedies was released, the school leaving age was raised to fifteen, *Gardeners' Question Time* was first broadcast, the University of Cambridge admitted women to full membership and soft loo paper went on sale for the first time, in Harrods – much to the nation's relief.'

We laughed and then a hush fell as, deliberately, she paused before saying, 'It was also in 1947 that the then Princess Elizabeth married Lieutenant Philip Mountbatten – two of the most remarkable people in our country's history.'

Then, looking over the top of her glasses, she nailed her colours to the mast: 'The Duke of Edinburgh's philosophy was clear,' she declared, "'Look up and look out, say less, do more – and get on with the job." And that is just what I intend to do.' And that is exactly what she has been doing this week and will continue to do in the months and years ahead.

I first met Camilla when we were both teenagers in the 1960s and I was at a boarding school in Hampshire and visited her grandparents at their rather grand manor house, Hall Place, nearby. About ten years ago, on the BBC radio comedy programme *Just a Minute*, out of the blue I was given the subject 'My Secret Crush' to talk about. Suddenly, spontaneously, for sixty seconds, I found myself talking about Camilla and that first teenage encounter in 1964. I conjured up a picture of the future Queen Consort in her riding jodhpurs in her grandparents' garden, hiding in the shrubbery smoking Woodbines.

Of course, it never occurred to me that Her Majesty (as she now is) might be listening. It turns out that *Just a Minute* is one of her favourite programmes and a few days after the broadcast she happened to bump into my wife – at a flower show for the Queen's Diamond Jubilee at our local church – and said to her, 'Tell Gyles I don't deny I was smoking, but it definitely wasn't Woodbines. I deny the Woodbines absolutely!'

She doesn't deny that she was a naughty girl at times. She remembers her (quite strict) grandmother with affection and happy holidays at Hall Place, with her much-loved younger sister, Annabel, rolling down the Hampshire hills, catching butterflies, making mischief. Annabel remembers that her beloved teddy bear was once buried in the garden by Camilla, who only owned up to it decades later. Says Camilla, 'Yes, Tiddy Bar – he had a very happy resting ground.' 'I've not forgiven her,' insists Annabel, 'it still rankles to this day!'

King Charles III listens to *Just a Minute*, too. In fact, he told me he used to leave voicemail messages for William and Harry in the style of *Just a Minute*, doing his best to say what he had to say in under sixty seconds, without hesitation, deviation or repetition.

Charles and Camilla share a sense of humour and they share a love of poetry, literature and theatre, too. And a love of gardening and the countryside. In some ways, they have more in common than did the Queen and Prince Philip, who had separate hobbies and enthusiasms. Prince Philip found his wife's corgis infuriating and did not share her passion for horse racing. At Royal Ascot he would do his duty, accompanying the Queen along the course in her open carriage, but once they were there, he would either race back to Windsor Castle by car or disappear into a room at the back of the Royal Box to watch the cricket. Camilla endeared herself to the Queen by sharing her love of dogs and racing.

Like Prince Philip, the Queen Consort runs a busy diary with a very lean team. She has a handful of younger women running her office and a small group of girlfriends of her own age who can serve her now as ladies-in-waiting – not, I think, that she will have official 'ladies-in-waiting': that is not her style. She brought three of them to her birthday lunch and they were fun and funny like her. Her son, Tom Parker Bowles, and his daughter, Lola, came to the party, too, as a surprise, bringing in the birthday cake. The Queen Consort is close to Tom and his sister, Laura, and to her five grand-children, but very much like Prince Philip, knows she has to leave the next generation to do their own thing. As the Duke of Edinburgh said to me of his offspring, 'You've just got to let them get on with it. I try to keep out of these things.' I have seen the Queen Consort's grandchildren with Charles at Clarence House, jumping up and ragging him. He obviously loves them. I have also seen the lovely photograph of Harry and Meghan that has pride of place in the Clarence House drawing room.

Like Prince Philip, Camilla also has her own bolt-hole. Just as the Duke of Edinburgh would escape on his own to his own 'cottage', Wood Farm, an unpretentious farmhouse close by the sea on the Sandringham Estate, two miles from the 'big house', Camilla still has her own private home, Ray Mill House in Wiltshire, a fifteen-minute drive away from Highgrove. She can disappear there and simply be herself.

Like Prince Philip, she is very familiar with court life, but far from wedded to it. Philip was an outsider (a prince of Greece) when he married Princess Elizabeth in 1947, but he had royal blood in his veins stretching back generations. Camilla was also an outsider with her own royal connections, descended from, among others, Arnold Joost van Keppel, 1st Earl of Albemarle, a favourite (and possibly a lover) of William III, and Charles Lennox, 1st Duke of Richmond, one of the illegitimate sons of Charles II by his French mistress, Louise, who became the Duchess of Portsmouth.

Famously, of course, Camilla is the great-granddaughter of Alice Keppel, the last love of our new King's great-great-grandfather, Edward VII. 'A lively crowd, eh?' she said to me of her family once, laughing. It was at one of the drinks parties I give to mark the birthday of the Victorian playwright, Oscar Wilde. For a while, Camilla's great-grandfather, Alec Shand, was engaged to a girl called Constance Lloyd, who went on to marry Oscar Wilde. It was at that party that I introduced the future Queen Consort to Baga Chipz, one of the stars of *Ru Paul's Drag Race*, and to April Ashley, one of the first British people known to have gender reassignment surgery at the beginning of the 1960s. They got on like a house on fire. Camilla is brilliant with people. It's always all about them. It's never about her.

Another of the new Queen Consort's several times great-grandfathers was Thomas Cubitt, the builder who reconstructed Buckingham Palace. Queen Victoria loved him. When he died, she said, 'A better, kinder-hearted or more simple, unassuming man never breathed.'

Elizabeth II called Camilla 'a very special lady'. I think she is special, as you can tell. She is totally normal and completely unspoilt. She is like Prince Philip in that she is outward-looking, optimistic and not remotely self-centred or self-absorbed. Philip regularly boosted the Queen's morale by telling her how lovely she looked and how well she was doing. He also threw in what he called his occasional 'two penny-worth'. Camilla does the same with Charles, offering praise, encouragement and common sense as required. (According to my wife, men seem to need this a lot more than women do.)

But there are differences between the last royal consort and this new one. Prince Philip loved flying. Camilla hates it, squeezing her husband's hand anxiously on take-off, distracting herself with Travel Scrabble through the turbulence. Camilla is easy company always – which Prince Philip wasn't. He could be cantankerous. He could be quite frightening. While he came to loathe the press, Camilla (who has had a pretty rough ride in the media over the years) does not appear to hold any grudges. The Duke of Edinburgh was impatient with photographers – 'Take the fucking photograph!' Camilla as Duchess of Cornwall was happy to do selfies – to the dismay of her protection officer. As Queen Consort that may change. If it does, it won't be her doing.

She is going to be the least stuffy queen in history – and exactly the consort the new King needs: as charming as the Queen Mother, as committed as Queen Mary, as kind-hearted as Queen Alexandra, and, with her immediate predecessor,

Prince Philip, as her role model: looking up, looking out, doing more, saying less, getting on with the job.

I have been lucky to know these remarkable royal consorts. Though, naturally, I call her 'Your Majesty' and 'Ma'am', I hope she regards me as a friend. What the Duke of Edinburgh made of me, if anything, I cannot tell you. He called me 'Gyles'. I called him 'Sir'. His last letter to me, written from Windsor Castle, was full of characteristic dry humour and his trademark double exclamation marks (!!); it was signed 'Yours ever'. But I am mindful of the former prime minister James Callaghan's observation: 'What senior royalty offer you is friendliness, not friendship. There is a difference.'

There were times when I felt quite close to Prince Philip – like a proper friend, or as much of a friend as you can be with a man who is thirty years your senior and the husband of the head of state. He showed me many acts of kindness. For example, when I told him I hoped to be a member of parliament, after he had spluttered 'What on earth for?', he asked 'Do you know anything about it?', and when he discovered I didn't, he sent me and my wife tickets to the State Opening of Parliament where, incredibly, we sat in the gallery of the House of Lords, on little gold chairs, as special guests of Her Majesty The Queen.

And a few days after I was elected as the Conservative MP for the City of Chester, he and the Queen happened to come to my constituency, on 16 April 1992, for the Royal Maundy Service at Chester Cathedral. At the service the sovereign ceremonially distributes small silver coins, known as 'Maundy money', as symbolic alms to elderly recipients. The name 'Maundy' and the ceremony itself derive from Christ's instruction, or *mandatum*, at the Last Supper that his followers should love one another. The Queen valued the service highly and only missed it five times during the course of her long reign.

When she and Prince Philip came to Chester in 1992, the Duke of Edinburgh caught sight of me at the back of the crowd of civic dignitaries gathered in the Town Hall and pulled me forward to meet Her Majesty – much to the irritation of the Liberal Democrat Lord Mayor and the Labour Councillors, who were infuriated that, against the odds, I had won the parliamentary seat just a week before.

Five years later, when I lost my seat in the 1997 New Labour landslide, Prince Philip got in touch to commiserate and to ask me about my future plans. I told him I was going back to my old life – broadcasting and writing books. 'Is there anything I can do to help?' he asked me. 'You could give me a newspaper interview,' I said. He did. It was wide-ranging and personal – and well-received. And it led to him asking me to write a short biography of him that one of his charities (the Outward Bound Trust) wanted to publish to mark his eightieth birthday. Working on that with him (and with his friend and private secretary, Brian McGrath, and his librarian and archivist, Anne Griffiths) led to the book I published about him and the Queen in 2004: *Philip & Elizabeth Portrait of a Marriage.*

'This is Gyles Brandreth,' said the Duke, introducing me to his wife on one occasion. (It was the Royal Variety Performance at London's Dominion Theatre on Monday 26 November 2001.) Her Majesty proffered me a tightly gloved hand and murmured an almost inaudible, 'How do you do?' Her consort continued cheerily, 'Apparently, he's writing about you.' He paused and leant towards his wife's ear: 'Be warned. He's going to cut you into pieces.'

The Queen looked startled. The Duke chuckled. I smiled. I was accustomed to his sense of humour. I liked it. I liked him. I admired him as much as any man I have known. It was knowing him as I did that led me to write that first book about him, and his wife, and their remarkable marriage – the longest-lasting marriage of any sovereign and consort in history. In writing this new book, inevitably I am revisiting that first one, but this is different because it is more personal, less circumspect, and it includes my conversations and small-talk with the Queen – all recorded at the time, on the day, in the diary I have been keeping since 1959.

As you will discover if you read on, I enjoy other people's diaries and quote from them quite frequently. Royalty may not remember all the people they meet, but people who meet royalty invariably recollect the moment, usually in some detail, and, if they are diarists, they keep a record of it, too. Here, for example, is an account by the political diarist, Clerk of the Privy Council under three sovereigns and, incidentally, gifted amateur cricketer, Charles Greville (1794–1865), of a conversation he enjoyed with Queen Victoria at Buckingham Palace in March 1840:

Q: 'Have you been riding today, Mr Greville?'
G: 'No Madam, I have not.'
Q: 'It was a fine day.'
G: 'Yes ma'am a very fine day.'
Q: 'It was very cold though.'
G: (like Polonius): 'It *was* rather cold, Madam.'
Q: 'Your sister, Lady Francis Egerton rides I think, does not she?'
G: 'She does ride sometimes, Madam.'
 (A pause, when I took the lead though adhering to the same topic.)
G: 'Has your Majesty been riding today?'
Q: (with animation): 'O yes, a very long ride.'
G: 'Has your Majesty a nice horse?'
Q: 'O, a very nice horse.'

Making small-talk with the monarch is not easy. One hundred and fifty years later, in 1990, at a drinks party hosted by her godson, Geordie Porchester (son of the 7th Earl of Carnarvon, the Queen's racing manager and friend, who died on 11 September 2001), I found myself with Elizabeth II, alone, in a corner of the room. I was an aspiring member of parliament at the time, but had spent the day rehearsing for the Christmas pantomime at the Wimbledon Theatre in southwest London. (I was playing Baron Hardup in *Cinderella*.) The Queen was coming up to her Ruby Jubilee, the fortieth anniversary of her accession. Standing where we were, there was no obvious means of escape for either of us, and, both a little weary (I had had a long day; she had had a long reign), neither of us could think of anything very interesting to say. Later that night, in my diary, I recorded our exchanges. (Believe it or not, this was before I had read Greville's diary.)

GB (getting the ball rolling): 'Had a busy day, Ma'am?'
HM (with a small sigh): 'Yes, very.'
GB: 'At the Palace?'
HM (sucking her lips): 'Yes.'
GB: 'A lot of visitors?'
HM (apparently biting the inside of her lower lip): 'Yes.'
(PAUSE)
GB (brightly): 'The Prime Minister?' [It was John Major.]
HM: 'Yes.'
(PAUSE)
GB: 'He's very nice.'
HM (nodding): 'Yes, very.'
(LONG PAUSE)
GB (struggling): 'The recession's bad.'
HM (looking grave): 'Yes.'

GB (trying to jolly things along): 'I think this must be my third recession.'

HM (nodding): 'We do seem to get them every few years … and none of my governments seems to know what to do about them.'

(A MOMENT OF TINKLY LAUGHTER FROM HM, A HUGE GUFFAW FROM GB, THEN TOTAL SILENCE.)

GB (suddenly frantic): 'I've been to Wimbledon today.'

HM (brightening briefly): 'Oh, yes?'

GB (determined): 'Yes.'

HM: 'I've been to Wimbledon, too.'

GB (now we are getting somewhere): 'Today?'

HM: 'No.'

GB (Oh well we tried): 'No, of course not.' (PAUSE) 'I wasn't at the tennis.'

HM: 'No?'

GB: 'No, I was at the theatre.' (LONG PAUSE) 'Have you been to the theatre in Wimbledon?'

(PAUSE)

HM: 'I imagine so.'

(INTERMINABLE PAUSE)

GB (a last, desperate attempt): 'You know, Ma'am, my wife's a vegetarian.'

HM (what will she say?): 'That must be very dull.'

GB (what next?): 'And one of my daughters is a vegetarian, too.'

HM (oh no!): 'Oh dear.'

The Queen had a wry sense of humour. Her voice in conversation was softer, less artificial, less strangulated, than the voice we heard when she was opening Parliament or giving her Christmas Day broadcast. Physically, she was small, and became smaller with age, but, until her last years, she was sturdy. Close up, she always appeared younger than she was. Her dress sense and her helmet of permed silver hair may have come from a bygone era (increasingly she looked like her grandmother, Queen Mary), but her skin was good, and her make-up straightforward, simple, and modern.

Happily, most of my conversations with the Queen were less halting than that one – and though royal protocol requires that one should let the royal personage lead any conversation and make the first remark, in my experience Elizabeth II didn't seem to mind at all if you made the opening gambit before she did. In fact, she seemed to welcome it, which was how over time I found myself talking to Her Majesty about pantomimes, and politics, and pizzas, *Countdown* and the Commonwealth, my jumpers and her dogs and horses. Not knowing much about the world of horse racing, when I found a line that seemed to work I ran with it. I told her I had been to Dubai as a guest of the ruler, Sheikh Mohammed bin Rashid Al Maktoum, and that he had shown me around his famous Godolphin stables. 'I envy you,' she said. She knew the Sheikh well because of their shared love of racing. 'I went on my birthday,' I said. 'Did he give you a present?' she asked. 'Yes,' I said, 'but it wasn't the white Rolls-Royce he had lent me for the week.' 'What was it?' she asked. 'It was something he said my wife would treasure.' The Queen looked at me wide-eyed: 'Pearls? Diamonds?' 'No,' I said, 'it was a small book of love poetry – poems written by the Sheikh himself and then translated into truly awful English by the retired British brigadier who worked as his ADC.' She laughed at that and told me she had received some 'quite strange' presents in her time, including all sorts of animals, from antelopes to zebra, and what she described as an 'Aladdin's cave' of gems when she visited the Gulf states in 1979. 'Millions of pounds' worth of jewellery and gold and silver,' she said. 'I'm not sure what happened to it. It's probably locked up in a basement at the Foreign Office.' (What I want to know is what happened to the little statuette of her son, Prince Charles, standing alongside a ceramic figure of Postman Pat, that – almost incredibly – the Kingdom of Jordan presented to Her Majesty on her ninetieth birthday in 2016.)

To make her smile, on another occasion I told the Queen about our family dogs: the sophisticated French poodle we called 'Phydeaux' and the ageing mongrel who thought his name was 'Down Boy'. She did smile (in fact, she laughed) and then told me that Prince Philip had a dog called 'Sargent' and asked me to guess what some of his other dogs were called. 'Major?' I suggested, 'Corporal?' 'No,' she explained, 'Beecham, Boult. They're not named after army ranks, they're named after musical conductors – Sir Malcolm Sargent, Sir Thomas Beecham, Sir Adrian Boult.'

Thanks to Prince Philip, I was given privileged access to Her Majesty, to walk with her, to talk with her as she went about her official duties, and to chat with her at assorted private events and parties. I also came into contact with her in my own right when I was an MP and in the government whips' office as a Lord Commissioner of the Treasury. One of the Lord Commissioner's duties is to sign the government's cheques – the mandates authorising government expenditure. It was explained to me by Treasury officials that with the larger amounts – the mandates involving billions of pounds of expenditure – I would not be signing the cheques alone. Two signatures were required, a second as well as my own. 'The Chancellor of the Exchequer's?' I asked. 'Or the Prime Minister's as First Lord of the Treasury?' 'No,' I was informed, 'It is HM Treasury. You will be signing the large cheques with

HM – with Her Majesty.' Later, I said to the Queen, 'You know, Your Majesty, the way the government insists on the two of us signing these huge cheques . . . I can't help wondering which of the two of us it is the government doesn't entirely trust?'

I think she was amused. I know she was amused by the daily handwritten message sent to her from another member of the government whips' office whenever parliament was sitting. The whip who is Vice-Chamberlain is required to send a report to the sovereign supplementing the official parliamentary record published by Hansard. This 'message', as it's known, was much more informal and was designed to give the Queen a flavour of the mood of the House of Commons, who was doing well, who wasn't, how the wind was blowing. The Vice-Chamberlain in my day was a lovely man called Sydney Chapman who kindly sent Her Majesty some of my jokes when he thought they would amuse her. She was certainly amused when I told her that political correctness required that Sydney Chapman should properly be known these days as Sydney Personperson.

The fun of spending time with the Queen was both finding out how much fun she was and discovering unexpected things about her. She really did love all the early James Bond films – 'before they got so loud'. She really could sing 'When I'm cleaning winders' and the other songs George Formby sang to his banjolele when she was growing up during the war – and with Formby's authentic Lancashire accent, too. (She was the Duke of Lancaster, after all.)

This week, early one morning, standing outside Buckingham Palace while the Queen's body lay in its coffin in the Bow Room before it travelled to Westminster Hall for the lying-in-state, I was asked by a BBC reporter why it was, I thought, that so many people were up so early, coming in their hundreds and thousands to pay their last respects to Her Majesty.

I said I reckoned it was partly because people wanted to share in an historic moment. Republican or monarchist, like it or not, royalty is a thread running through our island story for a thousand years. William the Conqueror, Richard III, Henry VIII, Elizabeth I, 'Good King Charles', 'Mad King George', Queen Victoria – we have been brought up on the stories of our kings and queens. The death of Elizabeth II is an historic moment. We feel it particularly, too, I think, because her reign has encompassed all our lives: she has been there for as long as almost all of us can remember. But most of all, I said, I think people are coming here because of who she was, 'Elizabeth the Great', 'Elizabeth the Steadfast', a remarkable human being: a woman of integrity – decent, dutiful, discreet, conscientious, consistent, kind. In a world where there is so much that is bad and dark – I mentioned the war in Ukraine – people are reaching out to the Queen because of her essential goodness. She was an exemplar of goodness.

But how did she come to be this remarkable person? What was it made her who she was? 'The destination of all journeys is their beginning,' wrote the novelist, Angela Carter. We will begin at the beginning then, with her family and her forebears. The Queen's journey reached its final destination on Monday 19 September 2022 when she was laid to rest alongside the Duke of Edinburgh in the memorial chapel created by her in 1962 and named by her in honour of her father, George VI, within St George's Chapel at Windsor Castle. The marble slab is simply engraved: 'ELIZABETH II 1926–2022'. Her journey began on Wednesday 21 April 1926 in Mayfair, London, with little or no thought that one day she would be a queen, let alone such a queen.

CHAPTER ONE

Princess Elizabeth Alexandra Mary

The future Queen Elizabeth II was born in a handsome eighteenth-century townhouse in Mayfair in the early hours of Wednesday 21 April 1926. Just off Berkeley Square, 17 Bruton Street was then the London home of the Earl and Countess of Strathmore, and their daughter, their ninth child, Elizabeth Angela Marguerite, was the new baby's mother. Aged twenty-five, she was also the Duchess of York, having married the Duke of York, the second son of King George V, three years earlier, on 26 April 1923.

For the Duke of York, who was now thirty, the baby was a very special anniversary present. 'We always wanted a child to make our happiness complete,' he wrote to his mother, Queen Mary, '& now that it has at last happened, it seems so wonderful & strange.'

For the Duchess of York, it was not an easy birth. It had taken her time to conceive. She had found pregnancy uncomfortable, confining and 'very dull'. She was tiny (not quite 5 foot 2 inches in height) and small-boned. The obstetrician to the royal family, Sir Henry Simson (a Scotsman, born in Bengal, a keen golfer and rugby player, which the King appreciated, but more pertinently, one of the founders of the Royal College of Obstetricians and Gynaecologists), in consultation with Sir George Blacker (an Irishman, born in Dublin, twice mentioned in despatches during the First World War, which the Duke of York appreciated, but, again, more pertinently, a surgeon and editor of the standard work on midwifery), had decided in advance that the Duchess's breech baby should be delivered by caesarean section. The baby was born at 2:40 a.m. The Duke of York and Lady Strathmore were in the room for the birth and 'much relieved' that everything had gone to plan.

Downstairs, in the drawing room, the Home Secretary sat waiting for news of the safe arrival. Sir William Joynson-Hicks, known to all as 'Jix', was a conservative Conservative, best remembered for clamping down on nightclubs he regarded as dissolute and literature he considered obscene – notably the work of D. H. Lawrence and Radclyffe Hall's lesbian novel, *The Well of Loneliness*. The writer H. G. Wells said Jix represented 'absolutely the worst element in British political life … an entirely undistinguished man … an obscure and ineffectual nobody'. On the night of 20/21 April 1926, however, he was unquestionably a 'somebody', the member of the government required by custom long established to 'witness' the birth of any baby in direct line of succession to the throne and the last holder of his office to be on hand for the birth of a baby destined to become a sovereign. The custom continued until the birth of Princess Alexandra (the daughter of the King's fourth son, the Duke of Kent) in 1935, but had been abandoned by the time Prince Charles was born in 1948.

Soon after 3:00 a.m., Jix left Bruton Street to report the glad tidings to the prime minister, Stanley Baldwin, while the Duke of York relayed the good news to his parents at Windsor Castle. The new princess was third in line to the throne – after her father and his older brother, the Prince of Wales – but there was no serious expectation that she would eventually become Queen. The Duchess of York was still young and would no doubt go on to have more children, including a boy who would take precedence. (The rule of royal primogeniture, giving first-born boys precedence over first-born girls in the line of succession, was not changed until 2013.) The Prince of Wales was only thirty-one and still a bachelor. In time, he was expected to marry and have children, too.

George V and Queen Mary were delighted to hear of the safe arrival of their first granddaughter. 'Such a relief and joy,' the Queen wrote in her diary. Their Majesties travelled up from Windsor that afternoon to meet the little princess for the first time. She is 'a little darling,' reported the Queen, 'with a lovely complexion and pretty fair hair'.

Through the day, crowds of well-wishers gathered in Bruton Street to catch sight of the royal comings and goings. Messages of congratulation were received from across the Empire, as well as from ten reigning European sovereigns and the Emperor of Japan, among many others. The royal birth was front page news and a happy distraction from the main story of the day: the impending General Strike.

By 1926 the relative prosperity that had followed the First World War and heralded the so-called 'roaring 'twenties' was over for most of the general population. Following the minor boom came a major bust. In 1925, the re-introduction of the Gold Standard by the Chancellor of the Exchequer, Winston Churchill, kept interest rates high and made British exports expensive. The economy was in decline. By the mid 1920s unemployment had risen to over 2 million. Coal reserves had been depleted during the war and Britain was now importing more coal than it was mining. Britain's coalmine owners announced their intention to reduce their workers' wages while increasing their hours. The miners rejected the owners' terms: 'Not a penny off the pay, not a minute on the day' was their battle-cry. In support of the coal miners, the General Council of the Trades Union Congress called a general strike. It began at midnight on 3 May. Some 1.7 million workers – mostly in heavy industry and transport – took part. Fearing economic paralysis and potential social unrest, Baldwin's government – with Churchill as Chancellor and Jix as Home Secretary in the vanguard of the battle – took on the strikers, mobilised the army and galvanised a legion of middle-class volunteers to maintain essential services.

Privately, the King had some sympathy for the miners' plight – 'Try living on their wages before you judge them,' he said – but he did not go so far as to condone the strike itself. Indeed, with his private blessing, court equerries and lords-in-waiting were excused royal service to volunteer for Jix's brigade of special constables. For a week, the country held its breath and nervous royalists wondered whether the strike presaged the kind of revolution that had led to the overthrow of the Russian Tsar by the Bolsheviks in 1917. They need not have worried. After nine days, the government prevailed and the trades unions gave up in defeat.

The new royal baby was born ten days before the strike began and christened a fortnight after it ended, on Saturday 29 May, in the private chapel at Buckingham Palace. Using water from the River Jordan in the Holy Land, the christening was performed by Cosmo Lang, the Archbishop of York, a staunch ally of the royal family – so close, said some, he was 'more courtier than cleric'. The new princess, dressed in the satin and lace christening robe that had been made for Queen Victoria's eldest daughter, was named Elizabeth Alexandra Mary, after her mother (there was no thought of Elizabeth I in the choice), her grandmother, Queen Mary, and her great-grandmother, Queen Alexandra, who had died of a heart attack, aged eighty, the previous November.

Her godparents included her royal grandparents, George V and Queen Mary; her other grandmother, Lady Strathmore;

her royal aunt, Mary, the Princess Royal, the Duke of York's younger (and only) sister, who had married the Earl of Harewood in 1922; a non-royal aunt, Lady Elphinstone, her mother's older sister; and Arthur, Duke of Connaught (1850–1942), Queen Victoria's last surviving son.

What everyone seems to have remembered most about the christening was how much the baby cried. 'Of course, the baby cried,' said Queen Mary. The Queen's long-serving lady-in-waiting, the Countess of Airlie, reported that (to the amusement of the Prince of Wales who was in a joshing mood that day) the baby's old-school nurse shocked 'the modern mothers present' by trying to calm the squawking child by dosing her with dill water. This was the first and last – and only – occasion on which the future Elizabeth II was seen to cry in public.

'She doesn't cry,' her husband, the Duke of Edinburgh, told me eighty years later. It was in 2006, when the film, *The Queen*, starring Helen Mirren in the title role, had just opened to critical acclaim. There is a moment in the movie where the Queen is seen sitting alone on a hill near Balmoral and a beautiful Highland stag appears nearby. In the picture, this is in the aftermath of Diana's death and, apparently overwhelmed by the pressure of recent events, the Queen bursts into tears.

'They just make it up,' said Prince Philip wearily. He hadn't seen the film, nor had she, but he had read about it. 'The Queen doesn't cry,' he repeated. 'You can have feelings without blubbing,' he added.

I thought of Prince Philip's observation during the Queen's funeral service at Westminster Abbey in September 2022. Grief and sadness were apparent in the faces of all the members of the royal family, but (rightly or wrongly) crying in public is not the Windsor way. The only person seen to conspicuously shed a tear that day was Prince Harry's wife,

Meghan. Back in 2006, referring to Helen Mirren, the Duke of Edinburgh said, 'An actress might cry and think it rings true. All I'm saying is that it isn't accurate. The Queen doesn't cry.'

Warming to his theme, the Duke moved from the makers of *The Queen* to the media in general. 'They're obsessed with people showing their emotions in public. They're determined to get a picture of the Queen with tears in her eyes – and if it's a cold day they might succeed. They want a photo that suits their story. Do you remember the pictures at the decommissioning of *Britannia*?' The Royal Yacht, launched by the Queen in 1953, was taken out of service in 1997. The Queen certainly had affection for the vessel: it had taken her and other members of the royal family on some 696 foreign visits and 272 trips around British waters, including many happy holidays. According to *Hello!* magazine and most of the media, the farewell in Portsmouth brought tears to the sovereign's eyes: 'Overcome with emotion, she was seen wiping her eyes as her beloved yacht was taken out of service.'

'It was the middle of December,' snorted Prince Philip. 'It was bloody cold. We all had tears in our eyes.'

Prince Philip also told me that on 21 April 1926, the day on which the future Queen Elizabeth II, his future wife, was born, his parents, Prince and Princess Andrew of Greece, happened to have lunch at Windsor Castle with the King and Queen.

'I didn't know that,' I said. 'That's a charming coincidence.'

'Not really,' he said. 'They were cousins, after all.'

CHAPTER TWO

Queen Victoria

At the Queen's funeral in September 2022, among the most notable of the royal mourners from other countries was Queen Margrethe II of Denmark, born in 1940, and now Europe's longest-serving head of state and only reigning queen. She is also Colonel-in-Chief of a British regiment and only the seventh Lady of the Order of the Garter since 1901, when Edward VII appointed his wife, Queen Alexandra, to the Order as the first. A few years ago, when I visited Queen Margrethe at her palace in Copenhagen, she told me, unsurprisingly, drawing on yet another cigarette (she is a committed smoker, though only in private nowadays), how much she admired Elizabeth II and the Duke of Edinburgh, and reminded me, incidentally, that she was related to both. She said, 'I love coming to their parties in London, especially when they are just family gatherings, for wedding anniversaries and that sort of thing. If it's just royalty in the room, once the door is closed you know you're all there because you are related, however distantly. You feel safe. You can say what you like, you can be yourself. Royals understand other royals. We all know what it's like. In the old days when royals only married other royals, there were disadvantages, of course, but there were advantages, too. Everyone had been brought up in the same sort of way. It can be difficult if you're an outsider. My husband has found it difficult, I know.' He was a French career diplomat given the style and title of 'His Royal Highness Prince Henrik of Denmark', but the marriage, which lasted more than fifty years until his death in 2018, had 'many ups and downs,' Margrethe told me. She added, smiling while lighting another cigarette, 'Your Queen and Prince Philip are cousins. I think that helps.'

Both Elizabeth II and her husband, the Duke of Edinburgh, were great-great-grandchildren of Queen Victoria, whose reign, of course, until Elizabeth's, was the longest in our history.

Victoria lived more than eighty-one years, from 24 May 1819 to 22 January 1901. She came to the throne aged eighteen, in 1837, and gave her name to a century, its achievements and constraints, its values and aspirations. Britain's first and only Queen-Empress was small (not five feet tall) and round (at her heaviest topping 200 lbs), but she cast a long shadow. Whenever Queen Elizabeth II appeared on the balcony of Buckingham Palace she looked out over the Victoria Memorial, designed at the time of the old queen's death, but not opened until the reign of George V and only completed in 1922. Whenever Elizabeth II drove in or out of Windsor Castle, she passed the bronze statue of Victoria erected to mark the Queen-Empress's Golden Jubilee in 1887.

Elizabeth II had plenty in common with her great-great-grandmother, not least her longevity, sense of duty, acceptance of destiny, love and admiration for her husband, sometimes complicated relationship with her eldest son, and sustaining faith. 'England has become great and happy by the knowledge of the true God through Jesus Christ,' wrote Victoria. 'For me,' said Elizabeth II, 'the teachings of Christ and my own personal accountability before God provide a framework in which I try to lead my life.'

Duty drove Elizabeth II, but it was her faith that sustained her. There was not a Christmas broadcast in which she did not speak of it – starting with her first, in 1952, when she was only twenty-six. 'Pray for me,' she said, looking ahead to her coronation the following year, 'that God may give me wisdom and strength to carry out the solemn promises I shall be making, and that I may faithfully serve Him and you, all the days of my life.'

In the mid-1950s, when the American evangelist Billy Graham came to London he met the Queen and told her one of his favourite stories – about her great-great-grandmother. In Billy Graham's version, 'Victoria went into the slums of London and visited the home of an elderly lady. When the Queen rose to leave, she asked, "Is there anything I can do for you?" The woman said, "Yes, ma'am, Your Majesty, you can meet me in Heaven." The Queen turned to her and said softly, "Yes. I'll be there, but only because of the blood that was shed on the cross for you and for me." Queen Victoria, in her day the most powerful woman in the world, had to depend on the blood of Christ for her salvation; and so do we.'

To Elizabeth, as to Victoria, her Christian faith was fundamental to her life. Both sovereigns said their prayers on their knees at their bedsides every night, not as a matter of form, but as a matter of belief. And for Elizabeth, as for Victoria, her marriage – sanctified by God – was the most important relationship of her life.

Elizabeth married her cousin, Prince Philip of Greece and Denmark, in November 1947, when she was twenty-one and he was twenty-six. Victoria married her cousin, Prince Albert of Saxe-Coburg and Gotha, in February 1840, when they were both twenty-one. Victoria adored Albert and it is clear from her journal that, at least when she was young, her approach to the physical aspects of love was anything but 'Victorian':

I NEVER NEVER spent such an evening!!! My DEAREST DEAREST DEAR Albert sat on a footstool by my side, & his excessive love & affection gave me feelings of heavenly love & happiness, I never could have *hoped* to have felt before! He clasped me in his arms, and we kissed each other again and again! His beauty, his sweetness and gentleness – really how can I ever be thankful enough to have such a *Husband*!

I doubt that Elizabeth II in her journal ever wrote about Prince Philip quite like that. It does not feel like her style, but I do know from friends and family members who knew Elizabeth and Philip when they were young that – in the words of Patricia Mountbatten, Prince Philip's first cousin on his mother's side – 'They absolutely adored one another – you could see it in both their eyes.' They were never ones for public displays of affection – there are no photographs anywhere of them holding hands or kissing except by way of a greeting on the cheek – but Countess Mountbatten told me that Prince Philip had told her, more than once, how 'gorgeous' his young wife was and 'what fun they had together'.

In 2021, in her Christmas broadcast nine months after her husband's death, the Queen spoke of 'my beloved Philip' in a way she had never done before in public. 'His sense of service, intellectual curiosity and capacity to squeeze fun out of any situation, were all irrepressible,' she said. 'That mischievous, inquiring twinkle was as bright at the end as when I first set eyes on him.' She loved her man as much as Victoria loved hers.

Elizabeth had four children and, so her childhood friend Sonia Berry told me, one miscarriage. Victoria, despite the discomforts and indignities of childbirth ('I think . . . of our being like a cow or a dog at such moments,' she said), had nine children. The first of them was born on 21 November 1840, nine months and eleven days after her wedding night.

'Oh, Madam,' said her physician, Dr Locock, 'it is a Princess.' 'Never mind,' answered the Queen weakly, 'the next will be a Prince.' It was. Eleven and a half months after the birth of Princess Victoria (known first as Pussy, then as Vicky), on 9 November 1841, Bertie, the Prince of Wales, the future King Edward VII, was born.

When Prince Albert died, on 14 December 1861, the Queen was only forty-two. Bereft, she closeted herself at Windsor Castle, and her sustained seclusion – at Windsor, at Balmoral, at Osborne House on the Isle of Wight – did not endear her to the press or public. She became the maudlin 'widow of Windsor', accused by some of indulging her grief and becoming neglectful of her duties to her people.

Elizabeth II's response to widowhood was very different. When Prince Philip died at Windsor Castle on 9 April 2021, just two months short of his one hundredth birthday, he and Elizabeth had been married for more than seventy-three years. The Queen was nearly ninety-five and well accustomed to death. She knew and accepted that life, as she put it, 'consists of final partings as well as first meetings.' Many of those closest to her had died over the previous two decades: her sister, her mother, her much-loved racing manager, Lord Carnarvon, among them. In 2021, along with her husband, she lost so many of her nearest and dearest: her first cousin, Mary Colman, aged eighty-eight, and Mary Colman's husband, Sir Timothy, a Knight of the Garter, aged ninety-one; the manager of the Royal Studs at Sandringham, Sir Michael Oswald, aged eighty-six; Lady Farnham, one of her longest-serving ladies-in-waiting, aged ninety; and the Dowager Countess of Grafton, aged 101.

In 1946, Fortune Smith married Hugh Fitzroy, Earl of Euston, who became the 11th Duke of Grafton on the death of his father in 1970. As we will discover later in our story, before Philip proposed, the teenage Elizabeth was quite sweet on Hugh. Her friendship with the Graftons was lifelong, comfortable and profound. Fortune joined what the Queen called 'my team' as a Lady of the Bedchamber in Coronation year, 1953, and succeeded the Dowager Duchess of Devonshire as Mistress of the Robes in 1967.

The Mistress of the Robes is the senior lady in the Royal Household. Once upon a time responsible for the queen's clothes and jewellery, as the title implies, the post now has the responsibility for arranging the rota of attendance of the ladies-in-waiting on the queen, along with various duties at state ceremonies. Over the years, the role has almost invariably been fulfilled by a duchess. In the past, whenever the queen was a queen regnant rather than a queen consort, the Mistress of the Robes was a political appointment, changing with the government. Queen Victoria had to endure twenty changes of Mistress of the Robes. It is different now and Elizabeth II had only two Mistresses of the Robes throughout her reign.

When I was travelling with the Queen's party on one of her regional tours in 2001, we overheard someone in the crowd asking if the Duchess of Grafton, seated next to the Queen in the royal Bentley, was the Queen's sister. This really delighted the Duchess. 'I do feel like her sister,' she said to me, proudly. They were very close.

When the Duke of Grafton died, the Dowager Duchess moved to Whitelands House, a block of flats in London, on Cheltenham Terrace, just south of Sloane Square. Fellow residents were pleasantly surprised to occasionally see the Queen emerging from the lift after a visit to her old friend. In February 2020, just before the first Covid-19 lockdown, Her Majesty delivered the sovereign's traditional card to a centenarian in person.

In 2021, when her husband died, Elizabeth II did not give

way to grief. Unlike Victoria, she did not hide away: she got on with the job. Indeed, she told one of her ladies-in-waiting, she was 'grateful to have a job to get on with'.

At the time of Prince Philip's death, there were Covid-19 lockdown restrictions in force across the United Kingdom. On the eve of her husband's funeral, it later transpired, officials in Downing Street were enjoying alcohol-fuelled staff parties late into the night. At Windsor Castle, the Queen, by contrast, was obeying the government's pandemic rules to the letter, only associating with members of staff within her 'bubble' and, at the funeral itself, sitting in her pew in St George's Chapel on her own, 'socially distanced' from the other twenty-nine mourners permitted to be part of the congregation.

Much was made of the stark image of the Queen, masked and dressed in black, sitting all alone at her husband's funeral, but, in truth, she did not feel 'isolated' or 'alone' in St George's Chapel that day as some of the press described her. For the Queen, a church was the one place where she never felt alone. In church, she was with God and at times of travail a church, for her, was the place to be to find comfort and consolation. It did not trouble her to be seated on her own. As Queen, she was accustomed to sitting apart from others.

As Queen, too, she was accustomed to her own company. Even when her husband was alive, she often spent evenings on her own. Immediately after his funeral, she returned to her apartment in Windsor Castle in silence. 'I helped her off with her coat and hat,' her dresser, Angela Kelly, remembered, 'and no words were spoken. The Queen then walked to her sitting room, closed the door behind her, and she was alone with her thoughts.'

When Prince Albert died, Queen Victoria retreated from the world. When Prince Philip died, Queen Elizabeth II went towards it. She continued with her official duties, working through her paperwork every day, signing letters and state papers, making phone calls, taking Zoom calls, meeting ambassadors on screen when they presented their credentials.

In the immediate aftermath of Prince Philip's death, Vice-Admiral Sir Tony Johnstone-Burt, the cheery Master of the Household and part of the Queen's Windsor 'bubble', told me, 'My principal duty with HM has been to keep her spirits up – so I've been watching *Line of Duty* with her . . . I'm "the Explainer"! It's very funny.'

The ninety-five-year-old widow of Windsor laughed as she struggled to understand the convoluted plotting and sometimes incomprehensible dialogue in the popular 'police procedural' television series. She enjoyed watching television, she told me: 'It keeps me in touch – when I can understand what's being said. There's an awful lot of mumbling on television now. It's not my hearing. They just don't seem to speak as clearly as they used to do.'

'Life goes on,' said the Queen, 'It has to.' 'All that lives must die, passing through nature to eternity,' is how Queen Gertrude put it in *Hamlet*. Though (unlike King Charles III) not particularly keen on Shakespeare, that was Elizabeth II's philosophy, too. 'We are all visitors to this time, this place,' she said in a broadcast in the run-up to her Platinum Jubilee in 2022, when, inevitably, she knew she was not long for this world. 'We are just passing through. Our purpose here is to observe, to learn, to grow, to love, and then we return home.'

Nor was Elizabeth II in favour of excessive or prolonged mourning – what Claudius in *Hamlet* termed 'unmanly grief', saying what Elizabeth believed: 'It shows a will most incorrect to heaven.'

Following the Duke of Edinburgh's death, the Queen thanked God for the blessing of her husband's long life and got on with the business of living her own as best she could. She knew it was her Christian duty to do so. 'There is no magic formula that will transform sorrow into happiness,' she said, 'but being busy helps.'

Frustratingly for her, because of the Covid-19 restrictions in force in 2021 she felt she should not go to the Epsom Derby at the beginning of June that year, only the fourth time that she had missed the race in seventy-five years. And for the first time in her reign, she missed out on Royal Ascot, too. She went to her first Royal Ascot in 1946 and, with the exception of 2020 when it was held behind closed doors, had not missed a day of the meeting since her coronation. She watched the racing on television, and 'working from home', continued with her duties, welcoming, among others, the Australian prime minister, Scott Morrison, to Windsor during Ascot week. I was on parade at Royal Ascot in 2022 when she told Sir Francis Brooke, her official Representative at Royal Ascot, and the sixth to hold the office during her reign, that she 'hoped, *so* hoped' to be there on the final Saturday. It wasn't to be and her cousin, the Duke of Kent, eighty-six, did the honours instead. 'We miss her so much,' said Francis Brooke. 'We love her. It's as simple as that.'

From the death of her husband, for the rest of her days, Queen Victoria was dressed in mourning. Her great-great-granddaughter's approach was very different. Not only did Elizabeth keep herself busy that first summer after Philip's death, with the help of one of the other key members of her pandemic 'bubble', her dresser, Angela Kelly, she also chose to dress, as the Queen herself put it, 'as cheerfully as possible' – in yellow and pink and powder blue, in summery dresses with pretty floral designs.

In bright green (appropriately in the run-up to the forth-coming international Climate Change conference in Glasgow), in October 2021 she opened the Scottish Parliament in Edinburgh. A few days later, all in pink this time, she opened the Welsh Senedd in Cardiff. The Prince of Wales and the Duchess of Cornwall were also on parade for both visits. 'We weren't required,' the Duchess said to me soon afterwards, laughing. 'We were there to help out if necessary. It wasn't necessary. The Queen did it all. She wanted to. She's unstoppable.'

For six months following Prince Philip's death, the Queen did so much, so purposefully and with such a determination not to give way to any form of self-pity (which, she said, 'My husband would certainly not have approved of'), that she probably did too much. In the autumn she had a sudden 'energy low'. She felt exhausted. Her doctors ordered her to 'rest a bit, not to push herself so much, to take it easy.'

She had planned to attend 'COP' (the 'Conference of Parties' who had signed up to the United Nations declaration on climate change) in Glasgow in person, but, in the event, had to record a video message instead. She had hoped to attend the Festival of Remembrance at the Royal Albert Hall and the Remembrance Sunday service at the Cenotaph – fixtures in her calendar – but was persuaded not to. 'I've got to be sensible,' she said. 'Sensible' is what she always was.

CHAPTER THREE

In the blood

'Sensible' is what Elizabeth II always was – from childhood to old age. How come? All her life she was a much steadier person than many of her forebears.

Queen Victoria, even before her husband's untimely death, could be temperamental, emotional, and volatile. There were times when her family, and her ministers, feared for her sanity. There were times when observers suggested that Elizabeth was too controlled and that her reluctance or inability to show emotion created difficulties for some, if not all, of her children. We will explore this later. I will only report now that her daughter, Princess Anne, says simply, 'That's complete tosh.'

What is not in dispute is that both Victoria and Elizabeth were able, intelligent and perceptive. Victoria was more susceptible to flattery than Elizabeth. 'Gladstone treats the Queen like a public department,' said Benjamin Disraeli, 'I treat her like a woman.' Of course, Queen Victoria preferred Disraeli. Through her reign, Elizabeth was more amused than seduced by the flattery on offer from some of her prime ministers, as we will discover in due course. She appreciated the charm of Anthony Eden and Harold Wilson in the 1950s and 1960s, for example, but, as her private secretary for many years, Lord Charteris put it to me: 'They were wily ones, but they didn't pull the wool over her eyes.'

Queen Victoria, notoriously, could be wilful to the point of obstinacy. She would not give up her devoted, drunken, Highland servant, John Brown, however much her family wanted her to do so. She would not abandon her Indian secretary, Abdul Karim, 'the Munshi', however anxious the Indian Office and others were at his constant presence at her side. Elizabeth was not wilful in the same way – though her ladies-in-waiting did find the Queen's dresser, Angela Kelly, a nuisance at times. Kelly, who joined Elizabeth's team in 1996, and from 2002 was officially 'Personal Assistant, Adviser and Curator to Her Majesty The Queen (Jewellery, Insignias and Wardrobe)', became very close to the sovereign and was with her to the last.

Born in Liverpool in 1957, the daughter of a Liverpool dock worker, Angela Kelly was at least a generation younger than the ladies-in-waiting and from a quite different background to theirs. Her no-nonsense Northern manner, her easy access to the Queen and her effortless familiarity with Her Majesty irritated some at court. They particularly resented the way Kelly felt able to step out of line to adjust the Queen's clothes or drop a word in her ear at what they considered to be inappropriate moments. They could do nothing about it because the Queen regarded her dresser and dressmaker – whose wardrobe choices were universally admired – as one of her closest allies and true friends.

The over-riding difference between Queen Victoria's long reign and Elizabeth's is that Victoria was sovereign and Queen-Empress at the height of the British Empire, in her day the largest empire in world history and, for more than a century, the foremost global power. When Victoria's grandson was crowned in 1911, the British Empire held sway over 412 million people, some twenty-three per cent of the world's population at the time, and covered almost a quarter of the earth's total land area. By the time of George V's granddaughter's coronation in 1953, the Empire had all but disappeared. The last remaining colonies were on their way to independence.

In the early twenty-first century, Elizabeth II was known as the grandmother of William and Harry – and Beatrice and Eugenie – and Peter Phillips and Zara Tindall – and Lady Louise Mountbatten-Windsor and James, Viscount Severn. In the late nineteenth century, Victoria was known as 'the grandmother of Europe' – and with good reason. Victoria had instinctive dynastic skills and used them adroitly. In the twentieth century, Elizabeth's children were able to marry whom they chose – and, first time round, they did not all make happy choices. In the nineteenth century, Victoria's children had to marry to a purpose to help forge or secure international alliances.

Victoria's first-born, Vicky, married a future German emperor. Bertie, the Prince of Wales who became Edward VII, married the Danish princess Alexandra, whose brother became King of Greece and whose sister was Empress of Russia. It was Victoria's third child, Alice, who married the Grand Duke of Hesse and launched the line that produced, among others, the last Russian Tsarina and Elizabeth's future husband, Prince Philip. Victoria's fourth child, Alfred, also married into the Russian royal family and, in time, his daughter became Queen of Romania. After Helena and Louise came two more sons: Arthur, Duke of Connaught (godfather to Elizabeth II), whose daughter became Queen of Sweden, and Leopold, Duke of Albany. Victoria's youngest, Beatrice, married Henry of Battenberg, and became the mother of the Queen of Spain.

As a mother, grandmother and great-grandmother, Victoria, perhaps more obviously than Elizabeth, was interested and involved, loving, concerned and conscientious. There is a lovely photograph of Victoria, taken in April 1886, with her daughter Princess Beatrice, her granddaughter Princess Louis of Battenberg, and her great-granddaughter, Princess Alice (Prince Philip's mother), aged one. They all look contented. The Queen is smiling happily.

There is no record of Queen Victoria ever saying, 'We are not amused.' On the contrary, her journals frequently include the phrase, 'I was very much amused.' Elizabeth Longford, one of Victoria's most respected biographers, told me there are 'many recorded instances' of the Queen laughing out loud, and heartily, often at stories or incidents that other Victorians might have considered quite *risqué*. Like Elizabeth II, Victoria enjoyed the absurd. She regularly repeated the story of the time her mother, the Duchess of Kent, had emerged from the dining room carrying a fork, mistaking it for her fan. Making small-talk, I repeated the story to the Queen once at a reception at Buckingham Palace. Amused (or at least seeming to be), Her Majesty claimed she hadn't heard it before and then told me the story of the silver statuette of Lady Godiva that Queen Victoria had commissioned for Prince Albert as a birthday present in 1857. The Queen told me her grandfather, George V, was especially fond of the statuette, still on display at Buckingham Palace, because, according to royal family legend, the myopic Queen Olga – mother of Prince Andrew of Greece and grandmother of Prince Philip – had peered closely at the naked figure of Godiva on horseback and murmured appreciatively, 'Ah, dear Queen Victoria.'

When Victoria was not amused it was all too often because of her son, Bertie. From his early days, Victoria and Albert viewed the young Prince of Wales as a problem child. He was not academic; he was not athletic; he did not inherit his father's appetite for work. Instead, he seemed to have inherited his assorted, dissolute, great-uncles' appetites for good food, fine wines, gaming and loose women. In 1861, when he was still nineteen and a young officer stationed with his regiment in Ireland, a compliant young actress, Nellie Clifden, was slipped between his sheets. Prince Albert heard about it and was appalled. What if the liaison were to result in a child? In his anguish, the Prince Consort wrote to the young Prince of Wales:

> If you were to try and deny it, she can drag you into a Court of Law to force you to own it & there with you in the witness box, she will be able to give before a greedy Multitude disgusting details of your profligacy for the sake of convincing the Jury, yourself crossexamined by a railing indecent attorney and hooted and yelled at by a Lawless Mob!! Horrible prospect, which this person has in her power, any day to realise! And to break your poor parents' hearts!

In 2022, when it became clear that Elizabeth II's second son, Andrew, the Duke of York, might be obliged to appear in court to defend himself against charges of sexually assaulting a girl of seventeen twenty years earlier, when he was in his early forties, the Queen accepted that she had no alternative but to strip her son of all the trappings of royalty – including the public use of his styling as a Royal Highness. If Andrew was to appear in court, the Queen's spokeperson made clear, it would have to be as a private citizen. As his father, Prince Philip, said to me, 'Appearing in court as a member of the royal family simply isn't on.'

Prince Philip was never accused of sexual assault in the way that Prince Andrew was by Virginia Roberts Giuffre, but, over the years, the Duke of Edinburgh was subjected to a steady stream of newspaper and magazine stories about his supposed extra-marital love-life. He found the stories hurtful and infuriating, but what could he do about them? As he saw it, suing the newspapers was not the answer. 'It's a cumbersome and costly process,' he said, 'and gives more coverage to the libel. "Queen's husband in court" – oh, yes? No smoke without fire . . .' Prince Andrew, who denied absolutely all the accusations levelled against him, avoided having to appear in court in person by coming to an out-of-court settlement with his accuser. While making no admission of guilt, he reportedly paid Virginia Roberts Giuffre £10 million and agreed to pay a further £2 million to a charity of her choice. Privately, he told family and friends that he wanted his 'day in court' to clear his name. The Queen and the Prince of Wales took the view that a court appearance would be fraught with danger given the questions that might be asked and would inevitably overshadow the Queen's Platinum Jubilee celebrations planned for that year. Since Her Majesty was having to foot the bill for much of the settlement, her view prevailed. Elizabeth's view was her husband's view: steer clear of the courts if you possibly can.

That was Victoria's husband's view, too. Prince Albert died only a matter of weeks after discovering Bertie's affair with Nellie Clifden. The Prince Consort died of typhoid, or possibly of cancer. In the extremis of her grief, Victoria attributed her husband's death to the distress he had been caused by their son. 'Oh! that boy,' she said, despairingly, 'much as I pity him I never can or shall look at him without a shudder . . .'

We shall come to Elizabeth II's feelings about Prince Andrew in due course. Here we are exploring the legacy of Elizabeth's immediate forebears: how who they were affected who and what she became.

At 5 feet 7 inches tall, Elizabeth's great-grandfather, Bertie, Prince of Wales, was both taller than his mother, Queen Victoria, and rounder. At his heaviest he weighed more than sixteen stone – 224 lbs. His nickname was 'Tum-Tum'. He enjoyed five substantial meals a day – breakfast, lunch, afternoon tea, dinner, supper – and smoked as many as twenty cigarettes and a dozen fat cigars between daybreak and sunset. He coughed and he wheezed, but he safeguarded his own health by requiring others not to smoke while he was doing so. Despite his weight and his wheezing, throughout his adult life he enjoyed a series of mistresses: occasionally actresses, like the young Nellie Clifden and the celebrated Lillie Langtry; more often, the willing wives of his complaisant aristocratic and racing friends.

On 10 March 1863, Bertie, aged twenty-one, married Princess Alexandra of Denmark. She was just nineteen, beautiful, tall, sweet-tempered, good-natured, a little vacant, chronically unpunctual, wonderfully tolerant. She endured her husband's selfishness, self-indulgence and promiscuity for almost half a century. When he was dying in the late spring of 1910, she allowed Alice Keppel to come to his bedside. Mrs Keppel was Bertie's last and most enduring mistress, and the great-grandmother, of course, of Camilla Parker Bowles, mistress three generations later to Bertie's great-great-grandson, Charles, Prince of Wales. In 1910, Queen and mistress shook hands and Alix, with extraordinary generosity, said to Alice, 'I am sure you always had a good influence over him.'

She probably did. Mrs Keppel was known for the way she could coax and tease the Prince of Wales out of his sulks and ill-humour. Charles when Prince of Wales was also known to have had sulking moments and bouts of ill-humour, and his easy-going, good-humoured mistress-turned-wife, Mrs Parker Bowles, had a similarly useful influence over him.

In 2005, when Charles married his long-term mistress, Elizabeth II did not know her new daughter-in-law that well. By 2022, when in her message marking the seventieth anniversary of her accession she declared it her 'sincere wish' that 'in the fullness of time' when Charles became King, Camilla should be known as Queen Consort, she had come to know Camilla well and to like her a lot. 'She's good news, isn't she?' I said to the Queen, somewhat presumptuously. 'She's rather special,' replied Her Majesty.

Over time, Elizabeth II came to recognise in Camilla the same self-sacrificing commitment to service that Prince Philip had displayed over so many years. Camilla told me that the Duke of Edinburgh was indeed her role model – not that she presumed to be his equal, 'not for a moment'. The Queen also discovered that Camilla was easy company because they had so much in common, not least a shared passion for horse racing.

Before she came to know Camilla properly, the Queen warmed more to Camilla's first husband, Andrew Parker Bowles, a polo-playing soldier and amateur jockey who, as a thirteen-year-old boy, had been a page at the Queen's coronation, and whose parents were good friends of Queen Elizabeth, the Queen Mother. Andrew Parker Bowles was always easy company. The Queen did not approve of her son having a mistress while he was married (not at all – and she told Diana so, in terms) and she was wary of Camilla until her position had been – in the Queen's phrase – 'properly regularised', but once it had been and the Queen could see how happy Camilla made her son and how good Camilla was in her role as Charles's mainstay and consort, she was keen to be seen to give her daughter-in-law her wholehearted backing.

Andrew Parker Bowles accepted his wife's affair with Prince Charles, much as George Keppel, a professional soldier like Andrew Parker Bowles, accepted his wife's relationship with Edward VII. There was a difference. For George Keppel, encouraging his wife to consort with the King enabled him to enjoy a lifestyle he might not otherwise have been able to afford. The Keppels lived in a fine house in London's Portman Square and George, obligingly, made himself scarce whenever Bertie came to call. Keppel – tall, elegant, moustachioed, with more than a touch of the music hall dandy about him – came from a family steeped in royal service, some of it respectable, some of it less so. William III – William of Orange – was bi-sexual and brought sixteen-year-old Arnold Joost van Keppel with him from Holland to England, allegedly as his catamite, in 1688. In due course he made the young man Earl of Albemarle. George Keppel's father was the 7th Earl of Albemarle and Treasurer in Queen Victoria's household.

George Keppel was also a descendant of King Charles II – as were and are so many. Charles II had no children by his wife Catherine of Braganza, but a considerable brood by his many mistresses. Charles III's first wife, Diana Spencer, for example, was descended from two of Charles's illegitimate sons: Henry Fitzroy, 1st Duke of Grafton (and forebear of the Queen's friend, the 11th Duke of Grafton) and Charles Lennox, 1st Duke of Richmond. This means that when Prince William, now Prince of Wales, succeeds his father as King, he will become the first blood descendant of Charles II to do so.

Just as there is a comparison to be made between Bertie's 'Little Mrs George', as he called Alice Keppel, and Camilla, the 'non-negotiable' love of Charles's life, who he sometimes called 'Mehbooba' (it's Urdu for 'my beloved'), so, too, there was an echo of Bertie's wife's life in that of Diana, Princess of Wales. Through their unhappiness at their husbands' infidelity, both Alix and Diana found consolation in the affection in which they were held by the public at large and in their deep and loving relationships with their own children.

Like Diana, Princess Alexandra was strikingly beautiful, much admired, and genuinely loved by the people. Like Diana, she did good works. In many ways, she pioneered the role of the caring royal consort. With the Alexandra Rose Day, she introduced a new form of charitable fund-raising to Britain. Despite the disability of increasing deafness as the years went by and the handicap of a slight limp, triggered by rheumatic fever when she was just twenty-two, like Diana, she was easy with strangers and especially comfortable with children.

Alexandra's own children were a special joy to her. She had six, the youngest of whom, a boy, died when only a few hours old. Her daughters called her 'darling Motherdear' and were so devoted that her husband feared they might never leave the nest. In the event, the eldest, Princess Louise, the Princess Royal, married the Duke of Fife, and the youngest, Princess Maud, married Prince Charles of Denmark, later to become King Haakon VII of Norway. Only the middle girl, another Princess Victoria, remained a spinster all her life.

It was the eldest son who proved to be the problem child. Prince Albert Victor, the Duke of Clarence, known in the family as Eddy, was born prematurely at the start of 1864 and died prematurely in the spring of 1892. He was neither bright nor ambitious and devoted most of his short life to the pleasures of the bedroom and the polo field. When the police raided a male brothel in Cleveland Street in central London, they discovered a clutch of the Prince of Wales's friends and associates among the regular clientele and learnt that Bertie's eldest boy, the young Duke of Clarence, had not long before visited the establishment in the (forlorn) hope of seeing a display of naked women. Eddy was notorious and his dissolute behaviour fuelled the rumours that he was 'Jack the Ripper', the man who murdered and mutilated a number of prostitutes in the Aldgate and Whitechapel districts of London in 1888.

Just as Albert and Victoria had hoped that marriage would magically transform their eldest son ('marry or burn' was the phrase they used), so Bertie and Alix hoped that matrimony would make a man of Eddy. Finding a bride for this particular prince was not easy. First, he rejected an anyway-reluctant Princess Margaret of Germany; next, he was turned down by Alix of Hesse (the one who went on to become the unfortunate last Tsarina of Russia); then, he fell passionately in love with Princess Hélène d'Orleans, who was a Catholic as well as French, and consequently (despite her readiness to become a Protestant) not remotely acceptable.

In due course, he was persuaded to propose to Princess Victoria Mary of Teck, known to all as May, who was three years his junior and not nearly so 'royal', but was willing, able, available and sound. Queen Victoria invited her to Balmoral and gave a grandmotherly seal of approval, judging May to be 'a superior girl – quiet and reserved *till* you know her well – & so sensible and unfrivolous.'

This was not how anybody would have described May's parents. Her mother, Princess Mary Adelaide, who was a granddaughter of George III, was garrulous, extravagant and greedy: she was reckoned to be at least the weight of Bertie, Prince of Wales. Her father, Franz, Duke of Teck, came from a family that had married beneath itself but resolutely refused to recognise the fact. Franz was argumentative, temperamental and sensitive about his status. The parents, as vulgar spendthrifts, embarrassed their daughter, who was a decent, discreet, dignified sort, fair-haired, blue-eyed, clear-skinned, handsome rather than beautiful, with a look we would now recognise in her great-granddaughter, Princess Anne.

Princess May agreed to marry Prince Eddy, but she was spared what would certainly have been an ordeal. In the run-up to the wedding, while shooting at Sandringham in the winter of 1891, Eddy was taken ill. He died of pneumonia on 14 January 1892. In his final fever, as May and his mother took turns to keep watch, repeatedly he called out, 'Hélène, Hélène.'

His fiancée was understandably disconcerted. His mother was understandably bereft. For years, in her bedroom, Alix kept the hat her hapless son had been wearing on his final shoot, and she preserved his quarters as they had been on the day he died: his toothpaste tube as he had left it, a fresh cake of soap ready by the washbasin. Her second son, George, wrote to her: 'Gladly would I have given my life for his, as I put no value on mine . . . Such a tragedy has never before occurred in the annals of our family.'

In truth, the private tragedy turned out to be a public benefit. Eddy was neither good-husband nor good-monarch material. Prince George turned out to be both. Princess May, having received Queen Victoria's seal of approval, was too good a catch to let slip, and, within eighteen months, May, having been engaged to one heir apparent, had married the next. It was a fortunate match. George later wrote to his wife: 'People only said I married you out of pity and sympathy; that shows how little the world knows what it is talking about.'

It is in these two – George V and Queen Mary – that we see several of the key character lines of Elizabeth II.

CHAPTER FOUR

King George and Queen Mary

On the morning of Saturday 7 May 1910, the future Edward VIII and his younger brother, the future George VI, aged sixteen and fifteen and known at home and to their friends as David and Bertie, learnt of the death of their grandfather, Edward VII. The boys woke up and looked out of the window of Marlborough House to see the Royal Standard flying over Buckingham Palace at half-mast. Moments later they were summoned downstairs.

David, the older boy (who became Edward VIII and then Duke of Windsor) later recalled, 'My father's face was grey with fatigue, and he cried as he told us that Grandpapa was dead. I answered sadly that we had already seen the Royal Standard at half-mast. My father seemed not to hear as he went on to describe in exact detail the scene around the deathbed. Then he asked sharply, "What did you say about the Standard?" "It is flying at half-mast over the Palace," I answered. My father frowned and muttered, "But that's all wrong," and repeating as if to himself the old but pregnant saying, "The King is dead. Long live the King!" he sent for his equerry and in a peremptory naval manner ordered that a mast be rigged at once on the roof of Marlborough House.'

This story makes an important point about the Royal Standard. When Diana, Princess of Wales, died in 1997, there was an outcry in the press about the Royal Standard at Balmoral not being flown at half-mast. The Queen was hurt and angered by the criticism – and she was not often given to anger. She felt it showed a lack of understanding of history and tradition. The Royal Standard never flies at half-mast. The flagpole at Buckingham Palace was bare because flags are only flown over a royal residence when the sovereign is in residence. The Queen could see no reason to break with precedent. After several days, against her better judgement, she was persuaded to change her mind and allow a compromise: the Union flag – not the Royal Standard – was flown at half-mast over Buckingham Palace. Except when the sovereign is in residence, when the Royal Standard is flown, the Union flag has been flown over Buckingham Palace ever since. When the Royal Standard is raised you know the sovereign is in the building. That is how, on the final day of Elizabeth II's Platinum Jubilee weekend, the crowd on the Mall got wind that the Queen was going to appear on the Buckingham Palace balcony for what turned out to be the very last time. As the Standard was raised and people began to notice it, the cry went up: 'She's in there! She's coming!' (Incidentally, immediately after King Charles III's accession, because I happened to be there, I noticed the Royal Standard flying above Buckingham Palace late into the evening, even though the new King had left the building and gone back to Clarence House for the night. Occasional mistakes happen, even in the best-ordered palaces.)

George V, Elizabeth II's grandfather, was a stickler for the established order of things – as his granddaughter was to be, by and large. As a boy, Prince George had been a naval cadet. He spent twenty years in the service and, according to his eldest son, throughout his life 'retained a gruff, blue-water approach to all situations, a loud voice, and also that affliction common to Navy men, a damaged ear-drum.' Apparently, 'Damn fool!' was his favourite expression. He had an explosive temper, a sailor's simple sense of humour, and a horror of change for change's sake. He liked things to be 'ship-shape'; he appreciated order. He was a creature of habit: carefully, he checked the barometer, every morning and every night. When his wife, Queen Mary (as Princess May was known after the accession), attempted to shorten her skirts in line with the fashion of the day, the King would have none of it. As their eldest son recalled, 'He disapproved of Soviet Russia, painted finger-nails, women who smoked in public, cocktails, frivolous hats, American jazz and the growing habit of going away for weekends.'

David's verdict on his father was a harsh one, possibly for understandable reasons, as we shall see in a moment. Bertie, the second son, was more respectful of his papa and Elizabeth, Bertie's firstborn, simply loved her royal grandfather. She was only nine when George V died, but she told me she remembered him 'with great affection'. 'He was great fun,' she said.

As she also said, in a different context, 'recollections may vary' and the word 'fun' rarely occurs in other descriptions of George V. Famously, the diarist, diplomat and MP, Harold Nicolson, said that for many years, George 'did nothing at all but kill animals and stick in stamps.' Certainly, his stamp collection was his pride and joy and shooting the great passion of his life. (Elizabeth was fond of stamps, too, but not to the same degree.) As a man with a gun he was almost unstoppable. For example, in the seasons of 1902/03 and 1903/04, not long after he had become Prince of Wales, he counted up 'What I shot' and it was a total of more than 12,300 head of game each year – up from 11,000 in his list of 'Game Killed by Me' in 1896/97. He reckoned the winter of 1913/14, just before the outbreak of the Great War, as the best pheasant-shooting season he had known: he fired 40,000 cartridges personally and noted that he had witnessed 80,000 birds killed. He was considered a brilliant shot (once he managed to kill nineteen birds out of one pack with just twenty-three cartridges) and a serious philatelist with a world-class stamp collection. Understandably, he specialised in stamps from the British Empire, featuring his own head and those of his father and grandmother. A lover of order and detail, he mounted his stamps with care and precision in 132 beautifully bound volumes. He pursued his hobbies, doggedly, year in, year out. He knew others regarded him as 'rather dull', but that did not trouble him.

'He *was* dull, beyond dispute,' according to Sir Alan 'Tommy' Lascelles, assistant private secretary and private secretary to four of the British sovereigns of the twentieth century, 'but my God, his *reign* (politically and internationally) never had a dull moment.'

Queen Victoria and Edward VII gave their reigns their names and their character. Not so George V and Elizabeth II. The quarter of a century between 1910 and 1935 and the seven decades following the Queen's accession in 1952 were extraordinary years of industrial, social, technological and international change, but are never thought of as the Georgian or New Elizabethan eras in the way that 'the Victorian age' and 'the Edwardian age' immediately conjure up a clear picture of both a time and a monarch whose personality somehow exemplified the period in question.

Elizabeth II did not stamp her personality onto the events of her lifetime. She lived through times of unique change – the end of Empire, the end of the Cold War, the sexual revolution that came with the advent of oral contraception, the rise of feminism, the information technology revolution – but made no particular impact on them. Her achievement was not to set a tone or define a time, not to effect change or influence events. There were causes she espoused and themes that she returned to – notably the importance of the Commonwealth and the value of community and of service to others – but she was not a change-maker or a trend-setter. Her achievement was to be herself and, by being who she was, and by giving a lifetime of unwavering and consistent service to the country and the Commonwealth, to illustrate the value of her values of consistency, decency, service and dedication. Significantly, she signed her Platinum Jubilee message to her people: 'Your Servant, Elizabeth R.'

George Gage said of George V: 'He was a very modest man personally, but he believed in the divine right of kings.' Elizabeth II, too, was a very modest woman, but she accepted her destiny as Queen as a sacred duty. At her coronation in 1953, the moment when she was anointed with holy oil was for her the most sacred and significant part of the ritual – and the only part which, at her request, was not shown on television. When Elizabeth took the Coronation oath, she did so with complete conviction. 'The things which I have here promised, I will perform, and keep, so help me God,' she declared standing at the altar in Westminster Abbey before bending forward to kiss the Bible.

To be a queen must be extraordinary. At the Coronation the Archbishop of Canterbury turned to the congregation in each direction of the compass and declared: 'I here present unto you Queen Elizabeth, your undoubted Queen: wherefore all you who are come this day to do your homage and service, are you willing to do the same?' Each time, the congregation replied 'God save Queen Elizabeth!'

From the moment of her coronation onwards, for more than seventy years, Elizabeth II was the object of adulation. People bowed and curtsied before her on a daily basis. When she went on international tours, hundreds and thousands – on occasion, millions – turned out to cheer.

'It didn't affect her at all,' the Duke of Edinburgh said to me. 'She never for a moment thought the cheering was for her personally. It's for the position she holds – it's for the role she fulfils, it's because she's Queen. That's all. She knows that. Her head hasn't been turned by being Queen – not at all. She's quite normal.'

For a king, George V was remarkably normal, too. On his accession in 1910, his first prime minister, Herbert Asquith, described him as 'a nice little man with a good heart', adding he 'tries to be just and open-minded.' David Lloyd George, as Chancellor of the Exchequer, stayed at Balmoral soon after the accession and found his sovereign to be 'a very jolly chap but thank God there's not much in his head.' The Lloyd George verdict on George V and Queen Mary: 'They're simple, very, very ordinary people.'

And they were happily married. 'My husband was not in love with me when we married,' Queen Mary said, 'but he fell in love with me later.' He definitely did. Unlike his father, Edward VII, and his son who became Edward VIII, George V was able to say, 'I'm not interested in any wife except my own.' He wrote to his wife on their thirty-fifth wedding anniversary in 1928:

> *I suppose no two people really suit each other better than we do, although I fear sometimes you must think me rather dull, but I have learnt to look to you to help me in my busy life & you never fail me, indeed I thank God for all the happiness that you have brought me during these 35 years.*

The dynamic between Elizabeth II and the Duke of Edinburgh was different from that between George V and his Queen Consort, but Elizabeth felt grateful to Philip for his support much as George did to Mary. As the Queen said of the Duke of Edinburgh at the time of their fiftieth wedding anniversary in 1997: 'He has, quite simply, been my strength and stay all these years.' And after his death in 2021, the Queen took to using one of her late husband's favourite walking sticks, not just to steady herself as she reached her mid-nineties, but also as a physical reminder of her lifelong 'strength and stay'.

Like her grandfather, Elizabeth II was in the best sense 'ordinary'. She was 'normal', to use Prince Philip's word. Like her grandfather, Elizabeth loved order even as a little girl. 'She was always very tidy,' one of her childhood friends, Sonia Berry, told me. 'She always put her toys away neatly – not something you could say of her younger sister.' Marion Crawford, the young Scots woman known as 'Crawfie' who joined the York household as Elizabeth's governess in the spring of 1932, remembered how carefully little Elizabeth lined up her toy horses, how neatly she folded her clothes, and how – night after night – she took care to position her shoes exactly parallel underneath her chair. After a family lunch one day, when their parents allowed the little princesses a spoonful each of sugar crystals, Margaret Rose, Elizabeth's little sister, born in 1930, ate all hers at once, but Elizabeth, before eating hers, arranged them meticulously, one by one, in a straight line according to size.

George V was a stickler for protocol and correct dress. Elizabeth II also had a reputation for noticing any discrepancies or inaccuraries when it came to uniforms. She had an eagle-eye for a misplaced medal or an order pinned on in the wrong place. I asked her about it once. She said, 'I think if you're going to wear a uniform you should wear it properly. It's important to get the details right.' At private dinner parties or state banquets, she always supervised the table settings personally, making sure the cutlery was placed exactly as it should be and the wine glasses lined up in the correct order. The cookery writer, Delia Smith, told me how, when she became a Companion of Honour, she was invited to stay overnight at Windsor Castle and how overwhelmed she was by the detailed care the Queen took of her guests. The Queen had arranged for royal recipe books from Queen Victoria's day to be on display for Delia to inspect and it was clear to Delia that Her Majesty had been involved in organising the display to the last detail.

In many ways, both George V and Elizabeth II led lives of unparalleled luxury. Materially, they wanted for nothing. But interestingly, beyond their personal passions – in his case, stamps and shooting; in hers, dogs and horses – their wants were modest. They were instictively frugal. During the First World War, the King insisted on food rationing at Buckingham Palace: meals were cut from twelve courses to three and the use of wine or sherry was banned from cooking. Meat was to be served no more than three times a week and the use of excessive hot water for baths very much frowned upon. 'I only get a hot bath once a week now,' claimed the King, '– and – well, you just cannot lather soap in cold water, can you?' Visiting a hospital in the early days of the war, he was invited to admire the new central heating system. 'How lucky you are,' he said. 'You know we have to live in the corner of one room to keep warm?'

Elizabeth II could not abide empty rooms being heated unnecessarily and preferred her rooms heated with electric fires where she could turn on just one or two bars of the fire as required. In the early 1970s, when most of Britain's electricity still came from coal, a dispute with the coal miners led to the halving of coal production and, in December 1973, the imposition by Edward Heath's goverment of a three-day week, with the aim of conserving coal stocks and keeping only truly essential lights on. Most businesses had to limit their electricity use to three days a week and were banned from operating for long hours on those days. The BBC and ITV had to stop broadcasting at 10:30 p.m. each night and the public was instructed to limit heating to one room and to keep non-essential lights switched off. Even the lights on the Christmas tree in Trafalgar Square were switched off until Christmas Day itself. Edward Heath told me that the Queen was more than happy to agree that she and her household would comply with the restrictions. 'She felt that people – especially the younger ones who hadn't experienced the war – were very profligate with their use of fuel. She was absolutely right.' Chatting to Her Majesty in the 1980s, she told me that when her children were younger she spent 'an awful lot of time going from room to room turning off the lights.' 'It really annoys me when people leave the lights on,' she said. 'It's just so wasteful.'

Prince Philip was also an enthusiast for order and economy. 'We're mocked for keeping our cornflakes in Tupperware boxes,' he told me, 'but it's stupid not to.' He was always looking for new ways to do things 'more efficiently, more effectively'. He shared his wife's hatred of waste, but she didn't share his gung-ho enthusiasm for modern gadgets and labour-saving devices. The Duke of Edinburgh was an impatient progressive, while the Queen was naturally conservative. He wanted to be as modern as tomorrow, while she had a lot of time for yesterday.

As she grew older, I think the Queen became less conservative, but one of her private secretaries said to me that he thought her conservatism was deliberate. He told me, 'She feels she should go at the pace of the slowest person in the kingdom, so that no one should feel left behind.'

'I dislike departing from traditions,' said Queen Mary firmly. On the whole, Queen Elizabeth agreed with her, 'except when it's necessary,' she said to me. 'And, of course, sometimes it is.' The Queen certainly agreed with her grandmother on the exhausting necessity of having 'to beam and smile' when on duty. When George and Mary first went as a couple to tour Australia and New Zealand in 1901, Mary found it quite a strain 'knowing that every word and look is being criticised'. The Queen, too, became aware quite early in her reign that if she wasn't smiling her face had a tendency to look unhappy. All her life, when in public and appropriate, she did her best 'to beam and smile' as her grandmother had done before her. Her Mistress of the Robes, the Duchess of Grafton, told me, 'Her face really aches at the end of a long day.'

Elizabeth's personality reflected several aspects of the personalities of both King George and Queen Mary and the style of her grandfather's reign – a new style, very different from that of his father, Edward VII, and grandmother, Queen Victoria – was the style Elizabeth II inherited. As part of his education, the future George V was made to study Walter Bagehot's celebrated book, *The English Constitution* (1867), the volume that sets out to explain the fundamentals of a constitutional monarchy in which the 'efficient' parts of the constitution, where power is exercised, are kept separate from the 'dignified' parts of the constitution designed to inspire the loyalty of the people.

Queen Victoria saw herself as an executive monarch, engaged in the politics of the day. To an extent, so did her son, Edward VII. Bagehot set out a new way forward which George V and his successors have lived by. 'We must not bring the Queen into the combat of politics,' said Bagehot. The monarchy must remain above the political fray and, to be properly respected and revered, must maintain a certain mystery. 'Its mystery is its life,' he wrote famously. 'We must not let in daylight upon magic.'

Bagehot was born in 1826, exactly one hundred years before Elizabeth, but even a hundred years after his death in 1877, Elizabeth II was living out her reign under the Bagehot rules. It is why she never gave an interview. It is why she came to regret the making of the 1969 fly-on-the-palace-walls documentary, *The Royal Family*. It is why, though an enthuastic photographer herself, often photographed holding her own Leica camera, she never allowed any of the photographs she took to be published during her lifetime. It is why books like the one her former governess, Marion Crawford, wrote about her, and like this one, where I am quoting informal conversations with her, were never welcome. She agreed wholeheartedly with her husband. 'Don't talk about your private self in public,' said Prince Philip. 'Just don't.' Do not let in daylight on magic.

That said, the Queen knew she had to be visible. She was often quoted as having said, 'I have to be seen to be believed', though she told me, 'I don't believe I ever said it. It sounds more like Queen Victoria to me.' But she accepted the principle: Elizabeth recognised, from first to last, that being seen by her subjects was fundamental to her role as sovereign. 'The use of the Queen, in a dignified capacity,' wrote Bagehot in 1867, 'is incalculable.' Elizabeth II maintained her dignity all her life. There are no photographs of her in curlers or a bikini. There are not even any photographs of her and her husband kissing or holding hands. There are no records of Her Majesty using bad language or losing her temper in public or doing anything that could for a moment be described as undignified. 'The media,' Prince Philip said to me, 'have done their best to turn us into a soap opera,' but Elizabeth did nothing, ever, to contribute to that.

For more than seventy years as Queen she was on public display – filmed and photographed, painted and applauded – but she never behaved like a performer. On several occasions I found myself waiting privately with the Queen and a lady-in-waiting and an equerry in one room – where she was, as it were, off-stage – before the moment came for the doors to open and for her to enter the next room and then be on stage. She never appeared to 'psych' herself up to make an entrance as an actor might. In my experience, a performer would be different on either side of the door: different off-stage from on-stage. Not so Elizabeth II. She was aware that her appearance mattered, she was conscious that she had to look her best, she knew she had to keep smiling, but she did not ever attempt to 'play the crowd' or play up to the camera. For someone much of whose whole life was spent being 'on show', she was extraordinarily unshowy – and unself-conscious. When I travelled with her on some of her Jubilee tours, I was struck by how, quite naturally, she would take her lipstick out of her bag and apply it, regardless of where she was or who was looking.

Occasionally, but very rarely, she became tetchy with photographers and film crews if she felt they were being intrusive or making an unnecessary fuss. In 2007, the BBC had to apologise to the Queen for wrongly implying that she had stormed out of a photo shoot with the American celebrity photographer, Annie Leibovitz. As agreed in advance, Her Majesty had worn a crown and her Order of the Garter robes for the sitting with the photographer, which was being filmed for a documentary, *A Year with the Queen*. Towards the start of the session Leibovitz was filmed saying to the Queen: 'I think it will look better without the crown because the garter robe is so . . .' Before the photographer could finish saying 'extraordinary', the Queen gave her a cool stare and interrupted:

'Less dressy, what do you think this is?', pointing to what she was wearing.

In a trailer for the programme shown to the press, this exchange was immediately followed by footage of the Queen walking down a corridor, telling her lady-in-waiting: 'I'm not changing anything. I've had enough dressing like this, thank you very much' – implying that the Queen had left the sitting because of the exchange with Leibovitz. In fact, the footage of the Queen in the corridor was filmed as the Queen made her way to the sitting. She did not storm out at all. As a consequence of the incident, the BBC1 Controller, Peter Fincham, who had told journalists the trailer showed the Queen 'walking out in a huff', resigned. Her Majesty had done no such thing and resented the implication that she had.

'She has the patience of a saint,' Prince Philip said to me. The Duke of Edinburgh did not enjoy having his photograph taken. The Queen accepted it as part and parcel of the job. For centuries, sovereigns have recognised the importance of visual imagery. In our mind's eye, most of us see Henry VIII as he was depicted by Hans Holbein – not that any of us have seen the original because it was destroyed by fire in 1698. The image is universally known through the many copies that were made of the portrait. Photography of a sovereign began in Queen Victoria's reign, but most of the pictures of Victoria with which we are most familiar are formal. It was in the reign of Elizabeth II's grandfather, George V, that a new kind of royal iconography was born: alongside the formal, posed portrait, the public was introduced to pictures of royalty in real situations with real people.

Cosmo Lang, Archbishop of York and friend of the King, staying at Balmoral in the summer of 1912, suggested it was time for the sovereign to be seen among his people, that 'it was not enough that they [the people] should assemble in the streets on ceremonial occasions to see him, but that he might, so to say, go to see them – move about with as little ceremony as possible through their own towns, villages and workshops.' So it was that the royal walkabout was born. In June 1912, George V and Queen Mary visited south Wales and met coal miners at work in the pits of the Rhondda Valley. The Queen had a cup of tea in a miner's cottage. They met working people and did so informally, not in 'tall hats and black coats', but in 'ordinary country clothes'. The visit was an astonishing success and the template for a new kind of royal tour. The people liked it, the press liked it, and the King and Queen, though exhausted by it – it was 'very fatiguing' said Queen Mary – found it both instructive and worthwhile.

That same summer, on 9 July 1912, at the Cadeby colliery near Doncaster, an explosion in the south-west part of the main pit killed thirty-five men, with three more dying later due to their injuries. Later on the same day, after a rescue party was sent below ground, another explosion took place, killing fifty-three men from the rescue party. The King and Queen, who were already visiting mining villages in the area, went to the pit the following day to see the situation for themselves and 'to express our sympathy personally.' 'It was awfully upsetting seeing the poor people who had lost relatives,' said the Queen, who emerged from the pit office with tears in her eyes.

Once I asked Lord Charteris, Elizabeth II's longest-serving private secretary, if the Queen herself ever felt she had put a foot wrong. He said, immediately, 'Aberfan. She got that wrong and she knows it.' In October 1966, in the South Wales mining village of Aberfan, a pit-heap collapsed, engulfing the village school and killing 146 people. The Queen expressed her anguish in a public statement and despatched her husband, Prince Philip, and her brother-in-law, Lord Snowdon, to the scene. She did not immediately go herself. It was nine days before she appeared in person in Aberfan. 'It was a mistake,' Charteris told me, 'and one she regrets. The scale of the tragedy called for an immediate response, but she is not a spontaneous person and she is not given to emotional gestures. Custom, form and precedent count with her. She tends to do what she has done before.'

The Netflix TV series, *The Crown* – 'that ghastly thing' is how Prince Charles described *The Crown* to me – devoted an episode to the tragedy of Aberfan and used it to illustrate what they portrayed as the buttoned-up Queen's inability to express emotion. 'I thought they portrayed her very, very callously,' said Jeff Edwards when he saw the episode. Jeff was eight at the time of the Aberfan disaster, and the last child to be rescued alive from the school. He met the Queen several times during her subsequent visits to the area and found her to be anything but unfeeling.

In *The Crown*'s version of events, the Queen (played by Olivia Colman) initially dismisses the suggestion that she should visit Aberfan. After pressure from the prime minister, Harold Wilson, she does eventually go, but on returning to Buckingham Palace, tells the prime minister that she had to pretend to weep for the crowd and the cameras. Jeff Edwards was not impressed. 'In the episode, the Queen says, "We don't do disaster sites, we do hospitals." When I heard that, I thought, "Well, that's rather callous." And knowing the person, I don't think she would have said that, personally.'

I am sure she would not have said it, nor would she have pretended to weep. I know, because the Duke of Edinburgh told me so, that both he and the Queen were aware that people often wanted to see her express emotion more openly, but, as he put it to me more than once, 'She's not a weeper and wailer, for God's sake, but that doesn't make her unfeeling.' I think the Queen herself would have echoed her grandmother, Queen Mary, whose own reserved nature Elizabeth in part inherited. 'The more I feel the less I say,' Mary once confessed to George in a letter, 'I am so sorry, but I can't help it, I often wish I could be less reserved.'

In the years following the tragedy of 1966, Elizabeth II visited Aberfan four times, the last time during her Diamond Jubilee tour in 2012 when she unveiled a plaque at Ynysowen Community Primary School and made a speech. 'I have travelled the length and breadth of this country during my sixty years as your Queen,' she said. 'Prince Philip and I have shared many of the joys and sadnesses of the Welsh people in that time and have always been struck by your sense of pride and your undimmed optimism.'

Elizabeth II learnt the lesson of Aberfan. On 13 March 1996, at Dunblane Primary School near Stirling in Scotland, a man named Thomas Hamilton shot dead sixteen pupils and one teacher, and injured fifteen others, before killing himself. It was – and remains – the deadliest mass shooting in British history. On 17 March, Mothering Sunday, the Queen, accompanied by her daughter, Princess Anne, attended a memorial service at Dunblane Cathedral, meeting the bereaved families who were there and then visiting the staff at Stirling Royal Infirmary as well as young survivors of the massacre and their parents. Michael Forsyth, then Secretary of State for Scotland, told me in the week of the Queen's funeral in 2022, that he had 'never been more moved' in his life than by the events of that terrible week in 1996. 'The Queen was quite extraordinary,' he said. 'To see her concern for the families, the quiet and caring way she talked to the parents and to the children, was deeply impressive. I don't think anyone else could have brought comfort to them in quite the way she did.'

On 14 June 2017, a fire broke out in the twenty-four-storey Grenfell Tower block of flats in North Kensington in West London. Seventy-two people died, with more than seventy others injured, in what was the worst residential fire in Britain since the Second World War. On 15 June, the Queen issued a brief statement: 'My thoughts and prayers are with those families who have lost loved ones in the Grenfell Tower fire and the many people who are still critically ill in hospital.' As George Carey, a former Archbishop of Canterbury, put it to me, 'The Queen always weighs her words. If she says something or someone is in her prayers, she means it. She will be on her knees praying, exactly as she has promised.' Within forty-eight hours of the fatal fire, the Queen, accompanied by Prince William, visited the Westway Sports Centre, the focal point of efforts to support those affected by the tragedy, to meet members of the emergency services, local residents and community representatives, and to sign the book of condolences.

Back in 1912, on 9 July, the day of the Cadeby pit explosion, George V was due to visit a mine nearby. Despite being advised to reconsider, the King insisted on going down a mineshaft as planned. 'Whatever happens,' he said, 'I have got to show I want to do all I can at this time to see for myself, as far as I can, the risks to which my miners are exposed.'

A sovereign must be seen to be believed.

CHAPTER FIVE

Bertie and Elizabeth

Georgie and May – King George V and Queen Mary – had six children:

The future Edward VIII (always known in the family as David), 1894–1972; the future George VI (known as Bertie and father to Elizabeth II), 1895–1952; Mary, later the Princess Royal (and mother of the Earl of Harewood), 1897–1965; Henry, Duke of Gloucester (father of the current Duke of Gloucester), 1900–1974; George, Duke of Kent (father of the current crop of Kents: the present Duke of Kent, Princess Alexandra, and Prince Michael of Kent), 1906–1968; and John, 1905–1919, who was born brain-damaged, suffered epileptic fits and died aged only thirteen after a severe epileptic attack at Wood Farm on the Sandringham Estate, where he was looked after by the family nursemaid, Charlotte Bill, known as Lala – and where, a century later, the Duke of Edinburgh lived during his retirement and where he and the Queen spent some of their last months together.

Back in January 1919, Queen Mary described her boy's death as 'simply heartrending', but felt it was a 'merciful release to the poor little soul of unrest'. The King said, 'It is of course very sad but no one could have wished him to have gone on living, but he was quite happy poor boy.' Even though Prince John had been fifth in line of succession, there was no extended mourning. The King was soon out with his guns again. 'I am thankful,' said Queen Mary, 'it is so good for him & gets him out.'

The rest of the family had been brought up in the main at York Cottage on the Sandringham Estate. As young parents, Georgie and May had been typical of their class and time. They saw their children twice a day: once, briefly, in the morning, and then, for an hour, at tea-time. May was a concerned parent, but not a cosy or a cuddly one. To her children (as to the public at large) she seemed somewhat removed, forbidding and formidable. She was a devoted and dutiful wife: she accepted her place and her husband's character. She knew that his gruff exterior concealed a kindly nature. He suffered from dyspepsia, smoked excessively and had a rough tongue. Their son David said his father had 'a most horrible temper': 'He was foully rude to my mother. Why, I've seen her leave the table because he was so rude to her, and we children would all follow her out; not when the staff were present, of course, but when we were alone.'

Queen Mary was naturally diffident and unassertive, and accepted (as much of the world did in her day) that women were the weaker vessels. She also, of course, respected her husband as monarch as well as master and expected her children to do the same. 'I always remember,' she said, solemnly, 'that as well as being their father he is also their King.' Her long-serving lady-in-waiting and friend, Lady Airlie, said: 'Her devotion to the monarchy demanded the sacrifice of much of her personal happiness.' In the 2020s, when achieving personal happiness is what life is all about for most of us in the peaceful and prosperous countries of the world, that kind of self-sacrifice seems alien. Elizabeth II, born in 1926, inherited her grandmother's view of these things. 'Service demands sacrifice,' she said in 2022. 'It is not enough simply to do our jobs.'

Queen Mary was a serious-minded traditionalist, restrained and disciplined, emotionally cautious. She and King George brought up their one daughter, Princess Mary, to be the same. Mary's son, George Harewood, remembered a family where emotional inhibition was the order of the day. 'We did not talk of love and affection and what we meant to each other,' he said, 'but rather of duty and behaviour and what we ought to do.' That was the Windsor way – and the world Elizabeth II was born into, a million miles from the world of Meghan Markle who, famously, said of her relationship with Prince Harry: 'We've just focused on who we are as a couple,' and 'This is for us. It's part of what makes it so special, that it's just ours.'

Princess Mary, Elizabeth II's aunt, was George V's favourite child and, to a limited extent, indulged. The King was much tougher on his sons, especially the elder two. He picked on them, mocked them, made sarcastic remarks about them, and generally found ways of finding fault with them at every turn. According to Bertie, 'It was very difficult for David. My father was so inclined to go for him. I always thought it was a pity that he found fault with him over unimportant things – like what he wore. This only put David's back up.'

Bertie was not spared. He was a left-handed child but, as was the custom of the time, was forced to become right-handed. He was also knock-kneed and, during his pre-adolescence, for several hours every day, and throughout the night, he was made to wear corrective wooden splints. He developed a pitiful stammer, which dogged him all his days, and infuriated his father. When Bertie was struggling to speak a word, his impatient papa would bark at him, 'Get it out, boy, get it out!'

David, as he grew older, and especially once he had become Prince of Wales, deliberately defied his father, doing his own thing in his own way, and seemingly taking perverse pleasure in irritating – even shocking – his unbending parent. Bertie was more compliant. He gave way to occasional outbursts of frustrated rage – known in the family as his 'gnashes' – but, on the whole, he kept out of trouble's way. Bertie was second-in-line, so, in any event, his public profile was lower, but his stammer also meant that he had less to say. He was shy, awkward, hesitant, in a way David was not. Famously, as a little boy, at lunch with his grandfather, Edward VII, David had dared interrupt the King in full flow. He was immediately reminded that children are to be seen, not heard, and to speak only when they are spoken to. Eventually, he was given permission to say whatever it was he had wanted to say. 'It's too late now, Grandpapa,' he chirruped. 'It was a caterpillar on your lettuce, but you've eaten it.'

King George's chaffing of his sons amounted to bullying. Queen Mary chose not to intervene, but others were bolder. Margot Asquith, second wife of Herbert Asquith, Liberal prime minister at the start of George's reign, told the King that his treatment of his sons would drive them to drink. During the First World War, to set an example, the King imposed a drinking ban on the entire royal household, but after the war, once they were adults, each of the four surviving royal princes drank much more than was good for him.

Henry, the third son, created Duke of Gloucester, at twenty-eight, in 1928, was reckoned the family dullard: a cavalry officer and a country gentleman, he drank too much whisky, but meant well and did no harm. Like Bertie, he had a speech impediment. Like David, he blamed his father. 'My father was the most terrible father,' he said, 'the most terrible father you can imagine.'

George, the youngest surviving son, was his mother's favourite and the most socially adept and easy of her boys. He had an artistic temperament, a fondness for high society and low living, and a loathing for the naval career into which he felt he had been forced by his father. He was a notorious ladies' man who was, apparently, equally at home among the homosexual set. He was once arrested, briefly, in a gay nightclub known as The Nut House. He even dabbled with morphine and cocaine. According to Sir Alan Lascelles, 'the air of a "spoilt child" never quite deserted him'.

In 1934, Queen Mary was 'delighted & excited' when Prince George became engaged to his second cousin, Princess Marina of Greece and Denmark. 'The women of that Danish family make good wives,' she told Lady Airlie. 'I hope all will be for the best & that he will settle down.' Princess Marina was twenty-seven and the daughter of Prince Nicholas of Greece and Denmark, the fourth of the eight children of King George I of Greece. This King George was born a Danish prince in Copenhagen, but to create stability in the region the Great Powers of the day promoted him as a suitable candidate to be King of Greece and he was elected as king by the Greek National Assembly in 1863 when he was only seventeen. He served his adopted country well for fifty years until he was assassinated in 1913 during the First Balkan War. He had two daughters and six sons, most of whom married into branches of assorted European royal houses. His fourth son, Prince Nicholas, married Grand Duchess Elena Vladimirovna of Russia, who was a first cousin of Tsar Nicholas II – as was he. Prince Nicholas's younger brother, Prince Andrew (also known as Andrea), married Princess Victoria Alice Elizabeth Julia Marie of Battenberg (known as Alice), the eldest child of Prince Louis of Battenberg and his wife, Princess Victoria of Hesse and by Rhine – whose mother was Princess Alice, Queen Victoria's second daughter. Prince Andrew of Greece and his wife, Alice, had five children: four daughters and, finally, in 1921, one son: Prince Philip.

The point is this: the wedding of Prince George of the United Kingdom and Princess Marina of Greece and Denmark at Westminster Abbey on 29 November 1934 marks the moment when we know that the future Elizabeth II and the future Duke of Edinburgh set eyes on one another.

'I don't remember much about it,' the Duke of Edinburgh said to me sixty years later.

'But that's when you first met?' I asked.

'We could have bumped into one another before that. We were cousins, after all. My mother was born at Windsor Castle, you know. My grandmother was living at Kensington Palace. My [Mountbatten] uncles were friends of the Yorks [Princess Elizabeth's parents]. We could have met any number of times. Anyway, it was certainly before the so-called "famous first meeting".'

'In 1939, at the Royal Naval College at Dartmouth?'

'Yes,' said the Duke with a weary sigh. It always infuriated him that the day in July 1939 when the King and Queen visited Dartmouth and Prince Philip, as a young naval cadet, was charged with looking after the royal children, was written up as the first encounter between him and his eventual bride. 'It wasn't. We'd met before, but that doesn't suit the way they want to tell the story.'

Prince Philip and Princess Elizabeth were married at Westminster Abbey in November 1947. Thirteen years earlier, in November 1934, Prince George – who had been created Duke of Kent in the run-up to the wedding – married Princess Marina. The eight-year-old Princess Elizabeth was at her uncle's wedding as one of the bridesmaids. The father of the bride was the thirteen-year-old Prince Philip's uncle. Philip was there to support the Greek side of the family: after the marriage service in the Abbey, there was a second service in the private chapel at Buckingham Palace which had been converted into a Greek Orthodox chapel for the ceremony.

Philip had come down to London for the wedding from Scotland, where he was a boarder at Gordonstoun School on the Moray Firth. We can see from the photographs that he was a remarkably handsome boy. By all accounts he was also a charming one: well-mannered, easy-going, outgoing, articulate, intelligent, athlectic, independent, entertaining. He must also have been remarkably resilient.

Born on the Greek island of Corfu in 1921, Philip's family was driven into exile when he was still a baby. He and his parents and his four older sisters went to live with his father's older brother, George, in Paris, but before Philip was ten the family split up. His mother had a breakdown and was sent to an asylum in Switzerland. His father moved to Monte Carlo. His sisters married different German princes. For the rest of his childhood, young Philip, when not at boarding school, had no settled home, but travelled between the homes of assorted relations: his grandmother at Kensington Palace, his Mountbatten uncles, his sisters and their new husbands in Germany. However much you pressed him on the matter, Prince Philip would make no complaint about any of this. 'It's simply what happened,' he said to me. 'The family broke up. My mother was ill, my sisters were married, my father was in the south of France. I just had to get on with it. You do. One does.'

In 1934 when Princess Marina of Greece married Prince George and in 1947 when Prince Philip of Greece married Princess Elizabeth, some within the British royal family expressed their reservations about their impoverished, exiled Greek cousins, but George V in 1934 and George VI in 1947 both went out of their way to be welcoming to their new in-laws. Princess Marina was sophisticated (she smoked in public) and modern (she and Prince George were the first royal couple to be photographed kissing on the cheek), but George V, though determinedly old-school, took to her. She was beautiful and charming and, to his mind, entirely suitable as a royal bride – which could not be said for Mrs Wallis Simpson, the twice-married American destined to marry the King's eldest son, the Prince of Wales.

Despite the King having forbidden it, David brought Mrs Simpson to the Buckingham Palace party held two nights before the royal wedding. He succeeded in introducing his mistress to his mother, but was intercepted by an equerry before he was able to present her to the King. 'That woman in my house!' the King shouted angrily after the event.

Through his twenties and early thirties, the Prince of Wales had a series of infatuations and affairs before his obsession with Wallis Simpson cost him the crown and changed the course of royal history. David's first heavy-duty love affair was with Freda Dudley-Ward, the liberal wife of a Liberal MP, and it is from their correspondence that we learn what we know about his younger brother Bertie's youthful indiscretions. Elizabeth II's father lost his virginity, it seems, in Paris towards the end of the 1914–18 war. According to David, that's where 'the deed was done'. Back in London, Bertie then enjoyed the company of several chorus girls and, on at least one occasion, in 1919, entertained Jack Buchanan's leading lady, Phyllis Monkman, star of the happily titled hit *Tails Up*, to a late supper in a private room in Half Moon Street.

David embarked on his affair with Freda Dudley-Ward in March 1918 and encouraged his younger brother to find himself a married mistress of his own. Sheila Chisholm was young, lively, Australian and game. She was married to Lord Loughborough and she had a baby son (Anthony, born in May 1917), but, nevertheless, she was up for some fun. David and

Freda, Bertie and Sheila, called themselves 'The Four Do's', and certainly did. 'What marvellous fun we 4 do have, don't we, Angel?' wrote the Prince of Wales to Mrs Dudley-Ward, '& f--- the rest of the world.' In 1926, Sheila and Lord Loughborough were divorced, but in 1919 he appears to have been unaware of what his young wife and the two kings-to-be were up to. 'After tea,' David reported gleefully, 'I managed to lure Loughie away on the pretext of wanting to play a few more holes of golf ... so as to give Sheilie a chance of being alone with Bertie ... I'm sure Loughie doesn't suspect Bertie at all!'

That was in June 1919. A year later, on 10 June 1920, Bertie, now twenty-five, and created Duke of York by his father, George V, only the week before, accompanied his mother, Queen Mary, to a Derby Night ball in Grosvenor Square. At around eleven o'clock, the young duke saw a smiling girl across a crowded room. She was chatting to his equerry. The duke asked to be introduced. Lady Elizabeth Angela Marguerite Bowes-Lyon, ninth child and fourth daughter of the 14th Earl of Strathmore and Kinghorne was nineteen, unattached, and pretty as a picture. Bertie later claimed it was love at first sight.

'It was always love at first sight. No one could resist her. No one. Everybody who met her fell under her spell. Always.' That was the verdict of the Hon. Margaret Rhodes, first cousin, childhood playmate and life-long friend of Elizabeth II, niece and sometime lady-in-waiting to Queen Elizabeth, the Queen Mother. Mrs Rhodes's mother was Lady Mary Bowes-Lyon, one of Lady Elizabeth's three sisters. Mrs Rhodes's daughter-in-law, Susan Rhodes, was appointed an Extra Lady-in-Waiting to the Queen in 2017 and, during the Covid pandemic, was part of 'the Windsor Bubble' and a good companion to the Queen in her final years.

Margaret Rhodes, who died aged ninety-one in 2016, was in her late seventies when I first met her, trim and bird-like.

She had a smoker's voice and the beady eye of one who had seen the world and, on the whole, been gently amused. Her elegant, slightly faded drawing room at the Garden House in Windsor Great Park was littered with signed photographs of assorted royals. Her small kitchen table was cluttered with old newspapers, correspondence, invitations, bills. In the downstairs lavatory, beneath the formal picture of the Queen and the Duke of Edinburgh on their wedding day, there was a well-thumbed copy of *The Prince Philip Throneside Book*. Mrs Rhodes was devoted to the memory of her aunt, Queen Elizabeth, the Queen Mother. 'Everybody adored her,' she said. 'Everybody.'

Certainly, I have met few who didn't. Twenty years after her death, aged 101 in March 2002, the Queen said of her mother: 'She had an infectious zest for living and an extraordinary capacity to bring happiness into other people's lives.' Lord David Cecil, who had been a childhood friend of the Queen Mother, told me that 'even as a girl, she had a certain twinkle as well as extraordinary sweetness. She made you feel part of a delightful conspiracy.' Woodrow Wyatt said to me, 'She is the most truly charming person in the world.' Sir John Mills told me, 'No one is more captivating. I have been lucky enough to meet some of the most glamorous women of our time. She outshines them all.' I asked one of her sons-in-law, Lord Snowdon, to sum her up in a single word and, without hesitation, he said, 'Fun.' I asked her other son-in-law about her at the time of her one hundredth birthday and he replied, more enigmatically, 'She certainly keeps going.' Prince Philip had reservations about his mother-in-law, in part because he knew that members of her family had had reservations about him in the 1940s, as we shall see, but largely because he felt she had an emotional hold over Prince Charles 'that's not always been to his benefit, in my opinion.'

In 1920, according to Mabell, Countess of Airlie, who knew her then, Lady Elizabeth's 'radiant vitality', combined with 'a blending of kindness and sincerity' made her 'irresistible to men'. When he came to know her, Prince Philip did resist her 'radiant vitality'. I think he thought it was overdone and he was grateful that his wife had inherited her mother's blend of kindness and sincerity without inheriting her manner, which, according to his cousin, Patricia Mountbatten, he found 'occasionally irritatingly gushing'. He was a cool customer (some, as we shall see, thought him 'a cold fish') who preferred his wife's calm restraint to his mother-in-law's playful exuberance.

At nineteen, Elizabeth Bowes-Lyon was considered pretty rather than spectacularly beautiful. She was small (5 feet 4 inches), but not petite. She had flawless skin, bright blue eyes, but shortish, rather dull, dark hair, cut in a noticeably unsexy fringe. She was anything but 'modern'. According to Lady Airlie, 'she was very unlike the cocktail-drinking, chain-smoking girls who came to be regarded as typical of the nineteen-twenties.' She came from one of Scotland's oldest, grandest families. Her forebears included Robert the Bruce. (As Lord Forsyth, former Conservative Scottish Secretary reminded me in the week of Elizabeth II's funeral: 'The Queen really was Scottish – descended from Robert the Bruce twice over, through her mother's line as well as her father's. Where she chose to die showed her complete commitment to the Union.') The Strathmore properties included Glamis Castle in Scotland; another, lesser castle, Streatlam, in County Durham; a fine, eighteenth-century country house, St Paul's, Walden Bury, in Hertfordshire; and a handsome town house in London, in St James's Square, between Piccadilly and Pall Mall.

Elizabeth Bowes-Lyon's father, Lord Strathmore, was a Scottish nobleman of the old school. He was God-fearing, courteous, kindly, conscientious, conservative, and only mildly eccentric. At breakfast he made his own cocoa and, at lunch, he ate plum pudding every day. Mrs Rhodes recalled the huge dining hall at Glamis and her grandfather at the head of the table: 'I can picture the food being sort of thrown onto the plates and him catching it. I remember, too, he had a wonderful droopy moustache and he smoked endless cigarettes. This was before the age of tipped cigarettes and we children kept watch as his cigarette burnt slowly down to see if it would set fire to his moustache. It never did.' Lord Strathmore took his duties seriously (as a landowner and Lord Lieutenant of Angus) and his recreations were exactly those you would expect: fishing, shooting and cricket. He was an authority on forestry. According to Mrs Rhodes, 'He really loved his trees. Queen Elizabeth used to tell the story of people telephoning Walden Bury and enquiring, "Is his Lordship down from Glamis yet?" "No," the butler would say, "His lordship only comes when the sap rises."'

Lady Strathmore, born Nina-Cecilia Cavendish-Bentinck, also came from good aristocratic stock. Her father, a clergyman, was heir to the 5th Duke of Portland. She, too, took her religion seriously: the chapel at Glamis was in regular use. She was also outgoing, unpretentious, warm, practical, and creative: she was an enthusiastic gardener and an accomplished pianist. Mrs Rhodes told me: 'She died when I was thirteen, but I can see her clearly – a lovely, voluminous figure, in a long black dress with a lace collar. She was a heavenly, smiling granny.' She seems to have been pretty perfect as a mother as well. According to Mrs Rhodes: 'Queen Elizabeth always spoke of her mother with enormous warmth and affection.' In a letter to Osbert Sitwell, she once wrote: 'I have nothing but wonderfully happy memories of childhood days at home.' She was ever grateful to her parents for providing 'Fun, kindness, & a marvellous sense of security.'

In July 1920, in the run-up to her twentieth birthday on 4 August, Lady Elizabeth Bowes-Lyon was, arguably, London's most eligible debutante. She had it all: breeding, looks, intelligence, vivacity, charm. She also had a certain maturity. She had seen something of life. During the 1914–18 war, one of her brothers was killed in action, at the Battle of Loos, and another was severely wounded and captured by the Germans. As part of the war effort, Glamis Castle was turned into a convalescent hospital for wounded soldiers and Elizabeth helped her mother care for the men. If Bertie, newly created Duke of York, fell for her instantly, as he later claimed, he was not alone. Other suitors also made the pilgrimage to Glamis. One of them was Ronald Barnes, 3rd Baron Gorell, who later claimed, 'I was madly in love with her. Everything at Glamis was beautiful, perfect. Being there was like living in a van Dyck picture. Time, and the gossiping, junketing world, stood still. Nothing happened . . . but the magic gripped us all. I fell *madly* in love.' Gorell listed Lady Elizabeth's principal qualities: 'Her charm was indescribable . . . She was also very kind and compassionate. And she could be very funny – which was rare in those circles. She was a wag.' Famously, as a little girl in want of pocket money, she sent a telegram to her father: 'S.O.S. L.S.D. R.S.V.P. ELIZABETH.' Much of Elizabeth II's sense of humour came from her mother.

The list of eligible young men who took a shine to the waggish, wide-eyed, heart-faced enchantress of Glamis was a long one. It included, among others, Prince Paul of Yugoslavia, a good friend of one of her brothers, who did most of his wooing, it seems, by paying court to Lady Strathmore (not a bad stratagem); Henry Gage, the 6th Viscount, who owned Firle Place, in Sussex, plus, he liked to say, 'about 10,000 acres'; the 10th Earl of Airlie's younger son, Brucie, who courted Elizabeth's attention by dancing on the dining-room table while playing the ukelele; Christopher Tennant, the second Baron Glenconner, who was a millionaire and a charmer (and whose first wife, Pamela, would produce Colin Tennant, the future owner of Mustique and friend of Princess Margaret); and James Stuart, the third son of the 17th Earl of Moray, who, at the age of nineteen, had won one Military Cross at the Battle of the Somme and a second at the Battle of Arras. James Stuart was more than a hero: he was reckoned – by many – to be the handsomest man in the kingdom. He was also the new Duke of York's equerry and the man who first introduced Bertie to Lady Elizabeth at the Derby Night ball in Grosvenor Square.

Of her many suitors, none was better connected than HRH Prince Albert, the Duke of York, but most were more obviously attractive: more outgoing, more articulate, less inhibited, less shy. How, then, did Bertie secure his bride? In the old way, it seems: by persistence. James Stuart was delightful: dashing, debonair, dangerous. He was a serial flirt. He was not reliable. Bertie was different. Bertie was dogged. Single-mindedly, he pursued Elizabeth for nearly three years. And he was not unattractive: he was slim, fit, well-dressed, well-mannered, a good shot, a brilliant dancer (this was an age in which that counted for something), a decent chap – kindly and courteous (in any age, that counts for a lot) – with sound instincts and an impeccable pedigree. He was, after all, a royal duke, the second son of the King.

Bertie proposed to Elizabeth three times. Twice she refused him. He did not give up and eventually, he secured his prize. On a Sunday walk in the woods at St Paul's, Walden Bury, in January 1923, she said 'yes', and did so whole heartedly. She belonged to a class and generation where every woman's destiny was to be a wife and a mother – and nothing more. To secure the ideal husband was everything. Elizabeth sensed that in Bertie she had found a good man and that theirs would be a happy match. She was right.

The Strathmores were not besotted with royalty. 'As far as I can see,' Lady Strathmore is said once to have said, 'some people have to be fed royalty like sea-lions fish.' She was not one of them, but nonetheless to be the mother of the first 'commoner' to marry legitimately into the royal family was undoubtedly 'something'. Bertie's mother, Queen Mary, was equally delighted. 'Elizabeth is charming,' she wrote in her diary, 'so pretty & engaging and natural. Bertie is supremely happy.'

The Duke of York and Lady Elizabeth Bowes-Lyon were married in Westminster Abbey on 26 April 1923. The political situation was uncertain and the economy fragile. The King declared that 'the arrangements should be of as simple a character as possible and that no unnecessary expense shall be incurred.' The wedding – the Abbey's first royal wedding since 1382, when Richard II had married Anne of Bohemia – was grand, but not ostentatious. The bride wore a dress of machine-made Nottingham lace, designed in medieval style by Queen Mary's dressmaker, with a veil of Flanders lace lent by the Queen. The groom wore the uniform of a group captain of the recently created Royal Air Force. The ceremony was filmed – in long-shot – for the cinema news-reels, but not broadcast on the fledgling BBC wireless. The Archbishop of Canterbury was concerned that 'disrespectful people might hear the service, perhaps some of them sitting in public houses with their hats on.'

In the run-up to the wedding, Elizabeth made what seems to have been the only unforced error of her public life. An enterprising reporter from the *Star* newspaper turned up at her parents' Mayfair front door and asked Lady Elizabeth for a brief interview. He was granted one. The King was not amused. 'Those filthy rags of newspapers' was how His Majesty regarded the press. Elizabeth never spoke on the record to a journalist again – and the coverage she received over the next eight decades was extraordinary and, almost always, adulatory. She had an instinct for doing what was right and doing it in a way that would be well-received. On her wedding day, as she entered Westminster Abbey, spontaneously she placed her bouquet of white heather and York roses on the tomb of the Unknown Soldier.

The guests at the wedding included a raft of royals, the cream of the aristocracy, a smattering of the great and the good, and thirty boys chosen by the Industrial Welfare Society to represent the ordinary youth of Britain. The Duke of York was President of the IWS and properly interested in giving sporting, recreational and training opportunities to young people. He founded – and attended – an annual summer camp where two hundred working-class lads and two hundred young chaps from public schools came together for an integrated adventure holiday. He pioneered 'social inclusion' seventy years before it became government policy. He undertook good works both because he believed in them and because that was what was expected of a king's second son in the aftermath of the Great War. He and his young duchess did their duty as required – he shyly, she gaily – but, once the excitement of the wedding was over, they neither sought, nor received, undue press or public attention. He was not the king and not ever expected to be. The Prince of Wales was not yet thirty. He was the glamorous one who was in the front line and in the spotlight. His younger brother could – and did – lead a relatively private life.

The Yorks honeymooned at Polesden Lacey, near Dorking in Surrey. The house was put at their disposal by its wealthy owner, Mrs Ronald Greville, later described by Cecil Beaton

(Elizabeth's favourite photographer) as 'a galumphing, greedy, snobbish old toad who watered at her chops at the sight of royalty'. Another of my favourite diarists, Harold Nicolson, described her as 'a fat slug filled with venom'. Elizabeth was more charitable. When Maggie Greville died in 1942, the Queen wrote to Osbert Sitwell: 'She was so shrewd, so kind and so amusingly *un*kind, so sharp, such fun, so naughty.' Mrs Greville, daughter of the brewing magnate William McEwan, left all her jewellery – including Marie Antoinette's diamond necklace – to the Queen, 'with my loving thoughts', and a bequest of £20,000 to Princess Margaret.

From Polesden Lacy, the honeymoon couple went on to Glamis. The weather in Scotland was atrocious and the new duchess contracted whooping cough, 'not,' she conceded, 'a very romantic disease'. This dampener behind them, the Yorks settled in to the life of near-unparalleled privilege – and occasional duty – that was to be their lot. Everybody was utterly enchanted by the Duchess. Most found the Duke a touch awkward. His equerry, James Stuart, who had also been, of course, his rival in love, said of the young Duke: 'He was not an easy man to know or to handle.' The Prince remained capable of sudden, unpleasant, bursts of anger, his notorious 'gnashes'. Margaret Rhodes remembered him 'for his totally schoolboy sense of humour.' She told me: 'He laughed like a drain at ridiculous things, but he had an explosive temper. I saw him once grouse-shooting in a butt. He hadn't shot very well. In fact, he'd shot badly. He threw his guns into the heather in his rage and frustration.' Elizabeth II was not known for bursts of anger, though her son was, especially when younger, particularly during the last years of his marriage to Diana. He has mellowed with age, though, as we saw during the exhausting week following the Queen's death, occasionally he still has flashes of irritability and ill-temper which the now Queen Consort does her best to assuage.

Charles III's grandmother, Elizabeth, did her best to tease her husband out of his ill-humour by taking his pulse and quietly counting: 'Tick, tick, tick, one, two, three.' Elizabeth was good for Bertie. On that, everyone agreed. Naturally, she was not without flaws. Her time-keeping was terrible. More than once, her husband was seen, impatiently pacing the hallway, checking the clock, muttering to himself, 'Where is that damned woman?' But such was her charm, and her lightness of touch, that, it seems, everyone forgave her everything. Even her father-in-law, the King, would indulge her. When, once, famously, she arrived late for dinner with His Majesty, she, of course, apologised. 'Not at all,' said George V, to everybody else's amazement. 'You are not late, my dear. I think we must have sat down early.'

Elizabeth was not over-awed by her father-in-law. 'Unlike his own children,' she said, after his death, 'I was never afraid of him.' George V and Queen Mary enjoyed Elizabeth's company. She was easy with them in a way that very few others were and they recognised how good she was for their son.

Elizabeth's particular gift to Bertie was to do all she could to help him conquer the speech impediment that was the blight of his life. She went with him on his regular visits to Harley Street to see his speech therapist, Lionel Logue. She lay beside him on the floor as he practised his breathing and relaxation exercises. She repeated after him the assorted tongue-twisters designed to help him jump the hurdles of especially challenging consonants. ('Let's go gathering heathy heather with the gay brigade of grand dragoons' was a particular favourite, apparently.) She checked the drafts of speeches he was due to deliver to eliminate the worst stumbling blocks – and, when he came to deliver those speeches, she was on hand, with an encouraging smile, willing him to succeed. He never wholly conquered his impediment, but, over time, he managed to contain it. Lionel Logue said, 'He was the pluckiest and most determined patient I ever had.'

In 2010 the film *The King's Speech* appeared. With Geoffrey Rush as the therapist, Logue, and Colin Firth as George VI and Helena Bonham-Carter as Queen Elizabeth, the picture told the story of the King's valiant struggles with his stammer. It was much acclaimed at the time. Elizabeth II was asked if she'd seen it. 'No,' she said crisply, 'they were my parents. I want to remember them as they were.'

CHAPTER SIX

Lilibet

The young Duke and Duchess of York did not much like the house assigned to them on their marriage in 1923. Originally built as a hunting lodge for George II, White Lodge in Richmond Park (now the home of the Royal Ballet School) was huge and unappealing, unwieldy and uncomfortable. Soon after Elizabeth's first birthday, in 1927, the family moved to 145 Piccadilly, overlooking Green Park, an impressive town house, running to five floors (with electric lift) and featuring assorted reception rooms, a fine dining room, a proper ballroom, a good library, twenty-five bedrooms (including several fit for a king) and an impeccably appointed nursery floor. The indoor staff included a housekeeper, a cook, three kitchen maids, a butler, an under-butler, two footmen, a valet for the Duke, a dresser for the Duchess, an orderly, a handy-man, a night-watchman and a couple of lads: one to wait on the senior servants, one to operate the in-house telephone exchange.

Up on the nursery floor, the little princess had her own retinue. In command was Clara Cooper Knight, known as 'Alah' (to rhyme with Clara), a traditional English nanny, originally from Hertfordshire, who had looked after Lady Elizabeth when she was a baby. Alah, now in her late forties (but looking older in the photographs), was assisted by a young Scots nursery maid, aged twenty-two, the daughter of a railway worker from Inverness, Margaret MacDonald, known as 'Bobo' – someone who would stay close to her royal charge for the next sixty-seven years.

Bobo got her nickname playing Hide and Seek with little Elizabeth. She'd surprise the young princess with a 'Boo!' The toddler would reply with a 'Boo! Boo!' that soon became 'Bobo'. And Bobo soon became indispensable to the little princess, both as nursemaid and companion. She slept in her bedroom until Princess Elizabeth was thirteen. She went on to be her dresser and, even in her eighties, was still bringing the Queen her early morning tea and laying out Her Majesty's clothes for her every morning. Even when she officially retired, Bobo continued to live at Buckingham Palace, and died in her own suite there, in 1993, aged eighty-nine. 'She knew me as a baby,' said the Queen. 'Of course, we were very close.' 'She even turned up on our honeynoon,' Prince Philip told me. 'Can you believe it?'

Quite soon, little Elizabeth would come to be known by her own diminutive: Lilibet – King George's pet name for his favourite grandchild, based on the way she pronounced her name when she first began to talk. Bobo was one of only a tiny handful of people outside the Queen's immediate family who called her Lilibet, not only when she was a toddler, but throughout her life. Lilibet was the Queen's very personal nickname, used only by those in her most intimate circle.

On 4 June 2021, at the Santa Barbara Cottage Hospital in California, Meghan, the Duchess of Sussex, gave birth to her second child and first daughter and she and her husband, Harry, Duke of Sussex, decided to call their newborn Lilibet Diana – in honour of the Queen, Harry's grandmother, and his mother, Diana, Princess of Wales. According to the Sussexes, Harry sought his grandmother's permission to use her intimate family nickname as the Christian name for her eleventh great-grandchild. The Queen's recollection was a little different. According to the Queen, Harry told her the Sussexes wanted to call the baby 'Lilibet' in her honour and she accepted their choice with a good grace, taking it as the compliment it was intended to be. Others in the family found the choice 'bewildering' and 'rather presumptuous' given that 'Lilibet' as a name had always been intimately and exclusively the Queen's. Later the Queen said, 'I hear they're calling her "Lili" which is very pretty and seems just right.'

Now the Queen is dead, Lili Mountbatten-Windsor is seventh in the line of succession to the British throne – one behind her brother, Archie Mountbatten-Windsor, and one ahead of her great-uncle, Prince Andrew, Duke of York. As a male-line great-grandchild, rather than a grandchild, of a monarch, she was not a princess during Elizabeth II's lifetime, but, technically, under letters patent issued by George V in November 1917, she could be entitled to become a princess upon the accession of her grandfather, Charles III – but that's not a likely prospect given that she is being brought up in America and the Sussexes have withdrawn from official royal life in the United Kingdom.

Back in the late 1920s, George V gave the little princess he called Lilibet the time, attention and affection he had denied his own children. He played with her – properly, down on all fours. He indulged her, sitting her at his side at breakfast and tea and feeding her titbits from his own plate. He took her with him on holiday, to Sandringham and to Balmoral – even to Bognor, in 1929, where he was recuperating from a near-fatal illness. Most significantly, perhaps, he shared with her his love of dogs and horses. He had a passion for racing and racehorses and loved nothing better than to take young Lilibet around the stud at Sandringham. For her fourth birthday, in April 1930, he gave her her first pony, a Shetland called Peggy.

According to the novelist Graham Greene, 'There is always one moment in childhood when the door opens and lets the future in.' For Lilibet, the moment when her grandfather gave her Peggy was probably it. 'Yes,' said the Queen many years later when I put the idea to her, 'that's probably when it all began. I do love my horses.' Horses – closely followed by dogs – were the abiding, sustaining passion of her life. What began with Peggy was followed by so many more. If she had been writing this book, not me, it would be largely about horses. As a young princess, she petted them, groomed them and rode them. As an adult, she bred horses of every kind: riding horses, racehorses, carriage horses, hunters, polo ponies, Highland ponies and Fell ponies, and rare breeds like Cleveland Bays. One of the most touching moments on the day of the Queen's funeral was when her black Fell pony, Emma, who the Queen had continued to ride well into her nineties, appeared at the roadside of the Long Walk in Windsor as the sovereign's hearse drove past. The pony's saddle had one of the Queen's headscarves over it and Emma lifted her foot as the Queen's coffin came into view.

The Queen named all her horses herself and could remember the parentage of every one. If you asked her in her old age about her favourites, she would mention Betsy – a spirited black-brown mare she used to ride in the 1960s – and Burmese – given to her in 1969 by the Royal Canadian Mounted Police, and ridden by her in Trooping the Colour for eighteen years before the mare retired to Windsor in 1986 – as well as Sanction – the horse she felt 'could read my mind' who died in the year of her Golden Jubilee in 2002 – and Doublet and Columbus, two horses that her daughter, Princess Anne, rode during her early days as an eventer in the 1970s. Princess Anne won the European Eventing Championships at Burghley on Doublet in 1971, leading the Duke of Edinburgh to compliment his wife on breeding both the horse and its rider. The Queen told me Princess Anne was less happy with Columbus: 'he was more of a man's ride,' she said. Columbus's stable name was The Monster. He won Badminton in 1974, despite leg injuries, ridden by Princess Anne's husband at the time, Mark Phillips. The Queen and her mother both loved Columbus. 'He had everything,' said the Queen. He also hunted and team chased and jumped round the old Grand National course with style. The Queen Mother liked to say he was 'the Grand National horse that never was'.

The Queen's recollections of her favourite ponies started with Peggy, her first Shetland pony, and ended with Emma. 'Emma was a wonderful servant to the Queen,' said Terry Pendry, for thirty years stud groom and manager of the Royal Mews at Windsor and the man who would go out riding with her at Windsor, Balmoral and Sandringham, and stood alongside Emma on the Long Walk in Windsor on the day of the funeral. 'The Queen knew more about horses than anyone I've ever known,' he told me. 'If she'd been a horse, she'd have been matriarch of the herd – the vault of knowledge. Her knowledge was so deep and it went right back to her childhood.'

The Queen loved her horses and loved talking about them. At a polo match at Windsor once, when Prince Charles was playing and the Queen was watching, the actor Ian Ogilvy was in the refreshment tent when Her Majesty wandered in – 'tweeds, headscarf, muddy wellington boots'. When he was presented to her, to make conversation, the actor suddenly remembered the name of one of the horses she used to ride on ceremonial occasions. 'I was wondering, ma'am – whatever happened to Bombardier?'

'Oh, my goodness,' said the Queen, her face lighting up. 'Well, it's funny you should ask, because I've just been to see him. He's very old, of course, but he lives here at Windsor, in his own field just half a mile away. So I went into his field, you see, and he came trotting over, as always, because we know each other terribly well, of course – great old friends, in fact – and I always take him a carrot or an apple or something – and I was just giving it to him, you see, when I heard this awful snorting and thumping noise and I looked up and there was this huge stallion charging at me! At full gallop! I had no idea what he was doing in Bombardier's field, but here he was, pounding towards me, and his eyes were all red and his ears were laid back and his enormous teeth were bared – just like *this*!' And here Ian Ogilvy claims to be one of the few of the late Queen's subjects to have seen Her Majesty 'performing her homicial horse routine'. 'And I knew without a shadow of doubt,' the Queen continued, 'that he was going to *kill* me so I ran, quite literally *ran*, as fast as I could to the gate and got out just seconds before he attacked me and – well, the fact is – you very nearly lost your sovereign.'

The Queen loved a story of a runaway horse. Waiting in the Mall to witness the return of the Queen's body from Balmoral to Buckingham Palace on 13 September 2022, Major-General Sir Sebastian Roberts, formerly Commanding Officer of the 1st Battalion of the Irish Guards and Major-General commanding the Household Division, told me his happiest memory of Her Majesty. Rehearsing for Trooping the Colour, the Queen's Birthday Parade, and riding a new horse, a powerful charger of 19.5 hands, the animal ran away with the commanding officer, careering down the Mall at 40 miles per hour. Eventually, with a cry of 'Pull the effing reins 'til the bridle comes out of his arse' from a seargent-major ringing in his ears, the Major-General managed to bring the horse under control. Later in the day, when Roberts recounted the tale to the Queen, he said, 'She laughed and laughed and laughed. I've never seen her laugh so much.'

She was always happy with horses. Margaret Rhodes – then Margaret Elphinstone – was ten months older than her cousin, and, when they were children, in the late 1920s, when Lilibet was staying in Scotland, at Glamis or Balmoral, they played together. 'What did we play? We endlessly played at horses. That was her idea. We galloped round and round the field. We were horses of every kind. Cart-horses, racehorses, circus horses. We spent a lot of time as circus horses.'

'Were there other games you enjoyed as children?' I asked her. Mrs Rhodes laughed and lit another cigarette and gazed into the middle distance. 'We played "Catching happy days". Do you know it? It's a game you play in the autumn. You just run around trying to catch the leaves as they fall from the trees before they hit the ground. It's a wonderful game. I remember, too, we invented a play. We put it on in Scotland and then again at St George's Hall at Windsor Castle. It was the story of one family through the ages. I remember carrying the Queen across the threshold. I was the young man in the play. Anyway, I dropped her. Of course, in those days, there wasn't the faintest idea she might be queen.'

In fact, by the end of 1930, the possibility that young Princess Elizabeth might indeed one day be queen was being openly discussed. In August 1930, the Yorks had produced a second child, but it was a girl. Rumour was rife: as adolescent naval cadets both Bertie and David had contracted mumps, which might have affected their fertility. Producing Lilibet and her sister – Princess Margaret Rose – had taken the Yorks all of seven years. Were they now likely to have a third child, and, if they did, would it be a boy? The Prince of Wales was thirty-six and still unmarried. Even if he found a wife in the foreseeable future, would he be able to father an heir?

The public, the press, even her parents, were speculating as to little Lilibet's destiny. Queen Victoria had succeeded her uncle. Would Princess Elizabeth succeed hers? Did she, even as a toddler, have the makings of a monarch? Osbert Sitwell recalled the Duke of York telling him: 'From the first moment of talking she showed so much character that it was impossible not to wonder that history would not repeat itself.' In September 1928, Winston Churchill – who would, one day, be Elizabeth II's first prime minister – stayed at Balmoral as a guest of King George and Queen Mary. He wrote to his wife: 'There is no one here at all, except the family, the household and Princess Elizabeth – aged 2. The latter is a character. She has an air of authority and reflectiveness astonishing in an infant.'

Margaret Rhodes remembered her as 'a jolly little girl, but fundamentally sensible and well-behaved. Princess Margaret was the naughty one. She was always more larky. She used to tease the servants. There was a wonderful old page and, as he carried the plates around the dining room, Margaret used to stare at him, trying to make him laugh. But she never got herself reprimanded. She got away with everything. She made her father laugh.'

Everyone I have met who knew the two princesses when they were little girls noted the difference between them. Anne Glenconner, daughter of the Earl of Leicester, remembers Lilibet and Margaret Rose coming with their parents to Holkham Hall, the Leicesters' neo-Palladian country house at Wells-next-the-Sea in Norfolk, twenty miles from Sandringham. 'Princess Margaret was always the naughty one. We'd run around the house playing games, riding our tricycles along the corridors, getting in the way of the footmen trying to do their work. Princess Elizabeth was older than us and she didn't approve. "Don't do that, Margaret, don't do that, Anne" – she was always telling us off.' Lady Glenconner showed me a photograph of the three little girls taken in the early 1930s. Princess Elizabeth is looking down at Margaret and Anne very disapprovingly.

From the age of five, Lilibet's closest friend outside the family was Sonia Graham-Hodgson, who became Sonia Berry. Sonia was the daughter of Sir Harold Graham-Hodgson, radiographer to the royal family, and a Mayfair neighbour of the Yorks. Sonia and Lilibet met in 1931, playing in Hamilton Gardens, behind Piccadilly. 'I was five and she was four,' Sonia recalled. 'I had no idea who she was, but I can see her now in a pink or red dress. She says I was wearing a blue coat, but we always argue over what we were wearing. I was the bossy one then – I rather rubbed in that I was eight months older. I was tall and she was rather small.'

Sonia and Lilibet played together in the gardens in Mayfair, in the nursery at 145 Piccadilly, and in the thatched Wendy House at Royal Lodge, Windsor. Sonia showed me photographs of the pair of them (uniformed nannies in attendance) walking hand in hand in the park. Another evocative picture showed them out cycling together: Lilibet, on her tricycle, looking very determined. 'We quarrelled like normal children,' said Sonia, 'but she was a thoughtful and sensitive child, and naturally well-behaved. She never seemed aware of her position and paid no attention to the people who stood by the railings to watch her play.' And the Yorks as parents, by the standards of their time and class, were noticeably hands-on. 'The Duchess, having had a very happy childhood herself, was all the more determined that, because the children were royal, they should have an ordinary childhood. The Duke never seemed shy, he didn't stutter and he played games, like Sardines. I remember my starchy nanny saying that she found it very undignified having to hide in a bush with him.'

When I went to visit Sonia Berry at her home in Bath she showed me some of the letters Lilibet had sent to her when they were little girls. They give a good flavour of the child and the childhood:

Please excuse blots, messes etc as I am just going to bed because we've just come back from Royal Lodge where there is about four inches of snow. We made an igloo, an armchair and an ice cake. Really I have no other time to write here because we're living in a whirl of excitement. I hope your mother is well. Longing to see you again. With lots of love from Lilibet xxxxxooooo

The following spring – in March 1936, when young Princess Elizabeth was not quite ten – in a clear hand (and without any spelling mistakes), she wrote to Sonia from Compton Place in Eastbourne, one of the homes of the Duke and Duchess of Devonshire:

I'm so sorry not to write sooner but we have done such a lot that I couldn't find time. We've had such fun here. We went to Beachy Head where the cliffs fall sheer down to the sea. Then we went to Burling Gap and played on the beach. We went to Seaford and saw a waiting steamer coming in to harbour. Then went to Cooden Beach where it was lovely. Papa and all of us, except Mummy who had a cold, went to a place called High and Over where the name suited it very well because you went high and then you went over. The next day we went to Cooden Beach again and we picked up a lot of shells and then we had tea in a hotel – wasn't that lovely? Tarts with cream and jam. It was lovely and I wished you were there. We've got a little chalet on the beach and it's perfectly lovely. Two big lounge chairs and two little basket chairs. I hope you are quite well and Woolly [Sonia's governess] I hope is better. Not having any more colliwobbles! Love from Lilibet.

It's clear: the Yorks were a happy family. They had reason to be. These were the years of the Great Depression, but – though the King ordered a general tightening of the royal belt – his family was mostly cushioned from the harshness of reality. The Yorks led comfortable, ordered lives. They already had a fine house in Mayfair and, in September 1931, the King had given them, in addition, a handsome weekend retreat in the mock-Gothic shape of the Royal Lodge in Windsor Great Park. They spent Easter at Windsor Castle; Christmas and the New Year at Sandringham; August and September in Scotland. There was nothing rackety about their lives. The Prince of Wales might desport himself on the continent with one or other of his mistresses, but the Yorks only ever went abroad on duty. They took their duties seriously. They took their role as parents seriously as well.

Yes, they would travel to foreign parts when they had to (in January 1927, when Lilibet was only nine months old, they went without her on an official visit to Australia and New Zealand that kept them away for six months), but when they were at home – and they were mostly at home – they were much more intimately involved in the care and upbringing of their children than many aristocratic parents of their generation. The Yorks gave time and attention to their daughters: they played with them, they bathed them, they read to them, they gathered round the piano after tea and sang songs together. Prince Philip barely saw his parents throughout his adolescence. Lilibet saw hers every day.

'Of course,' said Mrs Rhodes, lighting another cigarette and putting her head gently to one side, 'we were educated at home. The Queen and I were really the last generation of gels who didn't go to school. We thought school would be ghastly. You'd have to play hockey. We didn't want to play hockey. I had a French governess. The Queen and Princess Margaret had Crawfie.' Mrs Rhodes smoothed out her skirt with an anxious hand. 'I knew Crawfie. She was very nice really, but then she wrote the book. I haven't read it.'

A silence fell. 'It's rather good,' I said.

'It probably is,' said Mrs Rhodes, stubbing out her cigarette and laughing. 'I still haven't read it. I don't think I shall.'

'Crawfie' was Marion Crawford, the young Scots woman who joined the York household as Lilibet's governess in the spring of 1932. 'The book' is *The Little Princesses*, Crawfie's account of the childhoods of Lilibet and Margaret Rose based on her sixteen years of royal service and published – to the dismay and astonishment of the House of Windsor – in 1950.

Crawfie, born in Ayrshire in 1909, had trained as a teacher at Moray House in Edinburgh, working with young children from difficult backgrounds. She had plans to go on to train as a child psychologist. Tall, trim, intelligent, ambitious, she was introduced to the Yorks by another of the Duchess's older sisters, not Lady Elphinstone (Margaret Rhodes's mother), but Lady Rose Leveson-Gower, whose daughter, Mary, had been taking lessons with her. Crawfie was an excellent governess and a good friend to Lilibet and Margaret Rose, until, by publishing her book, she betrayed their trust – and became, overnight, a 'non-person'.

CHAPTER SEVEN

Miss Crawford and Mrs Simpson, Ms Giuffre and Ms Markle

In royal circles, there have always been 'people you don't talk about'. From the time of the abdication in 1936 until the time of their deaths, in 1972 and 1986, the Duke and Duchess of Windsor were regarded as *personae non gratae* by the rest of the royal family and mentioned in conversation rarely, if at all. 'Well,' said Tony Snowdon, Princess Margaret's husband, who adored his mother-in-law, Queen Elizabeth, 'the Windsors lived abroad, so it was quite easy to forget about them. As a family, I think the royal family is quite good at blanking out anything unpleasant or uncomfortable.'

These days, the names of Harry and Meghan, the Duke and Duchess of Sussex, do not crop up very often in court circles. When they do, courtiers flinch almost imperceptibly and change the subject – or, if that's not possible, refer to them obliquely as 'persons who live overseas'. Mention the Sussexes to other members of the royal family (and why would you?) and they simply smile briefly and say, 'We wish them all the best' – and nothing else.

As I write this, the members of the new King's communications team are bracing themselves for what may come when Prince Harry publishes his much-talked-about memoir, the 'accurate and wholly truthful' account of his life for which his publishers reportedly agreed to pay him an advance on royalty earnings of 20 million US dollars. 'I'm writing this not as the prince I was born, but as the man I have become,' said Harry when the book was initially announced. In fact, of course, he was not writing it at all: he was telling his story to a ghostwriter, Pulitzer prize-winning former *Los Angeles Times* journalist, J. R. Moehringer, who had previously worked on books for the tennis star, Andre Agassi, and the co-founder of Nike, Phil Knight.

Harry's book was promised for the autumn of 2022. I first feared that Elizabeth II's health was deteriorating more rapidly than we were being told early in the summer when news came that the publication of the tell-all Sussex memoir was being postponed. I assumed Harry had been informed that his grandmother was quite poorly and decided to pause publication in consequence. After her death, it was announced that the book would be further delayed so that he could write additionally about his grandmother's funeral.

The Queen, I know, was devoted to her grandson, Harry. She loved him, she thought him 'huge fun', and she truly wished him well in the new life he sought for himself in California. Whenever he called his grandmother from his address at 765 Rockridge Road, Montecito, he was always put through to Her Majesty immediately. She even 'understood' his desire to write his book, not only for the money but because he wanted to tell his story – to speak his truth. She never read them, but her attitude to books about the royal family changed over the years. When Crawfie published *The Little Princesses* in 1950, both the royal family and the royal household were appalled. In 2012 and 2019, when Angela Kelly published *Dressing the Queen: The Jubilee Wardrobe* and *The Other Side of the Coin: The Queen, the Dresser and the Wardrobe*, she did so with her royal boss's full blessing and approval.

Given her age and experience, as the years went by the Queen was increasingly able to take the long view. She did rather feel she had 'seen it all before' – as she told me in 1990 when we talked about the economic recession. I mentioned the challenges facing the new Chancellor of the Exchequer, Norman Lamont, and she remembered similar challenges faced by R. A. Butler, who had been Chancellor when she came to the throne in 1952.

She remembered, too, 'the fuss there was' in 1951 when her uncle, the Duke of Windsor, published his ghost written volume of memoirs, *A King's Story*. He wanted to tell his truth and he needed the money. 'Nothing's new,' said the Queen in a different context. The former Edward VIII did not attend Elizabeth II's coronation in 1953. He watched it on television in Paris and was paid to write articles about it for the *Sunday Express* and *Woman's Home Companion*. He produced another book, too: *The Crown and the People: 1902 – 1953*. In due course, in 1956, the Duchess of Windsor published her own book – *The Heart Has Its Reasons* – just as surely as Meghan will one day publish hers, possibly with a not dissimilar title. In 1956, the Windsors even gave a no-holds-barred television interview to the Oprah Winfrey of the day, Edward R. Murrow, appearing on the legendary broadcaster's *Person to Person* chat show.

The Windsors were regular visitors to New York, but spent most of their exiled lives in Paris. The Sussexes live further away, in California, which is useful: out of sight, out of mind. Prince Andrew lives at Windsor, unfortunately, so he is not so easy to avoid. On 29 March 2022, very publicly, the 'disgraced' Duke of York accompanied his mother to the memorial service in honour of his father, the Duke of Edinburgh. He travelled with her by car from Windsor to Buckingham Palace and then on to Westminster Abbey where he walked her towards her seat, holding her by the arm. The

Queen was happy to have her second son at her side: this was a family as much as a state occasion and it was in honour of the man who was his father as well as her husband. Indeed, Prince Andrew was named after Prince Philip's father, Prince Andrew of Greece and, in the Queen's view, though her son might be guilty of occasional poor judgement he had not been found guilty of any criminal offence. As we know, on 9 August 2021, Virginia Roberts Giuffre filed a civil lawsuit against the Queen's second son, alleging that she was forced to have several sexual encounters with him in the early 2000s after being 'trafficked' by Andrew's friend, the financier Jeffrey Epstein, when she was sixteen and seventeen years old. Andrew denied the claims absolutely, while agreeing to pay (with his mother's help) millions of dollars to settle the case out of court and avoid a trial during Elizabeth II's Platinum Jubilee year.

When the Queen died, each of her children published a personal statement about her. Prince Andrew's was accompanied by a black and white image of his mother holding him as a baby in March 1960. It was written in the form of a personal letter to his mother:

Dear Mummy, Mother, Your Majesty, three in one.

Your Majesty, it has been an honour and privilege to serve you.

Mother – of the nation, your devotion and personal service to our nation is unique and singular; your people show their love and respect in so many different ways and I know you are looking on honouring their respect.

Mummy, your love for a son, your compassion, your care, your confidence I will treasure forever. I have found your knowledge and wisdom infinite, with no boundary or containment.

I will miss your insights, advice and humour. As our book of experiences closes, another opens, and I will forever hold you close to my heart with my deepest love and gratitude, and I will tread gladly into the next with you as my guide.

God save The King.

Some of the turns of phrase in Prince Andrew's letter to his mother could have been penned by his former wife, Sarah Ferguson, Duchess of York, who still shares a home with the prince and whose first historical romance, *Her Heart for a Compass*, was published by Mills & Boon in 2021, but the part of the message he very much wanted the rest of us to take note of was where he spoke of the 'confidence' the Queen had shown in him.

Prince Andrew stepped down from public life over his friendship with Jeffrey Epstein in 2019. He was stripped of his honorary military roles, including as Colonel of the Grenadier Guards, and was obliged to give up his HRH style in public. But his mother stood by him to the last. She loved her boy. She retained her 'confidence' in him. Through the long weeks of lockdown during the Covid pandemic, Andrew and his mother, living close to one another at Windsor, would meet up and go together for long, companionable walks across Windsor Great Park. The Duke of York told the Queen the whole story of his long relationship with Epstein, all the ins and outs of it, and the details of the accusations made against him. The first time he gave her the full account of the whole sorry saga, she listened carefully and responded with just one word: 'Intriguing.'

The Queen never said more than was necessary, but she accepted her son's version of events. She was ready to believe him, and to help bail him out, but she also realised the reality of the situation. With such a cloud hanging over his reputation, 'fair or unfair, for the sake of the stability of the monarchy', he had to give up his royal duties and step back from public life.

Famously, in 1995, at a dinner held at Claridge's Hotel to mark Margaret Thatcher's seventieth birthday, John Profumo, the disgraced former minister who had lied to parliament and helped bring down Harold Macmillan's government because of his association with the 'call girl' Christine Keeler, found himself seated at the Queen's right hand – at Her Majesty's suggestion. Profumo had redeemed himself through good works in the thirty years since the scandal of the 'Profumo affair' of the early 1960s and the Queen wanted to make her support for Profumo visible. In the same way, when the press were writing stories about the Duke of Edinburgh and his 'friendship' with his carriage-driving companion, Penny Romsey, the Queen invited Penny to join her on the drive to church knowing they would be photographed together.

Over the years, even before the Epstein scandal, Prince Andrew was criticised in the press and, when he was, the Queen often rode to the rescue, recognising him with an honour or being seen with him in public. And even when her boy's association with the 'billionaire paedophile Epstein' was front page news, the Queen went out riding with her son and arranged that the two of them be photographed together.

The Queen was glad to have her second son at her side as she travelled to her husband's memorial service. The rest of the royal family was less happy to see Prince Andrew taking centre stage, not because of any personal hostility towards him, but because they feared the pictures of him side by side with the Queen would dominate the press coverage of the memorial service – and so it proved.

When it came to the Queen's funeral, there was less anxiety, simply because everyone knew that the focus would be so completely on the Queen that everything else would be a sideshow. The new King, of course, expected his brother, Andrew, to be present, and his son, Harry, also, but expected them on parade and mourning as family members, not in any way as 'working royals'. For that reason, neither was invited to the Buckingham Palace eve-of-funeral reception for visiting heads of state, and both were expected to appear for the lying-in-state and funeral in morning suits rather than uniforms. Eventually, knowing how much it mattered to Prince Andrew, and, even more so, knowing what his mother, the Queen, would have wanted, Charles III permitted the Duke of York to attend the vigil for the Queen in Westminster Hall wearing the military dress uniform of a Vice Admiral of the Navy, the only military rank he still holds. That concession made, the King then agreed that Harry could wear a uniform, too, when, along with the Queen's seven other grandchildren, he took part in a Westminster Hall vigil. He was dressed in the Blues No. 1 Uniform, with KCVO Neck Order and Star, Afghanistan Operational Service Medal, Golden, Diamond and Jubilee medals and Army Pilot Wings – but not the ER initials on the shoulder of the uniform which are reserved for those in 'active service'. Prince William sported the ER initials on his uniform and his younger brother was said to be 'heartbroken' and 'insulted' by what he conceived as a snub, especially as during his years of service Harry had seen rather more frontline military action than William had.

At the BBC, where I was helping with the coverage of the royal vigils at the lying-in-state in Westminster Hall, we were told before the broadcast: 'We're not mentioning the uniforms. Any of them.' When I protested that 'People might want to know about what the Princess Royal is wearing,' the response was emphatic: 'Too bad. We are *not* mentioning the uniforms.' And we did our best not to mention the Duke of York, beyond noting his presence when he was in shot.

His mother loved him to the last, of course, and, naturally, his former wife and their two daughters stand by him, and he still has good friends and loyal allies, but these days the Duke of York is someone who, in royal circles, it's better not to talk about.

It was the same with Crawfie. She did not break the law, but she did break the rules. In 1949, when she retired after sixteen years' service with the royal family, she was approached by an American magazine, the *Ladies' Home Journal*, with a handsome offer for her memoirs. She wrote to her former employer, Queen Elizabeth, for advice and Her Majesty's response, in a letter of 4 April 1949, was crystal clear: 'I do feel, most definitely, that you should not write and sign articles about the children, as people in positions of confidence with us must be utterly oyster. If you, the moment you finished teaching Margaret, started writing about her and Lilibet well, we should never feel confidence in anyone again.'

Crawfie, encouraged by her husband, disregarded the Queen's wishes and published, first articles, and then 'the book'. By the time Crawfie died, aged seventy-eight in 1988, Elizabeth II had forgiven her former governess, but I am not sure Queen Elizabeth, the Queen Mother, ever could. 'It was the beginning of the end,' she said. 'It opened the floodgates. It was an invasion of the children's privacy. It was an intrusion. It was a betrayal.'

There is nothing shocking in *The Little Princesses*. Far from it. The tone is altogether deferential, the literary style perhaps overly sweet and sentimental, but the observation is often shrewd and the details revealing. Here is Crawfie's account of her entry into the nursery world of Royal Lodge and her first encounter with Alah Knight, the formidable nanny, 'a tall, noble-looking woman', and little Princess Elizabeth, the heroine of her story, and ours:

Alah awaited me with that mixture of reserve and apprehension felt by all nannies when the governess is introduced. I like to remember that in all my years at 145 Piccadilly, London, and later at Buckingham Palace, Alah and I remained good friends; and if on her side the neutrality was sometimes armed to the teeth, I was always very careful not to tread on her toes.

Alah had entire charge in those days of the children's out-of-school lives – their health, their baths, their clothes – while I had them from nine to six. She had to help her an under-nurse and a nursemaid. These two girls are there still – Margaret MacDonald and Ruby MacDonald, two sisters, who have become the personal maids and friends of two sisters.

The night nursery was decorated in pink and fawn, the Duchess's favourite colour scheme. A small figure with a mop of curls sat up on the bed. She wore a nightie with a design of small pink roses on it. She had tied the cords of her dressing gown to the knobs of the old-fashioned bed, and was busy driving her team.

That was my first glimpse of Princess Elizabeth.

'This is Miss Crawford,' said Alah, in her stern way.

The little girl said, 'How do you do.' She then gave me a long, comprehensive look I had seen once before, and went on, 'Why have you no hair?'

I pulled off my hat to show her. 'I have enough to go on with,' I said. 'It's an Eton crop.'

She picked up her reins again.

'Do you usually drive in bed?' I asked.

'I mostly go once or twice round the park before I go to sleep, you know,' she said. 'It exercises my horses.' She navigated a dangerous and difficult corner, and went on, 'Are you going to stay with us?'

'For a little while, anyway,' I replied.

The account has the feel of a novella, but also the ring of truth. We are introduced immediately both to Lilibet's discriminating, observant eye and to her passion for horses. We can picture the child, the nanny and the governess quite clearly. Lilibet comes across as an intelligent child, a dutiful daughter and a responsible older sister. Her love of dogs and horses – practical as well as passionate – is essential to her happiness. 'Lilibet's first love of all was undoubtedly Owen the groom, who taught her to ride.' She was not yet six. 'What Owen did or said was right in her sight for many years.' Ninety years later, she had equal faith in her last groom, Terry Pendry.

In her book, time and again Crawfie comes back to her charges' contrasting personalities:

Of the two children, Lilibet was the one with the temper, but it was under control. Margaret was often naughty, but she had a gay bouncing way with her which was hard to deal with. She would often defy me with a sidelong look, make a scene and kiss and be friends and all forgiven and forgotten. Lilibet took longer to recover, but she had always the more dignity of the two.

The Duke [of York, her father] was immensely proud of her. He had a way of looking at her that was touching. But Margaret brought delight into his life. She was a plaything. She was warm and demonstrative, made to be cuddled and played with. At one time he would be almost embarrassed, yet at the same time touched and pleased, when she wound her arms round his neck, nestled against him and cuddled and caressed him. He was not a demonstrative man.

Lilibet took after him. She, too, was reserved and quiet about her feelings. If you once gained her love and affection you had it for ever, but she never gave it easily.

The Queen's father meant everything to her. She would openly acknowledge him as the most significant influence in her life. Most men who knew her (especially military and racing men) would tell you that the Queen was happiest in a man's company – but her ladies-in-waiting, or Bobo Macdonald, or Angela Kelly, or Sophie, Countess of Wessex, who became like a second daughter to her, might disagree. Listening to her in conversation, beyond her father and royal grandfather, the men I heard her talking to with most obvious easy enthusiasm were Prince Andrew and Prince Edward, her husband, the Duke of Edinburgh, and 'Porchey', her racing manager and acknowledged 'best friend'.

In January 1936, aged seventy-one, her beloved grandfather, George V died. His favourite grandchild was not quite ten.

As Crawfie noted:

Lilibet in her sensitive fashion felt it all deeply. It was very touching to see how hard she tried to do what she felt was expected of her. I remember her pausing doubtfully as she groomed one of her toy horses and looking up at me for a moment.

'Oh, Crawfie . . . ought we to play?'

The old King was much mourned. His face was red, his manner was gruff, his voice was loud, but he had done his duty with dignity and some skill. His reign encompassed the Great War, the Russian Revolution, civil war in Ireland, the Great

Depression, the advent of Britain's first Labour Government. He had risen to the challenges. He had dropped few catches. He had survived. He would be missed. 'The people of America are mourning, as if for their own King,' Virginia Woolf noted in her diary, 'and the Japanese are in tears.' The BBC suspended normal service and simply broadcast the sound of the ticking of a clock. The prime minister, Stanley Baldwin, addressed the nation and Virginia Woolf reckoned Baldwin hit the right note: 'He gave out the impression that he was a tired country gentleman; the King another; both enjoyed Christmas at home; and the Queen is very lonely; one left the other taken, as must happen to married couples; and the King had seemed to him tired lately, but very kind, and quiet as if ready for a long journey; and had woken once or twice on the last day and had said something Kind ('Kind' was the adjective always) and had said to his Secretary "How is the Empire?" – an odd expression. "The Empire, Sir, is well"; whereupon he fell asleep . . . The shops are all black. Mourning is to outlast the London season. A black Ascot.'

'Kind' was not necessarily the word his elder sons would have used to encapsulate the essence of their father. His relationship with each of them – which became very different – was never easy. He was much more comfortable with the women in his family. Perhaps they had the measure of him. The Duchess of York teased him. Playing horse and groom, little Lilibet led him around the drawing room by his beard. Until her death (a few weeks before his own) the old King and his unmarried younger sister Victoria chatted, daily, on the telephone. Once – Elizabeth Longford told me this story and assured me she had it on good authority – Princess Victoria telephoned the King at Buckingham Palace and said, 'Is that you, you old fool?' The operator interrupted: 'Beg pardon, your Royal Highness, His Majesty is not yet on the line.'

The reign of George V lasted more than a quarter of a century. The reign of Edward VIII came to an abrupt end after eleven months and twenty-one days. As Prince of Wales, David had been popular with public and press alike. He was good-looking, charming, socially adept; he appeared articulate, energetic and able; he came over as unstuffy and contemporary, both human and humane. Those who saw him at closer quarters got a different picture. Beatrice Webb, socialist pioneer and co-founder of the *New Statesman* magazine, met him at dinner in the summer of 1930 and recorded in her diary: 'He is neurotic and takes too much alcohol for health of body or mind. If I were his mother or grandmother, I should be very nervous about his future . . . his expression was unhappy – there was a horrid dissipated look as if he had no settled home either for his intellect or his emotions . . . He must be a problem to the conventional courtiers who surround him.' He was.

In January 1931, at Melton Mowbray in Leicestershire, at the country house of one mistress, Thelma Furness (the second wife of the 1st Viscount Furness), David met his next mistress, his last, the non-negotiable love of his life: Wallis Simpson. Mrs Simpson was thirty-five, American, chic rather than beautiful, the Baltimore-born second wife of a New York businessman, Ernest Simpson (who had an English-born father) and who had come to London to run the British end of the family firm.

Eighty-five years later, there were echoes of the Mrs Simpson scandal when Meghan Markle and Prince Harry began dating in July 2016. She, too, was a thirty-five-year-old American, with two established relationships behind her. Meghan had dated an American film producer, Trevor Engelson, from 2004 and married him in 2011. They were divorced in 2013, citing 'irreconcilable differences', and her next live-in relationship was with a Canadian celebrity chef and restauranteur, Cory Vitiello, which ended after two years in 2016, not long before she met Harry.

In the early 1930s, the deferential British media turned a blind eye to the developing relationship between the future King and his American lover. In court circles and London's high society, the affair was an open secret, but the British press – who knew all about it – breathed not a word. Things had changed by 2016. From the outset, Prince Harry was sensitive about the media coverage of his relationship with Meghan Markle. Once word got out, there was no stopping it. In November 2016, the prince instructed his communications secretary to release a statement on his behalf expressing his personal concern about pejorative and false comments being made about his girlfriend by both mainstream media and internet trolls. Later, in a letter to one of the British media regulators, Meghan's representatives complained about the harassment from journalists. But when the relationship became official – Prince Harry and Meghan first appeared together in public in Toronto at the Invictus Games and then their engagement was announced on 27 November 2017 in London – there was general rejoicing and a positive response across the media.

Edward VIII's determination to marry his American divorcee was received with ill-disguised distress and alarm by his family, press and (in the main) public alike in 1937. In 2017, Prince Harry's decision to marry his American divorcee was warmly welcomed by all and sundry. No great play was made of it, but it was generally reckoned 'a good thing' having a mixed-race person joining the royal family. Harry's father expressed his genuine delight; Harry expressed his dewy-eyed devotion; Meghan announced that she would retire from acting and become a British citizen. (This last has not happened and may not happen since, according to the official rules, you need to be resident in the United Kingdom for three consecutive years before you can apply for citizenship as a spouse.)

Elizabeth II's mother, then Duchess of York, was deeply unhappy at the prospect of her brother-in-law marrying Wallis Simpson. Elizabeth II, by contrast, was really delighted by the prospect of her grandson marrying Meghan Markle. She did everything she could to make her future granddaughter-in-law feel welcome. She was concerned for her future happiness. At their first meeting, the Queen said to Meghan: 'You can carry on being an actress if you like – that's your profession, after all.' But Meghan was ready for royal duty and, of course, the Queen was delighted by that. She was particularly delighted by the enthusiasm Meghan showed for the Commonwealth and the commitment she made to the Queen to do 'whatever you think we should be doing for the Commonwealth'. She promised the Queen that when it came to the Commonwealth she wouldn't let Her Majesty down.

The Queen liked Meghan and told lots of people so. The Queen (who, of course, had seen it all before) understood that Harry's girl might find adjusting to royal life 'challenging to begin with' (as she put it). 'It is very jolty, but you soon get used to it' – that was the Queen's experience (as we shall see) going back many years. To help Meghan, the Queen suggested that her daughter-in-law, Sophie Wessex, would be an ideal mentor. 'Sophie can help show you the ropes,' said the Queen. Meghan made it clear that she did not feel she needed Sophie's help. She had Harry. The Queen was a little concerned at that, and concerned, too, when word reached her that Meghan was reportedly occasionally a bit 'high-handed' with staff. The Queen put it down to pre-wedding nerves.

Harry and Meghan were married on 19 May 2018. Less than a month later, on 14 June 2018, the Queen took Meghan on her first solo outing – to my old constituency, the City of

Chester. The date marked the first anniversary of the Grenfell Tower tragedy and the Queen wore a green outfit by Stewart Parvin in memory of the victims of the fire. Meghan (in cream-coloured Givenchy) looked beautiful – and did her bit, effortlessly and well, to the manner born. She kept a step behind the Queen without fail, she smiled, she chatted, she coped with her hair in the blustery weather, she admitted she had never been to the north of England before but was 'loving it already'. 'Top marks,' said the Queen, who had chosen this day for her new granddaughter-in-law's induction to royal duty, in part because it was 'a fairly typical day', but mainly because the programme included a visit to a theatre – 'and she is an actress after all.' It was a very typical royal day – arriving by train in Runcorn, opening the Mersey Gateway Bridge and Chester's Storyhouse Theatre, unveiling plaques, having a civic lunch at Chester Town Hall, doing a bit of a walkabout, meeting some of the thousands of folk who had turned out to cheer. Meghan delivered in full measure and delighted the crowds, the Lord Lieutenant of Cheshire (a seasoned observer of the royals in action and my source for how well it all went) and, most important of all, Her Majesty.

That first visit to Cheshire was an undoubted success. The courtiers accompanying the royal party that day included Samantha Cohen, who I first got to know when she was working in the Buckingham Palace press office in 2001 and was soon to become Communications Secretary. Later, in 2010, she became Assistant Private Secretary to the Queen and then, in 2017/18, when she was planning to move from Buckingham Palace, was persuaded to stay on in royal service to help Meghan as she began her new life as a member of the Family Firm. Unhappily, as we know, it did not work out. During their short time as working members of the royal family, quite a number of staff left the Sussexes' service, including

Samantha Cohen and another private secretary, Amy Pickerill, two personal assistants and two nannies. Samantha Cohen, after she had left, reportedly said it had been like 'working for a couple of teenagers'. Others, unnamed, called Meghan 'an outrageous bully' and 'a narcissistic sociopath'. Meghan's solicitor denied the allegations, saying they were part of a 'calculated smear campaign'.

The only concern the Queen let slip in the early days of the Sussexes' marriage was to wonder to a friend if Harry wasn't 'perhaps a little over-in-love'. By all accounts Harry fell for his American divorcee pretty quickly. His grandmother Queen Elizabeth II's Uncle David's serious interest in his American developed more gradually. It began as a flirtatious friendship. The affair blossomed in the spring of 1934. By 1935 the prince was wholly infatuated. Within court circles, the affair was an open secret, but it was not a matter that was discussed within the Windsor family. As well as there being certain people best not to mention, there are certain subjects that are best avoided. Perhaps it was even worse then than it is now. As one of David's nephews, George Harewood, the then Princess Royal's son, pointed out: 'People kept much more private and much more quiet about things like that and were much more able to bottle up their feelings. I think the whole of my mother's family tended to bottle up their feelings very much.'

The Wallis Simpson crisis reached its climax in the autumn of 1936. In August, the new King – not yet crowned: his coronation was set for the following May – holidayed at Balmoral, with his mistress installed in the rooms that, a year before, had been occupied by Queen Mary. In September, he asked the Yorks to take his place at the official opening of a hospital in Aberdeen, so that he could meet Mrs Simpson, secretly, at the railway station. In October, Mrs Simpson secured her second divorce and became free to marry for a third time. In November, the King – Supreme Governor of the Church of England, which did not then recognise divorce – told his mother, his brother and the prime minister that he had decided to marry his American divorcee and, if necessary, to give up his throne in order to be able to do so. 'Oh,' stammered Bertie, 'that's a dreadful thing to hear. None of us wants that, I least of all.'

Of all this, until the beginning of December that year, the majority of the British public knew nothing. Around the world, especially in the United States, reports of the King's relationship with Mrs Simpson had been widespread. In the United Kingdom, a deferential press had breathed not a word of scandal. Up on the nursery floor at 145 Piccadilly, Crawfie and Alah and the little princesses sensed something ominous in the air, but no one told them anything. Evidently something was about to happen, but what was it? 'It was impossible not to notice the change in Uncle David,' said Crawfie, in retrospect. 'He had been so youthful and gay. Now he looked distraught, and seemed not to be listening to what was said to him. He made plans with the children, and then forgot them.'

On Thursday 3 December 1936, Crawfie went out and bought an evening paper. Standing on the doorstep, 'I remember I read the headline while I waited for the front door to open . . . THE KING AND HIS MINISTERS. GREAT CONSTITUTIONAL CRISIS . . . I do not know what we would have done at that time without the swimming lessons. They were a great diversion and took our minds off other matters.'

At Buckingham Palace and in Downing Street, as the drama of the Abdication unfolded, down at the Bath Club, Lilibet and Margaret Rose, aged ten and six, were learning to swim. Another regular at the Bath Club at the time was Georgina

Wernher, then a teenager, later a good friend of the Queen and Prince Philip, later still a godmother to Prince Andrew. 'I remember the Bath Club well,' she told me. 'Princess Elizabeth was always so nicely behaved. I remember she used to have a bag of sweets and, after swimming, would take the bag round, offering everybody a sweet.' Gina Wernher said, 'Princess Elizabeth was always level-headed. She has always been the calm at the centre of the storm.'

In the autumn of 1936 the storm surrounding the monarchy was considerable. The King could not marry Mrs Simpson and make her his queen. A morganatic marriage, allowing her the position of wife but not the status of Queen, might be possible, but would require legislation. The government advised against it. The King agonised. The press fulminated. The church pontificated. Mrs Simpson left the country to escape the furore. Queen Mary shook her head in sorrow and in anger. Bertie wept on his mother's shoulder, overwhelmed by the prospect of what was to come. Elizabeth retreated to her bed with a bout of influenza. At the poolside, Crawfie and Alah wrapped Lilibet and Margaret Rose in huge bath towels and, as each was awarded her Life Saving Certificate, rewarded the girls with hugs and a small box of chocolates.

The King was ready to sign the Instrument of Abdication. Edward VIII was about to become Prince Edward, Duke of Windsor. Prince Albert, Duke of York, was about to become King George VI. At 145 Piccadilly, Crawfie was standing in an alcove on the landing outside the Duchess of York's bedroom. The door opened.

Queen Mary came out of the Duchess's room. She who was always so upright, so alert, looked suddenly old and tired. The Duchess was lying in bed, propped up among pillows. She held out her hand to me. 'I'm afraid there are going to

124

be great changes in our lives, Crawfie,' she said . . . When I broke the news to Margaret and Lilibet that they were going to live in Buckingham Palace they looked at me in horror. 'What!' Lilibet said. 'You mean for ever?' . . . I had to explain to them that when Papa came home to lunch at one o'clock he would be King of England, and they would have to curtsy to him. The Royal children from their earliest years had always curtsied to their grandparents.

'And now you mean we must do it to Papa and Mummie?' Lilibet asked. 'Margaret too?'

'Margaret also,' I told her, 'and try not to topple over.'

When the King returned, both little girls swept him a beautiful curtsy. I think perhaps nothing that had occurred had brought the change in his condition to him as clearly as this did. He stood for a moment touched and taken aback. Then he stooped and kissed both warmly. After this we had a hilarious lunch.

'Of course, when the Yorks became King and Queen, the family had to move to Buckingham Palace,' Sonia Berry explained to me. 'That was quite a wrench. Lilibet had so many toy horses – dozens of them – she kept them all neatly lined up on the landing outside her bedroom – she groomed them so beautifully – and they had to be packed up. She left her favourite horse, Ben, with me, because she didn't want him to be packed up by the removal people. I didn't hear from her for a week or two, but then she wrote to me.'

The letter was dated Monday 1 March 1937:

Thank you very much for keeping Ben whilst we moved into Buckingham Palace. We're quite settled in now and we would like you to come to tea one day next week. We've been very busy and we could not find time for out-teas, but now we'll be able to find some.

Crawfie will ring up next week and would you please come to the Privy Purse door — that is the one next to Constitution Hill. I hope you will find it. Please do you think you could bring Ben with you. Could you bear it? I'm sure he enjoyed staying with you.

CHAPTER EIGHT

'Mummy and Papa – their Coronation'

George V, the second son of Edward VII, was forty-five when he became King in 1910, four years before the outbreak of the First World War. George VI, the second son of George V, was forty-one when he became king in 1936, three years before the outbreak of the Second World War. Wars that are won can do much to enhance the reputation of the reigning monarch. Bertie, as Duke of York, was unexceptional, a good family man, a decent chap, not over-stretched, but conscientious when duty called. Bertie, as King, was stretched to the limit and not found wanting. René Massigli, the French Ambassador to London at the time of Bertie's death just over fifteen years later, wrote in a report to the French Foreign Minister: 'If the "greatness" of a king can be measured by the extent to which his qualities corresponded to the needs of a nation at a given moment in history, then George VI was a great king, and perhaps a very great king.'

George VI – decent, dignified, determined – was the right man in the right place at the right time. He might lack his older brother's obvious glamour and panache, but you could see – and hear – from the way he wrestled with his speech impediment that he had courage. He might not be blessed with great imagination or any very obvious intellectual gifts, but he had palpable integrity. He looked to be what he was: a softly-spoken, well-intentioned, quietly uncomplicated, honest English gentleman. And one blessed with a matchless Scottish wife.

Famously, in his Abdication broadcast (which he scripted himself, though he showed the draft to Winston Churchill who may have added the odd rhetorical flourish), David had said, 'You must believe me when I tell you that I have found it impossible to carry the heavy burden of responsibility and to discharge my duties as king as I would wish to without the help and support of the woman I love.' Might the same not have been true of Bertie? Could he have coped as king without Elizabeth Bowes-Lyon as Queen? Certainly, he could not have coped as well. And, equally certainly, he found the burden to be a cruelly heavy one. When, later, someone commented on how well the exiled Duke of Windsor was looking, Queen Elizabeth responded, 'Yes. And who has got the lines now?' Sir Alexander Hardinge, who served as assistant and then principal private secretary to George V, Edward VIII and George VI, said of Bertie: 'As a result of the stress he was under the King used to stay up too late and smoked too many cigarettes – he literally died for England.'

There was no love lost between Queen Elizabeth and the Duke and Duchess of Windsor, but her niece, Mary Rhodes, who was also, later, her lady-in-waiting, and spent many hours with her, was anxious to tell me that 'Not once in all the years I was with her – not once – did I ever hear her say anything remotely unpleasant about the Windsors. I know she liked David and, I promise you, I never heard her say anything uncharitable about the Duchess. Becoming Queen was not what Queen Elizabeth wanted or expected, but, when it happened, she accepted it.' And grew into the role and, I suspect, over time, rather relished it.

Sensibly, Queen Elizabeth kept her feelings about Wallis Simpson – and much besides – to herself. The females of the family (Queen Mary, Queen Elizabeth, Queen Elizabeth II, Princess Anne) are good at that. Mrs Simpson was less circumspect. 'Really, David,' she wrote to the Duke of Windsor, having seen photographs and newsreel of the new Queen going about her duties, 'the pleased expression on the Duchess of York's face is funny to see. How she is loving it all.'

To his older brother's dismay, Bertie made it clear there was no prospect of Wallis ever being granted the title Royal Highness, nor of David returning to any kind of public life in the United Kingdom. Encouraged by Queen Mary – who had been quite horrified by David's behaviour – Bertie and Elizabeth ostracised David's closest and most ardent supporters, notably the celebrated hostess and shipping-line widow, Emerald, Lady Cunard.

In March 1937, three months into the new king's reign, Harold Nicolson, diarist and recently elected member of parliament, found himself (in knee-breeches and silk stockings – Court Dress) attending the grandest of dinners at Buckingham Palace: 'The dining-table is one mass of gold candelabra and scarlet tulips.' The meal was disappointing, but the wine 'excellent and the port superb'. After dinner, in the drawing room, Nicolson observed the new queen going the rounds: 'She wears upon her face a faint smile indicative of how much she would have liked her dinner-party were it not for the fact that she was Queen of England. Nothing could exceed the charm or dignity which she displays, and I cannot help feeling what a mess poor Mrs Simpson would have made of such an occasion. It demonstrated to us more than anything else how wholly impossible that marriage would have been.'

The evening over, Nicolson went home with friends and sat, over beer, late into the night, discussing 'the legend of monarchy'. At dinner, George VI had sat with Stanley Baldwin and David Lloyd George discussing affairs of state. In truth, he would have little impact upon them. The King was still head of state, the figurehead, the font of honour, but he was no longer a force to reckon with. Queen Victoria had been (in Prince Philip's phrase) 'an executive monarch' who could 'do things'. As a diplomat, as an operator on the European stage, Edward VII had been able to make a difference. Even George V had had opinions – and taken action – that, to an extent, affected the course of history. But by the time Edward VIII's reign had ended, exactly a century after Queen Victoria's had begun, the *power* of the monarch had all but disappeared. Edward VIII was forced to abdicate because the government and parliament of the day – in the Dominions as much as in Britain – would not let him do as he pleased. George VI was the first of a new kind of monarch: a symbol, not a player.

'Until the King became King,' Margaret Rhodes said to me, 'he was always "Uncle Bertie". Then, overnight, he became "Sir".' The simple fact of being King gave the hesitant Duke of York a new authority. The machinery of the monarchy – well-oiled and with its own momentum – swept him, relatively effortlessly, through the first few months of his reign. Privately, he felt the strain, but, so far as the public was concerned, it was a matter of 'business as usual'. Edward VIII's suddenly became the reign that never was. 'Least said, soonest mended' was the unstated national policy. 'The King is dead! (Well, moved to France which comes to the same thing . . .) Long live the King!' The Coronation, on 12 May 1937, was not Edward VIII's coronation *manqué*: it was wholly George VI's, and the day when the new king – according to several observers – seemed, for the first time, wholly to accept his destiny.

Lilibet, now eleven and Heiress Presumptive, seemed always to have accepted hers. Her life was to be different from here on in and there was nothing she could do about it. In public, even her closest friend, Sonia, now had to curtsy to her and could no longer call her Lilibet. 'When the family moved to Buckingham Palace', Sonia said to me, 'Princess Elizabeth's parents, who, previously, had simply been "downstairs" were now "miles away" and very much busier. Everything was different.'

'Was the young princess different?'

'She had always been quite serious, calm and organised. She was still fun to be with, but I think we were all suddenly aware that one day she might be Queen.'

According to Margaret Rhodes, 'I believe, briefly, she hoped that she might have a brother and be let off the hook, but I think she knew that wasn't very likely. She knew she would be Queen one day, but she thought it would be a long way off. She didn't talk about it much. In fact, I don't think she talked about it at all.'

What she did talk about, and take the keenest interest in, according to Crawfie, was her father's coronation. Crawfie read to her Queen Victoria's account of her own coronation in 1837. In 1937, as a present for her parents, in a neat hand, written in light pencil on lined paper, the little princess produced her own record of their great day:

> To Mummy and Papa
> In Memory of Their Coronation
> From Lilibet
> By Herself
> An Account of the Coronation

It's vivid stuff. The day begins with Lilibet, wrapped in an eiderdown by her faithful nursemaid Bobo, gazing out of her nursery window 'onto a cold misty morning'. Once they were breakfasted and dressed, the young princesses showed off their coronation outfits 'to the visitors and housemaids':

… I shall try and give you a description of our dresses. They were white silk with old cream lace and had little gold bows all the way down the middle. They had puffed sleeves with one little bow in the centre. Then there were the robes of purple velvet with gold on the edge.

We went along to Mummy's bedroom and we found her putting on her dress. Papa was dressed in a white shirt, breeches and stockings, and over this he wore a crimson satin coat. Then a page came and said it was time to go down, so we kissed Mummy, and wished her good luck and went down.

Lilibet and Margaret Rose in their coronation finery travelled in procession to Westminster Abbey in a glass coach: 'At first it was very jolty but we soon got used to it.' She watched the three-hour-long ceremony sitting alongside her grandmother, Queen Mary, in a specially created royal box:

I thought it all very, very wonderful and I expect the Abbey did, too. The arches and beams at the top were covered with a sort of haze of wonder as Papa was crowned, at least I thought so.

When Mummy was crowned and all the peeresses put on their coronets it looked wonderful to see arms and coronets hovering in the air and then the arms disappear as if by magic. Also the music was lovely and the band, the orchestra and the new organ all played beautifully.

What struck me as rather odd was that Grannie did not remember much of her own Coronation. I should have thought that it would have stayed in her mind for ever.

At the end the service got rather boring as it was all prayers. Grannie and I were looking to see how many more pages to the end, and we turned one more and then I pointed to the word at the bottom of the page and it said "Finis". We both smiled at each other and turned back to the service.

The service over, the princesses were escorted to 'our dressing room' and offered 'sandwiches, stuffed rolls, orangeade and lemonade' before taking the 'long drive' home.

Then we all went on to the Balcony where *millions* of people were waiting below. After that we all went to be photographed in front of those awful lights.

When we sat down to tea it was nearly six o'clock! When I got into bed my legs ached terribly!

The unique souvenir she presented to her parents (carefully tied together with pink ribbon) tells us much about the essential Lilibet. She is observant. She has a nice sense of humour. She lives in a world of nursemaids and housemaids and pages and accepts it completely. She goes out onto the balcony and '*millions* of people' are waiting below. The only thing she doesn't enjoy is being photographed. At the end of a long day her legs ache terribly. It's all a taste of things to come – and there's a telling phrase there, too, that, in many ways, sums up the phlegmatic approach to life that stayed with her – and sustained her – through the years: 'At first it was very jolty but we soon got used to it.'

Whenever Elizabeth II was asked what it was like to become Queen, she gave the same kind of answer. 'It was all a very sudden kind of taking on,' she'd say, but she never questioned her lot. Her father had been appalled by the prospect of becoming king. He neither wanted it, nor felt equipped for the role. His daughter was reconciled to her destiny from an early age. After fifty years as Queen she reflected, 'It's a question of maturing into something that one's got used to doing and accepting the fact that here you are and it's your fate.'

I once asked the Queen if, as a girl, she had ever felt overwhelmed at the prospect of what her life held in store for her. 'I don't think I ever thought about it really,' she said. We were on one of her Golden Jubilee walkabouts in the West Country at the time. 'Don't you ever get tired of it?' I asked. 'People are always very friendly,' she said. 'Not always,' I went on, rather tactlessly. 'Someone once took pot shots at you.' 'Thank you for reminding me,' she replied, with a short laugh. 'I think he had a few problems – and they were blanks. No one was hurt.'

At the Trooping the Colour ceremony in 1981, when the Queen was forty-five, and riding down the Mall on her horse Burmese, an unemployed young man, Marcus Sarjeant, aged just eighteen, fired six blanks from a starting pistol at Her Majesty. The horse was momentarily startled by the noise, but the Queen brought her under control almost at once and continued the ride with extraordinary *sang-froid*. (The horse, Burmese, was the mare given to the Queen by the Royal Canadian Mounted Police and ridden by her at Trooping the Colour over eighteen consecutive years from 1969 to 1986. She loved the horse. In 1982, famously, when the Queen went for a ride with the United States President, Ronald Reagan, she rode Burmese, while he was on another royal favourite, a black gelding named Centennial.) On 13 June 1981, in the Mall, moments after the shots were fired, Lance Corporal Alec Galloway of the Scots Guards seized Sarjeant and pulled him over the crowd control barriers, where Galloway and others disarmed and subdued him. Sarjeant (who had recently been turned down for both the police force and the fire brigade) told them, 'I wanted to be famous. I wanted to be a somebody.'

The Queen never wanted to be a somebody, but had no choice in the matter.

I once found myself talking to the Queen about the writer A. A. Milne, author of the famous *Winnie the Pooh* books written for his son, Christopher Robin, in the 1920s. The subject came up circuitously. The Queen was telling me that 'young Harry Herbert', second son of her racing manager, Lord Porchester, had really wanted to be an actor before following his father into the world of horse racing. She was telling me how Harry had formed his own theatre company, based at the Westminster Theatre in Victoria, close by Buckingham Palace. I suggested he should put on the musical, *Salad Days*. 'I hope he does,' said the Queen enthusiastically. 'I loved *Salad Days*.' She went to see it at the Vaudeville Theatre in the Strand with her mother and her sister in the mid-1950s. At the time, it was the longest-running musical in the history of the West End. Princess Margaret bought the sheet music and together she and the Queen sang songs from the show. 'We said we wouldn't look back' was one of their favourites.

'If I start looking behind me,' the Queen began to sing, 'and begin retracing my track, Remind me to remind you, we said we wouldn't look back.' Her Majesty was never one for regrets.

Anyway, I told the Queen how I was friend of Julian Slade, the composer of *Salad Days* and how I had written a musical with Julian Slade, too – about A. A. Milne.

'I loved his poems,' said the Queen, going straight into 'The King asked The Queen, and The Queen asked The Dairymaid: "Could we have some butter for the Royal slice of bread?"' She laughed happily at the recollection. 'They were my favourite nursery verses,' she said, slipping immediately into another one:

'James James Morrison Morrison Weatherby George Dupree
Took great care of his mother, though he was only three.'

At the end of the 1920s when Milne's poems were turned
into songs with music by H Fraser-Simson, and the songs were
published, with the permission of the Duke and Duchess of
York, they were dedicated to the young Princess Elizabeth.

I told the Queen that I had become a friend of A. A. Milne's
son, the real life Christopher Robin, who was born in 1920,
but had become famous as a character in his father's children's
story book in 1926, the year that Princess Elizabeth was born.
In later life, the real Christopher Robin blamed his troubled
adolescence on his father and on the global fame attached to
his name as a consequence of A. A. Milne's four best-selling
children's books: *When We Were Very Young, Now We Are Six,
Winnie the Pooh* and *The House at Pooh Corner.* He accused his
father of 'building his reputation by standing on a small boy's
shoulders'.

'That's rather sad,' said the Queen, who seemed to accept
her global fame to the extent that she never appeared particularly aware of it. The young Princess Elizabeth, like the young
Christopher Robin, received sackfuls of post from unknown
admirers. Like Christopher Robin, she was photographed,
written about and featured in newspapers and magazines
around the world. He, in effigy, appeared, with Pooh, in the
window of Selfridges department store in Oxford Street. She
appeared, with her pony, as a waxwork at Madame Tussaud's
exhibition in Marylebone Road. Unlike Christopher Robin,
however, Elizabeth did not complain: she accepted her lot.

And it was a bizarre lot to have to accept. Aged eleven,
when she was taken to a children's matinée at the Holborn
Empire, as she entered the auditorium, fifteen hundred

children got to their feet and sang a specially written children's verse of the national anthem. Aged twelve, she was attending the Buckingham Palace Garden Parties, walking dutifully behind her parents through a throng of three thousand excited subjects, who bowed and curtsied as she passed. Aged thirteen, she accepted her first official post: as President of the Children's League of the Princess Elizabeth of York Hospital, which had been named after her. From birth, she had been a public figure: as she grew up, without ever apparently questioning it, she became accustomed to public life, to exposure to public gaze, to being – literally – the centre of attention.

The Duke of Edinburgh told me that the Queen was never conscious of being 'the centre of attention'. 'It wouldn't occur to her,' he said. 'She was always herself.'

'From the age of ten that meant being the daughter of a king,' I pointed out.

'Yes,' he said, 'but she didn't behave like anybody special – ever.'

It is extraordinary, when you stop to think about it. On 12 May 1937, just three weeks after her eleventh birthday, in Westminster Abbey she watched the coronation of her parents as King and Queen of the United Kingdom and the Dominions of the British Commonwealth – and as Emperor and Empress of India – knowing that one day she was destined to inherit her father's crown, and yet, by every account of those who knew her best, 'she didn't behave like anybody special.' Prince Philip said to me: 'She was quite unspoilt.'

The young princess's account of her parents' coronation – a nicely structured composition, with sound punctuation and impeccable spelling – tells us something about her governess, Crawfie, too. Crawfie was a good teacher.

In February 1937, Crawfie, along with Alah and Bobo and

their young charges, moved from 145 Piccadilly across Green Park to Buckingham Palace. Number 145 had been a home, albeit a grand one staffed by eighteen servants. Buckingham Palace was the headquarters of an empire, with a staff in excess of four hundred. 'I still recall with a shudder that first night spent in the Palace,' said Crawfie. 'The wind moaned in the chimneys like a thousand ghosts.' Crawfie was disconcerted by the sheer scale of the place and not impressed by the (in every sense) Victorian quality of much of the accommodation. It was like 'camping in a museum', she said. The rooms were dark and musty. The light switch for Crawfie's bedroom was outside the door, two yards down the corridor. To reach the bathroom and lavatory you had to cross the passageway in your slippers and dressing-gown, and risk bumping into the Palace postman on his early morning round. Crawfie did not like it. She was homesick.

Lilibet was less troubled. To her, it was a home – this was where her grandparents had lived – and the corridors, while endless ('People here need bicycles' she said), were more fun than forbidding. 'There was very little restraint placed on the children,' Crawfie reported. 'The Prime Minister, coming to see the King on affairs of State . . . might easily find himself tangled up with two excited little girls racing down the corridors. Or one stoutish little girl panting, "Wait for me, Lilibet. Wait for me!" Perhaps Dookie, the Queen's devoted corgi, might take a nip at a passing leg. Dookie adored the taste of strange trousers.'

Gradually, the governess came to terms with her new surroundings. Improvements were made, walls were repapered, facilities were enhanced. The new Queen added her special touch. 'Elizabeth can make a home wherever she is,' said Bertie, proudly. 'Mice continued to be a menace,' said Crawfie, tartly. However, even she had to acknowledge that the gardens at the back of the Palace were a bonus, and there were still the weekends, 'now the best part of all our lives' when 'we escaped from the Palace' and went down to Royal Lodge, Windsor. 'At Royal Lodge, court etiquette was forgotten, and ceremony left behind. We were just a family again.' In fact, nothing was to be quite the same again.

The Yorks were now King and Queen; Lilibet and Margaret Rose were first and second in line to the throne. Queen Mary, who, since her own coronation, twenty-six years before, had always been the personification of majesty, and had long shown an interest in her granddaughter's upbringing, now insisted that touches of regality be introduced to the children's routine. Meals on the nursery floor were served by liveried footmen. The food was English, but the menus were in French. Crawfie continued to be in charge of the princesses' education, but Crawfie's staple fare – Bible, History, Grammar, Arithmetic, Geography, Literature, Poetry, Writing and Composition, with Music, Drawing or Dancing after lunch – was now supplemented by lessons in constitutional history (for Lilibet) and, later, for both girls, by special classes in French, provided by a Mrs Montaudon-Smith (soon known as Monty), and, later still, French Literature and European history, provided by a Belgian aristocrat, the Vicomtesse de Bellaigue (known as 'Toni': her Christian name was Antoinette).

Lilibet's personal tutor in constitutional history was Henry Marten, co-author of a much-respected standard *History of England* and Vice-Provost of Eton College, the celebrated boys' school conveniently situated not far from Royal Lodge. Marten described his royal pupil as 'a somewhat shy girl of thirteen who when asked a question would look for confidence and support to her beloved governess, Miss Crawford.' The teacher, a bachelor then in his sixties who had been a master at Eton since 1896, does not seem to have been wholly at ease himself, never managing to look his first-ever female student directly in the eye, frequently addressing her as 'Gentlemen', and, alternately, biting his handkerchief and nervously crunching lumps of sugar produced at regular intervals from his jacket pocket.

Marten's syllabus covered more than a thousand years of royal heritage, starting with the reign of King Egbert, the King of the West Saxons (802–839), 'the first to unite all Anglo-Saxons', and culminating with the two most significant events of modern times: the advent of broadcasting and the 1931 Statute of Westminster. According to Marten, the Statute, which recognised the independence of the Dominions within the Commonwealth, gave a new significance to the Crown as the one remaining link between the United Kingdom and the Dominions, and the arrival of broadcasting enabled the wearer of the Crown to sustain that link, in a personal way, by speaking directly to people around the world.

Princess Elizabeth was gradually being groomed for her destiny. Crawfie, meanwhile, was determined to keep the royal feet firmly on the ground: 'I suggested one day that it would be a very good idea for the children to start a Girl Guide Company at the Palace. Besides keeping them in touch with what children of their own ages were doing, I knew it would bring them into contact with others of their own ages and of all kinds and conditions.' So, in 1937, the Buckingham Palace Guide Company was formed, divided into three patrols, with a small Brownie pack tacked on for the benefit of Princess Margaret, who was still only seven. The girls – about three dozen in all – included royal cousins, royal friends, the children of courtiers and, according to Crawfie, 'those of Palace employees'. The Company met on Wednesday afternoons: in summer, in the Palace gardens; in winter, in one of the Palace's many echoing reception rooms. 'Just at first,' noted Crawfie, 'some of the children who joined started coming in party frocks, with white gloves, accompanied by fleets of nannies and governesses. We soon put a stop to all that.'

Princess Elizabeth was in the Kingfisher patrol and second-in-command to Patricia Mountbatten, Louis Mountbatten's elder daughter, who was two years her cousin's senior. 'Princess Elizabeth was a first-class Guide,' Countess Mountbatten told me. 'Really efficient and completely level-headed. You could really rely on her. She'd never let you down. She quickly became a leader in her own right.'

The girls enjoyed their guiding. 'The Company was formed so that Elizabeth and Margaret Rose could meet and mix with ordinary children,' Countess Mountbatten told me, with a charming little chuckle. 'Well, there's ordinary and ordinary, of course. I think the children were quite carefully vetted. I think they had to be "suitable". But we did do ordinary guiding things. The long corridors at Buckingham Palace were ideal for practising signals and we went on wonderful expeditions in the Windsor forest, trekking and bird-watching and cooking sausages over the camp fire. The King's Piper came and played for us and we did Highland dancing. That was fun.'

What was Lilibet like at thirteen? Henry Marten said she was shy and looked to Crawfie to give her confidence. Crawfie said that, at thirteen, 'when so many are gawky', Lilibet 'was an enchanting child with the loveliest hair and skin and a long, slim figure.' She was growing up. She was no longer biting her nails. She was almost as tall as her mother. Soon her wardrobe of 'very simple afternoon frocks' – 'usually of tussore silk, often hand-smocked, quite short with knickers to match' – would give way to something more sophisticated: a hemline below the knees, silk stockings in place of white cotton ankle socks, a beret instead of a winter bonnet or a summer straw hat. Lilibet and Margaret Rose who, according to Crawfie, 'were never in the least interested in what they were going to wear and just put on what they were told', no longer appeared, automatically, in matching outfits. The child was giving way to the young adult.

Was she a moody adolescent? 'No,' said Patricia Mountbatten. 'Far from it,' said Margaret Rhodes, 'she was always very controlled – or, should I say, in control?'.

Countess Mountbatten said, 'The Queen told me that she had been quite nervous of me when we were in the Guides together and she was my second-in-command. That surprised me, but, of course, she has always been guarded about her feelings. Even as a girl, she was careful how she appeared in front of others. For example, if she fell and hurt herself, she knew she mustn't be seen to cry.' 'Only once,' according to Crawfie, 'did she walk right into my arms, thinking of nothing but that for the moment she had to have a little comforting . . . "Oh, Crawfie, Grandfather Strathmore is dead," she said, and burst into tears.'

Like her father and, to an even greater extent her royal grandparents, King George and Queen Mary, Princess Elizabeth was not given to public displays of emotion. She was, from an early age, self-controlled, self-contained, self-sufficient. Was that healthy? We might not think so, living, as we do, in the let-it-all-hang-out twenty-first century, but things were very different a hundred years ago. The 'stiff upper lip' wasn't a joke then: it was a much-vaunted national characteristic.

Besides, as Margaret Rhodes pointed out to me, Lilibet had an outlet for her emotions. She might stand, as, by her own account, she did, for hours, gazing out of the window of Buckingham Palace, 'watching the people and the cars there in the Mall', saying little, but wondering 'what they were doing and where they were all going, and what they thought about outside the Palace'. But then, she could scamper off and play with the corgis and the Labradors – with Dookie and Spark, Flash and Mimsey, Scruffy and Stiffy – or go for a ride on Peggy or Comet. Margaret Rhodes stubbed out yet another cigarette and pondered, 'Perhaps she didn't repress her feelings. Perhaps she channelled them through her animals. Dogs are faithful. And they don't tell tales. I don't know. All I do know is that the real love of her life, then, as now, was dogs followed by horses.'

Corgis were central to Elizabeth II all her life. 'Dookie' was brought into the family by the Duke of York in 1933 – and called 'Dookie' as a variant on 'Duke', just as 'Lilibet' was a version of 'Elizabeth'. He was soon joined by Jane, a family favourite until 1944 when she was fatally struck by a car and replaced by Susan, an eighteenth birthday present for Lilibet, and the mother and grandmother of a long line of more than thirty corgis who were her constant and faithful companions for the rest of her life. They were royal corgis and treated as such. They had their own special 'corgi room' with individual baskets lifted off the floor to avoid the drafts and specially prepared meals (featuring beef and rabbit) and their own stockings at Christmas time. Not everyone loved them. They could nip and yap. Prince Philip told me he found them 'totally infuriating': 'Susan came on our honeymoon, you know. There were three of us in this marriage,' he said to me, laughing, and echoing Diana's famous line about her marriage to Prince Charles.

Wherever Elizabeth II went, the dogs went, too. 'They're barking all the time,' said Prince William, 'I don't know how she copes with it.' When he got engaged in 2017, Prince Harry said, 'I've spent the last thirty-three years being barked at,' but pointed out that the Queen's dogs had taken to Meghan right away.

The Queen understood dogs and bred them with pride and pleasure for many years. In 2001, I happened to be with her when she was visiting Haverfordwest, the county town of Pembrokeshire in Wales, and spotted a Pembrokeshire corgi in the crowd. 'I'm really pleased,' said the Queen. 'They're very special.' The moment was, without question, the highlight of her day. The Countess of Airlie, who was her lady-in-waiting on the day, told me, 'She's definitely got a sixth sense when it comes to dogs. She understands them completely and they recognise it at once.'

Her family and her staff all knew how important they were to her. When Prince Philip was in hospital, shortly before his death at the beginning of 2021, Prince Andrew gave his mother two puppies to distract her and keep her company: a corgi called Muick and a dorgi – a dachshund-corgi cross – named Fergus, who (with Prince Andrew's luck) died shortly afterwards from a heart defect it had had from birth. As a further present, marking what would have been Prince Philip's hundredth birthday in June 2021, Prince Andrew, with his daughters Beatrice and Eugenie, replaced Fergus with another corgi puppy. And when his mother died, the two corgis came back to live with him.

Dogs and horses – and the people who come with them: breeders, trainers, handlers, grooms – were central to her life. They kept her grounded. The animals – and those associated with them – were the principal source of her happiness throughout her long life. Sir Roy Strong, formerly director of the National Portrait Gallery and the Victoria and Albert Museum, met her on many occasions over the years. He told me, 'She only ever really came to life when the dogs came into the room.' He remembered meeting her once when she had just come from a large reception for leading literary figures. He asked her who was there. She said, 'I don't know. I forgot to wear my specs.' If you asked her (as I did) about the presidents and prime ministers she had encountered across the years – everyone from Harry S Truman to Vladimir Putin – she would not be particularly forthcoming. But mention Bill Fenwick, the retired head keeper of Windsor Great Park or Nicky Beaumont, Clerk of the Course at Ascot for many years, and she would rattle away happily for minutes on end.

I asked the Queen once to whom she owed most in her life and she said, at once, 'My parents, of course.' She was conscious that she had been blessed with parents who were loving – and united. 'My mother always gave me support and encouragement,' she said. 'And my father was everything to me.'

Inevitably, as King and Queen, however, her parents saw less of their daughters than they would have liked. In the summer of 1938, with the clouds of war gathering across Europe, Lilibet and Margaret Rose were left at home as Papa and Mama undertook their first foreign assignment: a state visit to France intended to reinforce the *entente cordiale*. In May 1939, with war now imminent (despite Chamberlain's determination to secure peace), the King and Queen were despatched on a longer and more ambitious expedition: to Canada and the United States. The American President, Franklin Roosevelt, invited the little princesses along for the ride. 'I shall try to have one or two Roosevelts of approximately the same age to play with them!' he promised.

In the event, the girls were left at home, perhaps wisely. The tour proved arduous and the transatlantic crossing, on board the Empress of Australia, potentially perilous. Off the coast of Newfoundland, the fog was treacherous. The Queen reported by letter to her mother-in-law, Queen Mary:

> *For three & a half days we only moved a few miles. The fog was so thick, that it was like a white cloud round the ship, and the foghorn blew incessantly . . . We were nearly hit by a berg the day before yesterday, and the poor Captain was nearly demented because some*

kind cheerful people kept on reminding him that it was about here that the Titanic was struck, & just about the same date.

George VI and Queen Elizabeth were the first reigning British monarchs to visit North America and their tour was a triumph. Even in Quebec, the cry went up: *'Vive le Roi! Vive la Reine!'* The Governor-General of Canada was Lord Tweedsmuir (better remembered as the novelist John Buchan) who chaperoned the King and Queen for much of the Canadian leg of the tour and drafted the text of the King's principal speeches. For Tweedsmuir, the most telling moment came at the unveiling of a war memorial in Ottawa:

> The King spoke admirably and clearly, as he has done each time since he landed. After the ceremony the Queen said to me that she wanted to go down among the veterans, and I thought, knowing what excellent fellows they are, that it would be worth chancing it. A most extraordinary scene followed. The King and Queen, and my wife and myself, were absorbed in a crowd of six or seven thousand ex-soldiers, who kept the most perfect order among themselves, and opened up lanes for Their Majesties to pass through. There was no need of the police, and indeed the police would have had no chance. It was a wonderful example of what a people's king means . . . One old man shouted to me, 'Ay, man, if Hitler could see this!' It was extraordinarily moving because some of these old fellows were weeping . . . The capacity of Their Majesties for getting in touch with the people amounts to genius.

Tweedsmuir was smitten. The King was a 'wonderful mixture' of 'shrewdness, kindliness and humour': 'He is simply one of the best people in the world. I never thought that I should feel the romantic affection for my sovereign that I felt for him.' The Queen 'has a kind of gentle, steady radiance which is very wonderful' and 'a perfect genius for the right kind of publicity, the unrehearsed episodes here were marvellous.' When he had dried his eyes and cleared his throat, the Governor-General reported to the British prime minister: 'The Statute of Westminster is now much more than a mere piece of paper, for we have been given a visual revelation of its meaning.' Henry Marten, Lilibet's tutor, would have been gratified. And what Tweedsmuir saw in her parents – shrewdness, kindliness, humour, and a kind of gentle, steady radiance – was what others would see in Elizabeth II across the seventy years of her reign. 'We are all more or less what our parents make us, aren't we?' she said, years later.

King George VI and Queen Elizabeth were as rapturously received in the United States as they had been in Canada. They took to the American President. 'He is so easy to get to know,' wrote the King, '& never makes one feel shy.' Roosevelt was equally charmed, and impressed – and possibly a little surprised – to find his British guests quite knowledgeable 'not only about foreign affairs in general but also about social legislation.' 'The British sovereigns have conquered Washington,' said the *New York Times*. Crowds turned out to cheer and an initially sniffy press was quickly won over. The misty-eyed Lord Tweedsmuir murmured to His Majesty: 'It is a pleasant saying in the United States at the moment that you have taken the "g" out of kingship.' The King himself, whose confidence grew as the tour proceeded, learnt from the experience. 'There must be no more high-hat business,' he reflected during the tour, 'the sort of thing that my father and those of his day regarded as essential as the correct attitude – the feeling that certain things could not be done.'

The King and Queen returned to England on 22 June 1939.

The imminence of war, combined with glowing coverage of the tour in the British press, ensured a properly patriotic and heart-tuggingly warm welcome home for the royal travellers. Lilibet and Margaret Rose had not seen their parents for seven weeks. In the 2020s that may seem a long time for parents and young children to be apart, but things were different ninety years ago. Then it was not unusual for middle- and upper-class girls and boys of the age of the young princesses (nine and thirteen) to be away at boarding school for twelve-week terms. There was a half-term 'exeat', but the children of diplomats, serving soldiers and the like, often did not see their parents for months at a time – and survived.

The girls, accompanied by Alah and Crawfie, travelled by train to Southampton. There they were taken, by destroyer, to meet their parents' ship mid-Channel. While Crawfie and the princesses ate cherries with the captain on deck, Alah retreated to a cabin ('I think she was not feeling very well,' Crawfie reported, lips pursed). At last, 'The *Empress of India* came in sight and we went below to tidy. The Captain's cabin amused us, with its, to us almost primitive amenities.' Back on deck, they saw the *Empress* 'heaving to' and the King and Queen amid-ships. 'The little girls could hardly walk up the ladder quickly enough,' recalled Crawfie, 'but when they reached the top they rushed to Mummie and Papa. They kissed them and hugged them again and again . . . The Queen kissed me and said how much the children had grown and how well they looked, and all the time the King could hardly take his eyes off Lilibet.'

In the ship's dining room happiness reigned. There was much merriment, and balloons and bunting, too. The King pushed some of the balloons through a porthole. Lord Airlie popped some of them with his cigarette. Champagne cocktails were served and Crawfie got a little squiffy. We can imagine what Alah thought. We are told the Queen said, 'Poor Crawfie, I ought to have warned you. They make them rather strong aboard.'

There was rejoicing in the streets as well. From Southampton to Waterloo, all along the railway route, Their Majesties' subjects turned out to cheer. From Waterloo to Buckingham Palace, the King and Queen travelled home in state. According to police estimates, some fifty thousand people crowded into the Mall to salute them, the men raising their caps and bowler hats (and furled umbrellas) in greeting, the women and children waving flags and handkerchiefs. As the royal carriage passed through Parliament Square, MPs of every party came out of the House of Commons to watch the parade. 'Such fun,' Harold Nicolson reported to his wife, Vita Sackville-West: ' . . . The bells of St Margaret's began to swing into welcome and the procession started creeping round the corner. They went very slowly, and there were the King and Queen and the two princesses. We lost all our dignity and yelled and yelled. The King wore a happy school-boy grin. The Queen was superb. She really does manage to convey to each individual in the crowd that he or she have had a personal greeting. It is due, I think, to the brilliance of her eyes. But she is in truth one of the most amazing Queens since Cleopatra. We returned to the House with lumps in our throats.'

The King and Queen were riding high. To date, this was their finest hour. Perhaps it needed to be: it was the prelude, after all, to Britain's darkest hour. War was looming. There was a whiff of romance in the air as well. On 22 July, exactly a month after their triumphal return from America, and five weeks and a day before the declaration of war on 3 September, the King and his family and their entourage – Crawfie and Alah and all – set off for a brief excursion on the Royal Yacht

Victoria & Albert. Their first port of call – part duty, part pleasure – was along the Devon coast, at the mouth of the estuary of the River Dart, at Dartmouth, at the Royal Naval College, where the King – a cadet at the College in the years before the Great War – was to carry out an inspection, and Princess Elizabeth, age thirteen, was to meet Prince Philip of Greece, age eighteen. Lilibet later claimed it was love at first sight.

CHAPTER NINE

Philip

What was Prince Philip of Greece and Denmark like in July 1939, when he had just turned eighteen? By every account: good-looking, good-humoured, well-mannered, outgoing, self-assured, but also self-sufficient, self-contained. He already had that bright 'mischievous, enquiring twinkle' that the Queen described at the time of his death more than eighty years later, but, even so, he was not easy to read: he did not give a lot away.

If he felt unhappiness at his family's – or his own – situation, he did not talk about it. Born in Corfu, exiled in Paris, educated in France, England, Germany and Scotland, living mostly at boarding school and, in the holidays, either with his sisters in Germany or his Mountbatten relations in Britain, he had parents he rarely saw. Throughout Prince Philip's adolesence Prince Andrea and Princess Alice lived apart from one another and their son did not live with either of them. In November 1937, he saw them together for the first time in six years – and together for the last time, too. This was when the family gathered in Darmstadt in Germany for the funeral of Philip's third sister, Cécile, aged only twenty-six, and her husband and two of their three children, all killed in an aeroplane accident on their way to a cousin's wedding. Cécile was Philip's favourite sister, perhaps because he knew her best. He spent most of his holidays with her and her family. Kurt Hahn, Philip's headmaster at Gordonstoun, broke the news of the tragic accident to the sixteen-year-old boy, who took it on board with stoical calm. 'His sorrow,' according to Hahn, 'was that of a man.'

Cécile's youngest child, her baby daughter Johanna, had been too small to take on the fatal flight in November 1937. She died, nonetheless, aged barely two, of a fever, in June 1939. Philip's mother, who was at her little granddaughter's deathbed, wrote to her son: '. . . we had such a sweet picture before our eyes of a lovely sleeping child with golden curls, looking for me so very like Cécile at that age that it was like losing my child a second time.' His mother, having disappeared from his life throughout his adolescence, was in touch with her boy once more. A week later she wrote to him again: 'I am quite exhausted by the strain and the sadness of it all.'

If Philip was affected by the strain and sadness, he showed no sign of it. In between the death of his favourite sister, Cécile, in 1937, and the death of her baby daughter, Johanna, in 1939, came the death from cancer of Philip's English uncle and guardian, his mother's brother, George, 2nd Marquess of Milford Haven, in 1938. He was forty-five. 'These things happen,' Prince Philip said to me more than sixty years later. 'Death is part of life.'

Prince Philip made no complaint about any aspect of his early years. 'I know you are determined to make a meal out of the so-called "deprivations" of my childhood,' he said to me, 'but I am afraid I can't help you there.' He always spoke of his parents with affection and respect (and kept handsome portraits of them both in his study at Buckingham Palace) and frequently expressed his gratitude for the education he received at Gordonstoun. Kurt Hahn, the school's founder, believed that young people were 'surrounded by a sick civilisation . . . in danger of being affected by a fivefold decay: the decay of fitness, the decay of initiative and enterprise, the decay of care and skill, the decay of self-discipline, the decay of compassion.' At Gordonstoun the regime was designed to tackle that decay and, years later, Hahn's radical philosophy and methods would play their part in shaping two of the national and international ventures with which Prince Philip became most closely associated: the Outward Bound Trust and the Duke of Edinburgh's Award Scheme. Prince Philip regarded Hahn as 'eccentric perhaps', an innovator 'certainly', and 'great beyond doubt.'

The admiration was mutual. In 1938, when Philip left the school – as 'Guardian', or head boy – the headmaster gave him a glowing final report: 'Prince Philip is universally trusted, liked and respected. He has the greatest sense of service of all the boys in the school.' Hahn described the seventeen-year-old as 'a born leader', a boy of 'intelligence and spirit', 'often naughty, never nasty', with 'a natural power of command', a 'sense of humour and a rapid understanding of human nature', but suggested Philip would 'need the exacting demands of great service to do justice to himself.' When he was engaged he had the 'power of meticulous application'; at other times he showed a 'determination not to exert himself more than was necessary to avoid trouble'. Hahn concluded that Philip would 'make his mark in any profession where he will have to prove himself in a free trial of strength.'

Years later, Prince Philip wrote to me: 'I did at least pass the Civil Service Exams to enter the Navy!!' Having passed those exams, on 1 May 1939, six weeks short of his eighteenth birthday, Prince Philip of Greece joined the Royal Naval College at Dartmouth and set himself on course for a career in the British Royal Navy. He told me that, left entirely to his own devices, 'I'd have gone into the Air Force without a doubt,' but there was an inevitability about him opting for the Navy.

As he explained to me, it was something of a family tradition: 'I was following my grandfather [Louis of Battenberg] and two uncles [George Milford Haven and Louis Mountbatten]. My Danish grandfather had been in the Danish Navy and my uncle George (of Greece) served in the Greek Navy.'

Philip was not a traditional Dartmouth cadet. They came to the College at thirteen and stayed for five years. Philip was a Special Entry recruit. These were public school boys, who joined up at eighteen, and would normally begin their naval careers on a training cruiser. However, in anticipation of war, HMS *Frobisher*, the cruiser in which Philip would have expected to train, was being re-fitted and re-armed, hence the presence of Philip – and the other 'Specials' – at Dartmouth over that memorable weekend when the King and Queen and their young daughters came to call.

On Saturday 22 July, the day the *Victoria & Albert* arrived at Dartmouth, Philip was invited to join the royal party – unsurprisingly, since he was a cousin of the King's, and his uncle, Louis Mountbatten, was in attendance on board the Royal Yacht. On 22 July, Mountbatten noted in his diary: 'Philip accompanied us and dined on board.' On 23 July, Mountbatten reported: 'Philip came back aboard V and A for tea and was a great success with the children.'

Philip entertained them ashore as well. According to Crawfie, the young princesses' ever-present governess: 'On the Sunday morning we were going to the College because there was to be a special service . . . I remember it was a lovely day, though it became a bit cloudy around eleven. Just about the time the service was scheduled to start and the boys had been paraded before the King and Queen, the Dartmouth College doctor said, "I am very, very sorry, but two of the boys have developed mumps." There was a long conversation as to whether the children ought to go into the chapel . . .'

Eventually, it was decided – 'better safe than sorry' – that Crawfie should take the girls across to the Captain's House and that Prince Philip would be detailed to entertain them. Lilibet and Margaret Rose were busy playing with the Captain's children's train set when Philip appeared. 'A fair-haired boy, rather like a Viking, with a sharp face and piercing blue eyes' is how Crawfie remembered him. 'He was good-looking, though rather off-hand in his manner. He said, "How do you do," to Lilibet, and for a while they knelt side by side playing with the trains. He soon got bored with that. We had ginger crackers and lemonade, in which he joined, and then he said, "Let's go to the tennis courts and have some real fun jumping the nets."'

Off they went, chaperoned by Crawfie. 'I thought he showed off a good deal,' she recalled, eleven years after the event, 'but the little girls were much impressed. Lilibet said, "How good he is, Crawfie. How high he can jump." She never took her eyes off him the whole time. He was quite polite to her, but did not pay her any special attention. He spent a lot of time teasing plump little Margaret.'

As well as Crawfie's account of this historic encounter, there are two photographs taken that weekend, each featuring Philip and Elizabeth, and each telling its own story. The first is a snapshot of the two of them alone playing croquet in the garden of the Captain's House. The focus of the picture seems to be ships moored in the Dart estuary, but in the foreground, glimpsed behind a parapet, are the two teenagers. The eighteen-year-old boy appears to be concentrating on his next stroke. The thirteen-year-old girl, standing by a hoop, in her neat double-breasted summer coat, small hands clasped together in front of her, is gazing at him intently. She does look happy.

The other photograph shows the entire royal party watching the cadets on parade. Sitting in the front row, staring somewhat vacantly into the middle distance, is Lilibet. She is wearing a solemn expression and what looks like a beret to match her coat. She seems very young. Three places along, seated next to a tiny Princess Margaret (who doesn't look plump at all), is the Queen, wearing a fabulous hat and chatting graciously to the Captain. Standing immediately behind them, side by side, are Louis Mountbatten and Prince Philip. Mountbatten is looking amused and avuncular. Philip is leaning forward, grinning, gesticulating with his right hand: he is, without doubt, in the middle of telling a funny story. He has the unmistakeable look of a charming young man who is often in the middle of telling a funny story.

That weekend the boy certainly made his mark. When the time came for the *Victoria and Albert* to set sail, permission was given to the cadets to commandeer what vessels they could – rowing-boats, motorboats, dinghies – and take to the estuary to give the royal visitors a memorable send-off. As the royal yacht made her stately progress out of the harbour she was escorted by an impromptu flotilla of small craft manned by enthusiastic young men. 'They followed the *Victoria and Albert* quite a long way,' according to Crawfie, who was on deck with the royal party. 'Then the King got very alarmed and said to Sir Dudley North [the Commander of the Royal Yacht], "It's ridiculous, and most unsafe. You must signal them to go back." Most of the boys did go back immediately, and all the others followed shortly except this one solitary figure whom we saw rowing away as hard as he could, who was, of course, Philip. Lilibet took the glasses and had a long look at him. In the end the King said, "The young fool. He must go back, otherwise we will have to heave to and send him back." At last Philip seemed to realise they did want him to go back – they were shouting at him through the megaphone – and he turned back while we gazed at him until he became just a very small speck in the distance.'

Prince Philip told me that the story, as told by Crawfie, was somewhat exaggerated – the small boats only followed the Royal Yacht for a few hundred yards, then turned round and went home – but he did not deny the essence of it. And nor did Lilibet. Looking back in later years, she acknowledged that it was from that weekend in Dartmouth that she began to take a special interest in Prince Philip. Of course, while through her field glasses on the deck of the *Victoria and Albert,* she may have gazed at him in his rowing boat until he disappeared from view, romance was some way off. He was eighteen and she was thirteen, and there was a war to contend with first.

At the beginning of August 1939, the prime minister, Neville Chamberlain, convinced that war was not, in fact, imminent, set off for a spot of salmon-fishing. (Salmon-fishing had long been a Chamberlain priority. Declining the office of Chancellor in May 1923, he wrote: 'What a day! Two salmon this morning and the offer of the Exchequer this afternoon.') On 6 August, the King, who liked and trusted a good hunting and fishing man, set off for Balmoral for his customary family holiday. The grouse were expected to be particularly good that year.

On 9 August, duty called, and the King came down briefly from Scotland to inspect the Reserve Fleet at Weymouth and, after the event, reported to his mother, Queen Mary: 'I feel sure it will be a deterrent factor in Hitler's mind to start a war.'

On 22 August news came that Germany and Russia had signed the Nazi-Soviet Pact. On 24 August Parliament was recalled and the King returned to London. The grouse had been magnificent. On 29 August he told a British ambassador who called at Buckingham Palace that he had never seen so many grouse, that he had bagged 1,600 brace in six days, that it was 'utterly damnable that the villain Hitler had upset everything'. Happily, now that Britain had signed a formal treaty of alliance with Poland, he was convinced there would be peace and that 'this time Hitler's bluff had been called'. Unhappily, His Majesty was mistaken.

On 1 September German troops crossed the Polish border. On 2 September Britain and France issued an ultimatum to Germany: withdraw or face war. A deadline was set for eleven o'clock on Sunday 3 September. Germany failed to respond with the undertakings demanded. The Second World War was under way.

CHAPTER TEN

Lilibet's War

'Hitler is a horrid man,' declared Princess Elizabeth in one of her regular wartime letters to her grandmother, Queen Mary. 'Who is this Hitler, spoiling everything?' demanded Princess Margaret. 'I remember trying to give the Princess a painstaking and unbiased character sketch,' said Crawfie, 'but it wasn't very easy.' The King and Queen were now based at Buckingham Palace, staying at Windsor Castle overnight and at weekends. Margaret and Lilibet remained in Scotland, at Birkhall on the Balmoral estate, with Alah and Bobo and Crawfie. 'Why had Mummie and Papa to go back, Crawfie?' asked Margaret. 'Do you think the Germans will come and get them?' Crawfie was predictably reassuring and Lilibet, apparently, 'was very calm and helpful, as usual, and at once ranged herself on the side of law and order.' (This, note, is Princess Elizabeth aged thirteen in 1939. Her nature did not change.) 'I don't think people should talk about battles and things in front of Margaret,' she said. 'We don't want to upset her.'

The princesses' parents telephoned their daughters every night at six o'clock. 'Stick to the usual programme as far as you can, Crawfie' was the Queen's instruction. 'Up there among the moors and heather it was easy to do this,' said Crawfie. 'The River Muick rippled merrily through the gardens just as usual in those lovely autumn days, while Poland was being over-run and "lights were going out all over Europe".'

Now and then the horrors of war managed to penetrate the peace of the Highlands. The children listened to the wireless. They heard the anti-British propaganda broadcasts made by William Joyce, the notorious 'Lord Haw-Haw', and threw books and cushions at the wireless set in protest. On 14 October they heard the news of the sinking of the *Royal Oak* at Scapa Flow with the loss of more than eight hundred lives. 'Lilibet jumped horrified from her chair,' according to Crawfie, 'her eyes blazing with anger . . . "Crawfie, it can't be! All those nice sailors."'

On 18 December, to their surprise and delight, they were summoned to Norfolk to join their parents for the traditional royal family Christmas at Sandringham. They did not know what the future would hold. No one did. They listened to their father as he made his Christmas Day broadcast, live, seated in front of two large microphones, dressed in the uniform of an Admiral of the Fleet. The hesitancy with which he spoke – at one point having to start a passage again from the beginning – made what he had to say all the more moving:

A new year is at hand. We cannot tell what it will bring. If it brings peace, how thankful we shall be. If it brings continued struggle we shall remain undaunted. In the meantime I feel that we may all find a message of encouragement in the lines which, in my closing words, I should like to say to you:

'I said to the man who stood at the Gate of the Year, "Give me a light that I may tread safely into the unknown." And he replied, "Go out into the darkness, and put your hand into the Hand of God. That shall be better than light, and safer than a known way."'

May that Almighty Hand guide and uphold us all.

The King's children were moved by what they heard. So were the British people.

The poem the King had quoted was by a Gloucestershire-born poet and academic, Minnie Louise Haskins, and it first appeared in a collection called *The Desert* in 1908. It was Lilibet who gave the book to her father and she told me it remained a favourite with her throughout her life. She had the words of the poem engraved on brass plaques and fixed to the gates of the King George VI Memorial Chapel at Windsor Castle, where her father was interred in 1952 and, fifty years later, the poem was read out at the funeral of her mother, Queen Elizabeth.

Elizabeth II was not as interested in poetry as her mother, or her husband (who read T S Eliot and Philip Larkin, which is perhaps not what you would expect from the press portrayal of the Duke of Edinburgh), or, indeed, as her son, Charles, and daughter-in-law, Camilla, both of whom have a real love of poetry. But the Queen was delighted when Camilla, in 2022, launched the Commonwealth Poetry Podcast, in a conversation with me and my daughter Aphra, recorded at Clarence House, talking about her experiences visiting different Commonwealth countries and celebrating her favourite poets – Robert Burns, Christina Rosetti, Walter de la Mare, and John Betjeman among them. 'But not Lord Byron,' said Camilla emphatically. 'I never got to grips with "Child Harolde".' (Incidentally, Queen Victoria resisted Lord Byron's work, too, and was said to be worried that her husband Prince Albert was developing a tendresse for Byron's only legitimate offspring, his distinguished mathematician daughter, Ada Lovelace.) Elizabeth II and our new Queen Consort did share a fondness for one particular poem: 'Right Royal' by John Masefield, poet laureate across four reigns, from 1930 to 1967. It's a narrative poem that tells the story of a steeplechase, the winning horse and the jockey's relationship with his beloved which is placed in jeopardy by the race. It was a favourite poem of Camilla's mother, who, of course, was of a similar generation to the Queen – born in August 1921, just eight weeks after Prince Philip.

George VI had a good war. At first, he was frustrated. 'I wish I had a definite job like you,' he wrote to Louis Mountbatten, now captain of HMS *Kelly* and commander of the 5th Destroyer Flotilla. 'Mine is such an awful mixture, trying to keep people cheered up in all ways, and having to find fault as well as praising them.' He was a constitutional monarch: his lot was to advise, counsel and warn the government of the day. He was Head of State and Commander-in-Chief of the Armed Forces: his role was to look the part, to lead by example, to be rather than to do. He delivered in full measure. He wore his uniform throughout the war. He paraded, he saluted, he inspected, he handed out medals whenever and wherever was required. When rationing was introduced, he made it clear that he and his family expected – wanted – to share the privations of the people.

And when, in September 1940, Buckingham Palace was bombed, it was akin to a blessing in disguise. 'The King & I saw 2 of the bombs drop quite close to us in the quadrangle,' the Queen wrote to Osbert Sitwell. 'They screamed past the window and exploded with a tremendous boom and crash about fifteen yards away. We both thought we were dead, & nipped quickly into the passage, where we found our two pages crouching on the floor. They rose at once & we then descended to the basement, pretending really that it was nothing.' It was quite something: the King and Queen were in the firing line and seen to be. As the Queen remarked, famously, after the bombing: 'Now I feel I can look the East End in the face.' 'Thank God for a good King,' someone shouted in the street as the sovereign inspected the damage done by yet another enemy air-raid. 'Thank God for a good people,' the King replied.

Princess Elizabeth was only a young teenager at the outset of the war, but on the wireless and through the newspapers and conversations with Crawfie and her parents, she followed its progress and reported to her grandmother on her own contribution to the war effort: 'We have been very busy knitting lately. We made a blanket for evacuees, jumpers . . .' Her spirit remained undaunted:

Darling Granny,
Poor old Buckingham Palace looks very sad with no windows and bits here and there gone completely . . . The news of the war has been very bad lately but we will never give in. Your very loving granddaughter, Lilibet

George VI and his family knew, liked and trusted Neville Chamberlain, the prime minister at the outbreak of war. When, in May 1940, he resigned, they were much distressed. After his farewell broadcast, the Queen wrote to him: 'My eldest daughter told me, that she and Margaret Rose had listened to it with real emotion – In fact she said "I *cried*, mummy."' Later, the King wrote to Chamberlain, now dying from cancer: 'You were my Prime Minister in the earliest years of my reign, & I shall ever be grateful to you for your help & guidance during what was in many ways a difficult period.' The Queen was unequivocal: 'How deeply I regretted your ceasing to be our Prime Minister.' The King was more circumspect: 'I have sympathised with you very much in seeing your hopes shattered by the lust & violence of a single man.' He was not referring to Winston Churchill – although the King shared Chamberlain's reservations about the arch-opponent of appeasement. Churchill, after all, wasn't just a maverick: he had also been one of Edward VIII's staunchest allies at the time of the Abdication. The King – whose constitutional duty it was to invite the parliamentarian best placed to form an administration to do so – would have liked to see Lord Halifax, the Foreign Secretary, as Chamberlain's successor, but he bowed to the inevitable. 'There was only one person whom I could send for who had the confidence of the country,' he noted in his diary, '& that was Winston.'

At first, their relationship was uneasy: at best, joshing; at worst, strained. In time, as they got to know one another better and to recognise each other's strengths, they became close comrades. When, five years later, on VE Day, 8 May 1945, they stood together on the balcony at Buckingham Palace, they did so as firm friends, conscious that each, in his own way, had played his part in the victory. Churchill's task, no doubt, had been infinitely more complex, challenging and significant, but the King's contribution – as a sounding board, as a figurehead, as a focus for national unity – was also key. Elizabeth II's devotion to her father's memory was lifelong, as was her admiration for Winston Churchill. I once asked her about her memories of VE Day. She said it was one of the days in her life of which she had the most vivid memories. She recalled stepping out onto the balcony at Buckingham Palace with her parents and sister to wave to the crowds cheering in the Mall. 'My father asked Mr Churchill to join us. I think it is the only time someone from outside the family has appeared on the Palace balcony. It was an extraordinary day.'

It was George VI who first described the House of Windsor as 'the family firm'. It helped that – while, yes, they lived in castles and palaces and were surrounded by flummery and flunkies – there were only four of them, and they seemed . . . well, almost ordinary. The King's shyness, diffidence and stammer served to underline his decency. The Queen's charm was simply irresistible. She wasn't slim and chic and brittle (as 'Queen Wallis' would have been): she was soft and round, regal yet real, classy but comfortable and comforting. And the two girls – moving slowly through adolescence but still, mostly, seen dressed in matching outfits – looked to be model daughters: quite unspoilt and thoroughly wholesome.

Lilibet and Margaret Rose lived through the war years at Windsor Castle. They arrived at the beginning of May 1940, as the Germans began their assault on Belgium and the Netherlands, and France prepared to fall, thinking they were to be there for a few days. They remained for five years. Where they were was an official secret. Press and public were simply informed that the royal children had been evacuated to 'a house in the country'. Some in government – fearful that they might be captured by the Nazis and used as hostages – wanted them evacuated to Canada. Churchill was opposed to the idea. So was the King.

Crawfie painted a lurid picture of the princesses' arrival at the ancient castle 'in the gathering twilight of that May evening':

We were tired, and it was very gloomy. Pictures had been removed, and all the beautiful glass chandeliers had been taken down. The State Apartments were muffled in dust-sheets, the glass-fronted cupboards turned to the walls. About the stone passages the shadowy figures of servants and foremen loomed, attending to the blackout. I remember one old man remarking to me dryly: "By the time we've blacked out all the windows here, it's morning again, miss." The two little girls clung to me apprehensively. Alah, as always when she was bothered or anxious, was cross.

The Queen's recollection of her war years at Windsor was rather different from Crawfie's. 'Windsor Castle was a fortress,' said Crawfie, 'not a home.' To the Queen it was a home, and a favourite home, too. It was frustrating to her, so she told me, that because Crawfie had 'written her book', every account of her childhood is seen, in part, from the governess's perspective. Emotionally, Lilibet was closer to Alah and to Bobo than to Crawfie. And closer, too, to her cousins, like Margaret Elphinstone, and to childhood friends like Sonia Berry and Alathea Fitzalan-Howard. And, perhaps, closest of all to Jane and Crackers and Carol and Susan and Ching – some of the dogs – and Jock and Hans, two of the ponies.

From 1938 Princess Elizabeth was taking formal riding lessons from the royal instructor, Horace Smith. She learnt to ride side-saddle. She was introduced to carriage driving. In 1943 and 1944, driving her own pony and cart, she won first prize in the Royal Windsor Horse Show. In 1942, the King took her up on to the Wiltshire Downs, to the Beckhampton Stables, to watch the royal racehorses being trained. She visited the royal stud at Hampton Court. She went to Newmarket to see more royal racehorses in training. In 1943, aged seventeen, she first rode to hounds. She still spent several hours each day closeted with Crawfie, conscientiously learning her lessons – and, twice a week, taking instruction on English history and the British constitution from Sir Henry Marten who came up to the Castle in his dog-cart – but, undoubtedly, during these years, she was most alive, most at ease, most happy, with her dogs and her horses, the sustaining passions of her life.

These adolescent years were also the ones during which another, quite different, sustaining force took a lifelong hold on the young princess. On 1 March 1942, when she was not quite sixteen, Lilibet was confirmed and took her first communion. Her father was Supreme Governor of the Church of

England, but not just in name. In his most celebrated broadcast, at the beginning of the war, he had said, 'I believe from my heart that the cause which binds together my peoples and our gallant and faithful Allies is the cause of Christian civilisation.' His daughter believed it, too. At his coronation – and hers – at the heart of the service, the sovereign is given a copy of the Holy Bible, with the words: 'We present you with this Book, the most valuable thing that this world affords. Here is wisdom; this is the royal Law; these are the lively Oracles of God.' Elizabeth II, not as a matter of form, but as a matter of faith, said 'Amen' to that.

So, Lilibet was a teenage girl who played with her dogs, groomed her ponies, said her prayers and lived in a castle. When once I asked her what she remembered of those war years at Windsor, she mentioned the Girl Guides (she became leader of her patrol) and the Saturday morning dancing lessons with Miss Vacani. 'They were fun,' she said. 'We loved Miss Vacani.' Betty Vacani (1908–2003) had inherited a society dancing school from her aunt and gave lessons to the children of all the best families, including the Royal family. The Queen told me she had so enjoyed the wartime classes herself that, in due course, she invited Miss Vacani to give a weekly class at Buckingham Palace for Prince Charles, Princess Anne and several children of the royal household. Miss Vacani was a passionate teacher and a favourite with the royal family because, unlike Crawfie, she was wonderfully discreet. She did reveal that Prince Charles was a particular favourite with her because of his seriousness and his commitment to the Highland Fling, but when asked about the abilities of Lady Diana Spencer – who, on leaving school herself, taught briefly at the Vacani School in Brompton Road (a few doors down from Harrods) – she would only say that Lady Di 'had a rather full social life, which distracted her from teaching dancing as a career.'

As a girl and beyond, Lilibet loved dancing and singing – and acting, too. This was a side of her we rarely saw, though when we did, we were impressed. Famously, when the Olympic Games were staged in London in 2012, the Queen made a truly dramatic entrance. Watched by the biggest global audience British television had ever known, the Queen was escorted to the Olympic Stadium by the country's most celebrated secret agent, 007 himself, James Bond. Bond (played by Daniel Craig) was seen arriving at Buckingham Palace in a black cab, running up the red-carpeted stairs, meeting two of the royal corgies, being greeted by the Queen's page, Paul Whybrew, and ushered into the royal presence. There, Her Majesty, with her back to the camera, kept Bond waiting a moment as she signed off a letter and the clock signalled the appointed time – when she turned round and said, 'Good evening, Mr Bond.'

It was only then that we realised it really was her. In our millions, we had all assumed it would be an actress, a look-alike playing the part – but it wasn't: it was the real thing. Her line delivered, the Queen stood up and made her way out of the room, accompanied by Bond and her page and her corgis and walked with purpose to the waiting helicopter that transported her from the Palace, over Westminster, past the statue of Winston Churchill in Parliament Square (Churchill looked up and gave Her Majesty a wave – she especially liked that touch), along the course of the river Thames, to the Olympic park in East London. There 007 opened the helicopter door and 'Her Majesty' (this time it was a stunt double) jumped out and made a parachute landing moments before the real Queen, now accompanied by the Duke of Edinburgh, made her formal entrance into the stadium.

It was an extraordinary few minutes, made all the more extraordinary because no one saw it coming. Sebastian Coe, who led the British bid to bring the Olympic and Paralympic Games to London in 2012, told me he was sitting next to Prince Charles at the opening ceremony, with Prince William and Prince Harry directly behind them. 'When the sequence began,' said Lord Coe, 'the Prince of Wales looked at me and laughed a bit nervously. When he realised it really was his mother up there on the screen with James Bond, he shook his head in total amazement. And when she appeared to jump from the helicopter, the two princes behind us started shouting, "Go, Granny, go!"'

Elizabeth II was always good at keeping secrets. The only member of her family who knew in advance about 'the James Bond moment' was Princess Anne, the Princess Royal, because she was on the International Olympic Committee. She also knew that her mother had a soft spot for 007 because watching a James Bond film was always a feature of summer holidays when the Queen took her family on a trip on the Royal Yacht *Britannia* around the coast of Scotland.

Danny Boyle, the film director responsible for masterminding the Olympic opening ceremony, came up with the original idea but had no idea whether or not it would appeal to the Queen. Lord Janvrin, the Queen's press secretary from 1987 and her private secretary from 1999 until 2007, told me he was sure she wouldn't have done it during the Queen Mother's lifetime. 'Why?' I asked him. 'Simply because she would have felt her mother wouldn't have approved – that it would have been a bit undignified. The Queen became less inhibited in several ways after her mother's death [in 2002], less constrained, more relaxed.' Seb Coe put the idea to Edward Young, the Queen's deputy private secretary at the time, who loved it. David Cameron, the prime minister, liked it, too, and promised to raise it with the Queen at his weekly audience with Her Majesty. As it happened, the Queen needed no persuading.

And when the day came for the filming at the Palace, she needed no coaching either. 'She was a one-take wonder,' said Danny Boyle. It was her idea that she should be finishing a letter before she spoke. Daniel Craig said, 'She was a natural. I was definitely more nervous than she was.'

There was a different Bond connection when it came to the Queen's next dramatic outing. In 2022, for the film sequence that introduced the 'Party at the Palace', the Saturday night concert that was one of the key events in the Platinum Jubilee long weekend of celebrations marking her seventy years on the throne, the Queen played herself in a delightful sketch in which her co-star was Michael Bond's creation, Paddington Bear. In the scene, Paddington (voiced by Ben Wishaw who speaks the part in the Paddington films) is taking tea with Her Majesty at Buckingham Palace and offers her one of his marmalade sandwiches – which it turns out the Queen doesn't need because she already has her own marmalade sandwich, hidden in her handbag. This time, much more in terms of acting was asked of the Queen than had been at the time of the Olympics – and she delivered in full measure. I happened to be working with Britain's most honoured film and stage actress at the time, Dame Judi Dench, and she said to me the day after she had seen it, 'Wasn't she good? I mean, really, *really* good. Her timing was perfect. Every look, every line was just right. It was completely on the money – none of it over-stated. Just wonderful.' She added, laughing: 'I'm quite worried. She's going to be offered all my work now.'

What did the Queen make of it? 'Great fun,' she said. She marvelled that such a large crew appeared at Buckingham Palace to film such a short sequence and she was truly amazed that word of it didn't leak out before the day of transmission. 'Everyone kept the secret,' she said, delighted. 'That was lovely.' And, afterwards, when one of her ladies-in-waiting asked her if she might have liked to have been an actress, she replied, 'Do you know, I think I might.'

Deborah Bean, for many years senior correspondence secretary at Buckingham Palace, told me that when the George Formby Society wrote asking if the Queen would consider becoming their President, she declined, but wanted them to know how well she remembered the ukulele-playing Lancashire entertainer who, when she was a girl, was, for several years, Britain's highest-paid performer. She recalled his films from the 1940s and meeting him when he came to Windsor Castle to entertain the royal family during the war. She said, 'I still remember all his songs and sing them!' She had two favourites – 'When I'm cleaning winders' and the one about 'Mr Wu', the Chinese laundryman – which she performed in a Lancashire accent, strumming an imaginary ukulele while singing.

This love of performing, which was kept well-hidden from the public for most of her life, was evident to family and close friends during her teenage years. Her parents took home movies of Lilibet dancing (ballet and tap, as well as improvised free dancing with plenty of twirls) and for five consecutive Christmases during the war, she and Margaret Rose appeared in home-made Christmas entertainments at Windsor. Four of these were full-scale pantomimes, with elaborate costumes and sets, performed over three nights in the Waterloo Chamber at Windsor Castle. They were produced by the headmaster of the Royal School in Windsor Great Park – a Church of England school founded by Queen Victoria and Prince Albert – and involved neighbourhood children and young evacuees as well as the two princesses.

In 1990, when I was last in pantomime professionally (playing Baron Hardup in *Cinderella*, with Bonnie Langford in the title role and Barbara Windsor as the Fairy Queen), I talked to the Queen about those wartime Christmas shows. 'We did *Cinderella*, too,' she said. 'In the first year of the war, we just did a simple nativity play, but in 1941 we did *Cinderella*. Princess Margaret played Cinderella. She was only eleven, but she was very good. I played the Prince Charming part, the principal boy – Prince Florizel.'

'Did you have a Buttons?' I asked.

'Yes, but he wasn't called that. He was called Buddy. That was Cyril Woods. He was very clever, very funny. And your part, Baron Hardup, we called him Baron Blimp. Mr Tannar played him.'

'And who were the Ugly Sisters?' I asked.

'The Blimp Sisters – Anne Chrichton and Alathea Fitzalan-Howard – they weren't ugly at all. It was very much our version of the story.'

The Queen remembered it all in great detail and, obviously, with much affection. Anne Chrichton and Alathea Fitzalan-Howard were teenagers, too, and friends of Lilibet. 'Mr Tannar' was Hubert Tannar, the head of the Royal School, who wrote the scripts and directed proceedings. ('A little too officiously,' according to some. Alathea called him 'that odious Mr Tannar'.) Cyril Woods was a local boy, one of the Royal School's star pupils, just fifteen in 1941, the same age as Princess Elizabeth. Cyril appeared as the comic lead in all the Windsor pantomimes. He went on to be the office-boy in the Supply Department at Windsor Castle and then worked in the Accounts Department at Buckingham Palace. He died at Windsor in 2001, after a lifetime of royal service working for the Crown Estate. 'We've kept in touch,' the Queen told me. Mr Tannar died in 1948, but the Queen kept in touch with his widow, Ethel, until her death in 1975.

'I am hoping Cyril Woods is going to write an account of those pantomimes,' the Queen said to me. 'They were rather special.' In 1942 the subject was *Sleeping Beauty*, with Lilibet again the principal boy, Prince Salvador, and Margaret Rose as Fairy Thistledown. In 1943 came *Aladdin* with the future queen in the title role and her sister as Princess Roxana. 'Cyril was just wonderful as the dame,' the Queen recalled. The young princesses sent him a first night telegram which (understandably) he treasured for the rest of his life. Addressed to C. Woods, 3 Richardsons Lawn, Great Park, Windsor, it read simply 'Congratulations Widow Twankey', and was signed simply 'Two Admirers'. Telling me the story nearly fifty years on, the Queen laughed, 'I hope he realised it came from us.'

I told the Queen it was H. J. Byron, a playwright and cousin of the poet Lord Byron, who had invented the character of Widow Twankey for a pantomime he wrote in the 1860s. It was then that she told me about Queen Victoria's reservations about Lord Byron. 'Quite a family, the Byrons,' we agreed.

The final Christmas show in 1944 was *Old Mother Red Riding Boots* with Lilibet as Lady Christina Sherwood and Margaret as the Honourable Lucinda Fairfax. This one was 'devised by Princess Elizabeth, Princess Margaret and Hubert Tannar' as a mash-up of half-a-dozen traditional pantomime stories. It was their most ambitious production, with music provided by the 'Salon Orchestra of the Royal Horse Guards (The Blues) under the direction of Captain A. J. Thornburrow' and Lilibet and Margaret performing a series of duets, some straight, some in 'swing time', some in cod Cockney accents. 'We had a lot of fun,' recalled the Queen a lifetime later, 'but I think we knew it was going to be our last. I was nearly nineteen and the war was gradually coming to an end.'

The young Prince Philip, staying at Windsor on leave in 1943, saw the production of *Aladdin*. I asked him what he remembered of it. 'Not much,' he said, with a dismissive shrug. Others remember the pantomimes as being very special events, remarkably elaborate and extraordinarily well done. All classes and conditions of people were involved – on stage, backstage and in the audience – but the shows were presented very much as star vehicles for the two princesses. Margaret Rose, the younger one, was seen as the more outgoing and more musical of the two, but Lilibet – by every account, except Prince Philip's – was the authority figure who held your eye when she was on stage and – in rehearsals and in performance – kept her eye on everything and everyone. She was the impressario. 'Her attention to detail has always been remarkable,' said her cousin, Margaret Rhodes.

Margaret Rhodes was a year older than her cousin Lilibet. 'I was at Windsor during the war,' she explained to me, 'because I was doing a shorthand and typing course at Queen's College which had moved out to Egham. I lived at Windsor and went in to Egham on the bus. And, later, I worked at MI6 and lived at Buckingham Palace. Queen Elizabeth's great achievement during the war was that she kept family life going, kept it as normal as possible. When we were about sixteen or seventeen, she had little parties with the young grenadier officers, so we could have a dance. And when the bombs were falling, she was always so calm. I remember there was a wonderful butler who would come in, bow and say solemnly, "Purple warning, Your Majesty," which meant that the Germans were closer than they ought to be. We had to go to the air-raid shelter, along miles of corridor. Queen Elizabeth would not be hurried. If people tried to hurry her, she simply slowed down.'

At Windsor, Lilibet and Margaret Rose believed they shared the privations of the people and, to an extent, they did. Their food may have been served to them by the nursery footman, but they were told it was subject to the rationing restrictions that applied to the public at large. There were lone light bulbs hanging from the ceiling in their chilly, draughty bedrooms.

Fires were limited and hot water was restricted, with a black line painted around the royal bathtubs as a reminder that the water should not be more than five inches deep. The children were also expected to contribute to the war effort. The funds from selling tickets to the Christmas pantomimes, for example, all went towards the Royal Household Wool Fund which provided comforts for the troops.

In October 1940, when Lilibet was fourteen and a half, she made her first broadcast, introducing a series of 'Children in Wartime' programmes for the BBC. 'She was so good about the endless rehearsals we had to have to get the breathing and phrasing right,' said Crawfie. Her voice was high-pitched, her accent high-falutin', but her performance was flawless. John 'Jock' Colville, then twenty-five and assistant private secretary to the prime minister, and, much later, private secretary to Princess Elizabeth herself, listened and was 'embarrassed by the sloppy sentiment' of the broadcast, but, by every other account, the people – in Britain, in the Dominions, in America – loved it. Lilibet was especially pleased that it met with her grandmother, Queen Mary's approval: 'Darling granny, I'm so glad you liked the broadcast. Everyone is saying how like my voice is to mummy's . . .'

The message was straightforward: 'Thousands of you in this country have had to leave your homes and be separated from your father and mother. My sister Margaret Rose and I feel so much for you, as we know from experience what it means to be away from those we love most of all.' According to Crawfie, 'Lilibet herself put in several phrases that were quite her, and everyone who heard this particular speech will remember the most spontaneous and amusing end. Lilibet, always anxious to bring her small sister forward, said, "Come on, Margaret, say good night," and a small, clear voice piped in rather pompously, "Good night, children."'

In fact, the end was not spontaneous. It was fully scripted and Margaret's farewell line actually read: 'Good night and good luck to you all.' Nor did Lilibet need to do much to bring her small sister forward. Margaret was naturally precocious. She was always the livelier and naughtier of the pair. She appears to have been encouraged in this by Crawfie who claimed, 'Margaret and I were very given to practical jokes and we each egged the other on.' The Heiress Presumptive did not approve. 'Lilibet was always too serious-minded,' said Crawfie. On one occasion, Margaret and Crawfie wanted to ring the alarm bell on the Castle terrace to see if it would bring out the guard from all over the castle. On another, they took one of the elderly gardener's brooms from his wheelbarrow and hid it in the bushes. 'Lilibet was always ashamed of us on these occasions,' reported Crawfie, without any apparent sense of remorse, 'and walked away from us rather pink in the face.'

Their cousin, Margaret Rhodes, said to me: 'The Queen and Princess Margaret were such different people. Occasionally, she [Lilibet] was driven mad by her, but they were sisters.' From an early age, Margaret was spoilt, outspoken, playful and flirtatious. Lilibet was not. During the war years at Windsor, young Grenadier Guards officers would sometimes join the girls and their governesses for lunch or tea. Margaret would chatter away gaily. Lilibet was more restrained, more formal, more dignified. Cosmo Lang, the Archbishop of Canterbury, who conducted her confirmation, spent some time alone with her and concluded, that 'though naturally not very communicative, she showed real intelligence and understanding.' Eleanor Roosevelt, wife of the American President, came to tea and reported that the Princess was 'quite serious and with a great deal of character and personality. She asked me a number of questions about life in the United States and they were serious questions.'

Lilibet was a serious young woman. She listened to the BBC news bulletins with care. She charted the progress of the war with her own large wall-map with little flags that were moved from place to place. As we have seen, under the instruction of Sir Henry Marten, she was taken through the niceties of *The English Constitution* by Walter Bagehot (1826–1877), required reading for monarchs-in-the-making. She was being prepared – and preparing herself – to fulfil her destiny.

To mark her sixteenth birthday, in 1942, she was made Colonel of the Grenadier Guards, in place of her great-great-uncle and godfather, the Duke of Connaught, who had died recently, aged ninety-one. 'It was a bit frightening inspecting a regiment for the first time,' she reported to a friend, 'but it was not as bad as I expected it to be.' She had her father at her side, and, in truth, all that was required of her was to stand stock still while the troops marched to and fro.

More of an ordeal for her would have been the small-talk she had to make afterwards, mingling with the officers and men, and the photographers she had to face. Ten press cameramen were admitted to the event and the unofficial court photographer, Cecil Beaton, was invited to take a special birthday portrait. It is a fabulous shot, both sexy and innocent: the sixteen-year-old princess, looking straight into the camera, is not quite smiling. She is in uniform, but her jacket is unbuttoned and her hat is at an angle that is almost provocative. The picture was reproduced around the world. A life of being photographed had begun.

In conversation, Elizabeth II gave the impression she was not comfortable with the idea of 'image making'. In reality, she understood and accepted the importance of what is now known as 'the optics' – getting the right look for the camera to help tell your story to the people. In the 1940s, George VI and his private secretary, Alexander Hardinge, allowed carefully wrought images of the young princess to be used as visual propaganda for both the war effort and the House of Windsor. Different kinds of image were required to tell different aspects of the story. Cecil Beaton – whose brilliantly lit and composed pictures (often with painted backdrops) had helped transform the bosomy, somewhat cosy and domestic Duchess of York into a fully fledged Queen – was used to give the world a romantic Princess Elizabeth. His eighteenth-birthday portrait has her set against an idealised skating scene, eyes wistfully cast down. Another photographer, Lisa Sheridan, was brought on board to produce more of a home-and-hearth series of pictures of Lilibet and Margaret Rose: nice girls, in sensible clothes, with perfect manners and adorable pets, the princesses-in-the-castle-next-door. When, in February 1945, Lilibet joined the Auxiliary Territorial Service as No. 230973 Second Subaltern Elizabeth Alexandra Mary Windsor, 'aged 18, eyes blue, hair brown, height 5ft 3in', she was photographed, on her knees, spanner in hand, on the ATS car mechanics course at Aldershot, learning how to change a wheel.

Nearly sixty years later, in October 2003, at the opening of an exhibition at the Imperial War Museum, the Queen was reunited with six of her wartime ATS colleagues. Betty Royle, aged eighty-two, said: 'I think she has never quite forgotten us, because those were the days when she had a kind of freedom.' Pat Blake, eighty-two, who had been an ATS sergeant, said: 'You've got to remember that in those days people knew little about royalty. There was no telly. Once in a while you saw them on a newsreel in a local cinema. She really did seem a remote person to us all . . . She and her sister seemed like fairytale people. The fact that we were going to work alongside her doing night driving, learning first aid, military law and theory and practice of mechanics was quite spellbinding . . .

She seemed very, very young – but she was very easy and just very unaffected and pleasant.'

In theory, on the course young Princess Elizabeth was 'to be treated in exactly the same way as any other officer learning at the driving training centre.' Well, she was – and she wasn't. She was taught alongside the others (who were instructed to call her 'Your Royal Highness' and then 'Ma'am to rhyme with jam'), and barked at when they were barked at, but, in class, she sat in the centre of the front row, and, at night, when the rest of the girls kipped down in the dormitory she was driven back to Windsor Castle. Her 'normal' life was anything but normal. For her wardrobe she was dependent on clothing coupons like everybody else, but, somehow, the royal household was issued with more coupons than everybody else. The world was told she received just five shillings a week in pocket money and more than half of that the kind princess donated to good causes. It was true, and it was good of her, but, of course, to her, money had no real meaning. She wanted for nothing. Her life was never – would never be, could never be – 'real'.

But the war was real enough. In August 1942, it claimed the life of her uncle, the Duke of Kent, killed on board an RAF Sunderland flying boat bound for Iceland where he was due to inspect RAF installations. In atrocious weather the craft flew into the side of a Scottish hill. The King was devastated. It was a family tragedy: the Duchess of Kent was a widow at thirty-five, with three small children, the youngest of whom, Prince Michael of Kent, was only seven weeks old. The Duke's nieces shared in the family sadness. 'Darling Grannie,' Lilibet wrote to Queen Mary, 'It was so very sad about poor Uncle George. His death was such an awful shock. We will miss him a great deal and he was always so very kind to us.' 'It was the second uncle they had lost completely,' Crawfie observed, 'for though the first, Uncle David, was not dead, they did not see him any more. The Royal conspiracy of silence had closed about him as it did about so many other uncomfortable things. In the Palace and the Castle his name was never mentioned.'

Lilibet's adolescence coincided with the Second World War. She was a child of thirteen at the outset in September 1939, a woman of nineteen when victory came in the summer of 1945. In the intervening six years, she grew up: she was confirmed; she made her first broadcast; she shot her first stag; she inspected her first regiment; she launched her first ship; she learnt to drive; in her ATS training she tested herself, for the first time (perhaps for the only time), against contemporaries from ordinary backgrounds; indeed she mixed, after a fashion, with ordinary people for the first time; she rode her horses; she loved her dogs; she learnt to dance; she became a Counsellor of State and, in her father's absence, visiting the Eighth Army in Italy in 1944, she performed her first constitutional functions, signifying the Royal Assent to Acts of Parliament. 'There was always a strong sense of duty mixed with *joie de vivre* in her character,' according to her French tutor, the Vicomtesse de Bellaigue. Princess Elizabeth had a good war, and she remembered it as, essentially, a happy time in her life.

To me the most telling witness of those wartime years is Alathea Fitzalan-Howard (1923–2001), one of those not-at-all-ugly Ugly Sisters in the Windsor Castle production of *Cinderella* in 1941. Alathea was a cousin of the Duke of Norfolk and, as a sixteen-year-old girl at the beginning of the war, went to live with her grandfather, Lord Fitzalan, at Cumberland Lodge in Windsor Great Park. Lord Fitzalan had been the last Viceroy of Ireland, the first Catholic to hold the post since the fall of James II. A widower, he and his daughter Magdalen (Alathea called her 'the Tigress') led a life dominated by their Catholic faith and their proximity to their royal neighbours by whose grace-and-favour they were living where they were. Happily for us (and posterity), Alathea kept a teenage diary that gives us both a portrait of Lilibet during those adolescent years and an insight into how those close to royalty – even when they are contemporaries and friends – can never treat royalty quite normally.

Sunday 21 January 1940
Lilibet rang up to ask me to skate. She, Margaret and the King picked me up in car and we drove to lake in front of house. Swept it first. Queen came down and watched. Played hockey with about six other people – policemen and chauffeurs etc from Royal Lodge. Great fun. Lilibet is so much nicer by herself than at Guides.

Wednesday 24 January 1940
Yesterday and today the princesses wore kilts and short green coats and their hoods. The princesses picked me up by drive gates and we skated like yesterday at Frogmore. Great fun skating. I can go backwards a bit now.

Thursday 15 February 1940
The princesses came to tea. Monty came with them as Crawfie in London. [Monty was Mrs Montaudon-Smith, second governess to the princesses.]. Played games in the hall – blind man's buff, charades etc. … Then detective came for them and they walked back in the dark.

Fun and games, governesses and detectives: a royal childhood in wartime, and Alathea, though two years older than Lilibet, was sharing in it. There was ice-skating, Girl Guides, dancing lessons, drawing lessons, playing party games, learning magic tricks, doing jigsaws, playing Monopoly – and beginning (very innocently) to meet young men, too. Lt Colonel Sir Grismond Picton Philipps, known as 'Jackie', was equerry to George VI and commander of the Castle Company, in charge of guarding the King at Windsor. He and his wife, Joan, were the source of much of the castle's social life for the young princesses and their friends.

Friday 7 June 1940
I changed (into my pinafore dress) and biked to Castle again. Lilibet and Margaret and Crawfie met me at the door and we walked down to the guardroom for tea with some officers. Enormous tea, we thought the supply of food was never coming to an end – cakes galore – ices – cherries – with which we had competitions. Once Lilibet and I looked at each other and nearly laughed. Most wonderful drawing and carvings on the walls and Lilibet and Margaret wrote their names in pencil above the fireplace. Lilibet and Margaret for the first time (that I've seen) weren't dressed alike.

The young officers, of course, were young men of the right class. Putting on their fund-raising concert parties, the princesses also met ordinary youngsters: local schoolchildren and evacuees. Not everyone approved.

Tuesday 2 July 1940
I went to the York Hall for a rehearsal of the concert on Saturday. The princesses came and Lilibet will tap dance in 'An Apple for the Teacher' (she's the teacher). Margaret is in it too. They both play the piano on the stage and then Margaret is the Dormouse in the Mad Hatter's Tea Party. We all come in the finale. I'm a waitress and Lilibet plays the piano and 'God Save the King'. It's very good, but everyone I've met says it's making them much too cheap. They really

shouldn't do it. They ought to get up little plays of their own with their friends but not dance with all the evacuees like this.

In April 1941, Alathea was seventeen and Lilibet was about to turn fifteen.

Thursday 3 April 1941
I biked to drawing and we finished modelling our clay horses. It was the last lesson for this term. Afterwards, we played a French tableau game with Monty and then cards till tea. They said something about Philip, so I said: 'Who's Philip?' Lilibet said: 'He's called Prince Philip of Greece' and then they both burst out laughing. I asked why, knowing quite well! Margaret said 'We can't tell you' but L said: 'Yes we can. Can you keep a secret?' Then she said that P was her 'boy'. Monty asked me if I had one and in the end, I told them it was Robert Cecil [who was twenty-four at the time and later became 6th Marquess of Salisbury], which amused L. M said she was so glad I had a 'beau'! We all laughed terribly. L says she cuts photos out of the paper! I must say she is far more grown-up than I was two years ago. When I left, Lilibet said: 'We part today the wiser for two secrets' and I biked home feeling very happy and also proud at being let into such a great secret, which I shall never betray.

Prince Philip told me – adamantly – that he had no romantic interest in Princess Elizabeth at this time. He visited Windsor Castle on leave because he was a cousin and a family friend – and because he was invited. Whatever others might have said or thought, he maintained the idea of marrying Princess Elizabeth was not 'even remotely' on his radar until the end of the war. That said, Lilibet was certainly sweet on him – though not only on him. She and Alathea both took a lively interest in Hugh Euston, a young Grenadier Guards officer two years Prince Philip's senior, and later, of course, Duke of Grafton, one of the Queen's closest friends and the husband of her long-serving Mistress of the Robes.

Monday 5 May 1941
Letter from Sonia [Graham-Hodgson] saying she's been to tea with the princesses and they talked about young men. L[ilibet] told her that I'd told them about Robert and she said she also adored Hugh Euston, so S said that I did too, so they laughed and laughed! L told her that she had a beau but didn't say who, so I must still keep that a secret from Sonia.

Thursday 23 October 1941
I biked to the Castle for drawing. It was lovely to see them again; we painted designs on our clay horses. They wore their old brown check skirts and red Aertex shirts, which they ought not to do – their clothes have gone down a lot since the war. They talked about their new lot of officers and are v. sorry Hugh's gone. Lilibet said she'd had her hair permed – it looked v. nice in front but too stiff behind. She told me that Philip, her beau, had been for the weekend and that I must come and see him if he came again! She said he's very funny, which doesn't sound my type actually – the only thing that does bore me about the royal family is that they all will tell one jokes that they've heard on wireless etc. No one else I know is in the least interested in those sort of silly jokes, but then the K and Q and the princesses are v. simple people.

The teenage Alathea was nothing if not judgemental, but her (plentiful) observations about the royal family's fondness for silly jokes, broad humour, practical jokes and raucous party games were spot-on. The Queen told me she loved meeting the popular entertainers her parents invited to Windsor in the 1940s. She mentioned 'big-hearted' Arthur Askey, Tommy Handley from *I.T.M.A.* and the female impressionist Florence Desmond as particular favourites. (It was the example of Florence Desmond that encouraged the young princess to do humorous impressions of her own.) Prince Philip told me that he and the Queen both had a soft spot for Tommy Trinder. We know that in the 1950s, Prince Charles adored The Goons.

In November 1941, the month she turned eighteen, Alathea confided to her diary: 'Lilibet said she thought I was her best friend now, which delighted me. She said that Sonia used to be but she never saw her now – poor S . . .' Alathea revelled in her closeness to Lilibet, but also worried about it. Should she continue to call her friend by her pet name now she was older? Would Alathea be considered a possible lady-in-waiting to the Princess in the fullness of time? What did the future hold? 'Surely,' she asked herself one day after lunch at the castle, when she had sat at the table with the King of Greece as well as George VI, 'after such a brilliant girlhood I could not be condemned to a life of obscurity? Since God has ordained for me to sit at my ease with the crowned heads of Europe, surely he must mean me to be great?'

By 1942, when Lilibet was sixteen, Alathea felt constrained to drop the L (for Lilibet) in her diary and refer to her friend as P.E (Princess Elizabeth). She also began to realise something that I have frequently noticed over fifty years of meeting royals: when they are with you there can be an intimacy that is disarming, but then, suddenly, they're gone – whisked away to the next appointment without so much as a goodbye. 'P.E calls me her best friend,' Alathea complained, 'but if friendship means seeing people on informal but not intimate terms, to her, it means more than that to me – it means confidences exchanged, joys and sorrows shared, lasting remembrance!'

Elizabeth was guarded from childhood, both instinctively reserved and careful – very careful – about sharing confidences. This self-restraint came to her naturally and was ingrained and a lifelong trait. I mention it here because people often ask, 'What did she really think about Princess Margaret – or Prince Andrew – or Harry and Meghan?' and the truth is: we do not know. Even with close family (I have this from her husband and her children), she was rarely judgemental and, on personal matters, in Prince Philip's phrase, inclined to 'say less rather than more'. Beyond interpreting her body language and relaying the odd remark apparently made to a page or prime minister or lady-in-waiting, it simply isn't possible to know what Her Majesty felt about certain sensitive issues. On the whole, and as a rule, she kept her feelings – or at least the detail of her feelings – to herself. For example, in 2022, when she heard that Harry and Meghan would not be attending the memorial service for the Duke of Edinburgh, she reportedly said, 'Thank goodness.' What did she mean? Thank goodness they're not coming? Or thank goodness, because they're not coming the press coverage won't be all about them? I suspect the latter, but I don't know. I do know that in 2020, when she read that Pope Francis had used his Sunday morning homily to urge the faithful to steer clear of gossip, calling it 'the devil's work and more deadly than the coronavirus', she heartily agreed.

Tentatively, I once raised all this with the Duke of Edinburgh. I suggested to him that he and the Queen were both 'emotionally self-sufficient'. He agreed, but added 'being emotionally self-sufficient does not make one unfeeling'.

In the early summer of 1942, not long after Sub-lieutenant Prince Philip of Greece had been mentioned in despatches

RIGHT: Queen Victoria at Osborne House on the Isle of Wight with her great-grandchildren, who were the children of the then Duke and Duchess of York (later King George V and Queen Mary): Princess Mary (later Countess of Harewood), Prince Edward (later King Edward VIII), Prince Albert (later King George VI), and Prince Henry (later the Duke of Gloucester) as a baby.

BELOW: Wedding Day, 26 April 1923: Elizabeth Bowes-Lyon, the new Duchess of York, and her parents, the Earl and Countess of Strathmore, and Prince Albert, Duke of York, and his parents, Queen Mary and King George V.

Royal christening, 29 May 1926: a future King and Queen with a future Queen – the Duke and Duchess of York with a baby Princess Elizabeth Alexandra Mary.

A royal wave in May 1928: Princess Elizabeth out for a ride with nanny 'Alah' Knight.

The Prince of Wales (the future Edward VIII) with his niece, Princess Elizabeth, in September 1933, coming back from church at Balmoral.

'Us four': Elizabeth and Bertie, Margaret and Lilibet.

Princess Elizabeth with Princess Margaret Rose, who is holding one of the family dogs, a Cairngorm terrier called Chu-Chu, in June 1936.

LEFT: 'Us four' and friends in the grounds of the Royal Lodge, Windsor, June 1936. RIGHT: Puppy love: Princess Elizabeth with her corgi in July 1936, five months before her uncle's abdication.

Coronation Day, 12 May 1937: crowned heads on
the balcony of Buckingham Palace.

Father and daughter – King and Heir Presumptive – George VI and
Princess Elizabeth, out riding, 1938.

Princess Elizabeth dressed as Prince Florizel with Princess Margaret as Cinderella in the royal pantomime at Windsor Castle, 21 December 1941.

Royal broadcast – Princesses Elizabeth and Margaret making a broadcast to 'the children of the Empire' during the Second World War, 10 October 1940.

Auxiliary Territorial Service 2nd Subaltern Elizabeth Alexandra Mary Windsor, on the ATS car mechanics course at Aldershot, 1945.

Princess Elizabeth playing tag on board the HMS *Vanguard*, 1947.

TOP: Father and daughter: King George VI and Princess Elizabeth, 1946.

RIGHT: Princess Elizabeth's 21st birthday speech, broadcast from Cape Town, South Africa, 29 April 1947.

RIGHT: Royal engagement –
Princess Elizabeth and her
fiancé, Lieutenant Philip
Mountbatten RN, at
Buckingham Palace, after
their engagement was
announced, 10 July 1947.

BELOW: Royal wedding –
Princess Elizabeth, Duchess
of Edinburgh, and Philip
Mountbatten, Duke of
Edinburgh, after their
wedding at Westminster
Abbey, 20 November 1947.

Four generations: Queen Mary, King George VI, Princess Elizabeth and
Prince Charles after his christening, 15 December 1948.

Princess Elizabeth, aged twenty-three, greeting Winston Churchill, aged seventy-five, at Guildhall, London, 23 March 1950.

LEFT: Peek-a-boo: Princess Elizabeth and Prince Charles hiding behind a pillar, playing hide and seek on the eve of Princess Anne's christening, 20 October 1950. RIGHT: Princess Elizabeth holding her daughter, Princess Anne, at her christening in Buckingham Palace, with the Duke of Edinburgh, 21 October 1950.

The prime minister, Winston Churchill, waits to welcome Queen Elizabeth II
on her return from Kenya following the death of George VI and her accession
to the throne, London, 7 February 1952.

Queen Elizabeth II making her first ever Christmas broadcast
from Sandringham House, Norfolk, 25 December 1952.

The Coronation of Queen Elizabeth II, Westminster Abbey, 2 June 1953.

On the balcony: happy and glorious, watchful and wary – the Queen and the Duke of Edinburgh, Prince Charles and Princess Anne at Buckingham Palace on Coronation Day, 2 June 1953.

LEFT: The Coronation Commonwealth Tour reaches Bermuda: the Queen and the Duke leave the House of Assembly in Hamilton, Bermuda, November 1953. RIGHT: Elizabeth II greeted by a young girl at an official welcome at a quayside in Fiji, December 1953. Behind the Queen are the Governor of Fiji, Sir Ronald Garvey, and, as ever, the Duke of Edinburgh.

In 1954, an estimated 20,000 Maori people from across New Zealand came to see the Queen and the Duke of Edinburgh at Arawa Park, Rotorua.

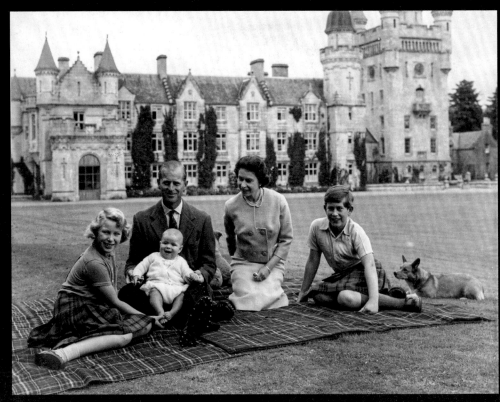

On the rug: Princess Anne, Prince Philip, Prince Andrew (aged seven months), the Queen, Prince Charles and a corgi outside Balmoral Castle, 8 September 1960.

for his contribution in the Battle of Cape Matapan in the south-east Mediterranean and awarded the Greek Cross of Valour, while war continued across Europe and the Far East, at Windsor Castle Alathea was having one of her most intimate conversations with her unique royal friend.

Sunday 7 June 1942
Had a last lovely supper in nursery, then P.E and I went to her room and lay on the beds talking. We began about her family which she's never breathed about before and I said things to her I would never had thought I would say! She said she wondered if she'd ever marry, and I assured her she would and she said if she really wanted to marry someone she'd run away, but I know she wouldn't really – her sense of duty's too strong, though she's suited to a simpler life. I would love to know how far she or her family have gone into the marriage question for her but I would never go a step further than she leads me herself. She may be right in her position, in not making too intimate friends. But tonight I learnt to know a new Lilibet; I saw behind the outward calm and matter-of-factness into something lovable and sincere – I knew this aspect of her would fade with daylight but it is one I shall never forget and my affection for her has become the deeper for it. We said goodnight at quarter to eleven and I lay awake in bed for ages, thinking. I've made a great effort since I've been here to call them P.E and P.M and as they haven't told me not to I concluded it must be right. It's sad the old Lilibet days are over but I know the time must come when it would be impossible.

That is a snapshot of Elizabeth II at sixteen and all the essential elements of her nature and personality are there – her sense of duty, her desire for a simpler life, her outward calm and 'matter-of-factness', her lovability, her sincerity, her practical approach to relationships in her position: 'not making too intimate friends.'

Alathea and Princess Elizabeth were close – and confiding. Alathea was nineteen and had never been kissed by a boy. 'I thought of P.E – she, like me, talks with men without ever encouraging them nearer but then she has people to look after her career and I haven't.' Alathea was unlucky in love, unlike her friend. (She was not as pretty as the princess, either, and more outspoken.) Alathea was unlucky, too, in that her fondest wish did not materialise. She hoped that when the time came she would be asked to become the heiress presumptive's lady-in-waiting. It was not to be. Was it because she was Catholic? No. Was it because her temperament did not seem quite suitable? Possibly. Most likely, it was because she wasn't yet married and those at court who decided these things – the Queen and the King and their advisers – had a preference for ladies-in-waiting with husbands and the right experience of the world.

On 11 July 1944, six weeks after Princess Elizabeth's eighteenth birthday, Alathea read in the Court Circular in *The Times* that Lady Mary Palmer had been appointed as Her Royal Highness's first lady-in-waiting. Alathea was appalled, her disappointment (verging on despair) only slightly assuaged by the realisation that Elizabeth herself had not been involved in selecting Mary Palmer: 'The week before last at drawing P.E said that M.P was coming for the weekend, as the *King's* guest – she couldn't think why and the only thing they were sure about was that she was Lord Selborne's daughter and had a big nose – which makes me certain she knew nothing of the appointment.'

In time, Alathea came to quite like Mary Palmer, who was twenty-four and soon to be married – and whose elder brother, William Wolmer, had been killed eighteen months before by a stray artillery shell during an army training exercise on the South Downs. Mary was bright (she had been to St Paul's Girl School), creative (she played the piano-accordion and loved to crochet) and sensible, with the right heritage (her grandmother was a Cecil, courtiers since the reign of Elizabeth I), as well as useful secretarial skills and a level head. Judging from photographs of the period, she had a pleasant appearance, too, and an unremarkable nose. More significantly, her father, the 3rd Earl Selborne, was working with David Bowes-Lyon, Queen Elizabeth's brother, at the Ministry of Economic Warfare at the time – and, as we shall see, David (a colourful character, much loved by some, less so by others), liked to have influence in royal family affairs.

Overlooked as a potential lady-in-waiting, Alathea nevertheless remained a good friend. In November, the Princess came to her 21st birthday dinner:

Thursday 25 November 1944

It was the first time P.E had ever been out to dinner and she said it was lovely to come here first – it is certainly a great honour for us. She looked absolutely charming in a dress of pale yellow chiffon, simply made and her pearls and two diamond stars either side of the neck. Her face was made up and she looked v. pretty, with a dignified grace peculiar to herself. After dinner I showed her my presents, while the men were still in the dining room and she gave me the most lovely handkerchief sachet, made of pink net and white lace with pot pourri inserted. I am delighted with it. We began by playing a paper game and then went on to acting clumps and charades, which were a great success and we all laughed a lot. They didn't leave till quarter to twelve, so they must have enjoyed it and there certainly never was a dull moment.

I went to bed radiantly happy and shall remember this day all my life . . .

Alathea went to Princess Elizabeth's wedding in 1947 (she did not marry herself until 1953 and then not happily) and remained friends with Elizabeth for the rest of her life, but as the war years came to an end the special closeness they had once enjoyed began to end, too.

Thursday 15 February 1945
Biked up to the Castle for drawing. Only P.M and me today and we continued with our lino-cuts. Went out with Crawfie and groomed the foals and came in for tea. P.M caught mumps at Sandringham but is now recovered and P.E developed it here last Saturday and has it slightly worse than her sister. When I was going away, P.M opened the door and tried to pull me in and I just caught a glimpse of P.E sitting in an arm chair by the fire and spoke to her through the door. P.M told me Prince Philip sent P.E a photograph of himself for Christmas and she danced round the room with it for joy!

According to Prince Philip, it wasn't until around 1945 'or probably 1946' that he began to consider seriously the possibility of marriage. 'There was a war on,' he said. 'I was rather concentrating on that.'

CHAPTER ELEVEN

Philip's War

Prince Philip of Greece had a good war. His mother, Princess
Alice, who had returned to live in Athens in November 1938,
had hopes that her son might choose to serve in the Greek
navy. From Philip's point of view, that was not an inviting
prospect. The Greek navy was tiny. Philip's knowledge of
the Greek language and people was sketchy. He was a prince
of Greece, but he had spent most of his life in England,
France and Germany. Where did his loyalty lie? He could
see there was a dilemma and he was torn – but not for long.
King George II of Greece (the son of King Constantine I,
Prince Andrea's eldest brother) let him off the hook. Philip
had started his naval training in Britain. The King decided it
was only sensible he should continue it there.

Philip had no regrets about the decision. Like his future
wife, he was not much given to 'regrets'. Nor was he given
(despite the presence of C S Forrester's *Hornblower* novels on
his bookshelves) to recounting tales of his wartime adventures
on the high seas. He was 'mentioned in despatches', but he
would not want to exaggerate his contribution or achievement.
In 1948, when, as the Duke of Edinburgh, he was presented
with the Freedom of the City of London, he looked back on
his war service and said, 'In every kind of human activity there
are those who lead and those who follow . . . I would like to

accept the Freedom of this City, not only for myself, but for all those millions who followed during the Second World War. Our only distinction is that we did what we were told to do, to the very best of our ability, and kept on doing it.'

Having graduated from Dartmouth as the best cadet in his course, his first appointment, as an eighteen-year-old midshipman, in January 1940, was to an old battleship, HMS *Ramillies*, then in Colombo, Ceylon, and working as an escort to convoys that were part of the Australian Expeditionary Force moving from Australia to the Middle East. The ship, a veteran of the Great War, was uncomfortable; the appointment – at least in the eyes of a young man eager for action – unexciting.

It turns out that his uncle, Louis Mountbatten, had proposed to George VI that Philip be sent to a ship on the China station. When I raised this with him, Prince Philip bridled at the suggestion that Mountbatten was the orchestrator of his career. Uncle Dickie took an avuncular interest, certainly – 'He put in a good word where he could, I've no doubt' – but Prince Philip made it clear to me that he hoped that whatever he achieved in the Navy he achieved through his own best endeavours. In fact, he was not entirely sure that being a prince, and nephew to a noted 'operator' like Mountbatten, may not have been positively to his disadvantage.

In 1940, after four months in *Ramillies*, Philip served briefly in HMS *Kent*, in a shore station in Ceylon, and in HMS *Shropshire*. 'Action' continued to prove elusive. 'We have something to look forward to,' he noted, optimistically, in his log book at one point in his time in *Kent*: 'there is an enemy raider in the Indian Ocean and there is just a chance our tracks will cross.' They didn't. The only 'fun' to be had was thanks to the swirl of the ocean: 'On one occasion a particularly heavy sea completely smothered the bridge and platform, and even the crow's nest felt the spray from it. Steaming with the sea on the beam and at twenty-one knots the rolling was greatly emphasised, and a lot of innocent fun was had in the mess, watching the Goanese stewards diligently laying the table, and then the plates, knives, forks, spoons, butter dishes, toast racks and marmalade landing in a heap on the deck.' It was stories like this with which he regaled Princess Elizabeth in his letters and when he visited her on leave. He did not talk about heroics at all. 'In fact, he rarely talked about the war,' the Queen told me. 'At least, not the dark side. He talked about the funny side. He talked about the funny side of everything.'

The catering arrangements were clearly taken seriously in HMS *Kent*. When the ship was off Bombay, the 1st Lieutenant noted in his log: 'It rained most of the Morning Watch. Luckily had Prince Philip as the snotty [slang for 'midshipman'] and he makes the best cup of cocoa of the lot.'

Prince Philip's own account of his war service was typically matter-of-fact: 'I remained in the East Indies Station until June 1940, when the Italians invaded Greece and I became a combatant. I was appointed to HMS *Valiant* in the Mediterranean Fleet . . . *Valiant* saw quite a lot of action during the latter part of 1940, including Malta convoys, the bombardment of Bardia, and the night action off Cape Matapan in March 1941, and the evacuation of Crete in May.' It was for his contribution to the success of the Battle of Matapan, manning the searchlight on board his battleship, that Prince Philip, not yet twenty, received his 'mention in despatches'. According to his cousin and exact contemporary, Alexandra of Greece (who married Peter II of Yugoslavia in 1944), when she congratulated him on the honour, 'he simply shrugged'.

Between engagements, Philip returned to England to take his sub-lieutenant's courses and exams at Portsmouth – and to visit his assorted British relations, in London and Windsor. He worked hard and he played hard. In the exams – covering seamanship, signals, navigation, gunnery and torpedoes – he secured the top grade in four sections out of five. In March 1942, staying in London with the Mountbattens, he went out on the razzle with his cousin, Dickie's other nephew, David Milford-Haven, who was also in the Navy. The young men borrowed the Mountbatten Vauxhall to help transport themselves around the more fashionable West End and Mayfair nightspots and, at 4:30 a.m., collided with a traffic island, wrote off the car, and returned to their uncle's residence, bloodied if unbowed. 'So,' reflected Mountbatten, 'after facing death many times over at sea, they got their first wounds in a London blackout.'

In June 1942 Philip was appointed to the destroyer HMS *Wallace* and, that October, when *Wallace*'s 1st Lieutenant was appointed elsewhere, the Commanding Officer asked that Prince Philip take his place. At just twenty-one, Philip became one of the youngest first lieutenants in the Royal Navy. HMS *Wallace* was one of the destroyers on convoy duty on the British east coast, constantly moving up and down 'E-Boat Alley', as it was known, from Sheerness to Rosyth and back. It wasn't glamorous, but it was necessary, arduous, and, given the effectiveness of the German E-boats' torpedoes, not without its hairy moments.

At the beginning of July 1943, the *Wallace* joined the armada of ships (and 150,000 men) amassed off the coast of Sicily ready to invade the island. According to Harry Hargreaves, a yeoman aboard the *Wallace,* 8 July was the night when Prince Philip of Greece saved the day. 'The stars were bright and the sea was black,' recalled Hargreaves. 'There was only one problem: the water shone and sparkled, and our progress created a long, glowing trail which made it extremely easy for enemy aircraft to spot us.' At midnight the first plane struck. 'We were sitting ducks. It was inevitable that one of the bombs would hit us. We had little chance of survival and all 163 of us on board thought we were facing death.'

After the first attack – which hit the side of the ship – the enemy aircraft disappeared. 'We knew it would return in minutes – with other aircraft.' At this point, according to Hargreaves, Philip came up with 'a brilliant plan that was destined to save our lives.' He got a group of men to lash together large planks of wood to make a raft, attaching smoke floats at each end. They launched the raft into the sea and activated the smoke floats. 'Billowing clouds of smoke and small bursts of flame made it look like the flaming debris of our ship floating in the water.' The *Wallace* then steamed away from the raft for 'a good five minutes' before the captain ordered the engines stopped. When, shortly afterwards, the enemy aircraft returned, 'I heard the scream of bombs falling,' Hargreaves recalled, 'but they were aimed at the raft, not at us. The 1st Lieutenant's ruse had worked.' In later years, the Queen had no recollection of Prince Philip telling her anything about any of this. 'He didn't like to talk about himself and found praise of any kind embarrassing,' she said.

Harry Hargreaves had no inhibitions when it came to singing Prince Philip's praises. He recalled that on the day they first met, when the *Wallace* was docked at Tilbury, Philip rustled up a meal of sausages and powdered egg for them both, despite the fact that Philip was an officer and Hargreaves 'merely a yeoman': 'He was a down-to-earth, ordinary man. He had no airs or graces, and when the captain told me he was a prince, I said, "He doesn't look like that to me."'

In 1944, as the war in Europe moved decisively the Allies' way, Philip was appointed to a brand-new destroyer, HMS *Whelp*, still building in Newcastle when he joined her, and, subsequently, set off with her for more exotic climes: the Far East and the climax of the war against Japan in the Pacific.

On the way, *Whelp* called at Colombo and Philip spent a memorable Christmas Eve with Uncle Dickie, now Supreme Commander, South East Asia, and Mountbatten's new chief of staff, Lieutenant General Frederick 'Boy' Browning (the novelist Daphne du Maurier's husband who, in 1948, became the first Comptroller of Princess Elizabeth's Household.) According to Philip Ziegler, Mountbatten's official biographer, the night went gloriously awry because 'the Singhalese cook, overawed by the occasion, took refuge in drink and served dinner cold, late, and back to front: Christmas pudding at midnight, turkey at 1 a.m. Nobody minded – least of all Mountbatten.' This was a story Prince Philip did share with Princess Elizabeth.

His uncle Dickie was increasingly a father figure for Philip. Earlier in December he had had to break the news to his nephew that his actual father, Prince Andrea, was dead. Andrea, aged sixty-two, unreachable in Vichy France, had died of a heart attack in his bedroom at the Hotel Metropole in Monte Carlo in the early hours of 3 December. His lady-friend, the Comtesse Andrée de la Bigne, was with him. His widow, Princess Alice, living, reclusively, in Athens, received the news two days later. Somehow she got word to Dickie, who sent a naval message to Philip on board HMS *Whelp*. The message was deciphered precisely as follows: 'So shocked and grieved to hear of the death of your (?) father and send you all my heartfelt sympathy. Following has been received from your mother: "Embrace you tenderly in our joint sorrow. Your loving mama."'

Princess Alice was a woman with a good heart – and much admired by Elizabeth II. 'She was a remarkable woman,' said the Queen, who invited her mother-in-law to come and live at Buckingham Palace towards the end of her life, when the Greek colonels' coup of 1967 forced her into exile (again) and when she had no money of her own to speak of because she had given it all away. 'She was a do-er,' the Queen said to me (when I was writing my biography of Prince Philip). 'She got things done. She was quite a character, too.'

During the war she worked in one of the largest soup kitchens in Athens; she worked in a refuge for orphans; she organised a group of district nurses to provide care in the poorest areas of the city. She was in no way ostentatious about her good works. She was quietly determined, dogged, devoted, and ready to take risks. When the Nazi threat to the Jews of Athens was at its height, Princess Alice offered refuge to a family of Cohens. When neighbours enquired, she said that Mrs Cohen was a former Swiss governess to her children. When the Gestapo questioned her, she simply exaggerated her deafness and looked uncomprehending.

She never talked about hiding the Cohens. When I tried to talk to Prince Philip about his mother, he was reluctant to be drawn. When I persisted, he said, 'Mm' and changed the subject, asking me if I had yet read a new book that told the story of the Royal Yacht *Britannia*.

It is clear to me that from his father Prince Philip inherited his appearance, his charm, his humour, his flirtatious way with the ladies. But with his mother he shared a wider, and perhaps more significant, range of characteristics. He guarded his privacy. He kept his own counsel. He did not wear his heart on his sleeve. He hid his light under a bushel. He found it uncomfortable to talk about himself – and had a feeling that it would have been both unmannerly and unmanly to do so. His manner was deceptive. He was a kindly person, and a caring one. He was more sensitive than he wanted us to think or know. He could be prickly and perverse, stubborn and wilful. He could also be visionary. His spiritual life was important to him. He was his mother's son. That was my impression, but

I believe the Queen would have agreed with this assessment.

From April 1941, when Athens was occupied by the Germans, Alice was able to get permission to visit her sister in Sweden and her daughters in Germany and Switzerland. In 1937 Hermann Goering had attended the funeral of Alice's daughter Cécile and her husband. At the outset of the war Sophie's husband had been a member of the Nazi Party and a member of the SS – the *Schutzstaffel*, 'Hitler's bodyguard'. Theodora's husband, Berthold, was a German, too, but not a Nazi. The oldest sister, Margarita, had the oldest husband, Gottfried (known as Friedel), who was already in his forties when war was declared. Relatively speaking, through the hostilities, they managed to keep a low profile and out of harm's way. In October 1944, when, three and a half years after being driven out, British troops returned to Greece, Alice's daughters were, once again, behind enemy lines. Throughout the war years, Philip was unable to make contact of any kind with his sisters. While Greece was in German hands, he was unable to see his mother. He was twenty-three, and in a ship bound for Colombo, when his father, whom he hadn't seen for five years, died in a hotel bedroom in the south of France.

'You're a poor bloody orphan just like me,' thought Mike Parker when he met Philip at the time, 'a poor bloody orphan.'

Mike Parker was an Australian, from Melbourne. Born in June 1923, he was two years older than Prince Philip – just as Alathea Fitzalan-Howard was two years older than Princess Elizabeth and, as Alathea was to Lilibet, so Mike Parker was to Philip: a wartime best friend and probably our best witness to what Philip was like during those years.

They met in 1942, as fellow 1st Lieutenants – Philip in HMS *Wallace*, Parker in HMS *Lauderdale* – on convoy duty on 'E-boat Alley'. Parker's father was a captain in the Royal Australian Navy. Parker came to Britain to join the British Royal Navy to prove his independence. 'I was an orphan,' Parker liked to say, 'because I came from Australia. Philip was an orphan because he came from nowhere. His parents weren't anywhere to be seen.'

The two men had much in common. They were young. They were ambitious. 'We were highly competitive,' said Parker. 'We both wanted to show that we had *the* most efficient, cleanest and best ship and ship's company in the Navy'. And they shared a sense of humour. They both laughed a lot. (It is clear from Alathea's diaries that she felt Prince Philip laughed too much and too loudly.). For a prince, Philip was remarkably unstuffy. As an Australian, Parker did not stand on ceremony. In an unlikely way, each felt he was the other's equal. The traditional middle-class British naval officer was relatively well-heeled. Not so Philip of Greece and Parker of Melbourne. 'He was better off than I was,' said Parker, 'but compared with many people he didn't have a brass razoo!'

Prince Philip dated the beginning of their close friendship to 1944, when, by coincidence, they found themselves in sister ships – Philip in HMS *Whelp,* Parker in HMS *Wessex* – on their way to the Pacific as part of the 27th Destroyer Flotilla under Admiral Sir James Somerville. They were looking forward to some action against the Japanese; they arrived just in time for the Japanese surrender in September 1945. In Tokyo Bay, *Whelp*'s final wartime assignment was to ferry newly released prisoners-of-war to light fleet carriers who then brought them back to Britain.

On their way to the Far East and after the Japanese surrender, Philip and Mike Parker took shore leave together, both in North Africa and in Australia. In 1990, interviewed for a biography of Prince Philip, Parker recalled: 'Of course we had fun in North Africa, but never anything outrageous. We'd drink together and then we'd go and have a bloody good meal.

People are always asking, "Did you go to the local estaminets and screw everything in sight?" And the answer is, "No! It never came into the picture. There was so much else to do."' He did admit, however: 'There were always armfuls of girls.'

What exactly did he mean by that? When I asked him, Mike Parker simply exploded: 'Nothing, for Christ's sake.' Commander Parker (as he became: and MVO, CVO and Order of Australia, too) died at the very end of 2001, aged eighty-one, a plain-speaking Australian to the last. 'Jesus, I wish I'd never used that phrase,' he said to me. 'Yeah, there were always "armfuls of girls", showers of them, but nothing happened – nothing serious. What I meant was this: we were young, we had fun, we had a few drinks, we might have gone dancing, but that was it. In Australia, Philip came to meet my family, my sisters and their friends. There were girls galore, but there was no one special. Believe me. I guarantee it.'

In 1945 Philip was twenty-four, a bearded Adonis. According to his cousin, Alexandra of Yugoslavia, who wasn't there, 'Philip, with a golden beard, hit feminine hearts, first in Melbourne and then in Sydney, with terrific impact.' According to Mike Parker, who was, 'Philip was actually quite reserved, quite restrained really. He was always good company, but he was self-disciplined, too. And self-contained. And careful. He didn't encourage gossip. He certainly didn't wear his heart on his sleeve. He didn't give away a lot. There have been books and articles galore saying he played the field. I don't believe it. People say we were screwing around like nobody's business. Well, we weren't. You didn't. We didn't. That's the truth of it.' Besides, in 1943, Mike Parker got married. 'In those days, if you slept with a girl, you married her.'

My friend Robin Dalton (1920–2022) – in due course a London-based literary agent and film producer; in 1945 a twenty-four-year old Australian girl working as secretary to the commanding officer of the ordnance department of the Southwest Pacific Area – remembered it a little differently. In her *Incidental Memoir*, she wrote: 'What would seem like shocking promiscuity – not only physical but emotional – in peacetime, was felt as a beneficence of the heart. The fact that it was also rarely that one was caught out in one's perfidious spread of affection blinded one to the dangers. The pleasures were freshly minted each week, as the turnover in admirers was brisk. If possible, our affections were limited to one per squadron, or PT boat, or Marine battalion, and the chief dread was that their leaves would overlap. They seldom did. We did not consider ourselves promiscuous. We were in love.'

Robin Dalton was in love with Philip's cousin, David Milford Haven (1919–1970), the son of Philip's Uncle George, the older brother of Louis Mountbatten who had died in 1938. 'We met in 1944, in Sydney, at a cocktail party on one of the warships. He was a signals officer working for Admiral Vian. He was adorable. It was love at first sight.' Their affair lasted five years. 'I met Philip through David,' she told me. 'They were like brothers, you know.' She told me that Philip had two special girlfriends in Australia at the end of the war: 'A society girl called Sue Other-Gee, and then Sandra Jacques – that was a terrific love affair.'

'A very full love affair,' Robin added, knowingly. When I raised an eyebrow, she went on: 'I'm sure they slept together, but I don't know it for a fact. I wasn't in the bedroom – but I did see them on the dance floor. They could hardly have been closer!' Perhaps there was a licence to be more uninhibited in Australia? Dame Barbara Cartland, the romantic novelist and step-grandmother to Diana, Princess of Wales, told me in the 1990s that Louis Mountbatten had told her that Prince Philip had even fathered a child in Australia at the end of the war. 'Are you sure?' I asked her. She was in her mid-nineties at the time. 'Well,' she said, 'you can't be completely sure about anything, can you? But it's possible, isn't it?'

It certainly is, though Gina Kennard (1919–2011), daughter of Sir Harold Wernher and Countess Anastasia de Torby, who knew Prince Philip well from the 1920s onwards, had her doubts. Sixty years after the war, sitting in the elegant drawing room of her third-floor flat off Sloane Square in London, she said to me: 'It was a different world. Unmarried girls didn't sleep with their boyfriends. It really wasn't done. You went for dinner, you went dancing, you went shooting, you had fun, but you knew where to draw the line. Of course, some girls stepped over the boundary, but that was the exception, not the rule.' Gina and her sister, Myra, and their friends were brought up in an age when the Church of England's traditional teaching on sexual morality went virtually unquestioned and mostly unchallenged. Married women (like Dickie Mountbatten's wife, Edwina) might have affairs (indeed, Gina's first husband, Bunny Phillips, had been one of Edwina's lovers) and, because there was a war on, some unmarried sweethearts might indulge their boys on the way to the front, but, on the whole, most nice girls expected to be married as virgin brides. And there were practical considerations as well as moral ones: contraception was uncertain, illegitimacy a stigma, abortion illegal.

I asked Gina Kennard if Prince Philip had been her boyfriend when they were young. She laughed. 'Everybody said he was in love with me. My mother used to say that his mother – who was a saintly person, deaf but lovely – would have been very happy for Philip to marry me, but it never came up. I said to him recently, "Are you still in love with me?" and he said, "Yes, of course, I am." The truth is, he was wonderfully attractive – he still is – and we were friends, best friends, and we went out together and had just the best time, but nothing really serious happened. It wasn't like that. He was young and handsome and, of course, I loved him. At that age, you fall in love all the time, don't you? Philip knew lots of girls. There was Osla Benning, wasn't there? We were just young people having fun.'

According to Alexandra of Yugoslavia, Philip started 'having fun' when he went on holiday to Venice in the year before the war and, aged seventeen, stayed with Alexandra and her mother, Aspasia (widow of Prince Alexander of Greece, nephew to Philip's father, Andrea). Andrea cautioned Aspasia that his boy had exams to pass and urged her to 'keep him out of girl trouble'. In the event, in Alexandra's account, Philip discovered 'blondes, brunettes and redhead charmers' and 'gallantly and I think quite impartially squired them all.'

Osla Benning was certainly one of Philip's youthful flames. She was a Canadian-born, London-based debutante, with 'dark hair, alabaster white skin, an exquisite figure and a gentle loving nature', according to Sarah Norton who shared a flat with her in 1939 – when Osla was just sixteen. Sarah, daughter of Richard Norton (soon to become 6th Lord Grantley) and goddaughter of Louis Mountbatten, introduced Osla to the eighteen-year-old Philip and, from the start, 'they got on like a house on fire'. When I asked Prince Philip how he remembered times with Osla, he simply said, 'Fun'. By all accounts – including her own – she was larky, high-spirited and innocent. For the first two to three years of the war, when Philip wasn't at sea he'd see Osla in London when he could – and then he saw her less. And less. And in 1944 she became engaged to someone else. 'But you remained friends?' I asked Prince Philip.

'Yes.'

'And you kept in touch?'

'Yes.'

Osla did not marry her first fiancé. In 1946, she married a thirty-year-old diplomat, John Henniker-Major, later 8ᵗʰ Baron Henniker, and, in 1947, Philip became godfather to their first-born son, who was given 'Philip' as one of his Christian names.

Through the war years, while he was seeing Osla Benning and others, Prince Philip kept in touch with his young cousin, Princess Elizabeth. He wrote to her, 'from here and there'. He saw her, 'now and again'. That's about as much as I got out of him. At around the time of his golden wedding anniversary in 1997 he said to me, 'I don't remember much about it. It *was* a long time ago.' In 1970, talking to his official biographer, Basil Boothroyd (whom he liked and trusted), he said, with the diffidence and touch of defensiveness that were the hallmarks of any conversation about his personal life: 'During the war, if I was here [in Britain] I'd call in and have a meal. I once or twice spent Christmas at Windsor, because I'd nowhere particular to go. I thought not all that much about it, I think. We used to correspond occasionally. You see it's difficult to visualise. I suppose if I'd just been a casual acquaintance it would all have been frightfully significant. But if you're related – I mean I knew half the people here, they were all relations – it isn't so extraordinary to be on kind of family relationship terms. You don't necessarily have to think about marriage.'

However sketchy he claimed his recollections to be, Prince Philip was adamant on one point. He did not think about marriage in any serious sense until more than a year after the war, when he went to stay at Balmoral in 1946. 'I suppose one thing led to another,' he conceded. 'It was sort of fixed up. That's really what happened.'

By 'fixed up', he did not mean arranged by others. He meant that was the time when he and Princess Elizabeth came to a mutual understanding that met with the approval of their families. If he did have thoughts of marriage much before 1946, he kept them to himself. He certainly did not share them with Mike Parker, his contemporary and closest wartime friend. 'He was the same, then as now,' Parker told me in 2000, two years before his death, 'good at keeping his feelings to himself. He didn't tell me anything and I didn't ask. I might have had my suspicions, but until around 1946, when an engagement was in the air, I didn't know a thing.'

Others, however, had their suspicions as far back as 1941. Henry 'Chips' Channon was one such. A wealthy American from Chicago, Channon came to Britain aged twenty-one in 1918, married Lady Honor Guinness, and became an English MP. He liked to feel he knew everybody and everything. He was a waspish chronicler of the social scene and took a special interest in royalty. In January 1941 he found himself staying at the British Legation in Athens and noted in his journal: 'The Royal set-up at Athens is complicated: there is the isolated King who sees no-one; there are the Crown Prince and Princess (Frederika) who, madly in love, remain aloof from the world with their babies and their passion. She is a touch unpopular, being German (I met her first dining with General Goering in 1936); there is Princess Andrew who is eccentric to say the least and lives in semi-retirement: there is Prince Andrew, who philanders on the Riviera whilst his son, Prince Philip, is serving in our Navy . . .' This was the January when Philip, on leave from HMS *Valiant,* was staying in Athens with his mother. On the 21st Channon was taken to 'an enjoyable Greek cocktail party': 'Philip of Greece was there. He is extraordinarily handsome, and I recalled my afternoon's conversation with Princess Nicholas [Ellen, Philip's aunt, widow of Andrea's brother Nicholas]. He is to be our Prince Consort, and that is why he is serving in our Navy. He is charming, but I deplore such a marriage; he and Princess Elizabeth are too inter-related.'

Prince Philip deplored the kind of tittle-tattle in which 'Chips' Channon revelled. In January 1941, Philip was nineteen, Elizabeth was fourteen, and, whatever his matchmaking aunt or her gossip-mongering tea-time companions might care to invent, as far as Philip was concerned, marriage was not on the agenda. Channon, nevertheless, retained his watching brief. On 16 February 1944, he noted in his diary: 'My parents-in-law, the Iveaghs, called to see me, after having had tea with the King and Queen at Buckingham Palace . . . I do believe that a marriage may well be arranged one day between Princess Elizabeth and Prince Philip of Greece.' In October the same year, Channon's nose went into an overdrive of twitching when he found himself a guest of Princess Marina, Duchess of Kent, at Coppins, her country house in Buckinghamshire. 'As I signed the visitors' book,' he reported to his journal, with a note of triumph worthy of Sherlock Holmes, 'I noticed "Philip" written constantly. It is at Coppins that he sees Princess Elizabeth. I think she will marry him.'

Prince Philip had no time for *The Diaries of Sir Henry Channon*. He and Princess Elizabeth were cousins; they became friends; they got to know one another better; they became closer; in due course, they became engaged. 'That's about it, really,' he said to me, with a shrug.

CHAPTER TWELVE

Men

Getting an insight into Philip's feelings about his relationship with Elizabeth was never going to be easy. Getting an insight into her feelings about him is more straightforward – if you are content to go along with the well-worn legend (that she contributed to) that her heart belonged to Prince Philip from the moment she saw him on that momentous day at Dartmouth when she was just thirteen. Once she had set her course, she did not waver from it.

Horace Smith, her riding instructor, when she was both a child and a young woman, had the measure of her. He saw that she was single-minded, not one to take up interests 'lightly, only to drop them just as easily a short time later. If and when her interest is aroused, she goes into whatever subject it is with thoroughness and application, nor does her interest wane with the passing of time or the claim of other new matters upon her attention.'

As it was with her horses – and her dogs, and her faith, and her duty – so it was with Philip. Her first cousin, near contemporary and friend, Margaret Rhodes, said to me: 'Princess Elizabeth was enamoured from an early age. I've got letters from her saying, "It's so exciting. Mummy says, Philip can come and stay." She never looked at anyone else. She was smitten from the start.' 'Yes,' agreed Lilibet's grandmother,

Queen Mary, 'it does happen sometimes and Elizabeth seems to be that kind of girl. She would always know her own mind. There's something very steadfast and determined in her – like her father.'

'Once she had set her course she did not waver from it.' Is that really so? 'She never looked at anyone else'. That is the line that everyone takes and always has. It was repeated again in all the coverage at the time of her death. It was the line I took, too, when I first published *Philip & Elizabeth Portrait of a Marriage* many years ago. Since then, however, I happened one day to find myself filming a television documentary at a country auction house when I was shown a letter that was up for sale, vendor unnamed. The letter was from Princess Elizabeth to her first cousin, Diana Bowes-Lyon. It was dated Tuesday 30 November 1943 – so the young princess would have been a little more than halfway between her seventeenth and eighteenth birthdays. It begins as a 'thank you' letter:

Darling Diana,
I hope you will forgive me for not having written sooner to thank you for the handkerchief which you sent me. You know, it really was wicked of you to give me another one as I only wanted the other one as it belonged to a set, which I've had for years. It was angelic of you to give me a hanky but an unforgivable thing to do nowadays.

So far not so surprising. Anyone familiar with William Shawcross's splendid collection of the letters of Queen Elizabeth, the Queen Mother, will be familiar with the effervescent family style. Anyone familiar with Princess Elizabeth's ordered mind and thoughtful character will understand her delight at having her incomplete set of hankies made whole once more and her horror at the extravagance entailed at a time of war, privation and clothes rationing. The opening of the letter is interesting – and charming in its way – but it is with what follows that there comes the revelation:

I saw Andrew for a moment last week. And the more I see of him, the more I wish he wasn't my first cousin, as he's just the sort of husband any girl would love to have. I don't think one could find anyone nicer.

Well, there you have it. 'He is just the sort of husband any girl would love to have.'

And who was Andrew? He was Andrew Charles Victor Elphinstone, born 10 November 1918, the younger son of Queen Elizabeth's oldest surviving sister, Mary (May), and Sidney, 16th Lord Elphinstone. The Elphinstones had five children in all: Elizabeth, John, Jean, Andrew and Margaret – our Margaret Rhodes. Mrs Rhodes told me that she 'hero-worshipped' her brother Andrew, who had Victor added to his Christian names because his birth coincided with Armistice Day marking the allied victory at the end of the First World War. When Andrew was staying with the Windsors during the Second World War, in May 1944, Queen Elizabeth wrote to Elizabeth Elphinstone, to say: 'It is delicious having Andrew. He is such fun, & so intelligent & so good-looking.' He was bright – educated at Eton and New College, Oxford – and musical, too. 'He has just bought me a piano, or rather he found it & I paid for it and he plays on it, & I listen.'

And Lilibet listened, also. And she liked what she heard. She enjoyed her tall and handsome first cousin's company very much. As a boy he had suffered from a stammer. It had not been as debilitating as her father's, but it was a point of sympathy. And Lilibet was taken with her cousin, too, because, while he was fun to be with, he was so palpably decent. And he was fundamentally serious. He was destined to become a clergyman.

He was not destined to marry Lilibet. He saw plenty of her during the war years and, at parties and dances, met the other girls in her set. At one of the parties, he danced with Alathea Fitzalan-Howard who found him '*madly* attractive', but he wasn't drawn to her. The girl who took his fancy was a young war widow, Jean Gibbs (née Hambro) who (further adding to Alathea's despair) became Princess Elizabeth's second lady-in-waiting in 1944. Andrew and Jean were married in the summer of 1946. They had two children and Lilibet stood godmother to the first, Rosemary Elizabeth, in September 1947. It was one of her last engagements before her own wedding seven weeks later.

The Reverend Andrew Elphinstone died in March 1975, aged only fifty-six. From photographs he looks to have been a kindly as well as a handsome man. He became one of Princess Anne's godparents and remained one of the Queen's close friends for the rest of his life. 'I don't think one could find anyone nicer.' That was Lilibet's verdict in 1943. From what I have read and heard, that seems to be the general verdict.

It was not a line that everyone would have used about Prince Philip of Greece. He was fun, too, and intelligent, and quite as handsome as Andrew (if not more so), but much less easy to read. By 1943, Philip had made his mark, for sure, but I do not believe that Lilibet had yet quite made up her mind. Philip is there, alongside Andrew, in that same letter to Diana Bowes-Lyon: 'I still think he is charming and he is great fun. Hardly ever serious. But when he is, I think he talks good sense. We had a terrific time on Sunday night. We danced to the gramophone, which was great fun.' The war notwithstanding, it seems they danced to Austrian tunes. 'You go waltzing madly round the room, but it's not like an ordinary waltz as your partner holds you round the waist and you hold his neck. Sounds odd, but it holds you together much better and you feel safer on a slippery floor.'

As we know, in the week before Christmas 1943, when the Windsor Castle pantomime was *Aladdin*, and Lilibet, aged seventeen and three-quarters, in fetching tights and tunic, was 'principal boy', and Margaret Rose, thirteen, played the heroine, 'Princess Roxana', Philip, then twenty-two, attended the third and final performance. He sat in the very front row. Crawfie was impressed: 'He looked more than ever, I thought, like a Viking, weather-beaten and strained, and his manners left nothing to be desired.' Lilibet was positively pink with excitement. 'I have never known Lilibet more animated,' said her governess. 'There was a sparkle about her none of us had ever seen before.' According to Crawfie, 'From then on, the two young people began to correspond.'

But what did Crawfie know? The two young people had, in fact, been corresponding for some time. Writing to a friend in January 1944, Queen Mary insisted that the two young people had actually 'been in love for the past eighteen months. In fact longer, I think . . . But the King and Queen feel that she is too young to be engaged yet. They want her to see more of the world before committing herself, and to meet more men.'

'Poor darlings,' the King wrote of his daughters in his diary as the war rumbled to a close, 'they have never had any fun yet.' His Majesty need not really have worried. Princess Margaret was to have plenty of 'fun' in the years to come and Princess Elizabeth never complained that her life lacked excitement or romance. She was not a natural gaiety girl: she never felt she was missing out on what her mother's friend Noël Coward called 'cocktails and laughter – and what comes after . . .' As Alathea Fitzalan-Howard put it at the time: 'Lilibet is placid, unemotional, conscientious and, above all, untemperamental.'

As Margaret Rhodes put it to me years later: 'She was not a flibberty-gibbet, by any stretch of the imagination.'

And she did have fun, in her own way. At Windsor, as the war was ending, she was allowed her own space, beyond the nursery and the schoolroom. Crawfie described it: 'There was a little boudoir done in pink tapestry between the schoolroom and her bedroom . . . This she could use as her private apartment. Lilibet was enchanted . . .' At Buckingham Palace, as the war ended, she was given her own suite: a bedroom (in pink and beige, her mother's favourite colours), a bathroom, a sitting room, all of her own, along the corridor from Margaret's rooms, and Crawfie's and Bobo MacDonald's. Alah, the nanny, was no longer part of the nursery family: she died of meningitis, at Sandringham, at Christmas 1945. Lilibet was growing up – and having fun, albeit pretty innocent fun by today's standards. When Philip came to call, reported Crawfie, 'The three of them [Philip, Elizabeth and Margaret Rose] had dinner together in Lilibet's sitting-room, and later romped in the corridor.' Elizabeth was nineteen, Philip was twenty-four. According to Crawfie (who appears to have been as taken with the golden prince as her young charge):

> There was nothing of the polished courtier about him. He came into the Palace like a refreshing sea breeze . . . Presently he began to come up as a matter of course, and have dinner informally, in the old comfortable nursery fashion, in the old nursery, which Margaret now used as her sitting room. The food was of the simplest. Fish, some sort of sweet, and orangeade. Philip does not smoke and drinks very little.

After dinner, apparently, along the palace corridors, there would be what Crawfie liked to describe as 'high jinks':

Philip removed from the door the old card with 'Nursery' on it, and substituted another marked 'Maggie's Playroom'. They would play ball (a good many electric-light bulbs suffered) and race about like a bunch of high-spirited children. It was always a threesome, unless I took a hand and did something about it by removing Margaret on some pretext or other. I felt the constant presence of the little sister, who was far from undemanding, and liked to have a good bit of attention herself, was not helping on the romance much.

The playful presence of little Margaret notwithstanding, the romance was blossoming. In February 1945, Lilibet, approaching her nineteenth birthday, reported to her cousin, Diana: 'I am now the proud possessor of a very large photograph of Philip, which stands on the mantelpiece and glowers at me. I had to go through a lot of ragging when it arrived – though I admit Mummy said, "He is a good-looking boy", at which I agreed! I am sure all the housemaids at Sandringham looked at the photograph and said, "Ooh! I wonder who that is?"'

Princess Elizabeth did meet other men, as we have seen. Her parents encouraged her to do so. Her mother organised small dances, to which young courtiers, Guards' officers, and aristocrats were invited. Crawfie, apparently, tried to encourage Lilibet to give 'little cocktail parties of her own, in her own sitting room, to return the hospitality of her many friends', but could never persuade her. 'She was too accustomed to leaving it all to Mummie. Mummie always had done all the entertaining, and the habit was hard to break.'

Princess Elizabeth's paternal grandfather, great-grandfather and great-great-grandmother had been royalty who had married royalty. Her father, however, only second-in-line to the throne, had married aristocracy ('a different gether altothing', as Princess Margaret liked to quip), but his marriage was universally accepted as a success, and, consequently, it was generally accepted that it would be equally acceptable for Elizabeth, although Heiress Presumptive, to settle for an aristocrat (top-of-the-range, of course), as Papa did when he married Mummie.

Heading the list of potential candidates were two young Grenadier Guardsmen, both born in 1919, who were the heirs to the dukedoms of Rutland and Grafton. Each became a lifelong friend of the Princess, but both married other girls during the course of 1946. The Duke of Rutland's marriage lasted just ten years. The Duke of Grafton, as we know, was more fortunate. His marriage survived (and thrived), and his wife, Fortune Smith (daughter of Captain Eric Smith MC), became one of Elizabeth's closest companions as Lady of the Bedchamber to the Queen from 1953 to 1966 and Mistress of the Robes from 1967 until her death in 2021. The romantic novelist, Barbara Cartland, said that Charles Manners, 10th Duke of Rutland, was the epitome of the kind of handsome hero she liked to describe in her novels. As we have seen, both Princess Elizabeth and her wartime best friend, Alathea, had a bit of a thing for Hugh Euston (who became 11th Duke of Grafton in 1970) and missed him when was despatched to India for a long tour of duty as aide-de-camp to the Viceroy, Field Marshal Lord Wavell. In February 1945, when Lilibet was confined to bed at Windsor Castle, she wrote to her cousin, Diana: 'On the second day of mumps and a long letter from Hugh which made me feel much better. He gave a very amusing description of tiger shooting with Nepalese generals. It is awful to think he has been out in India for over a year, nearly eighteen months.'

The separations of war made building relationships difficult – and the war itself took its toll, too. In October 1944, just after Jean Gibbs' twenty-three-year-old husband, Captain Vicary Gibbs, had been killed in action in the Netherlands, Lilibet wrote to Diana from Balmoral Castle in Scotland: 'It's awful how all the particularly charming people seem to get killed. People who had a wonderful future before them. One sometimes gets rather despairing about one's friends as one hears about more casualties, but I do hope the war will be over very shortly. We are coming south next week, which we are not looking forward to wildly. It is so peaceful up here and the thought of coming down back to bombs and sirens, and complete blackout, is not a very pleasant one. However, I expect we shall get accustomed to it again.'

Another young Guards' officer of the same generation who did survive the war and became one of Elizabeth's closest friends was Henry, Lord Porchester. Known simply as 'Porchey', he was born in 1924, the grandson of the 5th Earl of Carnarvon, who had been a distinguished racehorse breeder (and co-discoverer of the tomb of Tutenkhamun in 1922), and the son of the 6th Earl who, following the family tradition, bred the 1930 Derby winner, Blenheim. Shortly before he died – on 11 September 2001, 9/11, the day of the infamous Al'Qaeda attacks on the United States – I asked Lord Carnarvon (who became 7th Earl on his father's death in 1987) how he first came to meet Princess Elizabeth. 'My father knew the King and I think the King thought I might be the right kind of chap to accompany the Princess to the races. I'm glad he did. We hit it off at once.' And ever after. From October 1945 – when he accompanied her to Newmarket – until the end of his life, Elizabeth and Porchey were regular racing companions, and special friends.

Horse-breeding has long been an interest of the British royal family. A royal stud was established at Hampton Court back in the sixteenth century. In the late nineteenth century,

Elizabeth's great-grandfather, Edward VII, as Prince of Wales, established a royal stud at Sandringham. In 1962, Elizabeth II, encouraged by Porchey, took on the Polhampton Lodge Stud in Hampshire to breed royal race-horses. In 1969, Porchey was officially appointed Her Majesty's racing manager. Porchey and Elizabeth shared a passion for horses, for racing, for breeding. 'We've learnt a lot together,' he told me, 'and from one another. And we've had a great deal of fun.'

Before she died, I asked Porchey's son, Geordie, now 8th Earl of Carnarvon (who was born in 1956 and was also one of the Queen's godchildren), what he felt the Queen gained from her relationship with his father. 'The Queen is completely at ease in the world of horses,' he said. 'It's a world she knows and loves. It's quite separate from the rest of the universe she inhabits. When she's in it, she is wholly absorbed by it. And I suppose my father was the centre of that part of her life. The Queen has a long and successful history as an owner and breeder. She knows the background of the stallions, she knows all the good bloodlines. My father had a photographic memory – he could remember the names of all the descendants of the great horses with no difficulty at all. The Queen and he could talk about horses for hours. They had a shared interest that was all-consuming – and a shared sense of humour. When my father and the Queen were together, there were always a lot of laughs. The Queen is more comfortable around men, anyway. She is easy with them, more chatty. And I think their relationship was special because they knew each other so well. They were happy together. You could tell. When he died, quite unexpectedly, the Queen came to his funeral. She very rarely goes to funerals, as you know.'

Princess Anne once said that Porchey was the one person in the world who could telephone the Queen and always be put through at once. In seven months, between 11 September

2001 and 30 March 2002, the Queen lost three key figures in her life: Porchey, her sister and her mother. With Porchey and her mother, the Queen shared a passion for horses and the world of racing: her telephone conversations with each of them were a regular, and very happy, feature of her adult life. (The only thing I ever heard Prince Philip complain about in relation to the Queen was the amount of time she spent on the telephone. 'She's never off it,' he grumbled.). Prince Philip was a serious equestrian with a passion for carriage-driving, but he never shared his wife's commitment to the turf or her interest in horse-breeding. He left that to Porchey.

On the day after the Queen's funeral in September, I happened to see Harry Herbert, now sixty-three, the once-upon-a-time would-be-actor son of Porchey, to whom the Queen had introduced me back in 1990. Now founder, chairman and managing director of HTR (Highclere Thoroughbred Racing), arguably Europe's leading racehorse ownership company, he was with his new wife, the television chef (and my *This Morning* colleague), Clodagh McKenna, forty-seven. Harry's first wife, Francesca, fifty-nine, known as 'Chica', is set to marry the present Duke of Norfolk, Edward Fitzalan-Howard, sixty-five, who as Earl Marshal, organised Elizabeth II's funeral and will be organising the coronation of Charles III. The close friends of the royal family are a small and close-knit group. Harry told me how happy and proud he and his mother and his brother, Geordie, and the rest of the family had been that the Queen stayed in proper touch with them all and continued to visit Highclere Castle even after Porchey's death. 'It was such a privilege to be brought up knowing the Queen. She was so special,' he said to me, 'and my father and the Queen really were best friends.'

CHAPTER THIRTEEN

Engagement

On 8 May 1945, VE Day, Prince Philip was on board HMS *Whelp* in the Far East and Princess Elizabeth was at Buckingham Palace with her parents. Dressed in her ATS uniform, she joined the King, the Queen, Princess Margaret and the prime minister, Winston Churchill, on the palace balcony, and waved to the cheering multitude below.

Later in the day, the King and Queen, a little reluctantly, allowed their daughters to go down into the streets and join the throng. According to the Comtesse de Bellaigue, who, with Crawfie and a Guards' major, were the princesses' chaperones for the expedition, 'The King drew the line about Piccadilly Circus, which was to be avoided.' According to Porchey, who was part of the party too, 'We went down Birdcage Walk, up Whitehall, up Piccadilly, into the Ritz Hotel and back to Hyde Park Corner down to the Palace. Everyone was very jolly, linking arms in the streets, and singing "Run, Rabbit Run", "Hang Out the Washing on the Siegfried Line", "Roll out the Barrel", that sort of thing . . .'

The Comtesse de Bellaigue said, 'I shall never forget running wildly down St James's Street, with a puffing Major of the Grenadiers, to keep pace with the Princesses. When we reached the Palace they shouted like the other people, "We want the King", "We want the Queen". On the whole we were not recognised. However, a Dutch serviceman, who attached himself to the end of our file of arm-in-arm people (the Princesses being in the centre of the file) realised who the Princesses were. He withdrew discreetly and just said, "It was a great honour. I shall never forget this evening." All our group got back to the Palace through a garden gate. The Queen was anxiously waiting for us. Her Majesty provided us with sandwiches she made herself.'

By the time the Princesses took to the streets again, thirteen weeks later, for a similar expedition on VJ Day, 15 August, 1945, Churchill was no longer prime minister. With victory in Europe achieved, the Labour Party, under Clement Attlee, reckoned the time had come to end the wartime coalition. Churchill had no choice but to dissolve parliament and call a general election. Polling began on 5 July, with the voting and counting period specially extended to allow the troops overseas to vote. When the result was announced on 26 July, it was a landslide victory for Labour. Churchill's Conservatives lost 160 seats. Attlee's Labour Party gained 230. The age of nationalisation was upon us: the Welfare State was about to be born: King George VI was a monarch with misgivings.

The King was instinctively conservative, wary of change and apprehensive about the pace and degree of his new government's socialist agenda. He appears to have done rather well at keeping his personal feelings under wraps. Herbert Morrison, chief architect of Labour's election victory, and second-in-command in the new administration, said the King 'accepted calmly and willingly the changes of political outlook and of personality in the kind of minister he had known throughout his reign.' Morrison found the monarch 'fair in his observations' and 'meticulously observant in his constitutional position'. Princess Elizabeth learnt much from her father's example – and King Charles III has made it crystal clear that while he knows he has been notorious for expressing some of his passionate opinions in letters and conversations with ministers during his long years as Prince of Wales, as King he will observe the constitutional proprieties as fully as his mother and his grandfather did. Charles III has studied Bagehot just as Elizabeth II had: 'The Sovereign has, under a constitutional monarchy such as ours, three rights – the right to be consulted, the right to encourage, the right to warn. And a king of great sense and sagacity would want no others.'

Privately, George VI said (to his brother, the Duke of Gloucester) that he found Clement Attlee's government 'difficult to talk to' and his new prime minister 'positively mute'. Churchill, of course, was positively verbose (and elaborately solicitous when it came to his dealings with any monarch), but the King had been wary of him, too, back in 1940. In due course – in fact, quite quickly – George VI and Clement Attlee came to understand, respect and, even, value one another. Michael Foot, who became an MP in 1945 and, later, leader of the Labour Party, knew Attlee well. He told me: 'Clem was not an emotional man. He was not given to public shows of feeling. The only time – ever – that I saw tears in his eyes and sensed a crack in his voice was when he spoke of the death of George VI.'

The King made it his business to work harmoniously with his prime minister. The relationship prospered. In November 1951, he honoured Attlee with the Order of Merit. In July 1945, however, he was simply appalled by Attlee's triumph and Churchill's defeat. 'I was shocked at the result,' he told Churchill, '& thought it most ungrateful to you personally after all your hard work for the people.' With a heart 'too full', he wrote at length (and by hand) to say 'how very sad I am that you are no longer my Prime Minister', concluding:

For myself personally, I regret what has happened more than perhaps anyone else. I shall miss your counsel to me more than I can say. But please remember that as a friend I hope we shall be able to meet at intervals.

Believe me,

I am,

Your very sincerely and gratefully,

GRI [1]

The King's world was changing.

With the war in Japan at an end, Philip and HMS *Whelp* came home. In January 1946, in Portsmouth, as the destroyer's 1st Lieutenant, Philip's immediate post-war duty was to preside over her decommissioning. His next postings – to Pwllheli in North Wales and Corsham, near Bath, in Wiltshire – were land-based and less romantic, but, he would insist, no less rewarding. He used to speak with particular pride of his time at the Corsham naval training establishment, HMS *Royal Arthur*. It was a school for petty officers and, by all accounts, Philip was an innovative, imaginative and effective instructor. 'We had some new ideas,' he said. 'It was satisfying work.'

Away from his naval base, he still had no home to call his own. When I first went to meet Countess Mountbatten and Lord Brabourne, they showed me their first visitors' book – from 1946, the year they were married – and there, marking his visit over the weekend of 20–22 December, was Philip's signature and, next to it, in the address column, he had written: 'No fixed abode!'

He had a base with his grandmother at Kensington Palace;

---

1   *Georgius Rex Imperator* – George King Emperor.

he stayed with his cousin, Princess Marina, and her family, at Coppins; regularly, at weekends, when the Mountbattens were away at Broadlands, he cadged a bed for the night at 16 Chester Street, their London house. According to the Mountbattens' butler, John Dean, the Mountbatten household servants all adored him: 'He was so considerate, so anxious to avoid giving trouble to people who, after all, were paid to look after the family, that we all thought the world of him and looked forward to his visits.'

Dean later went to work for Prince Philip as his valet and, eventually, 'did a Crawfie', publishing a memoir of his happy years as the prince's trouser-presser. From start to finish, the prince remained a hero to his valet. Dean noticed how, immediately after the war, Philip seemed to have very few clothes and what he had wasn't in the best nick. Philip would come up to town, in his black MG, with just his razor in his pocket. Overnight, Dean would wash and iron the young prince's only shirt and darn his threadbare socks for him. 'He was very easy to look after, and never asked for things like that to be done for him, but I liked him so much that I did it anyway.'

Philip worked hard. He played hard. He drove hard. In April 1946, he managed to borrow an army vehicle, to drive across war-torn Europe, to Salem, to attend his youngest sister Sophie's second wedding. 'Tiny', as she was known, left with five young children when her husband, Prince Christoph of Hesse, was killed in Italy in 1943, was marrying Prince George Wilhelm of Hanover, now headmaster of Salem, the school founded by Prince Max of Baden and Kurt Hahn, where Philip had briefly been a pupil before moving to Hahn's Scottish outpost, Gordonstoun, in 1934. After years of separation, Philip was reunited with his sisters. He was reunited with his mother, too. Alice travelled to London to stay with her own mother at Kensington Palace and to see her son again: it was the first time they had been together for five years. 'She is full of energy & good sense,' Alice's mother reported of her daughter, '& she and Philip get on well together.'

Philip also made a post-war pilgrimage, in 1946, to Monte Carlo – accompanied by Mike Parker – to meet up with his late father's lady friend, the Comtesse de la Bigne, and collect a few of Prince Andrea's personal effects: some books, some pictures, some clothes, a pair of hair-brushes, his ivory-handled shaving brush, his signet ring. Andrea left his son very little because he had very little to leave – other than debts. (The debts were not finally cleared until 1947, and then only thanks to help from Dickie and Edwina Mountbatten, and Sir Harold Wernher.)

When he died, Andrea had been laid to rest in the Russian Orthodox church in Nice. In 1946, his body was taken by Greek cruiser to Athens and buried in the gardens of the royal palace at Tatoï.

Andrea had been the son of King George I of Greece. In September, 1946, following a plebiscite, George I's grandson, Andrea's nephew, George II, was restored to the Greek throne. His renewed reign was short-lived. In April 1947, he suffered a sudden stroke and died, unexpectedly, aged fifty-six. His younger brother, Paul (husband of the formidable Princess Frederika of Hanover), succeeded him.

King Paul was Prince Philip's first cousin. Prince Philip was a great-great-grandson of Queen Victoria. If Princess Elizabeth was to follow the custom, long-established, of British monarchs-in-waiting marrying into European royalty, there was a certain inevitability about her match with Prince Philip. That is certainly how his immediate family all felt – in Greece, in Germany, in England. He acknowledged the fact himself. 'After all,' he said, 'if you spend ten minutes thinking about it – and a lot of these people spent a great deal more thinking about it - how many obviously eligible young men, other than people living in this country, were available?'

One of 'these people' thinking about it, long and hard, over several years, was Lord Louis Mountbatten. On more than one occasion, Philip had to urge his uncle to moderate his enthusiasm. In September 1945 he wrote to him: 'Please, I beg you, not too much advice in an affair of the heart, or I shall be forced to do the wooing by proxy.' In January 1947, as the prospect of the engagement grew closer, Philip wrote to Dickie about the impact his uncle's attitude might have on Lilibet: 'I am not being rude, but it is apparent that you like the idea of being the General Manager of this little show and I am rather afraid that she might not take to the idea as docilely as I do. It is true that I know what is good for me, but don't forget that she has not had you as Uncle *loco parentis,* counsellor and friend as long as I have . . .'

Other members of the family were almost as excited by the prospect of the union as was Dickie. But Philip gave them no encouragement. In February 1944, Philip's grandmother, Victoria, having had Philip to stay on leave, reported to Mountbatten: 'As he has not touched on the subject you spoke about to me with reference to his future, I also refrain from doing so.' In March, having seen more of Philip, she wrote again to Dickie: 'I touched on the subject on which you gave him advice, but he was not inclined to confide in me, so I did not press him.' In June, Alice wrote to her son from Athens, hoping to tickle some titbits from him: 'I heard you stayed with Marina [at Coppins] at Easter and paid an interesting visit, as well as lunching with a certain young lady & her parents before you left . . .' Philip did not rise to the bait.

Philip was his own man, resistant to all outside interference. Yes, his cousin Marina was helpful in providing a discreet venue for the young couple to meet. Where else could they meet, after all? He had no home of his own and they could hardly have romantic trysts in public places – but she was not party to any intriguing. In January 1945, she wrote to Dickie: 'Of course the less said about the question we have sometimes discussed the better – & as you say it must take its course.'

Lilibet did not hide her feelings from her mother or her sister or her closest friends. One of those friends was Myra Butter, Gina Wernher's younger sister, who had known both Lilibet and Philip from childhood. Lady Butter, who had been one of the princess's swimming lesson and girl guide companions in the 1930s, married Major David Butter MC of the Scots Guards in 1946. Princess Elizabeth went to the wedding – as did Queen Mary and Prince Philip and his mother. In 1948, Myra Butter's daughter, Sarah Elizabeth Zia, became the seventh of Elizabeth II's thirty godchildren. Myra Butter, who died in 2022 aged 97, shared with the Queen a lifelong passion for horses, as well as a gift for doing impressions. She told me, 'She was madly in love with Philip from the word go – and she loved him as he was. She didn't try to change him. You couldn't. She didn't. She accepted him as he was – and he accepted her as she was. That's why it worked so well. They respected one another as equals. She was a princess and then she was Queen. He walked a step behind her because of that, but he was never a step behind her as a person.' In 2021, asked what the Queen had lost with her husband's death, Lady Butter said, 'The world, I think. Incalculable.'

Naturally discreet, by 1946 Princess Elizabeth could not hide her feelings. Margaret Rhodes told me: 'She'd say, "Philip's written again" or "Philip's coming to stay – isn't that exciting?" She was happy to be in love.' On the mantelpiece in her sitting-room, she kept her framed photograph of Philip. 'Is that altogether wise?' asked Crawfie, 'A number of people come and go. You know what that will lead to. People will begin all sorts of gossip about it.' The teenage princess removed the offending portrait – and replaced it with another one, featuring her adored 1st Lieutenant hidden behind a full naval beard. 'There you are Crawfie,' she said, 'I defy anyone to recognise who that is.'

Philip had a picture of Lilibet, too, a small one, kept – according to John Dean, who discovered it in the prince's overnight travelling bag – in a scuffed leather frame. Philip did not discuss his love-life with his uncle's butler, nor even, if he could help it, with his uncle. Where young Philip did cooperate with Mountbatten was in the matter of achieving British nationality. Philip was a Prince of Greece, but, as we have seen, he did not feel Greek and, in terms of blood, was not Greek at all. He was Danish, German, Russian and English. He was born in Greece, but spent his early childhood in France and Germany. From his adolescence onwards, he was based in England. Once he had joined the Royal Navy, therefore, and started to make headway as a young officer, becoming a naturalised British subject seemed to be a wholly sensible move. Mountbatten took the initiative, and did so with the family's general approval. In September 1944, Victoria wrote to Dickie: 'I think it is the best thing for him & it will give a firm basis for his life, which without a fixed career or home country it was wanting in, poor boy.' Princess Marina concurred: 'I think it is a very good idea & apart from it being a help in his naval career it might also be an asset for other "matters".'

Turning Philip from Greek prince to British subject proved a more challenging undertaking than Mountbatten had envisaged. For a start, the blessing of both George II of Greece and George VI of Britain was an essential requirement, and, initially, at least, neither monarch seemed in a hurry to give it. In George II's case, it may have been a matter of national pride, a reluctance to have Greece lose any prince to another country. In George VI's case, it may have been because the King suspected that Mountbatten's concern over Philip's nationality was as much to assist his nephew with the 'other matters' as with his naval career.

This hesitation of the two kings, combined with sustained doubts in government circles about the wisdom of getting embroiled in any aspect of Balkan politics except when absolutely necessary, and simple bureaucratic delay (there was a war on and this was not a priority), meant that it took three years – and much to-ing and fro-ing and huffing and puffing, lobbying and letter-writing by Mountbatten – to arrive at a satisfactory outcome. Eventually, on 18 March 1947, the deed was done. The news of Philip's naturalisation was officially posted in the *London Gazette,* alongside that of several hundred others, many of them Poles who had fought with the British through the war, many of them German Jewish refugees. Once, when I asked Prince Philip how he thought he was seen by most people in Britain, he said, after a moment's consideration, 'Refugee husband, I suppose.'

Along with a new nationality he needed a new name. The surnames on offer on his father's side of the family had little to commend them. Prince Andrea was the grandson of the King of Denmark and the family name of the Danish royal house was Schleswig-Holstein-Sonderburg-Glucksburg. Another, more manageable, paternal family name was Oldenburg and a bright spark at the College of Arms suggested that 'Oldcastle', as its English equivalent, might find favour. It didn't. Instead (apparently at the suggestion of James Chuter Ede, Clement Attlee's Home Secretary), Philip agreed to take the already-established Anglicised version of his mother's surname, Battenburg. Prince Philip of Greece became Lieutenant Philip Mountbatten, RN.

In time (in the mid-1980s), his mother-in-law, Queen Elizabeth, would describe Prince Philip as 'an English gentleman – completely'. In the mid-1940s, she was less certain. Her younger brother, David Bowes-Lyon, to whom she was very close (Elizabeth and David were the youngsters of the family, seventeen and nineteen years younger than their oldest sister), did not believe that Philip was an appropriate husband for the future Elizabeth II.

According to Gina Kennard, 'David Bowes-Lyon was a vicious little fellow. He had it in for Philip right from the start. He was completely against him.' He was not alone. Lord Salisbury (whose ancestor had been on hand to advise Elizabeth I, after all) had profound reservations. As did Lord Stanley and the Earl of Eldon. As did most of the senior men at court. According to Myra Butter, 'Philip was only in his mid-twenties, but he was his own man. They didn't like that. They thought he was too outspoken. They said he was brash.'

Philip might now be eligible for a British passport, but he wasn't really British. He was German and you couldn't trust a Hun. Yes, he was royal, but Greek royalty was a standing joke. The Greek throne was notoriously unstable and the Greek royals undeniably the bottom of the pack. All right, he was serving in the Royal Navy – and that 'mention in despatches' was to his credit – but where had he been to school? Gordonstoun? What was that all about? And where were his parents, for God's sake? And wasn't he a *protégé* of Dickie Mountbatten's? Need more be said?

Many at court, and much of the Establishment, were wary of Mountbatten. As his daughter, Patricia, put it to me, with a smile, 'My father was a progressive and the one thing the courtiers were not was progressive.' Never mind 'progressive': the courtiers considered Mountbatten dangerously left-wing. And not quite as royal as he liked to think he was. Hadn't his grandfather, Prince Alexander of Hesse (whose own parentage was doubtful), run off with a lady-in-waiting – a Polish girl called Julie Hauke? She might have been elevated to the rank of Serene Highness eventually, but she was certainly a blot on the Battenburg escutcheon. ('I believe that the Battenbergs have always behaved somewhat peculiarly,' commented Heinrich Himmler after studying the Gestapo file on Mountbatten and his family.)

Mountbatten had a questionable pedigree and a rum set of *louche* and left-leaning friends – such as Tom Driberg, Labour MP and notoriously promiscuous homosexual. Mountbatten was also, in the eyes of those who did not take to him, inordinately full of himself, impossibly pushy, and incurably inclined to interfere where he wasn't wanted.

'Yes,' chuckled Patricia Mountbatten, 'my father had colossal energy and drive. He was a dynamo. He made things happen. He got things done. And he didn't go through "the usual channels". He by-passed the officials. That really infuriated them. If he wanted to speak to the King, he just picked up the telephone. I'm sure they thought he'd be a very bad influence on Philip and that Philip might prove to be a chip off the old block.'

Sir Alan 'Tommy' Lascelles (*Educ:* Marlborough; Oxford; *Address:* Sutton Waldron House, Blandford; *Clubs:* Travellers', Pratt's, MCC; *TA:* Fontmell-Magna), Assistant Private Secretary to the Prince of Wales throughout the 1920s, Assistant Private Secretary and Private Secretary to successive kings from 1935, encapsulated some of the family's and most of the courtiers' initial estimation of Lt Philip Mountbatten: 'They felt he was rough, uneducated and would probably not be faithful.'

In time, the King's Private Secretary warmed to Philip, describing him (to Harold Nicolson in June 1948) as 'such a nice young man', and 'not a fool in any way', saluting his 'sense of duty' and acknowledging him to be 'so much in love poor boy'. The King himself warmed to the young prince from the start. In the spring of 1944 he told Queen Mary: 'I like Philip. He is intelligent, has a good sense of humour & thinks about things in the right way.' The King's only real reservation in the early days of the romance was his daughter's youth, but by the summer of 1946 Lilibet was twenty, so when Philip, now twenty-five, came to stay with the royal family at Balmoral – and proposed to her, and was accepted – there was little the doting father could do but bow to the inevitable – and play for a bit more time.

The King agreed, in principle, to the union, but made two conditions: there could be no formal engagement until after the princess's twenty-first birthday in April 1947 and, before that, there would be a period of reflection while the King and Queen took their two daughters with them on a twelve-week tour of southern Africa.

The tour was memorable on several counts. Princess Elizabeth was unhappy to be going away – Crawfie reports 'tears in her eyes' at the moment of departure – but ready, as ever, to do her duty, and excited by the prospect of her first trip outside the British Isles. The timing, however, was unfortunate. As the royal family set off from Portsmouth – 'us four', as the King called them – on 1 February 1947, on board HMS *Vanguard,* the Royal Navy's newest battleship, the weather in the English Channel was appalling. The weather on the mainland was even worse. Britain was suffering its cruellest winter of the century.

By 12 February, when the royal travellers were basking in sub-equatorial sunshine, the news from home was dire: 'Heavy snowstorms and sub-zero temperatures are combining with a serious fuel shortage to bring Britain to its economic knees. More than four million workers have been made idle by power cuts, and with hundreds of coal trains unable to battle their way through 20-feet high snow-drifts, thousands of homes are without heat or light for long periods of the day.' The Thames at Windsor had frozen over. Buckingham Palace was candle-lit. The King volunteered to return home. The prime minister, Clement Attlee, said 'Thank you, but no thank you': a dramatic return would simply exacerbate the crisis, advertising it worldwide. Besides, the African trip was also designed, in part, to give the King – exhausted by the war and in failing health – a well-deserved opportunity for rest, recuperation and sunshine.

On board ship, when the calmer seas were reached, there was certainly some of that. The King and Queen relaxed. The princesses had fun. There are delightful photographs of Lilibet and Margaret Rose playing deck games with the younger officers. They look really happy. (There is a key to these people in those pictures: as a rule, the Windsors are most comfortable and carefree, not in conversation or contemplation, reading books or listening to music, but when they are playing games, playing sport, riding, shooting, having larks, enjoying practical jokes, taking part in Scottish country dancing.) Off-duty in *Vanguard*, picnicking in Southern Rhodesia, visiting the Orange Free State, Basutoland and Bechuanaland in a special 'White Train', almost as tourists, the trip had many highlights. The girls sent regular reports to Crawfie:

The letters I got back were a great pleasure to me. They were also a wonderful picture of the different make-up of the two sisters. Margaret [now sixteen] wrote with her usual gaiety, all about the fun they were having, how beautiful the White Train was, how warm the sun, how wonderful the food.

Lilibet wrote, immensely distressed by all that was going on in England in the bitter weather. It bothered her to feel she was far away having a good time, in a land so full of everything. She felt she ought to be at home.

The South African leg of the tour was the longest and most trying. The King was in sympathy with the ageing South African prime minister, Field Marshal Jan Christian Smuts, who was striving valiantly against the odds to achieve Anglo-Afrikaner unity. The Boers – whose Nationalist Party would defeat Smuts and his United Party government in the election of 1948 and usher in the era of apartheid – were not in sympathy with the King, nor with the 'mingling' of Europeans and non-Europeans in the crowds that came to greet him. The atmosphere was tense. The King was tired and tetchy. At Benoni, a gold-mining town in the south of the Transvaal, there was an unfortunate incident when a man broke from the jostling crowd and rushed towards the open royal car. The King, unnerved, began shouting angrily at the driver to get a move on. The Queen, fearing an attack, hit at the man with her parasol. The man was immediately felled by one of the attendant policemen, and half beaten-up, before it became apparent that he was not a would-be assailant at all, but an ardent royalist who was trying to present their Majesties with a ten-shilling note as a twenty-first birthday present for Princess Elizabeth. The King, distressed by the misunderstanding, sent to enquire after the unfortunate man, and, later, apologised for his own behaviour to his equerry, Group Captain Peter Townsend. 'I'm very sorry about today,' he said, 'I was very tired.'

The South African tour had a profound impact on Princess Elizabeth. It was her first first-hand experience of the reality of the British Commonwealth and Empire, of a divided country, of native people, of the tensions of African politics and the nastiness of white supremacists. The Nationalists – who sneered at the King's halting attempt to say a few words in Afrikaans at the opening of parliament – trumpeted the '*swart gevaar*' (the 'black danger') and campaigned to keep '*Die kaffer op sy plek*' ('the nigger in his place') and '*Die koelies uit die land*' ('the coolies – i.e. the Indians – out of the country'). Lilibet was not impressed.

The Princess was taken with Africa and the African people – and the feeling was reciprocated. According to Peter Townsend, the Africans really loved her. As she drove past, they shouted 'Leave the Princess behind!', 'Stay with us!' A popular song was composed in her honour:

> Princess, in our opinion,
> You'll find in our Dominion
> Greetings that surely take your breath,
> For you have a corner in every heart,
> Princess Elizabeth

The climax of the tour coincided with her twenty-first birthday. Field Marshal Smuts declared 21 April a national holiday. There was a birthday parade, a birthday ball, and a civic reception at City Hall in Cape Town; Smuts presented the Princess with a gemstone necklace and a gold key to the city; the Princess reviewed hundreds of troops, shook scores of hands, and delivered a short speech at a celebratory 'youth rally of all races.' She also made one of the key broadcasts of her life.

Her old tutor in constitutional history, Sir Henry Marten, had impressed on her the special significance to the modern monarchy of both the advent of broadcasting and the development of the Commonwealth. He must have been mighty proud of his diligent pupil's birthday broadcast to the Empire and Commonwealth. 'Although there is not one of my father's subjects, from the oldest to the youngest, whom I do not wish to greet,' she began, 'I am thinking especially today of all the young men and women who were born about the same time as myself and have grown up like me in the terrible and glorious years of the Second World War. Will you, the youth of the British family of nations, let me speak on my birthday as your representative?'

The essence of the message was unsurprising and comfortably generalised: in the dark days of the war, the British Empire had saved the world and 'has now to save itself'. With determination – faith, hope and endeavour – the future of the Commowealth might be yet more glorious, prosperous and happy than its past. Then came the peroration – much less predictable and much more personal – spoken, in a steady high-pitched voice, and heard, by many millions, around the world:

There is a motto which has been borne by many of my ancestors – a noble motto, 'I serve'. Those words were an inspiration to many bygone heirs to the throne when they made their knightly dedication as they came to manhood. I cannot do quite as they did, but through the inventions of science I can do what was not possible for any of them. I can make my solemn act of dedication with a whole Empire listening. I should like to make that dedication now. It is very simple.

I declare before you all that my whole life, whether it be long or short, shall be devoted to your service and the service of our great Imperial family to which we all belong, but I shall not have the strength to carry out this resolution alone unless you join in with me, as I now invite you to do. I know your support will be unfailingly given. God help me to make good my vow and God bless all of you who are willing to share in it.

She meant it, and you could tell. She did not write it. The author was Dermot Morrah (1896–1974), historian, and leader-writer and correspondent for *The Times*. Morrah sent his draft of the speech to Sir Alan Lascelles, the King's private secretary, who was travelling with the royal party on board the White Train. At first, the draft went missing. According to Lascelles, who wrote to Morrah from the train on 10 March, 'The steward in the Protea diner had put it in the bar, among his bottles, little knowing that it was itself of premier cru.' Lascelles saluted Morrah's achievement: 'I have been reading drafts for many years now, but I cannot recall one that has so completely satisfied me and left me feeling that no single word should be altered. Morever, dusty cynic though I am, it moved me greatly. It has the trumpet-ring of the other Elizabeth's Tilbury speech, combined with the immortal simplicity of Victoria's "I will be good."' Lascelles told Morrah how it had pleased Princess Elizabeth and her mother: 'The ladies concerned, you will be glad to hear, feel just as I do. The speaker herself told me that it had made her cry. Good, said I, for if it makes you cry now, it will make 200 million other people cry when they hear you deliver it, and that is what we want.' And so it proved. When the speech was broadcast, there was barely a dry eye on the planet.

On 24 April, as the royal party set off once more for home, Lascelles reported to his wife: 'From the inside, the most satisfactory feature of the whole business is the remarkable development of P'cess E.' He summed up her essential characteristics: 'A perfectly natural power of enjoying herself ... Not a great sense of humour, but a healthy sense of fun. Moreover, when necessary, she can take on the old bores with much of her mother's skill, and never spares herself in that exhausting part of royal duty. For a child of her years, she has got an astonishing solicitude for other people's comfort; such unselfishness is not a normal characteristic of that family.'

Elizabeth was – and remained – a conspicuously unselfish individual. But uniquely so? In 1936, Elizabeth's uncle David selfishly abandoned his duty to pursue the love of his life – no question – yet, nineteen years later, in 1955, Elizabeth's sister Margaret – certainly spoilt, and undoubtedly self-indulgent in many ways – sacrificed the love of her life when she agreed not to marry a divorcee in the becoming shape of her father's former equerry, Peter Townsend. Elizabeth's grandfather, George V, was not an easy parent, but he was a conscientious King, wilful but not notably selfish. His wife, Elizabeth's grandmother, Queen Mary, shared her husband's stern sense of duty, but liked to get her own way. Famously, when she came to call, if there was a *bibelot* in your drawing room that took her fancy, she expected you to present it to her. Elizabeth's mother was justly celebrated for her courtesy, charm and commitment, and while, on the whole, she did as she pleased, and led a wonderfully pampered – and noncha-lantly extravagant – life, enhanced by an enviable capacity for ignoring the unpleasant, she, like her daughter, was always soliticous for other people's comfort.

That said, when Crawfie – while her charges were in South Africa – came to see Queen Mary to tell her of her own plans to marry, the old Queen, now in her eightieth year, 'spearing for me a muffin on a small silver fork: Her Majesty never touches any food with her fingers', said at once, 'My dear child. You can't leave them!' Crawfie, now in her thirty-eighth year, pointed out that Margaret Rose, at seventeen, was nearly done with her schooling and that Princess Elizabeth was likely to get married before too long. The Queen was unmoved. 'I don't see how they could manage without you,' she said. 'I don't think they could spare you just now.' Queen Elizabeth, on her return from South Africa, was equally unbending. 'Does this mean you are going to leave us?' she asked the governess. 'You must see, Crawfie, that it would not be at all convenient just now. A change for Margaret is not at all desirable.' Crawfie hoped Her Majesty might say something about the family's plans for Lilibet's future, but, according to Crawfie, the Queen 'said nothing further, and I curtsied and withdrew.'

From my observation of them, the members of this family are masters of the art of saying nothing. Sometimes they do it to protect themselves. Sometimes they do it to indicate that a conversation is at an end. Often they do it to indicate disapproval. In Queen Elizabeth, the Queen Mother's very first letter to Prince Philip at the time of his engagement to her daughter, Her Majesty warned her future son-in-law of the challenges that lay ahead and that chief among them would be 'remaining silent when one is *bursting* to reply.'

Crawfie reflected on Queen Mary's silence and settled on a compromise. On 16 September 1947 she married her man (Major George Buthlay, a divorcee from Aberdeen, fifteen years her senior), but, after the honeymoon, the royal governess returned to her duties at Buckingham Palace.

She was not there much longer. By the end of 1948 Princess Margaret had turned nineteen and Princess Elizabeth had given birth to her first son. After sixteen years of loyal and effective service, Crawfie retired. She had been a good teacher: intelligent, imaginative, and quite adventurous by the standards of her time. Queen Elizabeth wrote thanking her for the 'devotion and love' and she was awarded one of the honours in the sovereign's personal gift, becoming a Commander of the Royal Victorian Order. (She had been hoping to become a Dame, but she was a little too junior for that, both in years and in station.) Her happiest reward – besides, of course, her fond memories of her years with the little princesses – was the lifetime tenure of Nottingham Cottage at Kensington Palace, a dream home of 'seasoned red brick . . . with roses round the door . . . in the little square garden' – or £100 per annum in lieu.

Crawfie took the cottage and loved it. Originally designed by Christopher Wren for the Earl of Nottingham, in 1689 the second Earl sold it to William III and Mary II who developed it as part of the Kensington House estate that became Kensington Palace. Before Crawfie, George VI's brother, the Duke of Gloucester had it as his London home. Later, the Duke of Edinburgh's private secretary, Brigadier Miles Hunt-Davis, lived there, as did Robert Fellowes, private secretary to the Queen and brother-in-law to Diana, Princess of Wales. The Cambridges (Prince William and Catherine) had it as their London base until soon after Prince George was born in 2013 when they moved into the much larger Apartment 1A in Kensington Palace, formerly Princess Margaret's home, and Prince Harry had the cottage (known as Nott Cott) as his post-army bachelor's pad. It's where he famously proposed to Meghan Markle while cooking a roast chicken for her and where they gave their first television interview after announcing their engagement. Initially, it seems, Meghan quite liked the cosy cottage, but I was told by a royal page that her attitude towards it changed after she and Harry had been to Apartment 1A for dinner with William and Catherine and had seen the scale and grandeur of the Cambridge residence. Nott Cott is a cottage and the ceilings are low. Meghan did not stay there long.

Nor did Crawfie. In 1949, Marion Crawford wrote *The Little Princesses*, her account of her years in royal service. The book was originally published in the United States and serialised in the *Ladies' Home Journal*. Queen Elizabeth's friend Nancy, Lady

Astor, happened to know the magazine's editors and was able to send Her Majesty a copy of the manuscript. The Queen was appalled. The invasion of her family's privacy and the betrayal of their trust left Her Majesty 'shocked and distressed'. Her private secretary wrote to Lady Astor: 'Such a thing is utterly alien to the spirit and custom of Their Majesties' households and staff and great regret is felt by all those who care for the sanctity of their family life at this unhappy breach of decency and good taste.'

Crawfie was not to be silenced. She received $ 6,500 for the US serialisation and £ 30,000 when the book appeared in the UK, serialised in *Woman's Own*. The money was good, and she was pleased with her own writing, but, in her heart, she knew she had done wrong. John Gordon, editor of the *Sunday Express*, tried to persuade her to write for him. He reported to the *Express*'s proprietor, Lord Beaverbrook: 'Persuasion is difficult at the moment because she has been brought to the edge of a nervous breakdown by all the trouble, but she will bend in good time.' She didn't – at least, not for the *Express* – but for *Woman's Own* she continued to exploit her erstwhile royal connections with a weekly column that ultimately proved her undoing. In the summer of 1955 she gave her readers vivid and personal accounts of both the Sovereign's Birthday Parade and Royal Ascot – annual events that, unfortunately for Crawfie, were unexpectedly cancelled that year due to a national rail strike.

Crawfie abandoned Nottingham Cottage (which Queen Mary had helped furnish for her) in the autumn of 1950. The Court's low opinion of the errant former governess was made plain. Her neighbours, according to John Gordon, 'were afraid even to be seen speaking to her. So she decided to pack up and go.' Five years later, when her reputation as a reliable royal correspondent was finally exploded, she retired to Aberdeen, childless, largely friendless and living in a marriage that turned out to be a disappointment. She died on 11 February 1988. There were no flowers from Lilibet or Margaret Rose at her funeral. It had been very different forty years before. At her wedding in September 1947, Crawfie had been showered with royal gifts, including a complete dinner service from Queen Mary, a coffee set from Lilibet and three bedside lamps from Margaret Rose.

Crawfie had been determined to marry her man and their majesties had no choice but to accept her decision, however inconvenient. Lilibet, in her way, was just as detemined. She had accompanied her parents to South Africa: she had done her duty: she had passed her twenty-first birthday and broadcast her solemn commitment to the world. Now she was coming home to claim her prize. One of the ladies-in-waiting accompanying the royal party reported that, as the *Vanguard* steamed into harbour, Lilibet 'danced a little jig of sheer delight at being home again.'

Philip was determined, too, in his own way. In June 1946 he had invited himself to Buckingham Palace and, after the visit, had written to Queen Elizabeth to apologise for his 'monumental cheek' in so doing – adding, as if to compound his cheek while claiming to be 'contrite', 'there is a small voice that keeps saying "nothing ventured, nothing gained" – well I did venture and I gained a wonderful time.'

Later that summer, after he had spent three weeks holidaying with the Windsors at Balmoral and the young couple had shared their feelings with one another and with the King and Queen, Philip wrote another thank you letter to his future mother-in-law. 'I am sure I do not deserve all the good things which have happened to me,' he said to the queen. 'To have been spared the war and seen victory, to have been given the chance to rest and readjust myself, to have fallen in love completely and unreservedly, makes all one's personal and even the world's troubles seem small and petty.'

In an age of comparative deference and discretion, long before the advent of the internet and the tweet, it took a while for rumours of the royal romance to spread. On 29 May 1946, Philip was photographed next to Princess Elizabeth at the wedding of her new lady-in-waiting, Mrs Jean Gibbs, to her favoured first cousin, Andrew Elphinstone, but Philip was described in the press as 'a figure still largely unknown to the British public'. They were photographed together again five months later, on 26 October 1946, at the wedding of Philip's first cousin, Patricia Mountbatten, to John Knatchbull, 7th Baron Brabourne. This time the picture appeared to tell a story: the young couple were caught on camera gazing into one another's eyes. Then they were sighted walking in the park at Windsor – holdings hands. The moment they realised that they had been spotted, they sprang apart, but their secret was gradually seeping out. When Princess Elizabeth went to visit a factory, on one of the solo official outings that she was now beginning to undertake, someone in the crowd called out, 'Where's Philip?'

On 30 April 1947, the Rodgers and Hammerstein musical *Oklahoma!* opened at the Theatre Royal, Drury Lane. Philip and Elizabeth went to the show and, as a consequence, forever after, 'People Will Say We're in Love' was said to be 'their song'. I know from conversations with her that the Queen had a good recall of popular songs of the 1940s, but I know, too, that the Duke of Edinburgh regarded the notion of 'our song' as 'sentimental codswallop' and was 'utterly infuriated' whenever it was played. In 2012, at the time of the Queen's Diamond Jubilee and the Duke's ninety-first birthday, I took part in a special edition of BBC television's *The One Show* broadcast live from Buckingham Palace. The producers were keen to feature 'People Will Say We're in Love' in the programme. I said, 'Why?' They said, 'Because it's their tune – it's their *favourite* tune.' I said, 'It isn't. I know it isn't.' They said, 'It is. It really is.' When I reported this to the Duke of Edinburgh he laughed somewhat despairingly: 'Once these myths take root there's nothing you can do to dislodge them.'

Did Prince Philip marry for love? It is not a question that I dared to ask him – nor one that he would have deigned to answer. But every one of those to whom I did put the question who knew him at the time – and knew him well – answered with an unequivocal, 'Yes.' Myra Butter, who had known them both since they were children, told me, 'She was head over heels in love with him. She couldn't hide it. And he was completely in love with her. It really was a fairy tale come true.' Philip's first cousin, Patricia Mountbatten, said to me: 'He may have had his doubts about what he was getting himself into – the whole business of marrying the King of England's daughter, I think that did concern him. But he had no doubts at all about Lilibet as a person – as a future wife. He adored her. He loved her deeply – you could tell. It was definitely a love match.' Mike Parker, Philip's closest male friend at the time, said to me: 'He loved her – absolutely.' Mike Parker was an Australian and added, for good measure: 'And he fancied her, too. No question about that.'

Prince Philip married Princess Elizabeth for love. I think, perhaps, that he married her for family, as well. As he often reminded me, he had 'a perfectly good family' of his own. 'I had parents, I had sisters,' he insisted. But from his adolescence onwards he saw very little of them. Through the years of the Second World War, he could not see his sisters: they were in Germany, literally sleeping with the enemy. His father was in Vichy France until his death in 1944. His mother was in Athens, occupied by the Germans until October 1944. In the summer of 1944, after he had spent part of his leave staying with the Windsors, Philip wrote to the Queen and told her how much he had valued his time at Balmoral: 'It is the simple enjoyment of family pleasures and amusements and the feeling that I am welcome to share them. I am afraid I am not capable of putting all this into the right words and I am certainly incapable of showing you the gratitude that I feel.'

'Showing' his feelings was not something that came easily to Prince Philip. Gina Kennard told me: 'Philip used to speak to me about Princess Elizabeth before they were engaged. He was extremely fond of her, always. He said, "I think we could do a lot together."' Robin Dalton told me: 'Philip's a cold fish. Always charming and fun, but I couldn't tell you what he really felt. All I know is that in 1945 David [Milford Haven] told me Philip was definitely planning to marry Elizabeth one day. He saw it as his destiny.'

And so it proved. On 7 July, 1947, from Buckingham Palace, Queen Elizabeth wrote to her sister May:

This is one line to tell you very secretly that Lilibet has made up her mind to get engaged to Philip Mountbatten. As you know, she has known him since she was 12, & I think that she is really fond of him, & I do pray that she will be very happy . . . We are keeping it a deadly secret, purely because of the Press, if they know beforehand that something is up, they are liable to ruin everything!

'At last things were moving,' wrote Crawfie. 'Suddenly that look of strain we had all been conscious of disappeared from Lilibet's eyes. One day she poked her head into my room looking absolutely radiant . . . "He's coming tonight," she said, and then she kissed me and danced away. Next morning was Wednesday, July the ninth. Lilibet came to my room much earlier than usual. I have never seen her look lovelier than she did on that day, not even on her wedding morning. She wore a deep yellow frock, a shade that has always suited her very well. She closed the door behind her and held out her left hand. Her engagement ring sparkled there. It was a large square diamond with smaller diamonds either side. At the same time it was too large for her, and it had to go back to be made smaller. It was a ring they had chosen secretly, but of course she had been unable to go and try it on.'

In fact, neither Lilibet nor Philip had been able to choose the ring personally. Philip's mother, on one of her visits to London, undertook the task. Princess Alice had managed to reclaim her own jewellery – deposited for safety's sake at an English bank in Paris in 1930 – and took a selection of her diamonds to a jeweller's in Old Bond Street, 'as Philip dared not show his face at the jeweller's,' she explained to her brother, Dickie, 'for fear of being recognised. I think the ring is a great success.'

On 9 July 1947 the engagement was formally announced from Buckingham Palace:

It is with the greatest pleasure that the King and Queen announce the betrothal of their dearly beloved daughter The Princess Elizabeth to Lieutenant Philip Mountbatten, RN, son of the late Prince Andrew of Greece and Princess Andrew (Princess Alice of Battenberg), to which union the King has gladly given his consent.

CHAPTER FOURTEEN

Wedding

How great was their pleasure? How glad was the King's consent? Was George VI truly happy with the engagement? Yes, overall, I think he was. Naturally, he was loath to lose a daughter – he was a fond father and they were good companions to one another – but he saw Philip's merits. He liked the fact that Philip was royal – and therefore 'one of us'. He liked the fact that Philip was making a career in the Royal Navy, as he had done. He appreciated his future son-in-law's intelligence, energy, and sense of humour. Above all, he saw that Lilibet was wholly in love and, now she was of age, could find no reason to deny her her heart's desire.

Queen Elizabeth, too, welcomed the engagement – although not in person on the day of the announcement. On 9 July she wrote to Philip from Buckingham Palace: 'I am *so* disappointed to be laid aside with this laryngitis, because I particularly wanted to see [you] & tell you how happy we feel about the engagement, and to say how glad we are to have you as a son-in-law. It is so *lovely* to know you so well and I know that we can trust our darling Lilibet to your love and care.' She signed the letter, 'Ever your affect aunt'. Whoever you are, it is never easy knowing what to call your mother-in-law.

To friends, acquaintances and well-wishers offering congratulations on the news of the engagement the Queen gave a uniform response: 'We feel very happy about it, as [Philip] is a very nice person, & they have known each other for some years which is a great comfort.' But, privately, Her Majesty had reservations. Fuelled by her younger brother, David Bowes-Lyon, and some of her closest aristocratic friends, and by the senior courtiers led by Sir Alan Lascelles, she was not entirely sure about her future son-in-law. Was Philip really right for Lilibet? Was he good enough? Was he, in truth, a suitable consort for a future Queen? To the senior courtiers, to the aristocrats in Queen Elizabeth's immediate circle, Philip did not feel like 'one of us'. He spoke perfect English, he had impeccable manners, but he was by no stretch of the imagination a classic English gentleman. He was neither an Etonian, nor a Guards officer, nor a hunting man. And what little was known of his parents was not encouraging. The royal establishment did not welcome Philip with open arms. Far from it. According to John Brabourne, 'They were bloody to him. We were at Balmoral that summer' – the summer of the engagement – 'and they were absolutely bloody to him. They didn't like him, they didn't trust him, and it showed. Not at all nice.'

'What was Philip's reaction to the hostility?' I asked.

'I think it hurt,' Lord Brabourne said to me. 'But he didn't let it show. He just got on with it.' It certainly rankled with Philip – and continued to do so, even into old age. He was snubbed by snobs. He was treated as an outsider, when he knew he was anything but. His father, after all, had been an ADC to Queen Victoria, Edward VII and George V. Prince Philip told me the story of the first time he visited Windsor Castle after his engagement, when a courtier, patronisingly, began to tell him about the history of the place. Philip interrupted and silenced the man, saying, 'Yes, I know. My mother was born here.'

Princess Alice was in England at the time of her son's engagement. She was staying with her own mother at Kensington Palace. She was happy to see Philip and, together, they spent hours sorting through cases of Andrea's old possessions – his papers and books, clothes and bric-a-brac – sent up from the south of France following Philip's visit to the Comtesse de la Bigne. Alice now spoke of Andrea almost as if they had never parted. She had high hopes for her son's future happiness.

The betrothal was announced on 9 July, because a Buckingham Palace garden party was scheduled for the 10th and the young couple could make their first public appearance there. Alice sent a happy report to Dickie, now in India in his new role as Britain's last Viceroy: 'It amused me very much to be waiting with the rest of the family, for Philip to come down grandly with Bertie, Elizabeth & Lilibet. The young couple made their rounds of the garden alone, accompanied by the court people & received ovations from the guests. This morning the two came alone to visit Mama, who was delighted as she is very fond of Lilibet & likes her character very much.' Alice told Dickie that Philip was at his most exuberant: 'He was so excited he hardly knew what he was doing.'

The engagement announced, preparations for the wedding began at once. By royal standards, it was not to be an extravagant affair. Times were hard: the winter had been cruel, the economy was fragile, rationing was the order of the day. Tom Driberg, the Labour MP, wrote to his friend, Dickie Mountbatten, to warn him that the government's backbenchers would not look kindly on public funds being lavished either on his nephew's wedding or on his subsequent lifestyle. From India (where he had been transformed from Viceroy to Governor-General following India's independence) Mountbatten sent a swift response to Driberg:

You can rest assured that he [Philip] thoroughly understands this problem and indeed he spoke to me about it when I was home in May. I am sure he is entirely on the side of cutting down the display of the wedding, and his own personal feelings are against receiving any civil list for the very reasons you give. I have, however, persuaded him that he should take something.

Mountbatten explained that Philip had virtually no money beyond his Navy pay and that his 'little two-seater' (his beloved MG) made 'a big hole in his private fortune'. 'As a future Prince Consort, however,' he went on:

I think you will agree that Third-class travel would be regarded as a stunt and a sixpenny tip to a porter as stingey [sic] . . . It really amounts to this: you have either got to give up the Monarchy or give the wretched people who have to carry out the functions of the Crown enough money to be able to do it with the same dignity at least as the Prime Minister or the Lord Mayor of London is afforded.

As it turned out, Philip was not destined to be Prince Consort. It would be ten years, in fact, before he would become a Prince of the United Kingdom. At the outset of his marriage, he did not go entirely without honours, however. The wedding was set for 20 November 1947. At the beginning of the month, the King reported to Queen Mary:

I am giving the Garter to Lilibet next Tuesday, November 11th so that she will be senior to Philip, to whom I am giving it on November 19th. I have arranged that he shall be created a Royal Highness & that the titles of his peerage will be: Baron Greenwich, Earl of Merioneth & Duke of Edinburgh . . . It is a great deal to give a man all at once, but I know Philip understands his new responsibilities on his marriage to Lilibet.

Mountbatten (who had become a Knight of the Garter himself at the end of 1946) returned from India for the wedding. On the eve of the great day, Mike Parker organised a stag-night for Philip at the Dorchester Hotel. He told me about it: 'It was a great night. Everyone was in naval evening dress. Mountbatten was the senior guest, alongside David Milford Haven and captains and 1st lieutenants of the 27th Destroyer Flotilla, the flotilla that wound up in Japan at the end of the war. It was a very happy occasion. It was an evening of comrades. Philip was an orphan of sorts and we were family. Philip was happy and we were happy for him.' At the beginning of the evening, the gentlemen of the press were invited to take photographs of the guests. When they had done so, Mountbatten suggested that the guests might now borrow the press cameras to take a group photograph of the gentlemen of the press. Having done so, the guests, at Parker's bidding, removed the flash bulbs from the cameras and smashed them against the wall, so preventing any further photography. 'We were just having fun,' Parker told me. 'It was a good-humoured evening all round.'

Philip and his best man, David Milford Haven, spent the night before the wedding at Kensington Palace. John Dean, the Mountbattens' butler who became Philip's valet, said, 'Their rooms were astonishingly poor and humble – floors scrubbed boards with worn rugs.' (Robin Dalton recalled her boyfriend David's room being 'in the servants' attic'. 'We had a flat together in Chelsea,' she told me, 'but in the run-up to the wedding it was thought advisable that David, as Philip's best man, move in with his grandmother. I remember David and me, on our nights together, creeping up the back stairs of her apartment at Kensington Palace as silently as possible.') John Dean recalled bringing Philip his early-morning tea promptly at 7:00 a.m. and finding his young master in happy form and not the least bit nervous.

Patricia Mountbatten's recollection was a little different. 'I saw him just after breakfast that morning,' she told me. 'We were alone together – we were cousins and we knew each other very well – and I said something about what an exciting day it was and, suddenly, he said to me, "Am I being very brave or very foolish?"' I asked Lady Mountbatten what she thought he meant by that. 'He was apprehensive,' she said. 'He was uncertain – not about marrying Princess Elizabeth, but about what the marriage would mean for him. He was giving up a great deal. In many ways, nothing was going to change for her. Everything was going to change for him.'

For a start, that very morning, he stopped smoking cigarettes – not that he had been a heavy smoker. The King was a heavy smoker. (It was a family habit: Queen Mary was a smoker, too.) Princess Elizabeth saw the effect cigarettes had on her father and did not want her husband to smoke. Philip was happy enough to oblige his bride-to-be – and disciplined enough to be able to do so overnight. At 11:00 a.m., fortified by a gin-and-tonic, and dressed in naval uniform, sporting the insignia of a Knight Companion of the Order of the Garter, and wearing the ceremonial sword that had belonged to his grandfather, Prince Louis of Battenberg, Philip, accompanied by his best man, set off for Westminster Abbey.

Over at Buckingham Palace, Elizabeth, too, had an early start. It was still dark when Bobo brought her little princess a cup of tea. 'I don't think any of us had very much sleep,' reported Crawfie. 'I went along to Lilibet's room very early, and found her in her dressing-gown, peeping excitedly out of the windows at the crowds.' Despite the bitter cold, people had slept out overnight to secure their view. Along the Mall and down Whitehall, the pavements were packed, fifty-people deep. 'I can't believe it's really happening,' Lilibet told Crawfie, 'I have to keep pinching myself.'

Norman Hartnell, who had designed the Princess's wedding dress, delivered it personally to the palace the night before. At 9:00 a.m. he and his entourage were on parade again for the final fitting. It took an hour and a quarter. 'She looked so beautiful,' recalled Margaret Rhodes, who was one of the eight bridesmaids. 'We were all dressed by Mr Hartnell, too. It was very exciting. There was rationing, of course, and we used up all our clothes coupons.' The bride's dress alone absorbed three hundred coupons and cost £1,200. Given the prevailing austerity, the extravagance was considered controversial by some. Most, however, went along with the Leader of the Opposition, Winston Churchill, who welcomed the wedding and all that it involved as 'A flash of colour on the hard road we have to travel.' Norman Hartnell used to enjoy telling the story of how his manager – who had travelled far and wide gathering materials for the dress – was stopped at customs on his return from a buying trip to the United States and asked if he had anything to declare. 'Yes,' the man replied, 'ten thousand pearls for the wedding dress of Princess Elizabeth.' The dress was made of ivory silk, decorated with pearls arranged as white roses of York, entwined with ears of corn embroidered in crystal. The effect was ravishing.

Inevitably, there were last-minute dramas, 'the tensions common to any home on a wedding morning,' according to Crawfie. The bride's bouquet was lost. A footman remembered receiving it and bringing it upstairs, but what happened to it after that, he couldn't recall. Panic ensued and then, suddenly, happily, the footman remembered he had placed it in a cool cupboard nearby for safe-keeping. Next, the precious tiara given to the Princess by Queen Mary snapped as it was being put on her head. More panic, until nervous hands managed to repair the damage. Finally – and most dramatically – the Princess went to put on the double string of pearls that her parents had given her as a wedding present – and realised that they were half-a-mile away at St James's Palace where all the wedding presents were to go on public display.

The Princess's recently appointed private secretary, Jock Colville, was summoned to her sitting-room. 'She stood there, radiant and entrancing in her wedding dress,' he recalled. Could he, somehow, make his way to St James's Palace and retrieve the necklace, she asked. 'I looked at my watch,' he said. 'I rushed along the corridor. I galloped down the Grand Staircase and into the main quadrangle of Buckingham Palace. Take any car, the Princess had called after me. So I ran towards a large Royal Daimler. "To St James's Palace," I cried to the chauffeur, and I flung open the door of the car. Before I could leap in, a tall elderly man, ablaze with Orders and Decorations, began to emerge. It was King Haakon VII of Norway. "You seem in a hurry, young man," he said. "By all means have my car, but do let me get out first."' When Colville reached St James's, the detectives guarding the royal wedding gifts were not inclined to believe his story. He pleaded with them. He asked them to telephone Buckingham Palace. The line was dead. With his heart beating and the minutes ticking by, he told them his name and, when they discovered it printed in the official Wedding Programme, reluctantly, they allowed him to escape with the necklace. Pushing his way through the crowd, apologising as he went, 'with one hand firmly pressed against the pocket of my tunic where the pearls lay', Colville made his way back to the car and reached Buckingham Palace with only moments to spare.

At 11:15 a.m. the Princess, carrying her bouquet, wearing her parents' pearls, her grandmother's tiara and Mr Hartnell's fairy-tale dress, clambered into the Irish state coach. Her father, slight and pale, but smiling, dressed in his uniform as an Admiral of the Fleet, sat next to her. Together, escorted by the Household Cavalry in full ceremonial dress uniform for the first time in six years, father and daughter travelled along the Mall and down Whitehall towards Westminster Abbey crowds, cheering them all the way. 'The King looked unbelievably beautiful,' Sir Michael Duff wrote to his friend, the photographer, Cecil Beaton, 'like an early French King and HRH the Bride a dream.' It was a poignant journey for them both, but more so for the King than his daughter. For Lilibet a new life was about to begin; for George VI an era was coming to an end. 'It is a far more moving thing to give your daughter away than to be married yourself,' the King told the Archbishop of York later that day.

The Archbishop, Cyril Garbett, officiating alongside the Archbishop of Canterbury, Geoffrey Fisher, described the wedding – to the congregation of two thousand in the Abbey, to the few thousand more watching a film of the occasion on fledgling television in the evening, and to the millions tuned in to the live broadcast on the wireless around the world – as 'in all essentials exactly the same as it would have been for any cottager who might be married this afternoon in some small country church in a remote village in the Dales.' Well, up to a point. The Princess had chosen traditional hymns ('The Lord is My Shepherd', sung to the tune of Crimond, was Crawfie's favourite moment) and vowed, until death, to 'love, honour and obey' her husband, 'for richer or poorer, for better or worse', so the essentials were certainly familiar, but everything else was truly beyond the ken of the average British cottager of the period. For a start, there were eight bridesmaids (led by Princess Margaret, walking alone, three paces ahead of the other bridesmaids, in recognition of her rank), two kilted page boys (Prince William of Gloucester and Prince Michael of Kent, who inadvertently stepped on the Tomb of the Unknown Warrior), and the guests – the men in uniform and morning suits, the women in full-length dresses with long white gloves and glittering tiaras – included a remarkable array of royalty, some still reigning, others retired, hurt. According to one of the bridesmaids, Pamela Mountbatten, 'Crown Princess Juliana of the Netherlands caused a stir, remarking that "Everyone's jewellery is *so* dirty," which may or may not have been the case; to me it was just remarkable that all those royal jewels had survived the war.'

On Lilibet's side of the family, her uncle David and his American wife, the Duke and Duchess of Windsor, were conspicuous by their absence. On Philip's side, the principal non-invitees were his three sisters and their German husbands. It was only two years since the end of the war, too soon for the British royal family to be seen extending the hand of friendship to the enemy. Philip's youngest sister, Sophie, had three brothers-in-law still awaiting denazification, one of them still interned.

Alice wrote a twenty-two-page description of the wedding for her daughters, to 'console them for their absence'. She was there, seated with her mother, the Marchioness of Milford Haven, and her sister, Louise, and her husband, King Gustaf VI of Sweden, and her brother, Dickie, who, with Edwina, and their younger daughter, Pamela, had come home briefly from India for the occasion.

From Philip's father's side of the family the contingent was smaller: of Andrea's seven brothers and sisters, all but one was dead. Philip's uncle, 'Big' George, was there from Paris, with his wife, Marie Bonaparte, and their daughter, Eugénie, alongside assorted first cousins, second cousins and cousins by marriage, including Queen Helen of Romania, Queen Alexandra of Yugoslavia and Queen Frederika of Greece.

There were so many foreign royals in the best seats for the wedding, that members of the British parliament had to draw lots to secure access to the 'parliamentary enclosure'. Chips Channon was one MP who managed to get in. 'I thought Princess Elizabeth looked well,' he noted in his diary, 'shy and attractive, and Prince Philip as if he was thoroughly enjoying himself.' A few days later, Channon gave a spectacular post-wedding party – 'a great, great success' by his own account: 'I "laced" the cocktails with Benzedrine, which I find always makes a party go' – and entertained some of the royalty who were in town, including the Queens of Spain and Romania. 'I am sorry that Queen Freddie [of Greece] and the Duchess of Kent [Princess Marina, Philip's first cousin] could not come,' he told his diary: 'They are on a secret visit to the affronted German relations to tell them about the Wedding.' They took Alice's twenty-two-page account with them.

Noël Coward was at both Channon's party and at Westminster Abbey, where he found, to his surprise and pleasure, that he was placed in the fourth row, next to Beatrice Lillie. Coward recorded in his diary: 'A gala day . . . The wedding was most moving and beautifully done. English tradition at its best.' The Coward verdict was the general one. As the young couple left the Abbey, Philip bowing smartly to the King and Queen, Elizabeth dropping a low, slow curtsy to her parents, they looked like figures from a story-book: a fairy-tale princess with her prince from a foreign land, destined to live happily ever after. Jock Colville was one of those who, in the run-up to the marriage, had been sceptical about its prospects. 'As the day drew nearer,' he confessed, 'I began to think, as I now sincerely do, that the Princess and Philip really are in love.' That's what the cheering crowds thought, too, as the Abbey bells pealed, and the bride and groom, beaming and waving, were taken back to Buckingham Palace in the Glass Coach.

At the Palace, the society photographer known as Baron took the official photographs before luncheon was served. It was billed as an 'austerity' wedding breakfast, with just three courses, each featuring unrationed food. The main course was partridge – *Perdreau en Casserole* – preceded by *Filets de Sole Mountbatten* and followed by *Bombe Glacée Princesse Elizabeth*. There were just 150 guests: family, close friends and courtiers. Crawfie was excited to be included:

> It was a gay and merry lunch party. The tables were decorated with smilax and white carnations, and at each of our places there was a little bunch of white heather, sent down from Balmoral. The famous gold-plate and the scarlet-coated footmen gave a fairy-tale atmosphere to it all, and I was in a veritable dream. The skirl of the bagpipes warmed the hearts of those of us who came from north of the Tweed. The French gentleman seated next to me, however, winced from time to time, but he bore it with fortitude.
>
> There were no long speeches. The King hates them and has always dreaded having to make one. He was brevity itself. The bridegroom, another sailor, had just as little to say. It was a very large room and there were no microphones, so few people even heard the little that was said. The French gentleman kept hissing in my ear, 'Qu'est ce qu'il dit?' I was unable to help him.

The younger members of the family, and their nannies, had a quiet lunch and 'a nice lie down' in another part of the

Palace. According to Crawfie, the page boys, Prince William and Prince Michael (the six- and five-year-old sons of Lilibet's uncles, the Dukes of Gloucester and Kent), were 'thoroughly overtired', 'grew peevish', and almost came to blows: 'Shocked nannies enveloped them in those vast white shawls royal nannies always seem to have handy. Like sheltering wings! They were borne off, but not before they had made ceremonious bows to the King and Queen. In royal circles manners are taught young.'

The little ones reappeared to see the bride and groom set off on their honeymoon. Mr Hartnell was especially proud of his going-away outfit for the young princess: a love-in-the-mist crêpe dress with blue velvet cloth travelling coat, blue felt bonnet trimmed with ostrich pompom and curved quills in two tones of blue. It needed to be warm because the November weather was bitter and, for the benefit of the crowds, the newly-weds were to travel from Buckingham Palace to Waterloo Station (en route for Winchester) in an unheated open landau. (It was foggy, but at least it wasn't raining and, under their lap-rugs, discreet comfort was provided by hot-water bottles and Lilibet's favourite corgi, Susan.) As, hand in hand, the newly-weds came down the Palace staircase, the family, cheering, gathered round and threw rose-petals. As the couple's carriage trundled through the Palace gates, the King and Queen stood watching, holding hands. Princess Alice kept waving until the carriage disappeared from view. In some ways, perhaps it was like any cottager's wedding. All three proud parents had tears in their eyes.

A few days later, back in Athens, Alice wrote to Philip: 'How wonderfully everything went off & I was so comforted to see the truly happy expression on your face and to feel your decision was right from every point of view.' And, from London, the King wrote, touchingly, to Lilibet, as she embarked on married life and he contemplated a future without his elder daughter at his side:

I was so proud of you & thrilled at having you so close to me on our long walk in Westminster Abbey, but when I handed your hand to the Archbishop I felt that I had lost something very precious. You were so calm and composed during the Service & said your words with such conviction, that I knew everything was all right.

I am so glad you wrote & told Mummy that you think the long wait before your engagement & the long time before the wedding was for the best. I was rather afraid that you thought I was being hard-hearted about it. I was so anxious for you to come to South Africa as you knew. Our family, us four, the 'Royal Family' must remain together with additions of course at suitable moments!! I have watched you grow up all these years with pride under the skilful direction of Mummy, who as you know is the most marvellous person in the World in my eyes, & I can, I know, always count on you, & now Philip, to help us in our work. Your leaving us has left a great blank in our lives but do remember that your old home is still yours & do come back to it as much & as often as possible. I can see that you are sublimely happy with Philip which is right but don't forget us is the wish of

Your ever loving & devoted
Papa

The newly-weds began their honeymoon at Broadlands, the Mountbattens' country house in Hampshire, not far from Winchester, by the River Test. They were not alone. As well as Lilibet's corgi, Susan, the young lovers' entourage included a personal detective, a personal footman, Bobo MacDonald (the Princess's nursery-maid turned dresser and confidante), and John Dean (the Mountbattens' London butler who was now Prince Philip's valet). John Dean and Cyril Dickman, the footman, looked after the luggage: the bride had fifteen cases, the groom just two. The detective did his best to keep the public at bay. At Winchester station, there were crowds waiting to cheer the young couple. At Broadlands, there were more sight-seers gawping at the gates. Despite the cold, eager rubber-neckers (loyal subjects as well as representatives of the press) hovered, day and night, at the edge of the estate hoping for glimpses of the happy pair. On Sunday morning, when the couple went together to a service at Romsey Abbey nearby, frantic royal-watchers scrambled across tombstones to get a better view. Several came equipped with chairs and step-ladders to enable them to peer through the windows into the Abbey itself. For the royal newly-weds, life in the goldfish bowl had begun.

According to John Dean, Prince Philip, in the early days of his marriage, did not wear pyjamas. We are told, too, by Patricia Mountbatten, that, once, when she remarked on Lilibet's flawless complexion, Philip laughed and said to his cousin, beaming, 'Yes, and she's like that all over.' Robin Dalton told me that David Milford Haven had told her that Philip had told him that Lilibet was 'very keen on sex, quite a goer'. Well, for both their sakes, let us hope so – but let us not pretend that we know. I can just about visualise Prince Philip giving a nod and a grin to David Milford Haven in response to a jocular enquiry on the subject, but I do not think he was the sort of man who would discuss intimate aspects of his married life with his men friends.

What happened between the sheets on the night of the royal wedding I cannot tell you. However, I can report, because there were witnesses, that the evening at Broadlands was not especially peaceful. The telephone rang incessantly;

the staff at Broadlands (in the absence of the Mountbattens in India) were not as well organised as they might have been; Bobo and Cyril and John were exhausted. The day had been a long one. The bridal couple retired as soon as supper was over: they looked weary but very happy, Lilibet especially so.

By several accounts, the bride and groom certainly had a jollier evening in Hampshire than the groomsman and bridesmaids had in London. Elizabeth's cousin, Margaret Rhodes, was one of the bridesmaids and she told me, 'We didn't have a girls' party before the wedding, but, on the day itself, we did have the traditional evening where the best man entertains the bridesmaids. It was not a success. The best man was Milford Haven, not my favourite man. Let's not talk about him.'

'Why not?' I asked Mrs Rhodes.

She assumed a very pinched look and said, rapidly, stubbing out her cigarette, 'We went to somewhere like Quaglino's and he was much keener on some dolly-bird at the other table than he was on us. He was not my idea of a gentleman.'

Milford Haven's girlfriend at the time, Robin Dalton, told me she feared that she was probably the 'dolly-bird at the other table'. (In her memoir of the wedding day, another of the bridesmaids, Pamela Hicks, describes her as 'a dazzling girl at the next table'.) Looking anything but pinched, Robin Dalton told me, smiling into her Bloody Mary, 'I think the party was at Ciro's in Orange Street, not Quaglino's. I do remember Princess Margaret getting cross because David was spending too much time with me. I wasn't a bridesmaid, of course. I was only at the wedding because David got me a ticket. I sat at the back with the servants. I had been married, albeit briefly. I was a divorcee, so not a suitable bride for a descendant of Queen Victoria. I couldn't accompany him into the Royal Enclosure at Ascot, even had I wished to. I loved David. He was so sweet and we had five happy years together. Then, understandably, and very suddenly, David got married to someone else, through the mistaken idea that she was very rich, leaving me with his dog, his car and both of us in tears. As a wedding present, I think Philip gave David a pair of cufflinks Philip had been given by the Duke of Gloucester.'

As best man, David's present to Philip and Lilibet was something both practical and sought-after: the most up-to-date (and expensive) record player on the market, the new 'Deccola'. According to Robin Dalton, 'David and Philip had very little money. They survived on their naval pay, and £5 a week each from Lord Mountbatten. One night at a dinner party, I sat next to a businessman who proudly told me he was manufacturing the Deccola. By the end of dinner, I had procured, free for David, the very first one off the production line and the manufacturer had procured valuable publicity because all the wedding presents went on prominent display.'

Philip and Elizabeth received around fifteen hundred wedding gifts, ranging from five hundred cases of tinned pineapple from the Government of Queensland to a turkey from a woman in Brooklyn who had heard that 'they have nothing to eat in England'. 'The people of Kenya' generously gave the royal couple a hunting lodge; the people of Britain generously sent Lilbet dozens of pairs of nylon stockings. The Aga Khan pleased Elizabeth with his present of a thoroughbred filly; Mahatma Gandhi impressed Philip with his gift of a personally woven piece of cloth, intended as a cover for a tea-tray. As she toured the exhibition of the presents displayed at St James's Palace, Queen Mary, not an admirer of Gandhi, decided the material was intended as a loin-cloth and was not amused. Philip protested, but the old queen did not want to be enlightened. She muttered, 'What a horrible thing' and, lips pursed, moved quickly on.

After five nights at Broadlands, the honeymooners returned briefly to London for lunch at Buckingham Palace with the King and Queen before setting off by train for Scotland and a further two weeks of honeymoon at Birkhall on the Balmoral Estate. Here, the young couple had a quieter, cosier, more secluded time. They went for walks in the snow. They warmed themselves by roaring log fires. They got to know one another. They had time alone – or, as much time alone as you get when there are servants always hovering. It is the privilege of princes to be waited on, but the price they pay for that privilege is a heavy one: someone is always close at hand, waiting, watching, listening, standing in silent judgement; sometimes reporting this and that to others in the servants' hall; occasionally reporting that and this to the world at large. Marion Crawford (governess), John Dean (valet), Paul Burrell (footman turned butler), in their way, in their day, showed real dedication as royal servants. They served their mistresses and masters with devotion, and then repaid the royal trust placed in them by spilling the beans in best-selling books, protesting their continuing loyalty all the way to the bank.

Philip had had an odd childhood, but, at boarding school, and in the Royal Navy, he had, to some extent, lived in 'the real world', fending for himself. Lilibet, on the other hand, was a girl, born before the era of female emancipation, brought up as a princess, living in palaces and castles, surrounded by servants. She, more than Philip, was wholly accustomed to being fed, and bathed, and dressed, and watched over, by others. At Broadlands, at Birkhall, at Buckingham Palace, the entourage was always there: the detective, the driver, the footman, the valet, and Bobo. Especially Bobo.

Margaret MacDonald was the daughter of an Inverness railway worker. As a child she lived by a railway line in a small railway company cottage. At twenty-two – in 1926, when

Princess Elizabeth was born – she joined the Yorks' household as nursery-maid and assistant to Alah Knight, the royal nanny. When Princess Margaret Rose was born in 1930, Alah, naturally, concentrated on the new baby, and Bobo (as Miss MacDonald was soon nicknamed) began what would become a lifetime of single-minded devotion to Princess Elizabeth. When Lilibet was a little girl, Bobo shared her bedroom. When the Princess grew up, Bobo became her dresser, confidante and friend. John Dean described her as 'a small, smart, rather peremptory Scotswoman' whose years with the royal household 'seemed to be imprinted on her face and stature'. She was formal – 'We have to keep a certain standing in the house,' was her line – and seemed formidable to some, but, according to Dean, she was 'quite friendly when thawed'. She was a redhead when young. Dean reported: 'She was a lovely dancer and very good fun, with a nice sense of humour, but even when we were staying in some village, and were out socially in the local pub, she always addressed me as "Mr Dean". She always referred to Princess Elizabeth as "My Little Lady".' In private, with the Princess, Bobo would call her mistress 'Lilibet', one of the very few outside the royal family to feel comfortable doing so. (Playfully, Princess Margaret occasionally called her sister 'Lil'.)

Officially, Bobo was simply Elizabeth's dresser. She looked after the royal wardrobe. She dealt with the royal dressmakers: Mr Hartnell, Hardy Amies, and, later, Ian Thomas. She kept them in their place, both by the manner with which she handled them, and by not allowing any one of them complete control over Elizabeth's appearance. 'You're here for the clothes not the accessories,' she would tell the designers, firmly. Bobo was a personally disciplined, conservatively inclined, frugally minded, Scotswoman: she saw no virtue in Lilibet being kitted out with expensive handbags. Officially, Bobo looked after Elizabeth's wardrobe. Unofficially, Bobo looked after Elizabeth. Her devotion was absolute, her commitment total, her access almost unlimited. By the time she died, in 1993, aged eighty-nine, she had become a legendary figure in royal circles: the one person to whom the Queen always listened.

For sixty-seven years, Bobo lived for Elizabeth. She loved her, protected her, respected her. She was wholly loyal and ever-present. At times she must have got on Prince Philip's nerves. Mike Parker said to me, 'Let's face it, he had a hell of a time with her. Miss MacDonald was *always* there. And in charge. Princess Elizabeth was Bobo's baby and that was that. But I don't think he ever complained. Anyway, he didn't to me. He didn't say a word. Not a word. He just put up with it.' Patricia Mountbatten told me that Bobo would prepare Lilibet's bath and then potter in and out of the bathroom while she was having it, effectively keeping Philip at bay: 'He couldn't share the bathroom with his wife, because Bobo saw it as her territory and I don't think Princess Elizabeth had the heart to say, "Bobo, please go away." I think Philip must have found it quite irritating.'

After two weeks at Birkhall, the honeymoon was over and Elizabeth and Philip (and the detective and the dresser, the footman and the valet, the seventeen cases and the corgi) returned to London in time for the King's fifty-second birthday on 14 December. 'The Edinburghs are back from Scotland,' Jock Colville noted in his diary. 'She was looking very happy, and, as a result of three weeks of matrimony, suddenly a woman instead of a girl. He also seemed happy, but a shade querulous, which is, I think, in his character.'

I go along with Colville's judgement. In many ways, Prince Philip was remarkably good-humoured and long-suffering. He put up with Bobo; he shrugged off his press coverage; he endured more than six decades of footling royal flummery and thousands of hours of mind-numbing small-talk with strangers and civic dignitaries. But he was 'a shade querulous'. He would grumble. He could be difficult. His impatience sometimes showed. And, though he denied it, he was always contradictory. He liked to be his own man.

On 1 December 1947, Queen Elizabeth wrote to him from Buckingham Palace – 'the first time I have written to you as my son-in-law'. This letter, running to several pages, she signed 'with much love, dearest Philip, ever your devoted Mama'. It is full of warmth and encouragement: 'I *do* hope that you won't find public life too trying; for the people *are* demanding when they like you, but you will have the comfort of knowing that you are giving so much towards the happiness and stability of the country.' The letter also contains a telling observation: 'I remember at Balmoral last year, you told me that you had always played a lone hand, and had had to fight your own battles . . .' To an extent, all his life he continued to play 'a lone hand' – notwithstanding his public advocacy of team games. Within a fortnight of his wedding, his new mother-in-law told him, 'You will now have a great chance for individual leadership, as well as "married couple" leadership which is so important as well. As a family we do try to work as a team, but each going their own way, and I am sure you will make very valuable contributions towards the common pool.'

In 1947, Princess Elizabeth was twenty-one and, though self-possessed, still quite shy. I asked her cousin, Margaret Rhodes, what she made of Philip when she first got to know him in the 1940s. 'I used to dread sitting next to him,' she told me, pulling a rather anxious face. 'He'd be so contradictory. You'd say something just to say something, and he'd jump down your throat. "Why do you say that? What do you mean?" Quite frightening, until you got used to it. I think he's always had that de-bunking element in him. It was just his way.'

'Was he like that with Elizabeth?' I asked.

'Yes,' said Mrs Rhodes, 'He was like that with the Queen. He'd say, "Why the bloody hell? What the bloody hell?" I think she did sometimes find it very disconcerting.'

Patricia Mountbatten — whose manner was more robust than that of Mrs Rhodes: she was her father's daughter — told me that while, in her experience, the Queen did not respond to her husband's intemperate outbursts in kind, she enjoyed it when others did. 'I remember a big party at Balmoral,' said Countess Mountbatten, 'a shooting party, when, at dinner, Philip and I had a right old ding-dong about South Africa. It was a terrific argument and the Queen kept encouraging me. "That's right, Patricia," she said, "You go at him, nobody ever goes at him."'

When the Duke was critical of his wife, berating her for paying attention to the dogs when she should be listening to him, or wondering out loud why she was spending so much time on the telephone, or telling her she was wearing the wrong clothes for a shooting expedition, the Queen was quite capable of answering back, saying to him, 'Oh, do shut up.' According to family and friends, over the years, she became bolder with him, and he gentler with her.

Why was Prince Philip contradictory and querulous? His cousin, Patricia Mountbatten, said, 'He has a very similar character to my father. He's a dynamo. He wants action. He wants to get things done. He likes getting his own way and it's frustrating for him when he doesn't.'

'And life at court was very, very frustrating for him at first,' according to Patricia's husband, Lord Brabourne. 'It was very stuffy. Lascelles was impossible. They were absolutely bloody to him. They patronised him. They treated him as an outsider. It wasn't much fun. He laughed it off, of course, but it must have hurt. I'm not sure that Princess Elizabeth noticed it. She probably didn't see it. In a way, marriage hardly changed her life at all. She was able to carry on much as before. In getting married, she didn't sacrifice anything. His life changed completely. He gave up everything.'

According to Lord Brabourne and the Mountbatten girls (Philip's first cousins), and according to Mike Parker and other male friends of Philip's at the time, as a young man Philip was funny, charming, wilful, dynamic and occasionally impatient. As a bridegroom, according to Pamela Mountbatten, he was 'so dashing that it made you realise why every girl in England seemed to think she was in love with him.' Of course, not every girl in England was. His best man's girlfriend, Robin Dalton, described him to me as 'a cold fish'. When I asked Princess Elizabeth's childhood friend, Sonia Berry, what she made of the young Prince Philip, her back stiffened and she answered crisply: 'No comment.'

According to Elizabeth's first cousin, Margaret Rhodes, Philip 'mellowed a lot' in his later years. He must have done. When I first became involved in the work of the National Playing Fields Association in the 1970s, I was warned that Prince Philip was a 'hands-on' president, but not always easy. He could be abrupt, I was told. In my experience he was sometimes demanding and occasionally testy, but he was never rude.

Yes, he could be impatient. 'Why hasn't this happened?' he would ask, eyebrow raised. 'What are we waiting for? Let's get on with it, for heavens' sake.' With those he knew like me, he would indicate his disapproval with a grimace or a sigh and a weary shake of the head, but, on the whole, with the general public, and with those he met undertaking his array of public duties, he was surprisingly equable: easy-going, unaffected and good-humoured. I would see him looking grouchy now and again (and keep my distance), but I only once saw him positively bad-tempered. He expected to find a folder of papers in their usual place on the desk in his study at Buckingham Palace. A footman had moved the papers. Philip gave him short shrift. I blanched. The footman retreated, chastened and abashed. Lord Brabourne said to me of Philip in his seventies: 'He's naughty now. He shouts at people sometimes.' Gina Kennard said to me: 'Let's face it, he can be really quite bad-tempered.' His son, King Charles III, can occasionally be testy and impatient, too. That is a characteristic he has inherited from his father, his royal grandfather (George VI) and great-grandfather (George V), not from his mother, who would express irritation with a grimace or an occasional sharp remark, but rarely, if ever, with an overt show of ill-temper.

Jock Colville's assessment of the mood and manner of the royal couple in 1947 is borne out by other witnesses: the bride was very happy: the groom, happy but a touch querulous. Philip still did not have a home to call his own. The plan had been for the newly-weds to have a country home at Sunninghill Park in Windsor Great Park and a London home at Clarence House, next to St James's Palace, overlooking the Mall. Unfortunately, the substantial house at Sunninghill Park burnt to the ground before the Edinburghs could move in, and Clarence House was in need of substantial refurbishment and repair. Eventually, they rented a comparatively small country house, Windlesham Moor, in Berkshire and, in May 1949, eighteen months after their wedding, moved into their London home, a handsomely restored Clarence House. (The restoration cost £78,000, rather more than the £50,000 voted for the work, somewhat grudgingly, by parliament.) Meanwhile, for their London base, they perched briefly at Clock House in Kensington Palace (the home of the Earl and Countess of Athlone, who were on a three-month trip to South Africa), and then spent a year living with the King and Queen at Buckingham Palace. For Lilibet, Buckingham Palace was 'home from home'. For Philip, given a bedroom and sitting-room of his own alongside his wife's established apartments, the arrangement was less satisfactory. Queen Elizabeth told him to think of it as 'Hotel Buckingham'. He did.

There was one area in which Philip, however, was able to do exactly as he pleased: the appointment of his first equerry-in-waiting. He chose his friend, contemporary and fellow naval officer, Mike Parker. 'I was honoured,' Parker told me, 'and I felt I could do the job. Philip and I were mates and I felt I could be a useful ally to him at court. The King was fine, very friendly, very helpful, but the traditional courtiers weren't always so easy. I had been planning to return to Australia, but my wife, Eileen, who was Scottish, didn't want to leave the UK, so it worked out all round.' Parker was Philip's right-hand man – equerry, ADC, secretary, friend – for ten years, until 1957, when the 'scandal' of his divorce from Eileen obliged him to resign.

Princess Elizabeth's secretary, Jock Colville, was chosen for her by the King's secretary, Tommy Lascelles. Born in 1915, educated at Harrow and Trinity College, Cambridge, Colville was a career diplomat who started out (as personable and bright young men from the Foreign Office sometimes do) as an assistant private secretary in Downing Street. He worked for Chamberlain, Churchill and Attlee in turn, so he knew his way around the corridors of power. He was also wholly at home with the Palace culture. His mother, Lady Cynthia Colville, was a lady-in-waiting to Queen Mary. As a boy, he was a Page of Honour to George V. Jock Colville was a class act, as smooth and British as Parker was rough and Australian, but they rubbed along well and came to see one another's strengths.

In 1948, Colville married Lady Margaret Egerton, known as 'Meg', daughter of the 4th Earl of Ellesmere, who had been recruited by Princess Elizabeth as her third lady-in-waiting. Lady Meg was eight years older than Princess Elizabeth and noted for her good sense and good humour – and lifelong discretion. When she was widowed in 1987, Queen Elizabeth, the Queen Mother asked her to become an extra lady-in-waiting, which she did. She had the down-to-earth Scottish countrywoman's approach to life that the Queen Mother and her daughter shared. And a similar sense of humour. Amused by the story, the Queen told me that she had heard, when Lady Meg was in hospital not long before she died in 2004, she was kept awake by a fellow patient groaning through the night. Lady Meg said to the nurse, 'I just pretend I'm in the Highlands, and he's a rutting stag.'

Completing the young royal couple's team, as Comptroller and Treasurer to the Edinburgh household, was an older man, Lieutenant-General Sir Frederick 'Boy' Browning, born 1896, a dashing war hero, considered by Baron to be the handsomest man he ever photographed, married to the novelist Daphne du Maurier, and Chief of Staff to Philip's uncle, Louis Mountbatten, on his South-east Asia Command. Mountbatten recommended Browning to his nephew unreservedly: 'Boy has drive, energy, enthusiasm, efficiency and invokes the highest sense of loyalty and affection in his subordinates. His judgement is absolutely sound, and he would sooner die than let his boss down . . . he is not a "yes man" or even a courtier and never will be. He will fearlessly say what he thinks is right . . . Frankly, Philip, I do not think you can do better.'

It was a strong team. It had to be. The Princess and the Duke, aged twenty-one and twenty-six, were about to embark on a curious and exhausting adventure: a relentless, endlessly repetitive roller-coaster ride of royal duties and good works, from which only death or revolution could release them. When I asked Prince Philip if he felt frustrated that his marriage had ultimately curtailed his naval career, he said: 'In 1947 I thought I was going to have a career in the Navy, but it became obvious there was no hope. The royal family then was just the King and the Queen and the two princesses. The only other male member was the Duke of Gloucester. There was no choice. It just happened.' Philip had joined the family firm: he had to play his part in the family business. 'You have to make compromises,' he said to me. 'That's life. I accepted it. I tried to make the best of it.'

For the first four and a quarter years of his marriage, the Duke combined his royal duties with his naval ones. He had plenty of energy, a well-run office and an enviable ability to successfully juggle the competing demands of the Admiralty and Buckingham Palace. He worked hard; he played hard. In May 1948, Chips Channon observed the Edinburghs dancing the night away at a fancy-dress party at Coppins. They were still going at 5:00 a.m. – two hours after everyone danced the Hokey Cokey 'hilariously'. According to Channon, Philip 'looked worn out', but he was the success of the ball, 'wildly gay with his policeman's hat and handcuffs. He leapt about and jumped into the air as he greeted everybody. . . His charm is colossal, like all the Mountbattens, and he and Princess Elizabeth seemed supremely happy.'

In 1948, with the Edinburghs living at Buckingham Palace, Philip could walk to work, and did. He started the year with a desk job at the Admiralty, as an operations officer 'pushing ships around'. Later in the year, he went on a Staff Course at the Royal Naval College, Greenwich, and chose to spend the week in Greenwich, coming home to Lilibet at weekends. Spending nights, and weeks, and sometimes months, apart from your spouse, is the lot of married servicemen and women. It may be unsatisfactory – it may cause tensions and difficulties in a relationship – but it is not unusual: in the Navy especially, it is the way things are. In the years to come, the time Elizabeth and Philip would spend apart would give rise to comment: to them it was simply an inevitable fact of life.

Understanding the lives of other people is not easy if their way of life is very different from your own. I have spent my married life sharing a bedroom – and a bed – with my wife. Why? Because we are middle class, and comfortably married middle-class couples of our generation always share the same bedroom. That's the way it is. Among the upper classes, especially three or four generations ago, it was different. Men and women led much more separate lives: they lived in larger houses; they had separate (if adjacent or adjoining) bedrooms. That's just the way it was. When Elizabeth and Philip moved into Clarence House they had separate but communicating bedrooms. It was what they – and their staff – would have expected. In his memoir, the Duke's valet, John Dean, described the arrangement as though it was the most natural thing in the world. Of an evening, John would be assisting Philip in his bedroom, while Bobo would be tending to Elizabeth in hers, and the royal couple 'would joke happily through the left-open door'.

In July 1982, an intruder – a thirty-one-year-old schizophrenic named Michael Fagan – found his way into Buckingham Palace and disturbed the Queen, alone, asleep in bed. This alarming incident prompted a double dose of outrage from the tabloid press: why was the Palace security so lamentable and where was Prince Philip? Why was he not on hand to come to his wife's rescue? Indeed, the 'revelation' that the Queen and her husband did not appear to share a bedroom caused more comment in certain quarters than the fact that a lunatic could wander off the street into the sovereign's bedroom without let or hindrance. The Queen, who, at the time, handled the intrusion with commendable calm, was nevertheless shaken. The popular press had the answer: 'Give her a cuddle, Philip' instructed one newspaper headline. In fact, when sleeping under the same roof, the Queen and Prince Philip usually did share the same bed. It just happened that on the morning of Fagan's intrusion, Philip had a crack-of-dawn start for an out-of-town official engagement and so spent the night in his own quarters.

Their long-standing friend, Gina Kennard, told me, 'At Balmoral that year – after that man got into her bedroom – the Queen began snapping at Philip. She was really quite snappy with him. Which was unusual for her. Not for him, of course. He's always been a bit snappy. But the man getting into her room was horrid.' It was. The intrusion occurred at around 7:15 a.m. on 9 July 1982. The Queen pressed the alarm button by her bed, but her overnight police guard had gone off duty at 6:00 a.m. and her footman was out walking the corgis. The intruder simply wandered in, wholly unhindered, drew the curtains and sat on the bed. He wanted to share his troubles with Her Majesty. (Later, he told police he had planned to cut his wrists in front of the Queen.) Eventually, when he asked for a cigarette, the Queen managed to manoeuvre him out of the bedroom and the alarm was raised. The incident prompted a review of Palace security, which was, in the words of the intruder himself, 'diabolical'. This was not Fagan's first dawn raid on the Palace: on a previous occasion, he had not got as far as Her Majesty's bedroom, but he had found his way to the state apartments, tried out the thrones for size and stolen a bottle of wine.

The Home Secretary at the time was Willie Whitelaw. Ultimately, he was responsible for the Metropolitan Police and the Queen's security. He offered his resignation. It was declined. Some years later, he told me, his eyes brimming with tears, 'I felt utterly ashamed, utterly miserable. It was the worst moment of my public life.' It must have been one of the most alarming moments of the Queen's life, too. The year before, a disturbed young man in his late teens, Marcus Simon Sarjeant, had fired six blank shots at her as she rode down the Mall to the Trooping the Colour ceremony. Now, another disturbed individual, barefoot, dripping blood and holding a broken ashtray, was standing by her bedside. Her calm response was extraordinary – and indicative. Once Fagan had been taken away by the police, Her Majesty got dressed and carried on with her day's duties – starting with an investiture scheduled for 11:00 a.m. Later, when people expressed their admiration for her remarkable composure under the circumstances, her stock reply was: 'You seem to forget that I spend most of my time meeting complete strangers.'

Throughout her reign she took the possibility of being in the firing line in her stride. At Christmas 2021, when the Queen was ninety-five and, because of concerns over the spread of a Covid variant, spending Christmas at Windsor rather than Sandringham, a masked and hooded intruder wielding a cross-bow – a twenty-year-old from Southampton, Jaswant Singh Chail – approached a police officer in the grounds of Windsor Castle and announced he had come 'to kill the Queen'. He was arrested and charged under the 1842 Treason Act. When the Queen was told about the incident, she said to one of her team in the Windsor Covid 'bubble', 'Yes, well, that would have put a dampener on Christmas, wouldn't it?'

Back in May 1948, Princess Elizabeth and the Duke of Edinburgh undertook their first official foreign assignment: a four-day visit to Paris, a trip designed – as had been the King and Queen's French tour in 1939 – to burnish the *entente cordiale*. It did the trick. The programme was packed and predictable: Versailles, Fontainebleau, a night at the Opéra, a trip down the Seine. There were lunches, dinners, receptions and a banquet – the stuff of every royal tour. The French press was charmed: the Princess was beautiful, the Duke was handsome, and they both spoke surprisingly good French – he, thanks to his decade in Paris as a child; she, thanks to the tutoring of Antoinette de Bellaigue. 'In four hectic days,' Jock Colville noted, with satisfaction, 'Princess Elizabeth had conquered Paris.' Forty years before the phrase 'the Diana effect' became common currency, and seventy before the Duchess of Cambridge became a tabloid darling, Colville watched Elizabeth going about her business and described what amounted to the same phenomenon: 'Quite mysteriously, a visit by a young princess with beautiful blue eyes and a superb natural complexion brought gleams of radiant sunshine into the dingiest streets of the dreariest cities. Princes who do their duty are respected, beautiful Princesses have an in-built advantage over their male counterparts.'

One of the things that saddened – and worried – the Queen and Prince Philip about Diana, Princess of Wales, was not that she was popular, but that she allowed her popularity to go to her head. They both saw, with much relief, that the same thing never happened to Catherine. Elizabeth was adored once, too – as much as Diana was, as much as Catherine is, perhaps even more so. In the late 1940s and early 1950s, in Britain, in France, in countries around the world, thousands – tens of thousands, sometimes *hundreds* of thousands – turned out to cheer her. Once upon a time, Philip and Elizabeth were seen – and talked about – and written up – as characters from a fairy tale. The difference between them and Princess Diana is that they did not take it personally. When I discussed this with the Duke of Edinburgh in his library at Buckingham Palace, he said to me, 'You won't remember this, but in the first years of the Queen's reign, the level of adulation – you wouldn't believe it. You really wouldn't. It could have been corroding. It would have been very easy to play to the gallery, but I took a conscious decision not to do that. Safer not to be too popular. You can't fall too far.'

Years later, when Catherine Middleton came along as a potential bride for his grandson, Prince William, the Duke of Edinburgh was, he told me, 'relieved to find her such a level-headed girl'. 'If you believe the attention is for you personally,' he warned, 'you're going to end up in trouble. The attention is for your role, what you do, what you're supporting. It isn't for you as an individual. You are not a celebrity. You are representing the royal family. That's all. Don't look at the camera. The Queen never looks at the camera. Never. Look at who you're talking to. Look at what you've come to see. Diana looked at the camera.'

I have been on walkabout with the Duchess of Cambridge. She does not look at the camera. Whenever she is interviewed, Catherine talks about the matter in hand, never about herself. By contrast, Meghan, in 2019, when on her first tour to Africa with Prince Harry, was asked on camera how she was feeling. It was not long after her first baby had been born and, looking vulnerable and close to tears, the Duchess of Sussex replied, 'Thank you for asking because not many people have asked if I'm okay . . .' Clearly unhappy and feeling overwhelmed by aspects of her new royal life, she explained, 'Any woman, especially when they're pregnant, you're really vulnerable, and so that was made really challenging . . . And then when you have a newborn, you know. And especially as a woman, it's a lot. So you add this on top of just trying to be a new mom or trying to be a newly-wed, it's um . . . yeah . . .' Tom Bradby, the interviewer from ITN, then suggested that it 'would be fair' to say therefore that she was 'not really okay, as in it's really been a struggle.' 'Yes,' answered Meghan, with a pained expression, before adding that she was thankful to have both her husband and her son by her side.

Many would say that if that was how she was feeling, she was right to share her unhappiness and vulnerability on camera – and salute her for her courage and her honesty. Others would argue that sharing her feelings so emotionally was a mistake, because in doing so she, Meghan, suddenly became the centre of the story, and, in terms of coverage, all the good work that she and Harry had been doing in Africa, the people they had been meeting, the causes they had been supporting, were all, instantly, eclipsed. 'Don't talk about yourself' was the Duke of Edinburgh's golden rule. Elizabeth II, of course, never gave a formal interview, but in public speeches and in private conversation she very rarely talked about herself. 'She just doesn't,' said her husband, 'and she is the happier for it.' As we shall see, on the one occasion she did share her private feelings with the world – in her *annus horribilis* speech in 1992 – because it was such an unusual occurrence, its impact was considerable and intended.

Back in 1948, the four-day trip to Paris was the Edinburghs' first overseas triumph. As a diplomatic and public relations exercise, it was an unqualified success. At a personal level, it was hell – but they didn't let on. If they had, that would have been the story. The weather in France was unbearable: it was the hottest Whitsun weekend of the century. The tour schedule was alarmingly crowded: the couple were allowed one night off – 'a private evening' – and it was not a success. According to Jock Colville: 'We went to a most select three-star restaurant; the French had been turned out, so we found a table, just a party of us all alone in this vast restaurant. Prince Philip spotted a round hole in a table just opposite us, through which the lens of a camera was poking. He was naturally in a frightful rage. We went on to a night club, again the French all turned out. One of the most appalling evenings I have ever spent. Everybody dressed up to the nines – nobody in either place – except the lens.'

Philip was in a rage and he had an upset stomach. Rumour had it that the kitchens at the British Embassy were to blame. Elizabeth stayed calm, of course. 'She is always calm,' according to her childhood friend, Sonia Berry. 'She might get annoyed about something, but as a rule she stays on an even keel. I have never seen her lose her temper.' Elizabeth stayed calm, but she, too, felt a little queasy. Perhaps she felt 'really vulnerable'. She had cause: she was three months pregnant.

Back in London, in June, she wrote to her cousin, Diana Bowes-Lyon: 'Life is very busy at the moment, but after this month I'm taking a rest for the baby's sake. I am so excited about it and I really can't believe it's true.'

CHAPTER FIFTEEN

Charles Philip Arthur George

'Her Royal Highness the Princess Elizabeth, Duchess of Edinburgh, was safely delivered of a Prince at 9:14 o'clock this evening. Her Royal Highness and the infant Prince are both doing well.'

On Sunday 14 November 1948, at a little after 11:00 p.m., Commander Richard Colville RN – a cousin of Jock Colville's, but an older man and less subtle, who had joined the Palace as Press Secretary to the King the year before – took the formal announcement, written out in his own neat hand, and, accompanied by Jock, scrunched his way across the Buckingham Palace courtyard to fix it to the railings. The waiting crowd – some three thousand strong – greeted the news with sustained cheers and an impromptu chorus of 'For he's a jolly good fellow.'

By daybreak, word had spread across the nation – and the world. In the United States, radio programmes were interrupted with the news. In South Africa and India, in Kenya and Canada, in Australia and New Zealand, guns were fired, bells were rung, bonfires were lit. In the streets of London, newsvendors cried, 'It's a boy!' and across the mountain ranges of Wales a chain of beacons was lit. On the high seas, the ships of the Royal Navy – every one of them – put out more flags and, on the River Thames, the humblest boats were festooned with celebratory bunting. In homes, and pubs and clubs and churches, there was – in a way that seems incredible to us now – genuine rejoicing. At Westminster Abbey, the bells rang out with a peal of five thousand changes. In the chamber of the House of Commons, the prime minister, Clement Attlee, on behalf of a grateful nation, saluted the virtues of the constitutional monarchy 'which have won the hearts of the people' and spoke of the 'great responsibilities' that would one day settle on the shoulders of the infant prince. The Leader of the Opposition, Winston Churchill, now seventy-four, rose to the occasion with a typical rhetorical flourish:

> Our ancient monarchy renders inestimable services to our country and to all the British Empire and Commonwealth of Nations. Above the ebb and flow of party strife, the rise and fall of ministries and individuals, the changes of public opinion and fortune, the British monarchy presides ancient, calm and supreme within its functions, over all the treasures that have been saved from the past and all the glories that we write in the annals of our country. Our thoughts go out to the mother and father and, in a special way, to the little prince, now born into this world of strife and storm.

And the little prince was a little *prince*. He might not have been. Under the then most recent rules governing royal status – George V's Letters Patent of 1917 – only grandchildren of the monarch in the *male* line could be styled HRH, which is why Princess Anne's children aren't HRHs, or a prince and princess, while Prince Andrew's offspring are Their Royal Highnesses Princess Beatrice and Princess Eugenie. According to the 1917 ruling as it stood, the child of the Duke of Edinburgh and Princess Elizabeth would have been neither an HRH nor a Prince: if male, he would have had the

Duke of Edinburgh's secondary title – Earl of Merioneth – as a courtesy title; if female, she would have been styled simply Lady whatever Mountbatten. Naturally, George VI wanted the heir to his heir to be properly royal, so he adjusted the rules to ensure that all his daughter's issue would be both HRH and Prince or Princess from birth.

At the moment of the little prince's birth, his father was in the Buckingham Palace squash court, having a game with his friend and equerry, Mike Parker. Philip and Parker had had more than one game that evening – and a swim in the Palace pool. Princess Elizabeth's confinement – in the Palace Buhl Room, specially converted into a well-equipped surgery – had been a painfully long one. The King's secretary, Tommy Lascelles, brought the good news hotfoot from the Buhl Room to the squash court. Philip raced back, with Lascelles and Parker trailing, on the way picking up the carnations and champagne he had at the ready, and went in to congratulate his young wife and admire his new son. 'It takes a man to have a son!' was the signal Philip sent to Parker when Parker's first child was born. Parker told me, 'Philip was thrilled to have a son. He was over the moon. Absolutely delighted.' That same night Philip sent a telegram bearing the glad tidings to his mother in Greece.

Princess Alice, now aged sixty-three, had recently moved to the Greek island of Tinos. She planned, she told her family, to 'withdraw from the world' and found 'a religious sisterhood of Martha & Mary', training girls to become nursing sisters. She was not a nun herself, but she dressed as one, and rose early every morning to attend to her devotions. Prince Philip said, in a typically matter-of-fact way, 'Wearing the habit meant that she did not have to worry about clothes or getting her hair done.' She led a life of comparative simplicity, in a modest house, where the electricity supply was erratic and there was no telephone. She was thrilled to receive her son's telegram. She wrote to him at once: 'I think of you so much with a sweet baby of your own, of your joy & the interest you will take in all his little doings. How fascinating nature is, but how one has to pay for it in the anxious trying hours of the confinement.'

Princess Elizabeth recovered quickly from her confinement. She spent ten days in bed recuperating (as new mothers were encouraged to do in those days) and breast-fed her son from the start. The Princess wrote to her former music teacher: 'The baby is very sweet and we are enormously proud of him. He has an interesting pair of hands for a baby. They are rather large, but with fine long fingers quite unlike mine and certainly unlike his father's. It will be interesting to see what they become. I still find it hard to believe I have a baby of my own!'

The first cot-side report to reach the public came from one of Elizabeth's aunts, her mother's younger sister, Rose, by now Countess Granville, who told a gathering of girl guides in Northern Ireland that the new mother was 'wonderfully well and radiantly happy' and the new prince 'could not be more angelic looking': 'He is golden-haired and has the most beautiful complexion, as well as amazingly delicate features for so young a baby . . . The Queen says that she thinks the baby is like his mother, but the Duke is quite certain that the baby is very like himself.' After a few days, in small clusters, palace servants were allowed to gather round the royal crib ('done up in buttercup yellow silk, with lace trimmings', according to Crawfie: 'The Royal Family do not observe the old tradition of pink and blue') and coo and ooh and ah at the bonny little prince, who had weighed in at a satisfactory 7lb 6oz. John Dean described the infant as 'a tiny red-faced bundle, either hairless or so fair as to appear so.' Crawfie thought that, like all royal babies in her experience, he bore a strong resemblance to George V, with 'an absurdly mature look, and ridges under his eyes'.

After the initial excitement of the royal birth – 4,000 congratulatory telegrams were received at Buckingham Palace within twenty-four hours of the news first breaking, closely followed by an avalanche of cards, letters, flowers, and assorted gifts, from teddy bears to hand-knitted bootees – a macabre rumour started. Around the land the whisper went: something is wrong with the child: he is disfigured, he might not live. Crawfie later wrote, 'The stories that went around at that time about him were entirely without foundation of any kind.' Crawfie believed the root cause of the stories was the royal family's own obsession with privacy, what she called a 'strange campaign of secrecy': 'For a long time no pictures were issued, and even the household did not know what the baby's names were to be.'

There was a news vacuum and on the streets it was filled with wild speculation. The baby might be 'healthy and strong, and beautifully made,' as Crawfie insisted, 'with a flawless, silky skin', but, if so, why not show him off to the world? And why not name him? The answer to both questions was a simple desire on the part of the Princess for privacy. Just as fifty years later, on the death of Diana, Princess of Wales, the Queen's first instinct was to shield her grandsons, protect their privacy and keep her own counsel, so, in November 1948, on the birth of Prince Charles, Princess Elizabeth instinctively wanted to guard her baby son's privacy. There would be photographs – of course – and the baby's names would be made known – naturally – but all in good time . . . Why should the Heiress Presumptive and her little boy have to dance at once to the public's tune?

Throughout her life the Queen fulfilled her public duty conscientiously and with complete commitment, and hoped, as a consequence, to be allowed some private space for her private life. Do we really need to know how the infant prince took to the breast (quite well, apparently), or whether and when he was circumcised (yes, on 20 December 1948: Dr Jacob Snowman performed the operation)? Of course, we don't need to know. It is none of our business. And yet, we are curious.

From the birth of her son to the end of her life, Elizabeth II did her best to maintain a degree of privacy for herself and her children. It was not easy. Hugh Dalton, the Labour MP and sometime Chancellor of the Exchequer, wrote in his diary in the week that Prince Charles was born: 'If this boy ever comes to the throne . . . it will be a very different Commonwealth and country he will rule over.' Dalton was prescient. Elizabeth had been born in the reign of George V, King-Emperor. She grew up in an age of deference and discretion, when bowing and curtseying to royalty was automatic, when you did not speak to a royal unless first spoken to, when her uncle David could conduct an open affair with a married divorcee and know that it would go unreported by a self-denying press. The world during Elizabeth II's lifetime changed. The Empire vanished, deference disappeared and newspapers printed what they chose. When Edward VIII and his girlfriend, on holiday together, swam naked off the coast of Albania, there were no *paparazzi* hiding on the hillside. When, half a century later, the Duchess of York, on holiday with her boyfriend in the South of France, appeared topless by their swimming pool, the revealing photographs, taken with telephoto lenses from the adjacent hillside, appeared on front pages in Britain and around the world. In the summer of 2012, when the Duke and Duchess of Cambridge were holidaying at the Château d'Autet, near Veins in Provence, another photographer with a telephoto lens managed to take a series of pictures of Prince William's wife, Catherine, topless – and holding a cigarette. The French edition of the magazine *Closer* splashed three of the photographs on its cover and, on the inside pages, published more pictures – with captions to match: 'On the terrace of Château d'Autet, Kate has decided to release the pressure, to get rid of convention, to free herself from the protocol, but also to get rid of her bikini top! At the time of feminist struggles, militants were burning their bras. Kate doesn't wear hers, and that's her absolute right. Exulted by the fragrance of lavender from the neighbouring fields, Kate takes advantage of those delicious moments of doing nothing and offers her breasts to the soft caress of the Provence sun.'

For Princess Elizabeth, back in 1948, the desire for privacy was more than a matter of personal preference and natural reticence. It was a matter of policy. Famously, as we know, in 1867, Walter Bagehot, writing about the role of the monarchy in *The English Constitution,* declared: 'We must not let daylight in upon the magic.' Bagehot believed that sustaining the mystique of the monarchy was essential to its authority – and survival. Elizabeth had studied Bagehot, and Commander Colville, who was the Palace press secretary from 1947 until 1968, believed in Bagehot's maxim completely. When Colville got the job he had no experience of press relations: he had been in the Navy for twenty-two years. For the next twenty-one years he dealt with the press in a manner that suggested that relations with them were the very last thing that either he or the royal family desired.

According to Kenneth Rose, a journalist and biographer who dealt with him on a regular basis, Commander Colville did not discriminate between hacks: 'All were made to feel that their questions were impertinent if not downright vulgar.' Colville would supply information about the sovereign's public engagements, and that was all. In his view, as he explained to the Press Council, the Queen was 'entitled to expect that her family will attain the privacy at home which all other families are entitled to enjoy'. Somewhat impertinently, the Press Council begged to differ, maintaining that 'the private lives of public men and women, especially royal persons, have always been the subject of natural curiosity. That is one of the consequences of fame or eminence or sincere national affection. Everything therefore that touches the Crown is of public interest or concern.'

All their adult lives, Elizabeth and Philip remained wary of the press. In private the Queen was easy company and quite unselfconscious. In the company of journalists or broadcasters she was always on her guard. She was encouraged to be wary of them by Prince Philip. 'If I'm doing something I care about,' he once said to me, 'I really hope the press won't come along too, because I know they'll only ruin it.' When I reminded him that he was the member of the royal family who, in the 1950s, first talked to the press, giving a series of newspaper, radio and television interviews, he said, 'Yes, I made a conscious decision to talk to the media – but not about me, only about what I'm doing, what I'm supporting.' When I told him that, fifty years on, that was no longer enough, that the modern media need something more sexy, they need 'personalities', he nodded. 'Yes,' he said, with a sigh, 'the press have turned us into a soap opera.'

In 1948, the soap opera had something of the fairy tale about it. A month and a day after the royal birth came the royal christening. On the morning of Wednesday 15 December, in the White and Gold Music Room at Buckingham Palace, wearing the flowing silk and lace christening robe his mother had worn for her christening twenty-two years before, the infant prince was baptised into the Church of England and named Charles Philip Arthur George. His godparents included the King, Queen Mary, the King of Norway, Prince George of Greece, the Dowager Marchioness of Milford Haven, Elizabeth's uncle, David Bowes-Lyon, and Dickie's daughter, Patricia Brabourne. Patricia told me that she thought Philip and Elizabeth chose 'Charles' as a name simply because they liked it. Boy Browning was one of those who felt the name was 'bad news', given the precedents of Charles I and II, to say nothing of the unhappy fate that befell Charles Stuart, 'Bonnie Prince Charlie'. Princess Margaret, however, was delighted with the choice of name, explaining that henceforward she would be known as 'Charley's Aunt', 'probably my finest title'.

After lunch, and the taking of the formal photographs (including a fine study of the sleeping prince in the crisply starched arms of his nurse), Queen Mary invited the assembled company to gather round Queen Victoria's photo albums to decide who among his forebears the new prince most closely resembled. She decided, without doubt, it was Prince Albert. Queen Mary took the keenest interest in family history. Her christening gift was a silver cup and cover given by George III to a godson in 1780, 'so that', she noted in her diary, with allowable satisfaction, 'I gave a present from my great-grandfather to my great grandson 168 years later.' Queen Mary entertained few doubts about her family's place in history. Baby Charles's other great-grandmother, Victoria Milford Haven, was more circumspect. She wrote to Dickie of her 'latest & important great-grandson': 'Let us hope he may live in a more peaceable & prosperous time than we & live to be some sort of reigning king.'

Alice did not attend the christening, but she received news of her new grandson's progress from other members of the family. She got a full report from her younger sister Louise, the Queen of Sweden, which she shared with Dickie:

She says that Lilibet was looking so well & fresh, a good recovery after a hard time she had, 30 hours in all. The baby is sweet with a well-shaped head, an oval face & a little bit of fair fluff of hair. She says he is like Philip, but Marina says he is like Lilibet, so you can choose. I am so happy for Philip for he adores children & also small babies. He carries it about himself quite professionally to the nurse's amusement.

By every account, Prince Philip was especially good with babies and small children. 'They like him and he likes them,' is what Countess Mountbatten told me. 'No question about it, Philip was a very good father to his children when they were young.' According to Lady Kennard, 'He was a wonderful parent. He played with his children, he read them stories, he took them fishing, he was very involved. I remember we stayed with them in Scotland when Charles must have been about one. The three of them were so happy together, easy and relaxed. Philip has been marvellous with his grandchildren, too. He's just good with the little ones.' In the summer of 2002, when the prime minister, Tony Blair, and his wife, Cherie Booth, went to stay at Balmoral, Philip took a special shine to the Blairs' two-year-old son, Leo. Proudly, Leo sang the whole first verse of the National Anthem to Philip and Philip responded happily by singing Leo the second verse. Cherie Blair told me, 'I have to say that both the Queen and Prince Philip are really, really good with little children. You couldn't fault them.' (Whether you could fault Mrs Blair is another matter. I was told, on good authority, that when the Queen came to see Leo in the nursery at Balmoral, Mrs Blair had instructed her nanny not to curtsy to Her Majesty.)

Philip and Lilibet were very happy with their new baby. Parenthood suited them. According to all of their friends to whom I have spoken – friends who knew them in the 1940s and 1950s – the first few years of their marriage were, in many ways, the happiest. 'Perhaps inevitably,' Gina Kennard said to me, 'Princess Elizabeth was not yet Queen, Philip was still in the Navy. They were young, they were relatively carefree.' And they were cosseted. They were devoted to little Prince Charles, but they did not have to tend to him unaided. He had two Scottish nurses in constant attendance: Helen Lightbody, who arrived on the recommendation of the Duchess of Gloucester, whose sons she had looked after, and Mabel Anderson, who placed an advertisement in a nursing journal and was amazed to find herself invited to Buckingham Palace for an interview with the Princess.

Before Charles was born, Elizabeth had declared, 'I'm going to be the child's mother, not the nurses.' Well, she was – but, inevitably, because she was a princess as well as a mother, because 'royal duty' called and all her life Elizabeth has made answering the call of royal duty her first priority, and because it was the way of her class and her time, much of the nitty-gritty of childcare was left to Mrs Lightbody and Miss Anderson. (Both nurses were maiden ladies. Because Helen Lightbody was the more senior, she was given the courtesy title of 'Mrs' as Alah Knight had been in her day.) Until Clarence House was ready for the family to move in to in July 1949, the baby lived and was looked after in the country, at Windlesham Moor, only seeing his parents when they came down from London at weekends. The breast-feeding had stopped in January, when Charles was not quite two months old. Elizabeth had contracted measles and the doctors advised that, until she was better, mother and child should stay apart.

The Edinburghs rented Windlesham Moor from a Mrs Warwick Bryant. It had useful grounds – fifty acres and a fine garden noted for its azaleas – but the house itself – two storeys, five bedrooms, four reception rooms, plus staff quarters – was by no means a mansion. According to John Dean, Philip was particularly happy there: 'I believe that in those early days the Duke was uneasy in the atmosphere of the Palace with its formalities, and that this heightened his pleasure in having a country home that was so different.' Clarence House, of course, was grander, but, again according to Dean, Philip made it 'his own'. The Duke, reported the valet, loved 'home-making' and was particularly keen on every kind of new-fangled labour-saving device. The facilities for the staff were 'wonderful', said Dean, 'as near ideal as could possibly be imagined.' Even so, the turnover in the ranks of the junior members of the household was quite high. The hours were long – when the royals were in residence, staff got just one half-day a week free and alternate Sundays off – and the wages were modest. The Edinburghs were not extravagant.

The Princess was a 'considerate employer', according to Dean, concerned about the health and welfare of her staff, but, overall, the Duke was in charge, the undoubted captain of the domestic ship, 'pleasant and courteous to servants', but quite demanding, and liable to speak his mind 'in naval fashion'. When the Duke called Dean 'a stupid clot', master and servant did not speak to each other for several days. Paul Burrell, who first went to work at Buckingham Palace as an under-butler in the 1970s and later became one of the personal footmen to the Queen, before going to work for the Prince and Princess of Wales, told me of the time when, as butler to Diana, he and his mistress were not on speaking terms for a matter of *weeks*. Years before Meghan Markle, as the new Duchess of Sussex, was accused of 'bullying behaviour' by royal staff members, more than one royal servant reported being 'barked at' by the Duke of Edinburgh and Paul Burrell gave a hair-raising account of a book being thrown in his direction by a ranting, screaming and foot-stamping Prince of Wales, who, minutes later, apologised shame-facedly, only to be told by Burrell, as he picked up the missile from the floor, 'If you can't vent your feelings on me, Your Royal Highness, who can you vent them on?'

No one ever accused the Queen of that kind of behaviour. John Dean, the Duke of Edinburgh's valet in the early years of the royal marriage, did not find Philip altogether easy to work for. 'He is difficult to dress,' he complained, 'because he's not interested in clothes and is set on his own ideas – he wears suede shoes with evening dress and he simply cannot tie a tie.' The Princess, in her dressing-room, would hear her husband and his valet arguing next door. 'Listen to them, Bobo,' she would say to her own, ever-present dresser, 'they're just like Papa and Jerram [the King's valet]. Only sometimes I think they're worse.'

In fact, the Edinburgh household was a contented one. At Windlesham Moor, Mr Huggett, the head gardener, and an ex-Guardsman, playfully encouraged the Princess to take an interest in his team's handiwork, saying, 'Ma'am, from one Grenadier to another, I think you ought to come round the garden after church,' while Philip encouraged general team spirit by getting the staff of all ranks to come together to play cricket on summer Sunday afternoons. At Clarence House, when films were shown in the Edinburghs' home cinema, the members of staff were invited to join the guests for the show. In the staff sitting-room at Clarence House, there was even a television set.

In 1949, there were very few households in Britain that could boast of having a television set, fewer still that could boast of having two. In an age of austerity, the Edinburghs wanted for nothing. Their country house was thoroughly comfortable; their town house was unostentatiously palatial. The high-ceilinged reception rooms were filled with elegant eighteenth-century furniture. The Princess's bedroom was freshly decorated in pink and blue (with a crowned canopy over the royal bed); the Duke's bedroom and bathroom featured light wood panelling, red furnishings, and framed photographs of the ships in which he had served; Prince Charles's nursery was all in white, with blue trimmings. The young couple took an active interest in the detail of the refurbishment of Clarence House. The Duke chose and arranged all the pictures, and personally supervised the installation of the kitchen and laundry-room equipment. The Princess helped mix the light lime-green paint for the dining room walls with her own hand and offered her own practical solution to the problem of the lingering smell of paint: 'Put a bucket of hay in there and that'll take it away.'

One of the witnesses to Philip and Elizabeth's early married life that I most enjoyed meeting during my royal researches was John Gibson. He began his working life as a kitchen porter at Buckingham Palace in 1946. He went on to train as a footman and observed the romance between Philip and Elizabeth as it blossomed. Before the wedding, when Philip came to Sandringham to stay, John noticed that Philip's socks needed darning and that he had to borrow a tie from one of the valets. When Prince Charles was born, in November 1948, John found himself working temporarily in Winston Churchill's household. John told me: 'When I heard the news on the radio I went in to tell Mr Churchill and he jumped up in the air and gave three cheers. He was over the moon for the Princess. He ran round the room waving his hands above his head and shouting, "Hooray! It's marvellous news!" Tell everybody to come in, John. And bring the champagne. We must toast the heir to the throne.'

Two months after Charles was born, John Gibson returned to royal service as 'nursery footman' at Windlesham Moor. 'I had sole responsibility for the royal pram,' he told me proudly. He assured me that Princess Elizabeth was 'very hands-on' with Charles, 'like a real mother – not a princess'. He could not fault the young royal couple: 'When they were on their own it was a very simple life. They were quite normal people really. They were waited on hand and foot obviously, but they sat at the table and they had a natter about what was going on in the day.' Princess Elizabeth loved lemon and sugar pancakes and chocolate cake. Much of the domestic conversation overheard by John related to home-making. 'They couldn't wait to get into their new home at Clarence House. They talked about it all the time. "I think Grandma is giving me a nice sideboard. I'm sure she is." Grandma was Queen Mary, of course.'

When John Dean, Philip's valet, had a day off, John Gibson would take the young Duke of Edinburgh his early morning tea. Philip would look in on Elizabeth in her intercommunicating room and tease her for not being out of bed yet. When they were up at Birkhall in Scotland, Philip and Elizabeth would drive over to Balmoral with the staff piled into the back of the shooting-brake. 'He'd drive like mad over the country roads,' according to John Gibson. '"Philip, Philip, slow down for God's sake, slow down, you're killing all the rabbits," she said. "What's the matter with you?"'

These were the golden years. Elizabeth conceived her second child towards the end of 1949. Princess Anne Elizabeth Alice Louise was born at Clarence House at 11:50 a.m. on Tuesday 15 August 1950. Elizabeth reported to a friend: 'Both Philip and I are very thrilled about the new baby and we only hope that Charles will take kindly to it. He has only seen Fortune Euston's baby at close quarters and he then tried to pull her toes off and poke her eyes out, all of which she took very kindly, having a brother of two who presumably did the same.'

Elizabeth and Philip were proud parents and happy ones. They were good parents, too. That is certainly the impression I got, speaking to, say, the Duchess of Grafton (Fortune Euston, as was) or Countess Mountbatten (one of Prince Charles's godmothers), but it is not the impression you will have gained if you have read any of the many books that have touched on the matter. Every one of them – without exception, I think – portrays Elizabeth as a well-intentioned but somewhat distant mother and Philip as a forbidding, formidable and usually absent father. Sarah Bradford, for example, in her widely acclaimed portrait of the Queen, says of the young mother's relationship with baby Charles: 'Elizabeth, although fond of him, was not particularly maternal.' Anthony Holden, in his acclaimed biography of Charles, describes the young children's routine at Clarence House like this:

The royal nursery settled into a rigid daily routine in the care of the two nannies, 'Mrs' Lightbody and Miss Anderson. Charles and Anne were got up each day at 7 a.m. sharp, dressed, fed and played with in the nursery until nine, when they enjoyed a statutory half-hour with their mother. They rarely saw her again until tea-time, when Elizabeth would try to clear two hours in her day. She liked to bath the children herself when her schedule permitted, after which they were dressed up again to be introduced to distinguished visitors. Even before his third birthday, Charles had learnt to bow before offering his cheek for a kiss from 'Gan-Gan', Queen Mary, and not to sit down in the presence of his grandfather. It was a formidable introduction to the complexities of any child's life – basking but sporadically, and unpredictably, in the attentions of his mother, with his father all but a stranger. Already a pattern was being set that would come to haunt Charles's life even in adulthood, even at times of his greatest need.

The tone and content of this account of nursery life at Clarence House is accepted as a reflection of the truth by nearly one and all – including Prince Charles who, in 1994, allowed his authorised biographer, Jonathan Dimbleby, to reveal that the Prince felt 'emotionally estranged' from his parents and, all his life, had yearned for the kind of affection that, in his view, they were 'unable or unwilling to offer'. Charles's strictures hurt his parents. The Queen, of course, said nothing, but I know – because Prince Philip told me – that it 'saddened' her. It made the Duke 'bloody angry', both because he reckoned it was unfair and because he thought it was 'bloody stupid' of the Prince of Wales to air his grievances in public. All that Prince Philip would say to me on the record about his and his wife's parenting skills was, 'We did our best.'

They certainly did do their best by their own lights, and by the standards of their class and generation, but the sad truth is that for too many years Prince Charles and his father weren't on the same wavelength. The Duke of Edinburgh thought his son self-indulgent. He felt he spent too much time thinking about himself, feeling sorry for himself, brooding about how tough it was to be the Prince of Wales. Philip thought Charles a 'whinger' and at times found it difficult to hide his irritation with the boy. I often heard the father being negative about the son, but I heard him being positive, too. Prince Philip loved his son and admired much of what he achieved with ventures like the Prince's Trust, but he never told him.

When the Duke of Edinburgh died, I sent the Prince of Wales a letter of condolence and told him how I hoped he knew how much his father had loved and admired him. I told him about a conversation I had had with Patricia Mountbatten

(Philip's cousin, Charles's godmother) in which she said to me, 'He loves him so much, but he won't tell him. I wonder if he's ever told him.' I don't think Philip ever told his son he loved him. I know Philip's father never told him he loved him. 'I wouldn't have expected him to,' the Duke of Edinburgh said to me. 'It wasn't necessary.'

Elizabeth saw her young children as much as any aristocratic mother of her generation and more, perhaps, than many busy working mothers today. And Philip, on the evidence of those who witnessed him in action as a young father in the late 1940s and early 1950s, far from being distant and forbidding, was hands-on and loving – more so than many of his stiff-upper-lip, Eton-educated, Guards officer contemporaries. The royal couple did not spend as much time with their children as they might have liked for the simple reason that, as well as being parents, Elizabeth was Heiress Presumptive to an ailing King and Philip was a serving officer in the Royal Navy.

George VI was fifty-three when Prince Charles was born in November 1948. He looked much older. In the preceding eighteen months he had lost seventeen pounds in weight. He was, he said, 'in discomfort most of the time', suffering from numbness and cramp in his feet and legs. He carried on with his duties – standing, in considerable pain, at the Remembrance Day service at the Cenotaph in Whitehall and reviewing the Territorial Army in Hyde Park – but summoned his doctors. Two days before Charles's birth, he was diagnosed as suffering from arteriosclerosis, a condition brought on by his chronic smoking. Two days after the birth, he agreed, reluctantly, to postpone a planned tour of Australia and New Zealand. In March 1949, he underwent an operation to help regulate the blood supply to his legs, and felt much better. Because of the continuing danger of a sudden thrombosis, he was advised to reduce his commitments, to rest more and worry less. He did his best. He promised his mother that he was trying to 'worry less about political matters' – he was an inveterate worrier – and avoid the bursts of bad-temper – his notorious 'gnashes' – that were brought on by frustration and irritation. 'Since he has become a recognised invalid,' a courtier told Harold Nicolson, 'he is as sweet and patient as can be.'

As the King curtailed his workload, so the pressures on the young princess increased. 'It was inevitable,' Prince Philip said to me. 'You've got to remember that the royal family then was just the four of them: the King and the Queen and the two Princesses. It's very different now. Now we have to avoid tripping over one another, so Charles goes off and does the arts, Anne does the prisons, and so on. Then, there was just the four of them – and the Duke of Gloucester – for everything. Because of the King's health, it was inevitable that we did more. There was no choice.'

But there were compensations. As well as dutiful days, there were glamorous nights. To mark Elizabeth's twenty-third birthday in April 1949, they went to see Laurence Olivier and Vivien Leigh in *The School for Scandal* at the New Theatre and then went on for supper and dancing with the Oliviers at the Café de Paris off Leicester Square. The American entertainer, Danny Kaye, then the toast of the town, danced attendance on them – literally. (John Dean reported watching the star of *The Court Jester* 'capering round Princess Elizabeth' at Windlesham Moor.)

They consorted with stars of stage and screen (as royalty has often done) and they had a lot of fun, too, in their own way with their own set. Gina Kennard told me, 'I remember lots of laughter, lots of old-fashioned gaiety. Country weekends. Shooting – not hunting in Philip's case. We used to pot at rabbits. Serious shooting, too, of course. Shoot suppers. Hunt balls. Proper house parties. With tennis. And croquet. And dancing. They are both wonderful dancers. You should have seen Philip's samba! And games. Sardines. Hunt the Thimble. So much fun.' And some dressing-up, too. At the American ambassador's fancy-dress ball, Philip came as a waiter and Elizabeth as a maid.

In the summer of 1949, the world was an uncertain place. The Cold War was upon us. The Soviet Union was testing the atomic bomb. In China, Shanghai had just fallen to Mao Tse-tung's People's Liberation Army. The British Empire was no longer what it once had been. India and Ireland had become republics. There were race riots in Durban. In Britain, the economy was enfeebled. The Chancellor of the Exchequer spoke of 'the crushing difficulties' faced by the British people as he prepared to devalue the pound sterling by a staggering 30.5 per cent. But at Windsor Castle the champagne still flowed. At the end of Royal Ascot, a royal ball. They danced till dawn. There was magic in the air. In his diary, Chips Channon described the scene:

> The rooms were banked with flowers . . . Windows were open on to the terrace . . . The doors were flung open, and we saw the King and Queen waiting to receive us, side by side: he seemed brown and she, though unfortunately very, very plump, looked magnificent in a white satin semi-crinoline number with the Garter and splendid rubies . . . We walked along a long passage with magnificent Canalettos and Zoffanys, by the dozen, many of which have been rehung and cleaned since the war . . . The King had his foot up on a foot stool to rest, though he seemed quite well and often danced . . . The Edinburghs made a somewhat late appearance (he had been to the Channel Islands or somewhere) and they looked divine. She wore a very high tiara and the Garter – he was in the dark blue

Windsor uniform, also with the Garter. They looked characters out of a fairy tale ... At a quarter to five, [the Queen] told the band to stop; everyone bowed and curtsied to the remaining Royalties and we left, and drove back in the dawn – looking back, the Castle rose romantic in the pink morning light. I was enchanted with the evening.

Philip had boundless energy. He could indeed make a flying visit to the Channel Islands ('or somewhere') and then dance till dawn. Patricia Mountbatten said to me, 'He was a dynamo.' Mike Parker told me, 'He crackled with energy. He made things happen. He made things jump.' As well as fulfilling his naval and his royal duties, he was beginning to take on a range of 'good works' – starting with the presidencies of the London Federation of Boys' Clubs and the National Playing Fields Association. He was not inclined to be a docile figurehead: he wanted to be pro-active and hands-on. Mike Parker said to me: 'He wanted to make a difference and, if necessary, he was ready to make a noise.'

Elizabeth was altogether quieter. She was still quite shy. She didn't have her husband's ability to swing into a room of strangers and talk easily to anybody. She sometimes felt, as they went out on official visits together, that the crowd would prefer to see the Duke than the Princess. She was wrong, of course. She was beautiful and she was the Heiress Presumptive. She knew her duty, and did it conscientiously. Encouraged by Jock Colville, she was now regularly reading Foreign Office telegrams because – as Colville put it to the King's secretary, Tommy Lascelles – they 'would give HRH an idea of world affairs which she cannot possibly get from the newspapers.'

She was also making speeches – speeches drafted by Colville and Lascelles – whose content, when not simply anodyne, reflected the essentially conservative views and values of the Establishment of the day. In October 1949, for example, the young princess and mother, aged twenty-three, addressed a massed meeting of the members of the Mothers' Union in Central Hall, Westminster, and, in her thin, high-pitched voice, deplored the 'current age of growing self-indulgence, of hardening materialism, of falling moral standards' and nailed her colours firmly to the unshakeable, unbreakable matrimonial mast: 'We can have no doubt that divorce and separation are responsible for some of the darkest evils in our society today.'

From first to last, Elizabeth II believed in the value of marriage as set out in the Book of Common Prayer. She saw it as 'an honourable estate, instituted of God', 'not by any to be enterprised, nor taken in hand, unadvisedly, lightly, or wantonly,' and ordained, first, 'for the procreation of children', secondly, 'for a remedy against sin', and, thirdly, 'for the mutual society, help, and comfort, that the one ought to have of the other, both in prosperity and adversity.' The Queen was a traditional Anglican and, she told me, her faith had, 'if anything, deepened over the years,' because experience had taught her 'the sustaining truth and value of the teachings of Christ.' The Duke of Edinburgh told me that 'without question' the greatest personal sadnesses of the Queen's life were the early death of her father and the failure of the marriages of her sister and her own three oldest children.

The Queen was a woman of traditional Christian principles, with high ideals. But she was also a realist (if sometimes a reluctant one) and a pragmatist (encouraged in that by her husband) and, as she put it, 'sometimes you have to accept the inevitable – marriages do break down.'

In 2022, for example, not long before her death, she was particularly sorry to hear that the marriage of the 18th Duke of Norfolk – hereditary Earl Marshal who masterminded her funeral and will be masterminding the coronation of King Charles III – had ultimately ended in divorce. The Queen – whose own coronation was masterminded by the 16th Duke – knew that the 18th Duke had 'tried so hard to make it work'.

'By God we tried,' said the Duke. 'For the sake of the family, and because we are Catholic, we really, really tried everything. It proved completely impossible and we had to move on.' 'At least they tried,' said the Queen to one of her ladies-in-waiting, 'you've got to try – for the sake of the children.' Edward Fitzalan-Howard, and his wife Georgina, were married in 1987 and had five children. They first separated in 2011 and the break-up was said to have been so acrimonious that they both declined the invitation to the wedding of Prince William and Catherine Middleton to avoid having to be together in the same room. By 2016 they were together again, apparently reconciled, in time for the wedding of their eldest son Henry, the future 19th Duke of Norfolk, who one day may be in charge of the coronations of William V and George VII. The Queen was 'delighted' with news of the reconciliation and then 'saddened' a few years later with news of the final divorce. The Queen knew everyone involved in the sad story: when the Duke's marriage failed, as we have seen, he formed a new relationship with Francesca Herbert, former wife of Harry Herbert, son of her racing manager and friend, the 7th Earl of Carnarvon, and brother of Geordie, 8th Earl of Carnarvon – whose first marriage (attended by the Queen and Princess Margaret) also failed. 'There's a lot of divorce around nowadays,' the Queen once said to her friend the Duchess of Grafton. 'I think it's catching.'

When marriages within her own family failed, she felt for all the parties involved, but particularly for the children. As Princess Margaret's children and her own grandchildren all attest, the Queen always went out of her way to give them love, encouragement and support. When the Duke and Duchess of York separated, the Duke of Edinburgh told me he thought Sarah was 'beyond the pale' and he could see 'no point' in continuing to see her. He was 'bemused' that the Yorks continued to live under the same roof after their divorce – he called it 'a funny sort of set-up' – but the Queen welcomed it 'for the sake of the children' and, while Prince Philip steered clear of Sarah, the Queen went out of her way to stay in touch. A lot of people have reservations about the Duke of York and Sarah Ferguson, but most people seem to agree that their daughters are what the Queen called 'good girls, nice girls' so, for all their other failings, the Yorks appear to have been good parents and, naturally, Her Majesty approved of that.

The Queen was instinctively conservative. She believed in the value of a traditional Christian marriage. That said, she was always tolerant of the traditions and beliefs of others and, as the years went by, increasingly accepting of the changing *mores* she saw around her. She was never homophobic, but until she was in her forties acts of male homosexuality were outlawed in the United Kingdom and at the time of her death homosexuality was still considered a sin in a number of countries within the Anglican communion. When she was growing up, her parents had friends who were known homosexuals, but their sexuality was never discussed. Queen Elizabeth, the Queen Mother is said to have said to Noël Coward at a garden party where young guardsmen were on parade and the playwright was apparently eying them with appreciation, 'I wouldn't if I was you, Noël – they count them before they go back in,' but Noël's partner, Graham Payn, told me, 'I'm sure she never said that. He would have told me if she had.' And Margaret Rhodes was emphatic that Queen Elizabeth would never have called out to two of her pages (as legend has it), 'When you two old queens have finished arguing, this old queen is ready for her gin and Dubonnet.'

Elizabeth II's staff regularly included men who happened to be gay – or simply single. Occasionally, according to one of them, Prince Philip made 'sarky comments' at their expense, but the Queen told him to 'shut up', adding 'they're very reliable'. The most reliable was Paul Whybrew, born in 1959, who spent more than forty years in the Queen's service. As Page of the Backstairs he was both an invaluable servant and a good companion, walking the dogs, mixing the drinks, serving the meals, occasionally sitting down with Her Majesty to watch a favourite TV programme. (He would lay out her copy of the *Radio Times* for her, so she could mark up which programmes she particularly didn't want to miss.) It was Whybrew who confronted Michal Fagan when he made his way into the Queen's private quarters in 1982. It was Whybrew who escorted the Queen and Daniel Craig (plus corgis) to their helicopter for the Olympic opening ceremony in 2012. He was recognised by the Queen with various honours over the years and was recognisable to all because of his upright bearing and considerable height. Inside the Palace he was known as 'Tall Paul', both because he was 6' 4" and by contrast with another of the Queen's personal pages, Paul Burrell, who was known as 'Small Paul'.

Paul Burrell entered royal service as a footman in the 1970s, when he was just eighteen. Personable and devoted, he was soon promoted and became one of the Queen's personal pages, alongside Paul Whybrew. Now openly gay, he told me that in his early days working for Her Majesty, she noticed his roving eye. 'I have seen you looking at the steward, Paul,' she said to him, 'You know he's married?' I do, said Paul. 'You should think about getting married, Paul,' said the Queen. 'There are lots of nice girls working here.'

In 1983, Burrell married one of them: Maria Cosgrove, who was working at Buckingham Palace as Prince Philip's maid. According to Paul, the Queen encouraged the match – 'Marriage is a wonderful institution, Paul, it really is – it will make you very happy, especially when the children come along' – and when she heard they planned to honeymoon in Rhyl, said 'Rhyl? Rhyl? We can't have you going to Rhyl. You must go to Balmoral.'

When they got to Balmoral, of course, they had to stay in the staff quarters – where they only had single beds. Nine months later, the first of the Burrells' two sons was born. In 2016, when their children had grown up, Paul and Maria, already separated, were divorced. In 2017 Paul married his new partner, Graham Cooper. Discreetly, a few months after the marriage, a wedding present arrived from Her Majesty. 'The Queen has always been incredibly broad-minded and accepting and generous,' said Paul.

CHAPTER SIXTEEN

Good times, bad times

In October 1949, Philip, now twenty-eight, was appointed First Lieutenant and second-in command of HMS *Chequers*, the Leader of the 1st Destroyer Flotilla in the Mediterranean Fleet at Malta. The appointment was a good one – Philip was the youngest of the 1st Lieutenants in the Flotilla – and reunited him with his old friend from HMS *Valiant*, the future First Sea Lord and Chief of the Defence Staff, Terry Lewin. 'I found him doing the job of Flotilla Gunnery Officer,' Philip recalled. 'We served together until August 1950 in what was a very happy Wardroom, four of whose members were destined to become Flag Officers.'

The posting also brought Philip back into daily contact with his uncle, Dickie Mountbatten, recently translated from Viceroy to Vice-Admiral. Mountbatten, having overseen the end of empire in India, was reconnecting with the Royal Navy in Malta in a relatively humble role as Commander of the First Cruiser Squadron. Philip arrived on his own in Malta and went to stay with Dickie and Edwina at the house they were renting, the Villa Guardamangia. The two men took a little while to get used to one another again. Philip, according to Dickie, was 'very busy showing his independence'. Within three weeks, however, everything was much jollier. 'Philip is right back on 1946 terms with us,' Mountbatten reported in a letter to his daughter, Patricia, 'and we've had a heart-to-heart in which he admitted he was fighting shy of coming under my dominating influence and patronage!' Mountbatten's joy was wholly unconfined when, towards the end of November, Princess Elizabeth came out to Malta to join her husband. 'Lilibet is quite enchanting,' declared Mountbatten, 'and I've lost whatever of my heart is left to spare entirely to her. She dances quite divinely and always wants a Samba when we dance together and has said some very nice remarks about my dancing.'

This is the period in Elizabeth's adult life that can perhaps be described as the most 'normal' – or, at least, 'the least unreal', the most like that of other young couples of Philip's and Elizabeth's generation. He was a serving officer: she was a naval wife. Buckingham Palace was a thousand miles away: the British press left them largely unmolested. 'It was a good time,' according to Philip. 'It was a fabulous time,' according to Mike Parker. 'I think it was their happiest time,' said John Dean: 'They were so relaxed and free, coming and going as they pleased.'

Of course, the very fact that Parker, as equerry, and Dean, as valet, were in Malta as well, is a reminder that, when it comes to royalty, nothing is ever entirely 'normal'. The Princess arrived in Malta comfortably attended: as well as Parker and Dean and the inevitable police officer, there was the ever-faithful Bobo MacDonald and a new lady-in-waiting, Lady Alice Egerton, sixth and youngest daughter of the 4th Earl of Ellesmere and sister of Meg Egerton, who had recently married Jock Colville.

The Edinburghs, plus retinue, stayed with the Mountbattens at the Villa Guardamangia where the indoor help included a butler, a housekeeper, three cooks, six stewards, two house-maids, two cleaning ladies and a valet. 'We are not too grossly overstaffed,' protested Dickie, who was accustomed to living on a fairly grand scale. Clearly, however, he felt a little sheepish about the valet, writing to Edwina: 'I fear you think I'm very spoilt wanting a valet and I do admit I am, but if one is working hard it does help if there is a second man in the house who can look after my clothes.'

John Dean, who was there looking after Philip's clothes, paints a very sunny portrait of the Edinburghs in Malta. There were parties and picnics, swimming expeditions and boat trips. Elizabeth went out for coffee and shopping and visits to the hairdresser with the other young officers' wives. Philip – encouraged by his uncle – took to the polo field and discovered one of the great sporting pleasures of his life.

Princess Anne was conceived in Malta. Prince Charles was just one year old and back in England, being looked after by his nurses and devoted grandparents. The King sent a progress report to Lilibet: 'He is too sweet for words stumping around the room.' Elizabeth had been in London for Charles's first birthday on 14 November. Six days later she flew to Malta to join Philip and, after a few duty nights as a guest at the Governor's residence, settled in happily to life at the Villa Guardamangia, 'although,' according to John Dean, 'she was probably a little sad at leaving Prince Charles behind.' She was away from her boy for five weeks. She stayed in Malta until 28 December when Philip and HMS *Chequers* (along with six other warships) were sent on manoeuvres to patrol the Red Sea. Neither Philip nor Elizabeth was with Charles for his second Christmas, and, when Elizabeth did get back to England, she did not rush immediately to Sandringham to be reunited with her little boy. She spent four days at Clarence House, attending to 'a backlog of correspondence', and fulfilling a number of engagements, including a visit to Hurst Park races where she had the satisfaction of seeing

'Monaveen', a horse she owned jointly with her mother, winning at 10-1.

As we know, Prince Charles, our new King, had mixed feelings about his upbringing. He felt he was neglected by his parents when he was small. His parents, understandably, saw it differently. When I raised it with him, Prince Philip shrugged and pointed out that, at the time, he was serving in the Royal Navy and that servicemen and their families are often apart. 'It's the way it was. It's the way it is.' Prince Philip also made it clear to me that all her life the Queen had 'done her best to balance the range of her responsibilities' – as a princess and monarch, as a mother and wife – but, of course, 'it has not always been easy.' The Princess was with Charles for his birthday. That was important. She was with Philip in Malta. That was important, too. And, as his father reminded me, Charles was far from being either neglected or unloved: when he was not with his parents, he was with doting nurses and grandparents who adored him.

At the beginning of 1950, Princess Elizabeth spent three months in England before returning to Malta – again without Charles – on 28 March. On her twenty-fourth birthday, 21 April 1950, at 8:45 a.m., in her bedroom at the Villa Guardamangia, her telephone rang. When she picked up the receiver she was greeted with a rousing chorus of 'Happy Birthday to You' performed by a group of young naval officers accompanied by some of the band of HMS *Liverpool*. According to Bobo, who was there (of course), 'Lilibet was wildly excited and kept saying, "Oh! Thank you, thank you! That was sweet but who are you?"' She was answered by a second chorus of the song, harmonised by the officers' Glee Club, then a burst of bagpipes. Bobo reported to Dickie Moutbatten – whose Flag Officer had been responsible for organising the surprise birthday greeting – that 'Lilibet first went white, then quite red, and ended up with tears in her eyes.' Mountbatten was enchanted with the birthday girl: 'I think she's so sweet and attractive. At times I think she likes me too, though she is far too reserved to give any indication.' Elizabeth's birthday treat was to watch her husband and her uncle playing polo.

The young wife spent six weeks with her husband in Malta and then returned to England on 9 May and did not see him again for three months until he, too, came home, for five weeks' leave, at the end of July. Princess Anne was born on 15 August at Clarence House. The birth was a cause for general rejoicing. Among the first callers was Philip's mother, Princess Alice, who had come over specially from Greece, determined not to miss the birth of her latest grandchild. She was dressed in her nun's habit and spotted by a sharp-eyed reporter from the *Daily Mail* who decided to describe her, intriguingly, as 'one of the few remaining mystics in the Greek church.' Earlier, in January 1949, when the *Daily Mail* first learnt about Princess Alice and the home and religious school for district nurses that she planned to found on the island of Tinos, they sent a reporter to interview her. He did not get very far. 'I don't like talking about my work,' she said. 'Duty is its own reward. I am not a politician or a film star. Taking pictures of me at work would be posing.' That was her son Prince Philip's attitude to the last – and a lesson he shared with his children and grandchildren.

It was a happy time for the whole family – with the possible exception of Prince Charles. This is how Sarah Bradford puts it in her biography of the Queen:

For Prince Charles, the return of his father closely followed by the appearance of a new baby must have been something of a shock. A photograph of the time shows him peering into the cradle with a slightly puzzled air. He was two years old and had not seen his father for nearly a year, his mother only at intervals. Now the appearance of a new sister as the focus of everyone's attention must have been very confusing; only his loving grandparents and his unchanging nursery retinue provided stability. His father left again for Malta on 1 September and in December his mother went out to join him. At Christmas Prince Charles and his new sister went as usual with their grandparents to Sandringham.

The Queen and Prince Philip did not dispute the facts. What they found frustrating was the gloss. There is another photograph of Charles, taken at the time, looking quite content. Princess Elizabeth was devoted to her son and knew that when she went away – always after several months at home and usually for no more than four or five weeks at a time – her boy was in good hands – the best. And her mother, Queen Elizabeth, sent regular and enthusiastic reports from the home front: 'What a joy Charles and Anne are to me . . . I shall miss them quite terribly when you return.'

In July 1950, a few weeks before Princess Anne was born, Philip was promoted to the rank of Lieutenant Commander and given his first command: the frigate HMS *Magpie*. Philip was ambitious and fiercely competitive. He was determined that *Magpie* would be the smartest, sharpest frigate afloat, and that her eight officers and 150 men pull their weight at all times. He led from the front. He demanded the best and gave his all. In the annual Mediterranean Fleet regatta, the officers and men of *Magpie* rowed to victory in six out of the ten races, with 'Dukey', as he was known to his men, rowing at stroke in the Destroyer Command Officers' race – which they won (of course) by half a length from a field of fifteen. As well as taking part in routine naval manoeuvres, *Magpie* – or 'Edinburgh's Private Yacht' as some called her – was sent on sundry ceremonial exercises. In December 1950, when Princess Elizabeth came to Malta, there was an expedition to Athens to call on Philip's cousins, King Paul and Queen Frederika. Elizabeth travelled on board the Commander-in-Chief's Despatch Vessel, HMS *Surprise*. One morning there was a jovial exchange of signals between the ships:

Surprise to *Magpie*: Princess full of beans
Magpie to *Surprise*: Can't you give her something better for breakfast?

The exchange reflects the family sense of humour, which tends to be broad rather than subtle. As we shall keep seeing, there is also a family weakness for practical jokes. When Queen Frederika came to dinner on board Mountbatten's ship in the summer of 1949, she made him an apple-pie bed. Six months later, when Mountbatten was staying with Queen Frederika and King Paul, he had his revenge. 'Put packet of brown sugar in Freddy's bed,' he noted, gleefully, in his diary.

Happy days. But the fun – and Philip's career – did not last. The King's health was gradually deteriorating. On 4 May 1951, when George VI and Queen Elizabeth went to the official opening of the Festival of Britain on the south bank of the Thames, the King looked grey and weak. Three weeks later, on 24 May, at Westminster Abbey, at the installation of the Duke of Gloucester as Great Master of the Order of the Bath, the King appeared seriously ill. His doctors diagnosed 'catarrhal inflammation' on the left lung and prescribed a course of penicillin injections. The King felt relieved, confident, he told his mother, that the condition would resolve itself with treatment.

In the event, his condition worsened. In July he started to undergo a series of tests that would eventually establish the presence of a malignant tumour in his lung. In July, too, the Edinburghs returned from Malta. The Princess and her husband were required for public duty. Elizabeth had revelled in the relative freedom she had enjoyed as a naval officer's wife. 'They're putting the bird back in its cage,' said Edwina Mountbatten. Philip had relished his year in command of his own ship. 'That's that,' he said to Mike Parker. 'It was bloody for him,' Mike Parker said to me, 'Absolutely bloody.' 'No,' Prince Philip said to me, 'It's what happened. That's all. It happened sooner than might have been expected, but it was inevitable. I accepted it. That's life.'

That autumn the King and Queen had planned to make a state visit to Canada and the United States. The Princess and the Duke were sent in their place. They were due to leave on 25 September, sailing on the liner *Empress of Britain*, but their departure was postponed as the King's condition deteriorated further. On Sunday 23 September, in a two-hour operation at Buckingham Palace, the King had his left lung removed. A crowd of 5,000 waited outside the Palace for news and, when it came at 5:00 p.m., the bulletin, written in black crayon, encased in a picture frame and hung on the Palace gates, told the truth, but not the whole truth: 'The King underwent an operation for lung resection this morning. Whilst anxiety must remain for some days, His Majesty's immediate post-operative condition is satisfactory.' In 1951, cancer was a word rarely spoken above a whisper. On 24 September, Harold Nicolson wrote in his diary: 'The King pretty bad. Nobody can talk about anything else – and the Election is forgotten. What a strange thing is Monarchy!' I thought about this seventy-one years later, in September 2022, when writing my diary during the ten days between the Queen's death and her funeral: a new prime minister had only been in office for two days, a new Chancellor of the Exchequer was having to get to grips with an alarming cost-of-living crisis, a brutal war was being waged in Ukraine – but all that went by the board, all that was forgotten. What a strange thing is Monarchy!

Back in 1951, Clement Attlee, the prime minister, had already told the King that he proposed dissolving parliament at the beginning of October to hold a general election on the last Thursday in the month. Despite the King's frailty, on 25 October, the election went ahead. Attlee's Labour Party lost. The Liberals were routed. Winston Churchill and the Conservatives were returned to office with a majority of 17. Churchill was coming up to his seventy-seventh birthday and had suffered a stroke. He was hard of hearing, not altogether mobile and not always wholly alert. He had no doubt, however, that he was ready for office.

The King was coming up to his fifty-sixth birthday and far from well. Lord Moran (Winston Churchill's doctor) reckoned 'he can scarcely live more than a year', but since the King himself was not told he had cancer, he was ready to believe the operation had cured him. He did all he could – mentally and physically – to rally his strength and determined on a policy of business as usual. On 8 October, with his blessing and encouragement, Princess Elizabeth became the first member of the royal family to fly the Atlantic when she and Philip went ahead with their postponed North American tour. It was essentially a visit to Canada – George VI was King of Canada, after all – with a brief foray into the United States thrown in for good measure. When the royal couple reached Washington DC, the 32nd President, Harry S. Truman, introduced the young princess to his elderly and nearly deaf mother-in-law. 'Mother!' boomed the President, 'I've brought Princess Elizabeth to see you!' The old lady beamed at the young princess. 'I'm so glad your father has been re-elected,' she said.

Travelling with the Edinburghs on the thirty-five-day, twelve thousand-mile, cross-continental tour was the Princess's new private secretary, Martin Charteris. Jock Colville, having completed his two-year secondment to Clarence House (and having happily married one of Elizabeth's ladies-in-waiting) had returned to the Foreign Office in 1949. Charteris had come on board because he knew Jock Colville and because his wife was friendly with the King's secretary, Sir Alan Lascelles. 'It was as simple as that,' he told me, forty years later, still chuckling. 'No vetting, no board interviews, no security clearance, no qualifications required, no training given. That's the way it was.'

Certainly, Charteris had no technical qualifications for the job – he was neither a courtier nor a diplomat – but he was evidently the right kind of chap. His background was thoroughly sound: born 1913, second son of Lord Elcho (killed in action, 1916), grandson of the 11th Earl of Wemyss; educated at Eton and Sandhurst, he was a career soldier who had a decent war, much of it spent in the Middle East, where he eventually wound up running Military Intelligence in Palestine. He went to work for Princess Elizabeth in January 1950 and stayed at her side for twenty-seven years. He loved her – in the best sense – and loved to talk about her – in the best way. He was wholly loyal (he was devoted to her), but his anecdotes about her, while always affectionate, were both well observed and usually revealing. He liked to tell the story of the day he went for his first interview with his prospective employer and how impressed he was by her style before they even met. Charteris arrived early at Clarence House for his 11:30 a.m. appointment. At 11:25 a.m. Boy Browning rang through to the Princess. 'Major Charteris is here to see you, Ma'am. Shall I bring him in?' 'Yes,' said the Princess, coolly, 'at half-past eleven.' Charteris told me – and anyone else who cared to listen – that the moment he set eyes on her he was smitten. 'She was wearing a blue dress and a brooch with huge sapphires. I was immediately struck by her bright blue eyes and her wonderful complexion. She was young, beautiful, and dutiful. I knew at once that I would be proud to serve her.'

She was dutiful, and prepared for the worst. On the flight to Montreal on 8 October 1951, Charteris took with him the documents of accession in case they should be required. The Princess was already privy to a range of state papers. Throughout her time in Canada, she carefully monitored the news from home, conscientiously reading the air mail edition of the London *Times*. The tour was not an unmitigated triumph. The programme was exhausting – it took in every province in the dominion – and the Princess was anxious about her father. The Canadian press, who had been bowled over by the effortless charm of Queen Elizabeth when she and the King had toured the country twelve years before, complained that the twenty-five-year-old princess was shy and unsmiling. 'Please smile more, Ma'am,' pleaded Charteris. 'But my jaws are aching,' sighed the Princess. (Exactly fifty years later, accompanying the Queen on a tour of the West Country, the Duchess of Grafton told me, 'She does find this constant smiling very exhausting, you know. After a day like today, her jaw really aches.') The royal couple did their best, of course. They scored well when – kitted out like characters from *Oklahoma!* by the ever-present Bobo and John Dean – they gave their all dancing a Canadian square dance. Philip did less well when – hoping to be humorous – he nonchalantly referred to Canada as 'a good investment'. Forty nine years later, in October 2002, when the royal couple were back in Canada for an eleven-day Golden Jubilee tour, Canadian newspapers were still quoting the remark.

Martin Charteris said to me, 'It was a long trip and it wasn't plain sailing. It wasn't easy for either of them.' Is it true, I asked him, that, at breakfast one morning on the Governor-General's train, the Duke called the Princess 'a bloody fool'. 'He might have done,' said Charteris, smiling. 'He had a naval turn of phrase.' Was he often ratty with the Princess, I asked. 'Not so much ratty,' said Charteris, 'as restless. He was impatient. He was frustrated. You must remember he had just turned thirty and he was obliged to give up a promising career in the Navy to do – what? He hadn't yet defined his role, found his feet as consort. He was certainly very impatient with the old style courtiers and sometimes, I think, felt that the Princess paid more attention to them than to him. He didn't like that. If he called her "a bloody fool" now and again, it was just his way. I think others would have found it more shocking than she did. Although she was very young, she had a wise head on her shoulders. She has always understood him – and his ways. And valued his contribution – which has been immense and is underestimated. I believe history will come to judge him well.'

Fifty-two years after Elizabeth and Philip's visit to President Truman in Washington DC, in November 2003, George W. Bush, 42nd President of the United States, made a state visit to the United Kingdom. The Queen and the Duke of Edinburgh, of course, hosted a state banquet in honour of the president at Buckingham Palace. During the reception, before dinner, there was a telling moment. On one side of the room stood the Queen and President Bush, alone, chatting quietly – amiably but with little animation – while two yards away, on the other side of the room, stood Prince Philip at the centre of a small group that included the First Lady, Laura Bush, and the American Secretary of State, Colin Powell. They were all laughing. Prince Philip was leaning forward, gesticulating with his hands, entertaining his guests, telling a funny story. This – exactly this – was what Prince Philip succeeded in doing for more than seventy years. While the Queen made intelligent, interested small-talk, always amiably, but sometimes a little awkwardly, the Duke kept the party going. 'He has done the state some service,' Martin Charteris said to me, 'I think the Queen appreciates his sense of humour, and values it.'

On the long train ride across Canada back in the autumn of 1951, Philip did his best to entertain his wife with a range of practical jokes. According to John Dean, these included surprising her with a booby-trapped can of nuts and chasing her down the corridor wearing a set of joke false teeth. When they flew to Washington DC on 31 October, the smiles were rather more forced when, at the British embassy reception in their honour, they were expected to shake hands with each of 1,500 guests.

In terms of public relations, however, the brief visit to the American capital was an unqualified success. 'We have many distinguished visitors here in this city,' declared the President, welcoming his British vistors to the White House Rose Garden, 'but never before have we had such a wonderful couple, that so completely captured the hearts of all of us.' Sir Oliver Franks, the British ambassador, reported to the King that when the sixty-seven-year-old President appeared with the twenty-five-year-old Princess in public he gave 'the impression of a very proud uncle presenting his favourite niece to his friends'. According to Martin Charteris, 'Truman fell in love with her.' Truman was captivated, certainly. Memorably, he said, 'When I was a little boy, I read about a fairy princess, and there she is.' When the royal couple had returned to Canada to complete their tour, the President wrote himself to the King in England, 'We've just had a visit from a lovely young lady and her personable husband . . . As one father to another we can be very proud of our daughters. You have the better of me — because you have two!'

The Princess and the Duke returned to England by sea in the middle of the month, missing Prince Charles's third birthday on 14 November. In a birthday photograph, taken at Buckingham Palace, the toddler prince and his grandfather, sitting on a sofa side by side, look very much at ease. The photograph when it was published, combined with the King's determination to think positively, and the Queen's ability to avoid the unpleasant by ignoring it (what Martin Charteris later called her capacity for being 'a bit of an ostrich'), encouraged the public to believe that the King's health was on the mend. On 2 December a day of national thanksgiving for the sovereign's recovery was celebrated in churches throughout the kingdom. When, early in November, Princess Elizabeth, in a transatlantic call from Canada, had spoken to her father on the telephone, she reported that he sounded 'much better'. When she saw him on her return home, later in the month, he 'looked awful', according to Charteris, 'quite dreadful'.

The King had hoped to travel to Australia and New Zealand in the spring of 1952, to undertake the antipodean tour his health had forced him to postpone in 1948. Now he knew that would be impossible. Again, Elizabeth and Philip would go in his place. On their return from Canada, by way of tribute to what they had already achieved, he made them both Privy Councillors. His own hope for the New Year was to enjoy a recuperative holiday in South Africa in March. First, there was Christmas and the ordeal of the 3:00 p.m. Christmas Day broadcast. Customarily, the King gave the broadcast live so that he could speak 'directly' to his people. Because of its significance, and because of his stammer, it was a ritual he dreaded. One Christmas morning he barked at his family: 'I can't concentrate on anything because I've got that damned broadcast coming up this afternoon.' This year, his difficulty with breathing precluded a live broadcast. A BBC engineer, Robert Wood, came to Buckingham Palace on 21 December and, over two hours, painstakingly pieced together the ten-minute recording. Wood said afterwards: 'It was very, very distressing for him, and the Queen, and for me, because I admired him so much and wished I could do more to help.'

Christmas at Sandringham was a family affair and, by all accounts, the King – particularly because he did not have the cloud of 'that damned broadcast' hanging over him – was in mellow mood throughout. He was well enough to go shooting. He showed a revived interest in the business of the estate. He caught up with official correspondence, writing to, among others, President Truman and his successor, General Eisenhower. He began the New Year in a positive and determined frame of mind.

On 29 January he travelled to London and saw his doctors who, remarkably, pronounced themselves 'very well satisfied' with their patient's progress. The next day, by way of celebration, there was a family outing to the theatre. The King and Queen took their daughters and their son-in-law (and the King's equerry, Peter Townsend) to the Theatre Royal, Drury Lane to see a performance of *South Pacific*. Next day, Thursday 31 January, the King and Queen, with the prime minister in attendance, went to Heathrow airport to see Elizabeth and Philip off to Kenya, on the first leg of their journey to Australia and New Zealand. They were due to be away for almost six months. In photographs of the farewell, the King, standing on the tarmac, windswept, hat in hand, looks gaunt and bleak and lonely. But Churchill, who was there, said he was 'gay, and even jaunty, and drank a glass of champagne.' 'I think,' Churchill added, 'he knew he had not long to live.'

On 1 February the King returned to Sandringham. It was the end of the shooting season. On 5 February he was out on the estate shooting hares and rabbits. In the evening there was a jolly dinner with the Queen and Princess Margaret, and members of the royal household, and one or two shooting friends. At 10:30 p.m. the King retired to bed. At midnight he was seen by a watchman in the garden standing at his bedroom window. At some time in the early hours of Wednesday 6 February, he died, in his sleep, of a coronary thrombosis. 'He died as he was getting better,' said Princess Margaret.

When George VI died, the Heiress Presumptive was in East Africa, in Kenya, about 100 miles north of Nairobi, at Treetops, a three-bedroomed 'hotel' set, amazingly, in the branches of a giant fig tree, overlooking a salt lick, a unique vantage point for observing the wild animals ranging below. 'She became Queen,' Harold Nicolson wrote in his diary, 'while perched in a tree in Africa watching the rhinoceros come down to the pool to drink.' In fact, at the very moment of her father's death, Elizabeth was either asleep, or taking a photograph of the sunrise, or having breakfast, watching, not watering rhino, but a troop of playful baboons who had captured paper rolls from the Treetops lavatory and were throwing them over the branches. The news from England did not reach her for several hours.

At Sandringham, the King's death was discovered by his valet at 7:30 a.m. when he took in his early morning tea. The Queen, a widow at only fifty-one, was heartbroken. 'He was so young to die,' she wrote to her friend Osbert Sitwell, 'and was becoming so wise in kingship. He was so kind too, and had a sort of natural nobility of thought & life which some-times made me ashamed of my narrower & more feminine point of view. Such sorrow is a very strange experience . . .'

The King's secretary, Sir Alan Lascelles, telephoned the assistant private secretary, Edward Ford, in London and instructed him to break the news to the King's mother and to the prime minister. At 10 Downing Street, Ford found Churchill, propped up in bed, cigar in hand, surrounded by paperwork. 'I've got bad news,' Ford said. 'The King died this morning. I know nothing more.' 'Bad news?' said Churchill. 'The worst.' He threw aside the papers he had been working on. 'How unimportant these matters seem,' he said. Later, when Jock Colville arrived, he found the prime minister in tears. Colville said that he tried to console Churchill with the thought of how well he would get on with the new Queen, but 'all he could say was that he did not know her and that she was only a child.'

The child meanwhile, still unaware that she was now Queen, had finished breakfast at Treetops, clambered to the ground down the rickety ladders (she was wearing jeans), and, with Philip and the rest of her party, had driven the ten or so miles back to Sagana Lodge – the royal couple's wedding present from the people of Kenya – to spend the rest of the morning fishing for trout in the Sagana River before preparing for the onward journey to Mombassa and the boat that was due to take them on to New Zealand and Australia via Ceylon. The party included Bobo and John Dean, Pamela Mountbatten as lady-in-waiting, Mike Parker as equerry, and a celebrated local 'white hunter', Jim Corbett, armed with a high velocity rifle, to guard the Princess both from rampaging elephants and the possibility of an attack by local Mau-Mau terrorists. Martin Charteris was staying nearby, at the Outspan Hotel in Nyeri, once the home of Robert Baden-Powell. It was at the Outspan, at lunchtime, that Charteris got the news – given to him, in a garbled version, by a local newspaper reporter. The King's secretary at Sandringham had sent a telegram to Charteris in Nyeri, but it never reached him. Edward Ford told me he thought this was because the telegram was in the form of a pre-arranged coded message: 'Hyde Park Corner', three words that would signify the King's death to those in the know. Ford reckoned the telegraphist mistook the message for the address.

From the Outspan, Charteris telephoned Parker at Sagana Lodge. Parker found a wireless, fiddled with the dial and, eventually, tuned in to the BBC. Philip was having a siesta. Parker woke him and gave him the news.

'I never felt so sorry for anyone in all my life,' said Parker. 'He looked as if you'd dropped half the world on him.' The Duke said nothing, according to Parker, 'nothing at all. He just breathed heavily, in and out, as though he were in shock.' Philip found Elizabeth and took her into the garden. He told her what had happened. 'Did he hold her?' I asked Parker. 'I can't remember,' he said. 'We were all in a state of shock. But she was quite calm, I do remember that. She said very little. They were out on the lawn together, alone, away from the rest of us. They walked slowly up and down the lawn, up and down, up and down, while he talked and talked and talked.'

When Martin Charteris arrived back at Sagana, he found them in the sitting-room. 'I can still picture the scene,' he told me. 'The Queen, sitting at her desk, pencil in hand, making notes. She was sitting upright, erect, utterly resolved. Her cheeks were a little flushed, but there were no tears. Philip was lying back on a sofa, silent, holding a copy of a newspaper wide open over his face.' Parker was busy making the arrangements for their immediate return to London. The new Queen was anxious to send messages back home and to Ceylon and New Zealand and Australia. She apologised for all the inconvenience she was causing. 'I'm so sorry we've got to go back,' she said to Pamela Mountbatten, 'I've ruined everybody's trip.' Martin Charteris asked her what name she wanted to use as Queen. 'My own name, of course,' she told him, 'Elizabeth.' Charteris said later, 'I never imagined that anyone could grasp their destiny with such safe hands.'

They changed, they packed, they got into their cars and drove to Nanyuki airport. By now, reporters and photographers had arrived at Sagana. 'I asked them not to take any pictures,' Charteris told me, 'and, as our cars left the Lodge, though the world's press lined the road, not a photograph was taken.' Pamela Mountbatten recalled: 'Local villagers stood outside their huts or lined the roads, calling out "Shauri mbaya kabisa" ("The very worst has happened"). That such sympathy was shown as we drove through what was to become Mau Mau territory was truly remarkable.'

They flew first to Entebbe. There they were reunited with the rest of their luggage, flown up from Mombassa – including the black mourning clothes which Bobo and John Dean had carefully packed against this very eventuality. 'But I remember,' said Pamela Mountbatten, 'there wasn't a suitable hat, so we had to send a telegram to London asking for one to be delivered to the plane when it arrived.'

For two hours they waited in the airport lounge while a storm abated and then, at last, climbed aboard the BOAC Argonaut aircraft for the long flight home. Little was said on the journey home. John Dean recalled that he saw the Queen get up once or twice and return to her seat looking as if she had been crying. And, if she had been, she chose to do it in the privacy of the aircraft's toilet. Martin Charteris told me, 'We slept for much of the first part of the journey. I discussed some of the details of the accession with Her Majesty. She was completely calm, utterly composed. For a long time she simply gazed out of the window.'

It was mid-afternoon on Thursday 7 February when the plane touched down at Heathrow. Waiting to greet his new sovereign was her prime minister, Winston Churchill, who had first become a member of parliament more than fifty years before, when Victoria was Queen. Elizabeth II, Victoria's great-great-granddaughter, a tiny figure in black, solemn and self-possessed, came down the aircraft steps alone. Philip lingered inside the aircraft door, hidden, watching and waiting until the new Queen had touched British soil. Only then did he emerge and come down the steps to join her. 'Oh yes,' he said to me, 'when the late King died, everything changed.'

Pamela Hicks (as Pamela Mountbatten became when she married the designer David Hicks in the 1960s) told me, 'We felt everything change immediately. At the Lodge, when we had just heard the news, Mike Parker and I watched the Princess and the Duke pacing up and down on the lawn together and when they came back in I gave her a hug instinctively – and then suddenly I thought "That's wrong – she's now Queen" and I dropped into a deep curtsy. She accepted the curtsy. She accepted what had happened at once. And when Martin [Charteris] asked her what she wanted to be called, she seemed surprised. Her father was named Albert, but he reigned as George VI. Her uncle was David, but he chose to be Edward VIII. It never occurred to her not to be Elizabeth. And, you know, she was twenty-five, the same age as Elizabeth I when she became Queen.'

CHAPTER SEVENTEEN

Elizabeth II

As darkness descended on London on that cold, dank February afternoon, the new Queen and her husband were driven from Heathrow airport to Clarence House where they found the old King's private secretary, Sir Alan Lascelles, waiting for them. He had a sheaf of state papers that he needed Her Majesty to sign. Within the hour, Queen Mary also came to call. She was eighty-four and frail, full of dignity and grief. The day before, her son, the King, had died. Today, she had come, not to hug her granddaughter, but to curtsy to her new Queen. 'Her old Grannie and subject must be the first to kiss her hand,' she said. Elizabeth's eyes pricked with tears as she accepted her grandmother's obeisance. Martin Charteris told me, 'For the young Queen, it was a moment that must have sorely tested her reserve and her resolve, but she loved her father and wanted to carry herself courageously as he would have done.'

Elizabeth said as much the following day, at St James's Palace, where her Privy Councillors gathered for the formal meeting of the Accession Council – many of them, according to Hugh Dalton, a former Chancellor of the Exchequer, who was there, 'people one didn't remember were still alive, and some looking quite perky and self-important.' (Having been a member of parliament in the 1990s and knowing a good number of Privy Councillors – there are currently around 730 of them, though not all could be accommodated at the Accession Council meeting for Charles III – I felt this exactly as I watched them gathering in the same room on Saturday 10 September 2022. There were many more women Privy Councillors in 2022 than there would have been seventy years before, and not all the men were in full morning dress – the former prime minister David Cameron stood out from the crowd in a blue suit – but other than that, it did feel like a gathering of elderly folk one had half-forgotten and, certainly, a number appeared both perky and self-important.)

In 2022, the King entered, accompanied by his Queen Consort and the new Prince of Wales, looking, in my view, every inch a King. In 1952, according to Hugh Dalton, the Queen, looking 'very small', entered alone and read the Declaration of Sovereignty in a 'high-pitched, rather reedy voice'. 'She does her part well,' said Dalton, 'facing hundreds of old men in black clothes with long faces.' Harold Wilson, another of the Privy Councillors and one of her future prime ministers, said it was 'the most moving ceremonial I can recall.' When she had read the formal Declaration, she added, 'My heart is too full for me to say more to you today than that I shall always work as my father did.'

King Charles III spoke at much greater length, but the essence of his message was the same:

> My mother's reign was unequalled in its duration, its dedication and its devotion. Even as we grieve, we give thanks for this most faithful life.
>
> I am deeply aware of this great inheritance and of the duties and heavy responsibilities of sovereignty which have now passed to me. In taking up these responsibilities, I shall strive to follow the inspiring example I have been set in

upholding constitutional government and to seek the peace, harmony and prosperity of the peoples of these islands and of the Commonwealth realms and territories throughout the world.

In this purpose, I know that I shall be upheld by the affection and loyalty of the peoples whose sovereign I have been called upon to be, and that in the discharge of these duties I will be guided by the counsel of their elected parliaments. In all this, I am profoundly encouraged by the constant support of my beloved wife.

Outside, on the ramparts of the Palace, the Garter King of Arms, in Tudor tabard, proclaimed the accession in similar terms in 2022 as in 1951. In 2022, Charles III acceded to the throne at the age of almost seventy-four. In 1952, his mother was still just twenty-five: 'Queen Elizabeth the Second, by the grace of God Queen of this Realm and of all Her other Realms and Territories, Head of the Commonwealth, Defender of the Faith.'

Inside St James's Palace, in 1952, Philip, only eight weeks a Privy Councillor himself, stepped forward to take his sovereign by the hand and escort her out of the chamber and down to her waiting car. 'In the back of the car,' according to one biography of the Queen, 'she finally broke down and sobbed.' The Duke of Edinburgh told me, 'Not true.' She may have shed a tear, but she did not break down and sob. 'Why does everything have to be exaggerated?'

There is no need to exaggerate the national sense of grief at the passing of George VI or the degree of admiration bordering on adulation expressed for the new Queen. When news of the King's death was broadcast, drivers stopped their cars, got out and stood to attention as a mark of respect. When his body lay in state in Westminster Hall, more than 300,000 people filed slowly past in tribute – a similar number to those who filed past the coffin of Elizabeth II when her body lay in state in Edinburgh and London in 2022.

'The world showed a large and genuine measure of grief,' said Jock Colville in the aftermath of the death of George VI. 'The King was universally loved and respected,' said Martin Charteris. 'He gave his life for his country.' 'The King's outstanding quality,' said Dean Acheson, the US Secretary of State, was 'his selfless dedication to duty.' 'He was a grand man,' President Truman noted in his diary, 'worth a pair of his brother Ed.' George VI had been King through the six long years of the Second World War and had not flinched. At his funeral at St George's Chapel, Windsor, the card accompanying Winston Churchill's wreath bore just two words, the inscription to be found on the Victoria Cross: 'For Valour.'

In his broadcast on the night of the King's death, Churchill, as prime minister, paid tribute to the courage and fortitude of the late King and then, with typical Churchillian bravura, heralded a new Elizabethan age: 'Famous have been the reigns of our Queens,' he rumbled prophetically. 'Some of the greatest periods in our history have unfolded under their sceptre.' Churchill might not yet know Elizabeth well, might consider her no more than a child, but, very quickly, he became utterly enchanted by her. 'You've got to remember,' Charteris said to me, 'Churchill was nearly eighty and the Queen was no more than twenty-five, but it was not simply her youth and beauty that entranced him. He was impressed by her. She was conscientious, she was well-informed, she was serious-minded. Within days of her Accession she was receiving prime ministers and presidents, ambassadors and High Commissioners – all those who had come to London for the King's funeral – and doing so faultlessly. She had authority and dignity as well as grace.' Within a year, Churchill was confiding to his doctor, Lord Moran: 'All the film people in the world, if they had scoured the globe, could not have found anyone so suited for the part.'

Among the many who came to London for the lying-in-state and funeral of the late King was his older brother, David (or 'Ed' as President Truman called him), whose abdication as Edward VIII, of course, had led to George VI's reign. The Duke of Windsor, as he had become, was now 57 and destined to live a further twenty years. Queen Elizabeth, privately, may have blamed her brother-in-law's selfishness for her own husband's premature death, but now she entertained him to tea and spent some time alone with him. He reported to his Duchess – who, diplomatically, had stayed behind in New York – that the widowed Queen had 'listened without comment' (they are very practised at that) '& closed on the note that it was nice to be able to talk about Bertie with somebody who had known him so well.' 'Officially and on the surface,' David told Wallis, 'my treatment within the family has been entirely correct and dignified.' Superficially, he acknowledged, he was handled impeccably by courtiers and relations alike – 'But gee,' he added, 'the crust is hard & only granite below.' (Is that how Meghan feels? We may know one day when she 'speaks her truth' in full.) Unsurprisingly perhaps – given that he had lived away from the Court for sixteen years, and that most of those at Court had little affection and still less respect for him – the Duke of Windsor found the mood and way of life at Buckingham Palace stiff and uncompromising. 'Gosh they move slowly within these Palace confines,' he said. He found the tone and atmosphere at Clarence House, the Edinburghs' base camp, much more congenial. 'Clarence House was informal and friendly,' he reported to Wallis. 'Brave New World, full of self-confidence & seem to take the job in their stride.'

According to Martin Charteris, 'the operation at Clarence House was a good one.' 'We were a good team,' said Mike Parker, 'Philip ran a tight ship.' As well as being the Edinburghs' office, Clarence House was also their home – and Philip's first and only family home since he had last lived with his parents in Paris when he was ten. Philip wanted to go on living there. He put his thoughts on paper in a note to Boy Browning. He proposed that Queen Elizabeth, the Queen Mother – as she decided she wished to be known – should remain at Buckingham Palace and that the new Queen and her family should remain at Clarence House. One day, he suggested, Clarence House might also be an appropriate London home for Prince Charles. (As it eventually became.) The business of the monarchy could be conducted from Buckingham Palace, while the family of the monarch could continue living where they were.

Sir Alan Lascelles was having none of it. 'God, he was bloody,' Lord Brabourne said to me, fifty years later. Lascelles was adamant: the traditional home of the British monarch was Buckingham Palace: it always had been: it should remain so. In fact, the Palace – built by the Duke of Buckingham in 1703 and rebuilt between 1825 and 1837 – had only been the official London residence of the sovereign since Queen Victoria's reign, but Lascelles, as the Queen's private secretary, had authority that Philip, as the Queen's husband, lacked, and – significantly – he also had the backing of the prime minister. Churchill said, 'To the Palace they must go.' So, to the Palace, they went.

At the Palace the new Queen's team were coping with the thousands of letters and telegrams of condolence that were arriving from all over the world. Pamela Mountbatten, who helped sort the correspondence, remembered that many of the letters were 'deeply moving' and 'a source of great comfort to the Queen.' She also recalled: 'Not all of the authors of these letters were quite so balanced, and among the piles organised under the collective headings of "children", "women" and "service families", we also had "lunatics" . . . One afternoon six of us were sitting in a circle on the floor going through the post when I opened a telegram that was signed "Mama in Chicago". "Oh, listen to this!" I cried, delighted at a diversion from our sad task. "One for the lunatic pile!" Unbeknown to me, the Queen had just entered the room and my laughter was met by stony silence. "Pammy," she "Mama is in Chicago just now ...". As she removed the telegram from my hand I remembered, to my horror, that Aunt Alice, Prince Philip'a mother, was indeed in Chicago, raising money for her religious order. We continued our work in silence.'

Pamela was a Mountbatten, of course. Her father, Lord Mountbatten, was the brother of Princess Alice, and the uncle of Philip Mountbatten, now Duke of Edinburgh. The new Queen's gimlet-eyed private secretary, the redoubtable Tommy Lascelles, sixty-five to her twenty-five, and servant to four sovereigns, was determined to ensure that in matters of state the influence of the Mountbatten family was contained. The prime minister, Winston Churchill (seventy-eight to her twenty-five), concurred, and Lascelles and Churchill were a formidable duo, which is why the young Queen chose to ignore precedent in a very sensitive area and do as her private secretary and prime minister advised, rather than as her husband – and perhaps she – wished. She decided that her children – and her children's children – should bear her family name of Windsor rather than his of Mountbatten. Philip was incandescent. 'I am the only man in the country not allowed to give his name to his own children,' he protested. 'I am nothing but a bloody amoeba.'

'It hurt him, it really hurt him,' Patricia Mountbatten said to me when I went to see her many years later. Sitting facing her and her husband, John Brabourne, in their drawing room at Mersham in Kent half a century after the event, from the pained expressions on their faces you would think the wound had been inflicted yesterday.

'Can you imagine doing such a thing?' asked Lord Brabourne. 'It so hurt him,' repeated Countess Mountbatten. 'He had given up everything – and now this, the final insult. It was a terrible blow. It upset him very deeply and left him feeling unsettled and unhappy for a long while.' 'A long while,' echoed Lord Brabourne. A silence fell in the room. The fire crackled. Suddenly, jointly, the Brabournes seemed to sense that they had gone too far. 'Of course, I don't blame the Queen,' said Lady Mountbatten. 'It was Churchill,' said Lord Brabourne, emphatically, 'encouraged by Lascelles. They forced the Queen's hand.' Lady Mountbatten said: 'I remember hearing the Queen say herself that she was in favour of the name Mountbatten-Windsor.'

The issue arose when it did, as it did, because, at a house party at Broadlands, within days of the old King's death and the new Queen's accession, Dickie Mountbatten was heard to declare 'that the House of Mountbatten now reigned'. Prince Ernst August of Hanover, who was there, swiftly reported this boast to Queen Mary – whose own husband, of course, George V, had created the House of Windsor in 1917. Queen Mary, outraged, summoned the prime minister's secretary, Jock Colville. Colville duly reported the dowager Queen's concerns to Churchill, who had his own reservations about Mountbatten – and was by no means alone. The Duke of Windsor, after the King's funeral, wrote to Wallis: 'Mountbatten – one can't pin much on him but he's very bossy & never stops talking. All are suspicious & watching his influence on Philip.'

Churchill decided on 'action this day' and immediately raised the issue with his senior ministers. According to the Cabinet minutes of 18 February 1952, 'The Cabinet's attention was drawn to reports that some change might be made in the Family name of the Queen's Children and their descendants. The Cabinet was strongly of the opinion that the Family name of Windsor should be retained; and they invited the Prime Minister to take a suitable opportunity of making their views known to Her Majesty.' The Prime Minister did exactly that and, within six weeks, despite her husband's furious protestations, the Queen made her position plain before the Privy Council: 'I hereby declare My Will and Pleasure that I and My children shall be styled and known as the House and Family of Windsor, and that my descendants who marry and their descendants shall bear the name of Windsor.'

'Philip was not happy,' said Charteris. 'Philip was spitting,' said Mike Parker. 'Personally,' reflected Dickie Mountbatten, 'I think it was Beaverbrook's hatred of me coupled with Winston's disenchantment with what I did in India that brought all this about.' Certainly, Lord Beaverbrook had Churchill's ear and, not long before George VI's death, John Gordon, the editor of the *Sunday Express,* had reported to his newspaper's proprietor that a member of the Greek royal family had told him that those 'dangerous people', the Mountbattens, were 'determined to be the power behind the throne when Elizabeth succeeds,' though he sensed they would not succeed as 'Elizabeth was developing into a strong-minded woman who would not be controlled by him.' Gordon told Beaverbrook that the Mountbattens were plotting to get Philip pronounced King or King Consort.

There is no evidence that Philip ever wanted to be called Prince Consort – let alone King Consort or King. He was content to be the Duke of Edinburgh, just as, many years later, his daughter-in-law, Camilla, now our Queen Consort, was more than content to continue to be known as the Duchess of Cornwall. It was Prince Charles who wanted her to be Queen when he became King and it was his mother, recalling the confusion over what to call her husband following her accession, who thought it best, as she put it, 'to settle the matter' in advance of the event – which she did in 2022, at the time of her Platinum Jubilee, with her declaration that it was her 'sincere wish' that, when the time came, Camilla should be known as Queen Consort.

The Duke of Edinburgh told me he was 'not particularly fussed' about what he was called, nor, he said, was he particularly concerned about the actual name 'Mountbatten'. It was not his father's name, after all. It was not his mother's name either. It was the anglicised version of his maternal grandfather's name. What concerned Philip was the principle that a father be allowed to pass on his surname to his children. He believed he had precedent on his side. Victoria of Hanover had married Albert of Saxe-Coburg-Gotha: their son, Edward VII, had reigned as a member of the House of Saxe-Coburg-Gotha.

He also, unfortunately, had precedent against him. During the First World War, George V showed that a sovereign could change the name of the Royal House at will.

'What the devil does that young fool Edinburgh think that the family name has got to do with him?' asked Queen Mary in the spring of 1952. In the spring of 1953, ten weeks before the Coronation, Queen Mary died. In the summer of 1953, shortly after the Coronation, Tommy Lascelles retired. In April 1955, Winston Churchill, aged eighty, resigned as prime minister. On 8 February 1960, eight years to the day after her Accession Council, and shortly before the birth of Prince Andrew, the Queen issued a new declaration of her 'Will and Pleasure':

While I and my children will continue to be styled and known as the House and Family of Windsor, my descendants, other than descendants enjoying the style, title or attributes of Royal Highness and the titular dignity of Prince or Princess, and female descendants who marry and their descendants, shall bear the name Mountbatten-Windsor.

It was a compromise. 'The Queen has always wanted,' announced the Buckingham Palace press office, 'without changing the name of the Royal House established by her grandfather, to associate the name of her husband with her own and his descendants. The Queen has had this in mind for a long time and it is close to her heart.' She had certainly been brooding about it. Harold Macmillan, her prime minister between 1957 and 1963, liked to tell the story of calling on the Queen at Sandringham and encountering the old Duke of Gloucester in the hall. 'Thank Heavens you've come, Prime Minister,' says the Duke. 'The Queen's in a terrible state. There's a fellow called Jones in the billiards room says he wants to marry her sister, and Prince Philip's in the library wanting to change the family name to Mountbatten.'

It was a compromise – and kindly meant – but it did not amount to much. Essentially, the Queen's descendants, if non-royal, could be called Mountbatten-Windsor. Dickie, delighted to find the door even slightly ajar, did his best to push it further open. In 1973, Princess Anne married Captain Mark Phillips. In June that year, Mountbatten wrote to Prince Charles: 'When Anne marries in November, her marriage certificate will be the first opportunity to settle the Mountbatten-Windsor name for good . . . if you can make quite sure . . . that her surname is entered as Mountbatten-Windsor it will end all arguments. I hope you can fix this.' It seems he did, for – though clearly contrary to the stipulations of the Queen's declaration of 1960 – it was as a Mountbatten-Windsor that Princess Anne was married.

In fact, the first properly named Mountbatten-Windsor did not appear on the scene until more than fifty years after the Queen's coronation. Lady Louise Alice Elizabeth Mary Mountbatten-Windsor, the daughter of the Earl and Countess of Wessex, was born on 10 November 2003 – and her Christian names nicely reflect both the Windsor and the Mountbatten heritage. Princess Louise (1848–1939) was the sixth child of Victoria and Albert; Princess Louise of Hesse-Cassel (1817–1898) married Christian IX of Denmark and was grandmother to Prince Andrea, Prince Philip's father. Prince Philip's mother was Alice; the Queen's mother was Elizabeth; the Earl of Wessex's great-grandmother was Queen Mary; the Countess of Wessex's mother was Mary Rhys-Jones. The Mountbatten family's delight at the arrival of the first unquestioned 'Mountbatten-Windsor' may have been a little dampened by the Buckingham Palace spokesman who, having announced the new royal baby's full name, added: 'She will, however, be generally known by the more easily remembered title of Lady Louise Windsor.'

Dickie Mountbatten was obsessed with the issue of the Mountbatten name. Mountbatten was a great achiever (and a great operator), but at times he had to be taken with a pinch of salt. Philip always understood that. Elizabeth understood it, too. They knew Mountbatten's strengths and his weaknesses and his foibles – and were enormously fond of him. In 1974, five years before he was murdered by the IRA, they took him on a cruise aboard the Royal Yacht. He was seventy-four, and delighted to be on *Britannia* once more, 'but what moved me most of all,' he wrote in his diary, 'is the increasing kindness of Lilibet and Philip who treat me more and more as a really intimate member of their immediate family.' They understood him and he, perhaps, understood them, too. When the cruise was over, Mountbatten wrote to Philip: 'You sometimes seemed rather disappointed, perhaps frustrated would be a better word, but I feel you underestimate your effect on the UK, and especially the Commonwealth. I hear more and more praise and appreciation from people in all walks of life.'

For Philip, in 1952, frustration and disappointment were already the order of the day. His children were not to inherit his name. He was not happy about that. He was obliged to move house. He was not happy about that. He was treated as something of an extraneous nuisance by both the Court and the prime minister – and there was very little he could do about that. Mike Parker said to me, 'There were a lot more of them than there were of us.' At Clarence House, Philip and Elizabeth had essentially shared a secretariat, and Philip was head of the household. It was his domain. At Buckingham Palace, it was very different. Elizabeth was Queen. The Palace was the sovereign's domain. Naturally, she inherited her father's household (huge and hidebound), to which she added Martin Charteris (more flexible and fun, but still relatively inexperienced), leaving Philip, pretty isolated, with just Parker and Boy Browning. 'You can imagine,' Countess Mountbatten said to me, 'Bobo MacDonald sitting by the bath-tub' – and 'Tommy Lascelles sitting in judgement', chipped in Lord Brabourne – 'it can't have been easy.'

It was not easy. In most households in Britain in the early 1950s, the husband and father was the dominant figure. He was the head of the household, the breadwinner, the lawmaker; he ruled the roost, he was the cock of the walk. For Philip, it was not like that. 'It was bloody difficult for him,' said Mike Parker. 'In the Navy, he was in command of his own ship – literally. At Clarence House, it was very much his show.

When we got to Buckingham Palace, all that changed.' 'It was an unsettling time for him,' said Martin Charteris. 'He had no defined role, while the Queen's role was clearly defined and she assumed it with an extraordinary and immediate confidence and ease. For the rest of us, it was wonderful to behold, but I can see that he might have found it somewhat disconcerting.'

According to Elizabeth Longford, soon after her Accession the Queen told a friend: 'I no longer feel anxious or worried. I don't know what it is – but I have lost all my timidity somehow becoming the sovereign and having to receive the prime minister.' She was now leading a life from which her husband was necessarily – constitutionally – excluded. When the prime minister came to the Palace for his weekly audience with the sovereign, the old man and the young queen would sit together, alone, sometimes for up to an hour. 'What do you talk about?' Jock Colville asked Churchill. 'Oh, mostly racing,' answered Churchill, with a twinkle. And polo, apparently. And the state of the world, of course.

The Queen was, for seventy years, supplied, daily, with a mass of 'state papers': Cabinet minutes, Foreign Office telegrams, documents, briefs, drafts – boxes of 'secret' documents relating to all manner of United Kingdom, Commonwealth and international affairs. Philip never had access to any of these. When I told him that, as a Lord Commissioner of the Treasury, I used to sign mandates that were then sent to Her Majesty for counter-signature, he was bemused. 'I had no idea she did that,' he said. 'I've no idea what goes on.'

In 2012, at the conclusion of her Diamond Jubilee year, the Queen went to 10 Downing Street to attend a meeting of the British Cabinet. Her father, George VI, had attended gatherings of the War Cabinet during the Second World War, but on 18 December 2012 Elizabeth II became the first monarch to attend a normal Cabinet meeting since George III in

1781. (George I chaired the Cabinet personally until 1717.) The Duke of Edinburgh did not accompany her. His absence caused some press speculation. Was the ninety-one-year-old Duke unwell? No, not at all. He was undertaking his own official engagements elsewhere. He was not privy to attend the Cabinet meeting because constitutional matters are entirely the sovereign's preserve.

The Duke of Edinburgh did not complain about this. He accepted it as a matter of fact. 'When the Queen became Queen, I was told "Keep out" and that was that.'

'So, what did you do?' I asked him.

'I tried to find useful things to do,' he said. 'I did my best. I introduced a Footman Training Programme. The old boys here [at Buckingham Palace] hadn't had anything quite like it before. They expected the footmen just to keep on coming. We had an Organisation and Methods Review. I tried to make improvements – without unhinging things.'

The Organisation and Methods Review involved the Duke and Mike Parker treading on a number of toes. 'Some of the old guard weren't too happy,' Parker told me. 'We met with a fair bit of resistance. But I think we made a few improvements, dragged some of them into the twentieth century. We explored the whole Palace. We didn't find a wicked fairy in a turret with a spinning wheel, but we did discover the wine cellar. It's deep underground and goes on for miles and miles. There were some great old vintages and menus dating back to the early days of Queen Victoria.'

The old guard at the Palace did not welcome the Duke of Edinburgh. The young Queen was sensitive to this and did what she could – within limits. When she married Philip Mountbatten in 1947 she made the traditional promise 'to love, cherish and obey' her husband, which was why he was so infuriated in the matter of the family name and why she, without hesitation, gave him full responsibility for and authority over the management of the family estates at Sandringham and Balmoral, and appointed him Ranger of Windsor Great Park. Outside the domestic sphere, what she could deliver for Philip was limited – or so she felt in those early days. In the House of Lords, for example, the consort's throne was peremptorily removed and put into storage. It was for the consort of Kings, not the husband of Queens, so the authorities decreed. When the young sovereign proposed that her husband succeed her as Colonel of the Grenadier Guards, she was told there was an old soldier (Lord Jeffreys, an Eton and Sandhurst man, a Boer War veteran and sometime Conservative MP) who was the preferred choice. Over time, the Queen's confidence grew. Eventually, the consort's throne was returned to the House of Lords for the Duke of Edinburgh to sit upon at the State Opening of Parliament. When Lord Jeffreys died in 1960, the Queen saw to it that the Duke of Edinburgh succeeded him as Colonel of the Grenadier Guards. But in the first years of her reign, while always ouwardly calm and apparently in control, she was inwardly tentative. As Lord Brabourne put it to me, 'She wasn't her own woman. She was Lascelles' creature. She did as she was told – and Philip paid the price. To an extent, their relationship paid the price. It caused tension between them, inevitably.'

Where she could, where she deemed it appropriate, she did her best to give her husband a role. In 1952, he was appointed Chairman of the Coronation Commission. The Commission had a definite function, overseeing the non-spiritual elements of the coronation. Philip believed it was 'a real job' and he took it seriously. Large numbers of Commonwealth and Colonial troops arrived in the country to take part in the event and were stationed in barracks across the land. The Duke decided to visit them all. He and Mike Parker looked at the logistics and reckoned they should go by helicopter. They borrowed one from the Royal Navy. 'It was just more practical,' the Prince explained to me, 'but it caused a ruckus. I didn't go through the proper channels. There was a lot of pettifogging bureaucracy.' Parker was hauled before the prime minister and given a severe dressing down. 'Is it your intention to destroy the entire royal family in the shortest possible time?' growled Churchill.

CHAPTER EIGHTEEN

Coronation Day

The Coronation when it came – on Tuesday 2 June 1953 – was more than a logistical triumph. 'Never has there been such excitement,' wrote Jock Colville, 'never has a Monarch received such adulation.' The country felt on top of the world – literally. The 29,002-foot summit of the world's tallest mountain had been reached at 11:30 a.m. on 29 May. The news arrived in London on the morning of the Coronation. The triumphant mountaineers were a New Zealander, Edmund Hillary, and a Nepalese Sherpa, Norgay Tensing, but the leader of the expedition, John Hunt, was British and the feat was hailed as a British achievement. Everest had been conquered and Elizabeth was to be crowned!

In London the day itself was dank and overcast, but the mood was universally sunny. Hundreds of thousands of people – happy and curious – braved the drizzle and filled the streets. Millions more – in Britain and around the world – followed the day's events on television. Never before in human history had so many people witnessed the same events at the same time.

Inevitably, there were a few republicans with reservations, but, sensibly, they kept their heads down. And the Duke of Windsor stayed away because he was not wanted. Elizabeth felt his presence would be inappropriate. He came to England to attend his mother, Queen Mary's, funeral on 31 March, but reckoned he had not received a warm welcome. Elizabeth would not pay him the £10,000 a year allowance he had been given by her father. A family dinner was held at Windsor Castle following Queen Mary's funeral. He was not invited. He wrote to his wife: 'What a smug, stinking lot my relations are and you've never seen such a seedy worn-out bunch of old hags most of them have become.' Seventy years later, Elizabeth II's grandson, Prince Harry, chose not to attend the Duke of Edinburgh's memorial service at Westminster Abbey, and when he and his wife, Meghan, came over from California for the Queen's Platinum Jubilee celebrations in June 2022, they were welcomed at some, but by no means all, the family gatherings. 'Family rifts are always sad,' the Queen once said to Margaret Rhodes. In later life, the Queen came to regret not having been closer to her uncle David in his exile, but while her mother was alive she avoided doing anything of which she might disapprove or which might distress her.

Elizabeth II lived so long that she did sometimes feel that she had 'seen it all before'. The Prince of Wales (who became Edward VIII) and the Duke of York (who became George VI) were brothers, born only a year or so apart in the mid-1890s, and very close when they were young. The present Prince of Wales (formerly William, Duke of Cambridge) and the Duke of Sussex (Prince Harry), are brothers, too, born only a year or two apart in the early 1980s, and they, also, were very close when they were young. With each set of brothers, the arrival of a thirty-five-year-old American divorcee changed the dynamic of their relationship and ruined everything. Whether Harry when talking privately to Meghan has ever been as vitriolic about his family as the Queen's uncle David was writing privately to Wallis, we shall never know – or perhaps we shall. Shortly before Elizabeth II's death,

Meghan let slip in an interview that she was not obliged to sign an NDA (Non-disclosure agreement) when she and Harry had stepped down from their royal duties in 2020 and, further, that when she had returned to their Windsor home at Frogmore Cottage for the Queen's Platinum Jubilee celebrations in the summer of 2022, she had found a journal that she had kept during her days as an active member of the Family Firm . . .

This sorry Sussex saga will run and run, just as the earlier sorry saga of the Duke and Duchess of Windsor did from the time of the Abdication in 1936 until their dying days. When we get to the coronation of Charles III, the issue of 'Harry and Meghan' – where they are seated, what uniform (if any) he will be allowed to wear, what her body language is telling us, etc., etc. – will be unavoidable. And, from the new King's point of view, regrettable.

Back in 1953, when Elizabeth II was crowned, the Duke of Edinburgh was Chairman of the Coronation Commission – but most of the detail was out of his hands. The pageantry was largely in the gift of his Vice-Chairman, Bernard Fitzalan-Howard, the 16th Duke of Norfolk, hereditary Earl Marshal and Chief Butler of England, a seasoned campaigner whose family titles dated back to 1139 (when King Stephen was crowned) and whose past personal triumphs included the management of the funeral of George V and the coronation of George VI. The Duke was only forty-four, but quite a character. When asked by a peer if his invitation to the coronation might be prejudiced because of his divorce, Norfolk replied, 'Good God, man, this is a coronation, not Royal Ascot.' When asked if it was true that the peers were hiding sandwiches inside their coronets during the service, he answered, 'Probably. They're capable of anything.' When one of the coronation rehearsals was running behind schedule, his voice echoed round Westminster Abbey: 'If the bishops don't learn to walk in step, we'll be here all night.'

There were a dozen rehearsals at the Abbey. The Queen attended several herself and learnt her moves from the Duchess of Norfolk who also acted as her stand-in. At Buckingham Palace – where the ballroom was marked out with ropes and posts replicating the Abbey's floor-plan – she put in hours of extra practice on her own. She listened to recordings of her father's coronation. She walked the course with sheets pinned to her shoulders representing the robes she would wear – and, at the final run-through with the Maids of Honour in the White Drawing Room at Buckingham Palace she had a curtain draped over her as a substitute train. To become accustomed to its weight, she sat at her desk wearing the actual St Edward's crown first used at the coronation of Charles II in 1661. It was heavy – 5lbs – and its weight was of significance, symbolising, according to Geoffrey Fisher, the Archbishop of Canterbury, the burden of the demands that would be made upon her 'to her life's end'. (It was because of the weight of the crown that Queen Victoria and Edward VII chose not to wear it at their coronations. Elizabeth II was made of sterner stuff.)

In attendance on the Queen throughout the ceremony were six Maids of Honour, unmarried young women of the Queen's age or a little younger whose principal role was to carry the Queen's twenty-one-foot purple velvet, ermine-trimmed train. The Maids all came from ancient aristocratic families: the daughters of the 10th Duke of Marlborough, the 5th Duke of Abercorn, the 8th Marquess of Londonderry, the 12th Earl of Haddington, the 5th Earl of Leicester and the 3rd Earl of Ancaster. Fifty years after the coronation, for a television programme in 2003, I hosted a tea party for the Maids at Claridge's Hotel, and their individual recollections of the great day had one memory in common: how calm and self-possessed the Queen was before and during the ceremony and how happy she was afterwards. They also all remembered that Prince Margaret looked 'a bit glum' and that Prince Philip 'fussed too much' – 'he rather got in the way'.

Anne Coke (coming up for twenty-one at the time, daughter of the Earl of Leicester, and later, as Anne Glenconner, lady-in-waiting to Princess Margaret and, later still, a best-selling author) had particularly vivid memories of the Duke of Norfolk, forty-four, the Earl Marshal, 'the supreme commander', and the Marquess of Cholmondely, seventy, the Lord Great Chamberlain, 'who was supposed to help with the Queen's costume changes but wasn't very good at it.' According to Anne Glenconner, 'The Duke knew what he was doing. He had ninety-four diagrams, each depicting different parts of the ceremony in which every minute was worked out and every movement within each minute prescribed. He even had the foresight to work out that his bald head would need to be powdered a few times on the day itself, due to the aerial shots the television cameras would take.'

George Horatio Charles Cholmondeley, 5th Marquess of Cholmondeley, a direct descendant of Sir Robert Walpole, Britain's first prime minister, was a character, too. Tall, handsome ('he seemed very proud of his looks,' according to Anne Glenconner, '– he always sat bolt upright with his head slightly to one side'), gifted as a soldier, and tennis and polo player, he had a passion for good handwriting and created what became known as 'the Cholmondeley italic script.' Given his elegant penmanship, it was all the more surprising that he was all fingers and thumbs when it came to helping the young queen with her wardrobe changes during the coronation. 'He was simply terrible at doing up hooks and eyes,' said Lady Glenconner, 'probably never having to dress himself, let alone anybody else. As the Duke of Norfolk repeatedly showed him what to do, the attempts only resulted in yet more fiddling, and the Duke becoming ever more exasperated.' In the end, the Duke ordered the hooks and eyes to be changed to poppers – and the poor queen paid the price. After the event, she told Anne Glenconner it had been 'tiresome' because every time the Marquess did up a popper he pushed Her Majesty 'rather violently'.

On the day, the Queen, now twenty-six, was 'completely calm', the Maids of Honour all agreed. 'The eyes of the world were on her, but she didn't seem nervous at all.' At the door of the Abbey, as the first procession was about to begin, the Queen turned to her young attendants, smiled and said, 'Ready, girls?'

And in they went, following Her Majesty, carrying her train, quickly realising they had to walk more slowly than they had expected – because the Queen on the day was processing more slowly than the Duchess of Norfolk had in rehearsal. They all agreed that the Queen looked 'simply beautiful', but they weren't so sure about themselves. They loved their dresses – designed by Norman Hartnell and made from ivory silk with gold embroidery – but the dresses were quite tight and not lined, so the underside of the embroidery made them 'uncomfortably scratchy'. And the young ladies were unaccustomed to the amount of make-up required to look normal under the television lights. 'With my black arched eyebrows and bright lipstick, I looked like George Robey as a pantomime dame,' Anne Glenconner told me.

Norman Hartnell was the star of high-end British fashion design from the 1930s to the 1950s, noted for his genius at combining rich fabrics with exquisitely patterned embroideries. He gained the Royal Warrant as Dressmaker to Queen Elizabeth in 1940 and created Princess Elizabeth's weddding dress in 1947. In October 1952, the new young queen invited Hartnell, then fifty-one, to design her coronation gown. 'I can scarcely remember what I murmured in reply,' he recalled, overwhelmed by the significance of the commission. The Queen expressed her wishes to him 'in simple conversational tones' (that was always her way) and left Hartnell to it. He then 'retired to the seclusion of Windsor Forest' (that was his way) and spent many days making trial sketches. 'My mind was teeming with heraldic and floral ideas,' he said. 'I thought of lilies, roses, marguerites and golden corn; I thought of altar cloths and sacred vestments; I thought of the sky, the earth, the sun, the moon, the stars and everything heavenly that might be embroidered upon a dress destined to be historic.'

Hartnell submitted nine different designs and the Queen accepted the eighth, but suggested embroideries in various delicate colours rather than all in silver. She also requested that in addition to the four national emblems, those of the Dominions of which she was now Queen should be added. The dress was both simple and elaborate: a short-sleeved white silk satin gown with sweetheart neckline, natural waist, wide circle skirt and embroideries arranged in three scalloped, graduated tiers bordered with alternating lines of gold bugle beads, diamantés and pearls. All agreed it was a wonder to behold.

The young queen's make-up was the responsibility of her 'Cosmetician and Beauty Adviser', Thelma Besant, an Australian, born in Melbourne in 1910, who came to London at the outset of the war to work for Cyclax, Britain's second oldest cosmetic company (after Yardley), founded in 1896 in the converted front room of a house at 58 South Molton Street, to provide beauty treatments for discerning ladies. By 1910 there were more than forty preparations in the Cyclax range, including skin and hair care products, face powders, eye lotions, lip lotions and soap, and by the 1940s Cyclax's

Molton Street clientele included, among others, some of the mothers of the future Maids of Honour to the next Queen and ladies-in-waiting to the current one.

As Princess Elizabeth turned eighteen in 1944, Miss Besant suggested to one of the Queen's ladies-in-waiting that the time might be right for the heiress presumptive to be given some advice on make-up and skin care. The Australian Cyclax consultant was invited to Buckingham Palace to discuss the matter and then invited to meet the young princess. They got on well and began a working relationship that lasted well into the 1950s and saw Thelma advising the Princess on her make-up for her wedding, her first public engagements, her coronation and her foreign tours.

It is clear from Thelma's unpublished memoir, that she admired the young princess's serious approach to whatever she undertook. Thelma was particularly taken with the photographs that had appeared in the press in 1945 when, at her own insistence, Princess Elizabeth joined the Auxiliary Territorial Service, and was pictured, dressed in overalls as part of her training, taking the spark plugs out of a car. As we know, she completed her course at No. 1 Mechanical Training Centre of the ATS and passed out as a fully qualified driver. Thelma must have met someone who had seen the young princess at work because she wrote in admiration of how 'she learnt to change wheels, to adjust carburettors, to grind in valves, to decarbonise an engine . . .' and reported, 'An army officer told me, "I would sooner drive with Hon Second Subaltern 230973 than any other woman in Britain." How he knew the number I don't know.'

The young princess had been drawn to Cyclax because she knew the firm had made a number of serious contributions to the war effort, including an effective burn treatment and a camouflage cream. And Cyclax took a special interest in the ATS because they had released a lipstick shade named 'Auxiliary Red' that was specifically designed for service women and is reckoned to have started the trend for the use of bright red lipsticks during the war.

The Princess liked the beauty adviser because she was a no-nonsense Australian with a sense of humour who understood the importance of helping the young royal to get her make-up right and be comfortable with it, not for reasons of vanity but so she wouldn't need to worry about it. She could concentrate on her duties, knowing her appearance was as it should be – and the young princess wanted that appearance to be 'natural and uncontrived'. The two always had comfortable exchanges when they met at the Palace and exchanged handwritten notes in between meetings as well. When Prince Charles turned one, Miss Besant sent him a present. Princess Elizabeth was delighted: 'I know he will greatly enjoy banging on the xylophone,' she wrote in her thank you letter from Clarence House, 'for he already prefers noisy things to woolly things!' On 24 April 1950, the Princess wrote to her beautician from Malta: 'I am most grateful to you for sending the two powder puffs for my birthday – they will be so useful . . . It is lovely to be out here in the warm sun – very unlike the weather at home, I gather – though we have also felt the influence of the bad weather from Europe. I haven't managed to get at all sunburnt, but have produced dozens of freckles on my nose, which my husband thinks is very funny!'

Miss Besant was a professional and she worked closely with the young Queen's designer, Norman Hartnell, and her personal dresser, Bobo Macdonald, to get the right foundation and colour of lipstick to work with each outfit and special occasion. For the Coronation, the key was to achieve a make-up that would be strong enough not to be washed out by the bright television lights and a colour scheme that would coordinate with both the scarlet Robe of Estate the Queen was to wear before the crowning and the purple silk velvet Robe of Estate she was to wear after it.

Thelma was allowed to visit the royal robe-makers, Ede and Ravenscroft in Chancery Lane, to collect samples of both materials. 'The Queen, Miss Macdonald, the cosmetic chemist and I were the only people to know about these patterns,' Thelma confided in her memoir. 'After I visited the Robe-Makers I felt like some secret agent carrying an important message. I put the envelope in a handbag with an inside zip and held it tightly under my arm. My imagination ran riot and I wondered, if I was run down near Fleet Street, how I would eat the two pieces of velvet – on the principle that "agents" are supposed to eat their instructions when captured.'

Happily, she was not run down that day and lived on to 1995, guarding the small samples of royal velvet to the end. Her only son, Merlin Holland, has them to this day. Merlin was seven at the time and, by invitation of the Queen, spent Coronation Day with his mother at Buckingham Palace, playing in the garden and watching the comings and goings from one of the top-floor windows facing out on to the Victoria monument on the Mall. He particularly remembers the dust-cart that circled round the Victoria monument early in the morning before the big parade, cheered on by the gathering crowd.

As well as guarding the samples of velvet, Thelma Besant guarded another secret for the rest of her days. She did not do the Queen's make-up on Coronation Day. The Queen did her own make-up. She wanted Thelma on hand at the Palace in case anything should go wrong, but she asked her cosmetic adviser if she thought she would be capable of doing it on her own, because it was such a significant day in her life she felt she wanted to be alone with her thoughts at the start of it.

It was a significant day for all concerned. Thelma Besant was married to Vyvyan Holland, the only surviving son of Oscar Wilde. The Victorian playwright's son, born in 1886, was also a witty writer, as you can tell from these previously unpublished extracts from his diary for Coronation week:

May 22 1953, Friday, London
Thelma had a good session with the Queen yesterday and also saw P. Charles, P. Anne and P. Margaret.

May 25, Monday, Bank Holiday
Merlin went to school in view of two days' holiday next week for the Crowning. We joined the Millers in the gardens in the afternoon and afterwards had drinks with them. Then Thelma got all Coronation minded and after eating some gulls' eggs we took an expensive taxi (15/-) to go to see the show in Parliament Square, Whitehall, etc. It is, of course, all very grand, but the whole thing is too mediaeval and bar-baric for my liking. It is only the fact of having a young Queen that makes the thing possible at all. With an old goat like Edward VII the situation would become absurd.

May 26, 1953, Tuesday, London
. . . Merlin wrote a letter to the Queen today thanking her for letting him come to the Palace on June 2.

I would bet anything that if the indications for June 2 weather are unfavourable there will either be no weather report at all or it will be faked.

May 27, 1953, Wednesday, London
Thelma this morning asked me, pensively: 'Do you think it is very undignified of me, going to Buckingham Palace instead of to the Abbey?' She is getting terrific publicity

over the Queen's make up: it is beginning to frighten even her . . . I have started a rumour that the footmen standing at the back of the Coronation Coach are really eminent physicians in disguise, just in case the Queen is taken queer.

May 28, 1953, Thursday, London
Full page (front) publicity for Thelma in the Daily Graphic. Also lots in News Chronicle, Evening News & Star. Getting really a bit too much.

June 1, 1953, Monday, London
. . . Thelma returned at about 8 pm in high fettle because Queenie wants her to go and help to tickle up the Royal Countenance for tomorrow's Coronboree, and she ate her cold lamb with gusto.

June 2 1953, Tuesday, Coronation Day, London
Up at 5 am and the preparation of food for Thelma and Merlin to take to the Palace. They left at 6:30 . . . The weather was, of course, filthy with occasional fine intervals. I myself went to 10 Wellesley House where Hazel Miller and the Martens were giving a television party with masses of champagn . . . The television was quite amazing. So was the luncheon, which consisted so far as I was concerned almost entirely of Virginia Peach fed Ham.

Thelma turned up at 7:30, quite exhausted and regaled us with Royal stories. She had quite clearly had a few in addition to the quarter bottle of gin which she took with her. . . A really exhausting day. Ethane Davies, who had my Coronation seat at Hyde Park corner, said that she enjoyed it on the whole, but got thoroughly soused. 'So did I,' replied Holland, 'but mine was done in champagne.'

June 4 1953, Thursday, London

I went into the King's Road at 2.30 to see Queenie pass by on one of her post Coronation drives through London. How sick she must be of crowds and people.

But, of course, she wasn't. Sometimes she admitted to being tired at the end of a long day, but Elizabeth II never complained – ever – of doing her royal duty. 'I can't believe I'm not getting paid for this,' said Meghan, in an aside, while meeting Australians on her first royal tour. That was not something the Queen would have said – or thought. The Queen believed in her role as sovereign. Indeed, she believed it was not simply a duty, but a sacred duty.

The Archbishop of Canterbury, Dr Geoffrey Fisher, the ceremonial head of the worldwide Anglican communion and a muscular Christian (at Oxford he was a noted footballer, rugby player and oarsman), went to great lengths to ensure that the spiritual significance of the Coronation was not obscured by the pomp and pageantry. In the run-up to the great day, he gave a series of sermons exploring and explaining the coronation liturgy. He was an experienced teacher (he had been headmaster of Repton) and in Elizabeth, of course, he had a willing pupil. Martin Charteris said to me, 'People will have their own memories of the Coronation – of the pageantry, the processions, the Queen of Tonga in her open carriage[2], the street parties and what have you – but for the Queen herself, the Coronation was not about celebration, it was about dedication. It was a religious event.'

---

2   Queen Salote of Tonga was a large lady and she travelled to the Abbey in an open carriage sitting opposite the comparatively diminutive Sultan of Kelantan. Someone asked, 'Who is that with Queen Salote?' 'That,' said Noël Coward famously, 'is her lunch.'

On the day itself, the Archbishop played his part with due solemnity – and maintained that solemnity in part thanks to Oscar Wilde's daughter-in-law, who supplied Lady Fisher with a bottle of foundation cream that the Archbishop's wife applied to her husband's shiny bald head so that it wouldn't glisten distractingly under the fierce television lights. A few days after the event, the Archbishop looked back on it all in awe: 'The wonder of it, the unforgettable bearing of the Queen, the overwhelming sense of dedication to God, of worship of God, consecration by God and communion with God, embracing everyone in the Abbey.' And beyond. In the United Kingdom in 1953, the Anglican faith was alive and well – and popular. In London in the early 1950s, more than forty per cent of all adults regularly attended church. Today, fewer than three per cent do.

Westminster Abbey, the setting for Elizabeth's coronation, was where William the Conqueror was crowned on Christmas Day, 1066. The essential elements of the ceremony were much as they had been for a thousand years. For the Queen, the most significant part of the service was the Act of Anointing, the moment, in the Archbishop's phrase, that brought her 'into the presence of the living God'. It was a moment, both intimate and sacred, that, at her own request, was neither filmed nor televised. As she sat on the Coronation Chair, under a canopy held by four Knights of the Garter, the Archbishop made a sign of the cross on both of her hands, on her breast and on her head. 'Be thy Head anointed with holy Oil,' he said, 'as kings, priests and prophets were anointed. And as Solomon was anointed King by Zadok the priest and Nathan the prophet, so be thou anointed, blessed and consecrated Queen over the Peoples, whom the Lord thy God hath given thee to rule and govern.'

For Philip, the most significant part of the service came a little later. This was, in every sense, the Queen's day – and, in truth, hers alone. He was there as her attendant lord. Dressed in the uniform of an Admiral of the Fleet, he accompanied her to and from the Abbey in the great Gold State Coach. He shared in the waving, not the crowning. This was her Coronation, not theirs. In the Abbey, she processed alone. She took the Coronation oath alone. She alone was anointed with holy oil. She alone was crowned. When the Coronation was done – when St Edward's crown had been placed upon her head – the nobility paid homage to their Queen. The first to do so was the Lord Archbishop of Canterbury. Next was the Duke of Edinburgh. He stepped forward and knelt before her. He placed his hands between hers and said, 'I, Philip, Duke of Edinburgh, do become your liege man of life and limb, and of earthly worship; and faith and truth will I bear unto you, to live and die, against all manner of folks. So help me God.'

He said it and he meant it. When, once, I asked Prince Philip what his life had been about, he narrowed his eyes and shied away from the question. I decided to persist. 'Supporting the Queen,' I suggested, 'isn't that what it's all been about?' He looked away – which was unusual for him: normally, he looked directly at you – and said, very slowly and almost inaudibly, 'Absolutely. Absolutely.' He may have been disappointed that his naval career was cut short. He may have been angered that he could not give his own name to his own children. He may have been infuriated by the way he was patronised by some of those he met at Court. But never – not once – in more than sixty years – did he flinch in the performance of what he saw as his one, essential duty: to support the Queen.

When Philip had completed his homage, he stood up, touched the Queen's crown and kissed her left cheek. Next to pay homage were the Dukes of Gloucester and Kent, followed by England's premier baron, Mowbray Segrave and

Stourton, whose titles dated back to 1283 (when Edward I was King) and whose appearance provided some unexpected light relief. The Archbishop recalled: 'He came down from his homage all over the place, bunching up his robe and, as the Queen said, with moth balls and pieces of ermine all over the place.' When the homage was over, the trumpets sounded and the congregation – 7,500 strong – called out: 'God Save Queen Elizabeth, Long Live Queen Elizabeth, May the Queen Live for ever.'

As the choir sang a valedictory *Te Deum*, the Queen stepped down from her throne.

In the St Edward's Chapel, she changed her velvet robes once more – the ceremony had involved a lot of dressing and undressing – and swapped the historic St Edward's Crown for the slightly lighter, but undeniably fancier, Imperial State Crown, studded with many of the most precious stones on earth – including the Black Prince's ruby, Elizabeth I's pearl earrings and Charles II's sapphire. 'During this recess,' according to Anne Glenconner, who had felt a little faint earlier in the proceedings (and had had to be steadied by Black Rod, the Second World War hero, Lieutenant-General Sir Brian Horrocks), 'the Archbishop of Canterbury got out a small flask of brandy and offered it around. The Queen, along with the other Maids of Honour, declined but I took a sip.'

Sober, calm, contained, bearing the crown jewels, carrying the sceptre in her right hand and the orb in her left, while the congregation sang the National Anthem, Elizabeth II processed through the Abbey to the West Door where the Gold State Coach again awaited her. She clambered aboard, accompanied by Philip, and, drawn by eight grey horses, the coach – a proper fairy-tale affair, over-the-top, baroque and bedazzling, with door panels painted by Cipriani in the 1760s – took them, slowly and steadily, on a circuitous seven-mile route back to Buckingham Palace. They were cheered, long and loud, by hundreds of thousands of the Queen's subjects, many of whom had camped out for several nights, in the cold and wet, to secure a good view of the passing parade. They were escorted by twenty-seven further carriages, twenty-nine military bands and thirteen thousand troops. The Chairman of the Coronation Commission reckoned it 'not a bad show'.

Back at the Palace, in the Green Drawing Room, Cecil Beaton was waiting to take the official photographs. 'In came the Queen,' he recorded in his diary, 'cool, smiling, sovereign of the situation.' Cecil Beaton is a useful witness because he has a photographer's eye and an artist's sensibility. 'The Queen looked extremely minute under her robes and Crown, her nose and hands chilled and her eyes tired. "Yes," in reply to my question, "the Crown does get rather heavy." She had been wearing it now for nearly three hours.' Beaton's description of Philip rings especially true:

> The Duke of Edinburgh stood by making wry jokes, his lips pursed in a smile that put the fear of God into me. I believe he doesn't like or approve of me. This is a pity because, although I'm not one for 'Navy-type' jokes, and obviously have nothing in common with him, I admire him enormously, and think he is absolutely first-rate at this job of making things comparatively lively and putting people at their ease. Perhaps he was disappointed that his friend, Baron, was not doing this job today; whatever the reason he was definitely adopting a rather ragging attitude towards the proceedings.

The recollection of the Maids of Honour when I met them all fifty years after the event was that the Queen remained serene throughout the day, focussed during the Coronation service itself, relaxed, good-humoured and mindful of others afterwards, whereas the Duke of Edinburgh was tense, tetchy and, when it came to the taking of the photographs, positively officious. Anne Glenconner said, 'Eventually Cecil Beaton snapped. He put down his camera, glared at the Duke of Edinburgh and said, "Sir, if you would like to take the photographs, please do." He then gestured to the camera and started to walk away. The Queen looked horrified, as did the Queen Mother, and realising he had gone too far, the Duke of Edinburgh moved off.'

Beaton was homosexual, and camp in manner, and his favourite royal sitter on Coronation Day – on any day, come to that – was Queen Elizabeth, the Queen Mother. He found her in 'rollicking spirits' and so immediately warm and helpful towards him that, at once, all his 'anxieties and fears' were dispelled:

The Queen Mother, by being so basically human and understanding, gives out to us a feeling of reassurance. The great mother figure and nannie to us all, through the warmth of her sympathy bathes us and wraps us in a counterpane by the fireside. Suddenly I had this wonderful accomplice – someone who would help me through everything. All at once, and because of her, I was enjoying my work. Prince Charles and Princess Anne were buzzing about in the wildest excitement and would not keep still for a moment. The Queen Mother anchored them in her arms, put her head down to kiss Prince Charles's hair, and made a terrific picture.

Charles III, as he now is, would endorse every word of Beaton's description of his grandmother. In the Abbey, Charles, not yet five years old, in white silk shirt and shorts, had watched the Coronation from the Royal Box, perched between his aunt and his grandmother. His other grandmother, Princess Alice, was nearby, 'a contrast to the grandeur,' Beaton noted, 'in the ash-grey draperies of a nun.'

For Princess Alice, it was a wonderful experience, moving and exciting. She ordered a special, brand-new nun's habit for the occasion. She was an interesting mix: she craved the simple life, but travelled widely; mostly she lived modestly, but sometimes she was immoderately extravagant; she advocated self-discipline, but she smoked like a chimney. For the Queen Widow (as Beaton called the Queen Mother) it was a more poignant occasion. At the Palace she was 'dimpled and chuckling, with eyes as bright as any of her jewels': at the Abbey, in her expression 'we read sadness combined with pride.'

Martin Charteris told me that he believed that the Queen Mother was jealous of her daughter. 'Queen Elizabeth was not yet fifty-two when the King died,' he reminded me. 'She was accustomed to being centre-stage, the focus of attention, universally loved. She was still loved, of course, and admired, but she was no longer the star of the show and I don't think she found that easy. In the early days of the new queen's reign, there was an awkwardness about precedence, with the Queen not wanting to go in front of her mother and Queen Elizabeth, of course, accustomed to going first.'

I want to quote one last time from Cecil Beaton's diary for two reasons: to illustrate Elizabeth's sense of humour and to suggest something about the Queen Mother's attitude to her son-in-law. Beaton had not expected to be asked to take the coronation pictures. Because Baron, 'a most unexpected friend of Prince Philip's', had been taking all the recent royal photographs, Beaton assumed that Baron would get this special assignment, too. When he didn't, when, in early May 1953, Beaton learnt that the job was going to be his, after all, the news came 'as an enormous relief':

The same night that this message was relayed to me, at a ball at the American Embassy, I saw the Queen [Elizabeth II] for a brief moment and thanked her. 'No, I'm very glad you're going to take them,' she said, 'but, by the time we get through to the photographs, we'll have circles down to here' (she pointed halfway down her cheeks), 'then the Crown comes down to here' (to the eye), 'then the court train comes bundling up here, and I'm out to here' (sticks stomach out). 'There are layers upon layers: skirt and mantle and trains.' She spoke like a young high-spirited girl.

I also had a short opportunity to thank the Queen Mother for what I am sure must have been her help in bringing about this 'coup' for me. She laughed knowingly with one finger high in the air.

I can picture her. She could be very naughty. And worse, perhaps. Famously, Sir John Wheeler-Bennett, the official biographer of George VI, remarked of her that there was 'a small drop of arsenic in the centre of that marshmallow'. Philip was the Chairman of the Coronation Commission. He might have preferred to have the official Coronation photographs taken by his friend, Baron, but, if so, he was thwarted. Beaton secured the assignment, not only because he was an exceptional photographer who wooed Queen Elizabeth with flattery and flowers ('I took enormous care to choose a bouquet of all the first spring flowers to be sent to that adorable human being living in that cold, bleak Palace' he recorded in his diary), but also because Baron was Philip's man and Philip was someone Queen Elizabeth did not entirely trust. When first he had appeared on the scene, she had had her misgivings about him – encouraged by her brother David and his set – but, according to several of Philip's friends, her doubts and reservations about her son-in-law persisted until the end of her very long life.

Her published letters betray none of this – unsurprisingly. According to her editor, William Shawcross, she 'made it a rule never to talk (let alone write) about her new relations, even to her Strathmore family.' Shawcross commends her 'wise discretion' and tells us that she maintained it for the rest of her life. Certainly, her letters to Philip are consistently affectionate – though she suffered the dilemma faced by many mothers-in-law. She was not quite sure what to call herself. In the 1940s she was signing her letters to Philip: 'Ever your devoted Mama Elizabeth' and 'Much love, Mummy or Mama' and 'Ever your loving Mum, Elizabeth'. In the 1950s she tried 'Your loving Mama, Elizabeth', 'Your loving m-in-l, E' and 'Your loving Mama in law, Elizabeth'. Eventually she settled for 'Your affec Elizabeth M' or, most often, a simple, 'Much love, Mama E'.

When Philip and Elizabeth were married, Queen Elizabeth told her son-in-law, 'We are so fond of you, and *so so* glad that you and darling Lilibet are so happy.' Margaret Rhodes told me that was the essence of it: 'Queen Elizabeth was happy that her daughter was happy. That's all she asked. That's what every mother wants, isn't it?' And the Duke of Edinburgh was a conscientious son-in-law. When George VI died, Philip sent the Queen Mother a 'comforting & wonderful' letter full of 'understanding and sweetness'. When Princess Margaret was married, Prince Philip walked his sister-in-law down the aisle and his mother-in-law thanked him 'with all my heart', not only for providing 'the arm of a strong and loving person' but also for 'being so sweet to her during the last years. It must have helped her a lot, for I think she felt terribly lost when her father died.' Philip was a committed family man, on the whole better at expressing his feelings in action or by letter than in conversation. He wrote thoughtful letters to his mother-in-law; he gave her presents (including two landscapes he had painted himself); he lent her books that he thought would be of interest to her. He always behaved towards her with dutiful affection and punctilious courtesy.

At around the time of Queen Elizabeth's one hundredth birthday, I happened to interview Prince Philip (seventy-nine himself at the time) for ITN Radio and tried to nudge him into saying something about his mother-in-law. Apart from insisting that he had no desire to live so long himself, he would not be drawn. I have had no reports of his having ever made any disparaging remarks about her, but several people have told me how, within their hearing, Queen Elizabeth made slighting comments about Philip and referred to him – not entirely humorously – as 'the Hun'. One of Philip's close female friends told me that the coolness between Prince Philip and Prince Charles was, in part, a by-product of the unspoken tension between Philip and his mother-in-law. Charles adored his grandmother and Queen Elizabeth was extravagantly, effusively, fond of Charles. There was an intimacy and mutual sympathy between them that Philip did not share. 'She laughed knowingly with one finger in the air.' Yes, there was a small drop of arsenic in the centre of that marshmallow.

On Coronation Day, the young queen was happy – so happy, according to Anne Glenconner, that when she got back to Buckingham Palace she began running along the corridors. Her Maids of Honour ran after her. Eventually, she collapsed on to a red sofa in the gallery on the way to the White Drawing Room where the photographs were to be taken, her dress billowing and settling down around her. 'We sat with her,' remembered Lady Glenconner, 'and when she kicked up her legs for total joy, we did the same. It was the happiest of moments.'

The Queen was happy; the Duke of Edinburgh was tetchy; Princess Margaret was sad. Later, Margaret told Anne Glenconner, who in time became her lady-in-waiting, 'Of course I looked sad, Anne. I had just lost my beloved father, and, really, I had just lost my sister, because she was going to be so busy and had already moved into Buckingham Palace, so it was just me and the Queen Mother.'

Princess Margaret was sad on Coronation Day – and pre-occupied. Cecil Beaton described her at Buckingham Palace that afternoon, sailing towards him, 'her purple train being held aloft by four pages', 'with pink and white make-up and a sex twinkle of understanding in her regard.' Perhaps Beaton knew her secret. Margaret was twenty-two and in love with a married man sixteen years her senior.

CHAPTER NINETEEN

Duty – and sacrifice

Group Captain Peter Townsend was born in 1914, at the outset of the First World War, and, in 1940, in the Battle of Britain, became one of the heroes of the Second World War. He was a fighter pilot who led the 'B' Flight of Hurricanes in the celebrated No. 43 Squadron. He was mentioned in despatches. He won the DFC and Bar. But the war took its toll: he had a nervous breakdown. 'I knew in my bones that I should never again be the pilot I once had been,' he confessed in his memoirs. 'I had gone too far down the hill ever to get to the top again . . . The more I flew, and there could be no relenting, the more fear, stark, degrading fear, possessed me. Each time I took off, I felt sure it would be the last.'

By 1944, he was no longer flying, but he was still a hero, and when the King expressed the desire to have an RAF officer as an equerry for the first time, Townsend seemed a first-rate choice. He was handsome, agreeable, distinguished and came from a solid, if middle-class, background. (His brother Michael, a naval captain, served with Philip in HMS *Chequers*.) He was also complex, troubled and deeply religious. The King took to him at once and Townsend was immediately sympathetic to the King: 'The King did not try, or even need, to put me at my ease . . . the humanity of the man and his striking simplicity came across warmly, unmistakably . . . sometimes he

hesitated in his speech, and then I felt drawn towards him . . .'
Townsend was said to be the only member of the Household
who could successfully soothe the King when he was overwhelmed by one of his 'gnashes'. He arrived at Buckingham
Palace anticipating a three-month attachment. He remained in
the King and Queen's service for nearly ten years. On the day
he came for his initial interview, in February 1944, Lilibet and
Margaret, then aged seventeen and thirteen, saw the beautiful, brown-haired, blue-eyed hero, who was just twenty-nine,
arrive at the Palace, and, as he came into view, so the story
goes, Lilibet whispered to her younger sister, 'Bad luck. He's
married.'

Townsend married young and unluckily. Rosemary
Townsend was attractive, vivacious and flirtatious. She was
also socially aspirational. She liked to flirt with the King.
According to Townsend, when he secured the job as equerry,
his wife's immediate reaction was: 'We're made.' In fact, they
were undone. Townsend gave his all to the royal family: he
was devoted to the King, charmed by the Queen, and, before
very long, innocently enamoured of the teenage princess:

> One day after a picnic lunch with the guns, I stretched out
> in the heather to doze. Then, vaguely, I was aware that
> someone was covering me with a coat. I opened one eye to
> see Princess Margaret's lovely face, very close, looking into
> mine. Then I opened the other eye, and saw behind her, the
> King leaning on his stick, with a certain look, typical of him:
> kind, half-amused.

In 1947, when the royal family took their three-month trip
to southern Africa, Townsend was in attendance, of necessity
leaving Rosemary behind. Rosemary had an affair with a young
Guards officer, and then another, with John de Laszlo, son of

the painter Philip de Laszlo, whose portraits of Prince Philip's parents used to hang in his study at Buckingham Palace. Townsend's marriage was breaking down and he was falling in love with the second-in-line to the throne. He was sixteen years older than Margaret and a married man. He should have known better. He should have resisted temptation. But he didn't. He was besotted:

> What ultimately made Princess Margaret so attractive and lovable was that behind the dazzling façade, the apparent self-assurance, you could find, if you looked for it, a rare softness and sincerity. She could make you bend double with laughing; she could also touch you deeply. There were dozens of others; their names were in the papers, which vied with each other, frantically and futilely, in their forecasts of the one whom she would marry. Yet I dare say that there was not one among them more touched by the Princess's *joie de vivre* than I, for in my present marital predicament, it gave me what I most lacked – joy. More, it created a sympathy between us and I began to sense that, in her life too, there was something lacking.

When the King died, Margaret was twenty-one years old and bereft. 'He was so kind and brave all his life,' she said, 'the very heart and centre of our family and no one could have had a more loving and thoughtful father.' His death left a void and Townsend filled it. Having served as the King's equerry, he was now appointed Comptroller of the Queen Mother's Household. At the end of 1952, he secured a divorce from Rosemary on the grounds of her adultery. He was the innocent party; he was the wronged husband; he was now a free man and he wanted to marry the new Queen's sister. With a sense of timing that, according to their detractors, serves to illustrate Townsend's naïvety and Margaret's selfishness, in the spring of 1953, in the immediate run-up to the Coronation, the young princess told her sister and her mother that she and Townsend were in love and wished to marry. Townsend later recalled: 'If they were disconcerted as they had every reason to be, they did not flinch, but faced it with perfect calm and, it must be said, considerable charity.'

Sir Alan Lascelles, the new Queen's private secretary, who was set to retire after the Coronation, was less understanding. 'You must be either mad or bad or both,' he told Townsend when he heard the news. Martin Charteris, then the Queen's assistant private secretary, said to me, 'I don't think he was mad or bad, but he was naïve. Incredibly so. He was a commoner and a divorcee. Rightly or wrongly, divorcees were not presented at court, were not invited to garden parties, were not formally introduced to royalty. I don't think there was ever a serious prospect of a marriage. If the King had still been alive, I don't believe the matter would have arisen. I don't think Townsend would have dared.'

Queen Elizabeth, the Queen Mother seemingly put the matter out of her mind – 'the old ostrich approach' as Charteris had it. The young Queen, not yet crowned, put the matter on hold. 'Under the circumstances,' she said, 'it isn't unreasonable for me to ask you to wait a year.' In the event, Margaret and Townsend waited more than two years before bowing to the inevitable.

Elizabeth wanted Margaret to be happy. As their cousin Margaret Rhodes put it to me, 'Margaret drove the Queen mad frequently, but she was her sister and she loved her.' Philip was not unsympathetic either. He was infuriated by the amount of publicity the romance generated, and annoyed, especially, that it was a photograph taken at Westminster Abbey on Coronation Day – of Margaret brushing Townsend's lapel 'with a tender hand' – that triggered the worldwide media interest in the story, but there is no evidence to support repeated press suggestions that he was positively hostile towards Townsend. When stories of his alleged plotting against his would-be brother-in-law appeared in the papers, Philip bleated, despairingly, 'What have I done? I haven't done anything.' In truth, he tried to keep out of the way. As he said to me once, with reference to his own children's marital difficulties: 'I try to keep out of these things as much as possible.' Martin Charteris said to me, 'Prince Philip had a sort of ragging, joshing way with Princess Margaret, treated her as the wayward younger sister, but I don't believe he interfered in any way. The Queen was naturally sympathetic towards the Princess, but I think she thought – she hoped – given time, the affair would peter out. Townsend really was unsuitable. He was older, he had two sons already. It just wasn't going to happen. Churchill wouldn't wear it. Salisbury wouldn't wear it. The Commonwealth wouldn't wear it. It wasn't going to happen.'

It didn't. Under the Royal Marriages Act of 1772, the Queen's sister required the Queen's blessing before she could marry. If the Queen decided not to sanction marriage, Princess Margaret could wait until her twenty-fifth birthday and then marry without the sovereign's consent provided she could secure the approval of Parliament. In 1953, when Margaret was still twenty-three, Churchill, whose momentary first instinct had been that 'the path of true love must be allowed to run smooth', quickly advised against the marriage. Lord Salisbury, a senior figure in the government, was adamantly opposed. The Commonwealth prime ministers, when consulted, expressed their misgivings. The Queen was Supreme Governor of the Church of England: her sister's union with a divorced man was not to be condoned.

For two years the issue simmered on, with the publicity surrounding it coming to the boil at regular intervals. In the hope that distance might lessen enchantment, under pressure from Lascelles and Churchill, the Queen agreed that Townsend be 'let go' from court. He was despatched to the British embassy in Brussels as air attaché. Margaret took up her public duties. She accompanied her mother on a tour of Rhodesia. Alone, she undertook a tour of the West Indies. For nearly two years the lovers remained apart, but in touch. They were love-sick and the malady lingered on. It all came to a head in the summer and autumn of 1955, as Margaret approached and passed her twenty-fifth birthday. The new prime minister, Anthony Eden (himself, incidentally, a divorcee) advised the Queen that the government still could not sanction the union – Lord Salisbury, for one, would resign if it attempted to do so – and, while the legislation required to enable the marriage to take place might be passed by Parliament, it would necessitate the Princess sacrificing her right of succession. Margaret was third in line to the throne. Eden advised the Queen that 'neither the proposed marriage nor her renunciation of her right to the Succession need in themselves affect her style and title as Her Royal Highness Princess Margaret or the provision made for her under the Civil List', but, inevitably, if she married Townsend, her status would be changed, irrevocably.

In the end, Margaret decided against the sacrifice. She met with Townsend on 22 October 1955. 'We were both exhausted,' he recalled, 'mentally, emotionally, physically.' He knew his Princess loved her life as a princess. He knew he could not expect her to abandon it for a life in Brussels as the not-quite-as-royal-as-once-she-was second wife of a middle-aged air attaché. They met again. 'We looked at each other,' he said, 'there was a wonderful tenderness in her eyes which reflected, I suppose, the look in mine. We had reached the end of the road.'

On 31 October, they met at Clarence House and had a last drink together, toasting the happiness they had shared and the future they would not. At 7:00 p.m. that same evening the young princess issued a public statement that, within hours, became the lead story on front pages around the world:

I would like it to be known that I have decided not to marry Group Captain Peter Townsend. I have been aware that, subject to renouncing my rights of succession, it might have been possible for me to contract a civil marriage. But, mindful of the Church's teaching that Christian marriage is indissoluble, and conscious of my duty to the Commonwealth, I have resolved to put these considerations before any others.

I have reached this decision entirely alone, and in doing so I have been strengthened by the unfailing support of Group Captain Townsend. I am deeply grateful for the concern of all those who have constantly prayed for my happiness.

Sarah Bradford, in her biography of the Queen, says, when she reaches this point in the story:

Amazingly, the royal family did not rally round Margaret on the night of her formal renunciation. She dined alone while her mother kept an official engagement at London University. The Queen Mother did not say goodnight to her daughter on her return. For some time they had barely been on speaking terms; for the Queen Mother, the Townsend affair had been as traumatic as the Abdication had for Queen Mary. Elizabeth telephoned for a brief conversation, after which Margaret returned to watching boxing on television. The King's death and his widow's subsequent withdrawal, Elizabeth's marriage and Margaret's romance had weakened the family bonds that had linked 'us four' so closely together.

Certainly, the 'family dynamic' had changed, but I believe that the Queen – who, I know, admired Sarah Bradford's biography of her father – would have quarrelled with the implications of the Bradford account of 'the night of the formal renunciation'. It does not take into account the way the Windsors do things – or at least did in the Queen's day. Of course, the Queen Mother fulfilled a long-standing official engagement. Duty always comes first. Of course, the Queen telephoned her sister, but the conversation was neither cursory nor unsympathetic. As Queen Elizabeth, the Queen Mother pointed out to Princess Margaret in a letter that October: 'It is so difficult talking of anything personal on the telephone, because one feels that so many people are listening most eagerly.' In the old days, before mobile phones, royal calls usually went via landlines through Palace switchboards, and anyone could have been listening in. In more recent times, there has been a different difficulty. Unless a telephone conversation is recorded, how can you be certain that a garbled version of it might not appear in somebody's 'my truth' memoir somewhere down the line? Because, in Elizabeth II's memorable turn of phrase, 'recollections may vary', the only way to ensure that you are not misquoted is to electronically record your conversations – but who wants to do that within the family circle?

And if – as the Queen felt and the Queen Mother felt, too – a telephone is not necessarily totally secure, a personal meeting is not always easy either. The Queen's position – and her lack of any kind of anonymity – meant that she could not simply jump into the car and go round to see people on a whim.

Townsend did not entirely disappear from Margaret's life. He went around the world, slowly, to help himself forget her, but found himself unable to do so. He contacted her once more in the spring of 1958. They met again at Clarence House, apparently with the Queen Mother's somewhat uncertain blessing. This was in March 1958, when the Queen and the Duke of Edinburgh were on a state visit to the Netherlands. Unfortunately, news of the reunion reached the press, and salacious, sensationalised coverage of the Princess's tryst at Clarence House quite eclipsed more responsible reporting of the sovereign's visit to Holland. Elizabeth and Philip were not amused. Margaret and Townsend knew there was no hope, and parted for a final time. Within a year, Peter Townsend, aged forty-five, was engaged to a Belgian girl, aged nineteen. Marie-Luce Jamagne looked uncannily like the teenage Margaret.

In May 1960, Princess Margaret, approaching thirty, married a man her own age ('and almost her own height', quipped friends: in fact he was several inches taller): Tony Armstrong-Jones, a gifted theatre and society photographer, and one of the most alarmingly charming people a girl (or boy) could hope to meet. They did not live happily ever after. Far from it. Their marriage was a roller-coaster ride: at times exciting, at times quite frightening: ultimately disastrous. As personalities they had much in common: both were charismatic, creative, charming, manipulative, selfish and self-absorbed. Their marriage was turbulent almost from the start, characterised by self-indulgence, recrimination and mutual infidelity. Most of those who knew them both branded some of Snowdon's behaviour towards his wife as 'cruel'. I knew Tony well: he was funny, gifted, and, until he had had too much white wine (he kept a glass on the go from mid-morning), good company.

But he was a serial seducer, mostly of younger women, but occasionally of younger men. He bedded his best friend's wife who gave birth to his illegitimate daughter three weeks after his marriage to Princess Margaret in 1960. Thirty-eight years later, he fathered another illegitimate child, a son this time, during his marriage to his second wife, Lucy Lindsay-Hogg. In the intervening years, he had any number of mistresses and one-night (as well as one-afternoon) stands. One of his long-term mistresses died by suicide on New Year's Eve in 1996. He also did good works for people with disabilities and doted on his (legitimate) children. He sent them to Bedales (my old school) and, having met both his daughters, I can tell you they are delightful. The Queen very much loved both Sarah Armstrong-Jones (now Lady Sarah Chatto) and David Linley (now the 2nd Earl of Snowdon), her sister's two children, seventh and fifth in line to the throne when they were born, and, especially after Princess Margaret's death, always made sure they were invited to any family gatherings. I once made the Queen laugh by telling her a story she claimed she had never heard before – but that both Tony Snowdon and Lady Olivier (the actress Joan Plowright, married to Laurence Olivier) assured me is true.

In the story, the Snowdons visit the Oliviers at their house in Brighton, and Lady Olivier and Princess Margaret are comparing notes on the progress of their baby boys. David Linley was born on 3 November 1961. Richard Olivier was born a month later, on 3 December 1961. Lady Olivier boasts that her Richard has spoken his first word and she says she is 'So pleased – and so is Larry – because Richard's first word was "Dada".' Princess Margaret responds with the news that by happy coincidence, her little David had just spoken his first word. 'And what was it?' asks Lady Olivier. 'It was "chandelier",' says Princess Margaret proudly.

The Queen thought that very funny and reckoned it was even possibly true, given the chandeliers in the ceilings at Kensington Palace. The nanny could have pointed it out to baby David in his cot and kept repeating, 'Chandelier!'

Princess Margaret and Antony Armstrong-Jones were married at Westminster Abbey on 6 May 1960. Noël Coward was there. The wedding was 'moving and irreproachably organized,' he confided to his diary. 'The Queen alone looked disagreeable; whether or not this was concealed sadness or bad temper because Tony Armstrong-Jones had refused an earldom, nobody seems to know, but she did *scowl* a good deal.'

According to one of her ladies-in-waiting at the time, the Queen was simply tired. She had hosted a big ball in her sister's honour at Buckingham Palace two nights' before and it was only twelve weeks since Prince Andrew had been born. Her third child had arrived a little earlier than expected, weighing in at 7lbs 3oz, but Her Majesty, according to her lady-in-waiting, had suffered 'post-natal side effects' because this baby, like Prince Charles, had been born using the now-discredited 'twilight sleep' method of childbirth.

The scowling sovereign notwithstanding, Noël Coward in 1960 was swept away by 'the pomp and circumstance and pageantry' of the wedding day, 'handled with such exquisite dignity.' I think it is worth quoting Coward's observations, because, now as then, as much in 2022 as in 1960, the pageantry of a royal moment – be it a wedding, a jubilee, or a state funeral – is something the British do uniquely well. It is a core element of 'Brand Britain'. 'There wasn't one note of vulgarity or anything approaching it in the whole thing,' reflected Coward. 'In America such a balance between grandeur and jollity would be impossible; in France or Italy hysterical, in Germany heavy-handed, and in Russia ominous. But in dear London it was lusty, charming, romantic, splendid and conducted without a false note. It is *still* a pretty exciting thing to be English.'

Antony Armstrong-Jones accepted an earldom eighteen months after the wedding, when Princess Margaret was about to give birth to their first child. The Queen very much encouraged him to keep his artistic career going alongside his royal commitments as her sister's husband – just as many years later she told Meghan she should pursue her career as an actress if that is what she wanted. Lord Snowdon went on taking fabulous photographs – including the one of the Queen that features on the cover of this book. In 1964, with Cedric Price and Frank Newby, he conceived Britain's first walk-through aviary for London's Regent's Park Zoo, its design inspired, he told me, 'by the very movement of birds – I love a graceful bird!' In 1969, as Constable of Caernavon Castle, with his friend Carl Toms, he designed and masterminded the Investiture of the young Prince of Wales.

'Was it fun?' I asked him.

'I was proud to do it,' he said. 'It was important. It was hilarious, too. We had to go to pompous meetings at St James's Palace, to get our plans approved by the Garter King of Arms. You had to call him "Garter". His actual name was Sir Anthony Wagner, so you can imagine our nickname for him. There was a frightful row about the dragons we wanted to put on the banners. Carl said, "The dragons must have a knot in their tails: all dragons have knots in their tails." Garter wouldn't have it. Garter stood his ground. Eventually I said to him, "Oh, come on, Garter darling, can't you be a bit more elastic?"'

Prince Charles was the twenty-first heir to the English or British throne to hold the title of Prince of Wales. The 1969 investiture was a revival of a ceremony which had first been used for the previous Prince of Wales in 1911. Charles's son, William, the new Prince of Wales, has made it clear already that he has no immediate plans for an elaborate investiture. He and Catherine are 'going to get to know Wales and the Welsh people properly' first. They have already lived in North Wales. William graduated from the Search and Rescue Training Unit at RAF Valley in Anglesey when he was training to become a helicopter pilot with the Royal Air Force's Search and Rescue Force. The couple's three children, Prince George, Princess Charlotte and Prince Louis, have now taken on the last name, Wales, and the family's hope is to get to know and understand the principality from the grass roots up and do so 'with humility rather than ceremony.'

The 1969 Snowdon-designed investiture was watched by 500 million people worldwide on television, but it received opposition from Welsh nationalist organisations and brickbats from some critics who felt the ritual had no heart and the central figures looked ridiculous. Prince Charles appeared awkward in his princely robes; the Queen's hat, in pale yellow silk, apparently inspired by a Tudor era French hood and designed by Simone Mirman, looked like an ill-fitting space helmet; and Lord Snowdon, in a bottle-green uniform he had designed himself, looked, according to the Duke of Edinburgh, exactly like the character Buttons from the pantomime *Cinderella*. From that day on, when in a joshing mood, Prince Philip regularly called his brother-in-law 'Buttons'. (In later years, to annoy him, other friends referred to him as 'Tony Snapshot'.)

Tony loved that green uniform and kept it readily to hand for the rest of his life. I was in the basement studio of his house in Launceston Place once when, with some cajoling, he persuaded his young assistant to dress up in it for him and pose on one of the investiture chairs he had kept from 1969 as a souvenir. She was in her twenties and he was in his seventies at the time. He did not let the Queen or Prince Philip see that side of his character when he was with them, but they had the measure of him from the start. They liked him, were amused by him, Prince Philip admired his creative and design skills, but they were dismayed – distressed in the Queen's case – when they learnt of his casual (and occasionally deliberate) cruelty to Princess Margaret. According to Margaret's lady-in-waiting Anne Glenconner (and others), he would leave 'horrid notes' around the house for his wife to find, including, famously, one headed, 'Twenty Reasons Why I Hate You'.

Nevertheless, the Queen (ever forgiving, and loving and caring for her sister's children) and the rest of the royal family turned out in force for Lord Snowdon's memorial service at St Margaret's, Westminster, in 2017. I was there, too, and found myself seated next to the playwright, Alan Bennett, who ten years before had written a short novel called *The Uncommon Reader*, a comic fantasy in which the Queen discovers 'serious reading' when some of her corgis stray into a mobile library parked at Buckingham Palace. When it was published, Patricia Mountbatten sent a copy to the Queen as a Christmas present. Her Majesty was grateful for the gift, 'but didn't get very far with it.' At St Margaret's, while we were waiting for the royal party to arrive, I asked Alan Bennett why he was there. 'I am wondering that myself,' he replied in his slow, gentle Northern drawl. 'I didn't know Tony very well, I'm not sure how much I liked him.' A silence fell. And then, just as the Queen was arriving, he added in a low voice, 'Tony took a wonderful photograph of me years ago and I've used it a lot on the back of my books. I suppose I've come to say "thank you".'

The Queen came to say 'thank you', too – for the good times, for the best parts of the Earl of Snowdon. 'Yes,' said Prince Philip, 'she's like that.'

The Snowdons' marriage failed and they were divorced in 1978. After twenty-seven years, David, the 2nd Earl of

The Queen and Prince Philip visiting the Taj Mahal during their visit to India, 29 January 1961.

BELOW: Queen Elizabeth and 'Porchey', Lord Porchester, the future Earl of Carnarvon, at Newbury Races, 1965.

TOP: The Investiture of Prince Charles as Prince of Wales at Caernarfon Castle, 1 July 1969.

RIGHT: The Queen, the Duke of Edinburgh, the Prince of Wales, Prince Andrew, Prince Edward and Princess Anne at Balmoral Castle, 22 August 1972.

The Queen and the Duke of Edinburgh at Balmoral Castle during the royal family's summer holiday, in August 1972 – one of a series of photographs taken to mark the couple's silver wedding anniversary in November 1972.

Silver Jubilee celebrations: two young men have the Queen rocking with laughter at St Katharine Dock, during one of the stops on her Silver Jubilee river progress on the Thames from Greenwich to Lambeth.

The Silver Jubilee
Thanksgiving Service:
the Queen at prayer
in Westminster Abbey,
7 June 1977.

Queen Elizabeth is carried in a war canoe down the main street in Tuvalu during her tour of the South Pacific, October 1982.

The Queen out riding with US President Ronald Reagan at Windsor Castle, 1982.

BELOW: The Queen giving Mother Teresa of Calcutta an honorary Order of Merit in New Delhi, 1983.

The Queen with young Prince William and Prince Harry in the royal box at
Guards Polo Club, Smith's Lawn, Windsor, 1988.

BOTTOM: Queen Elizabeth with Prime Minister John Major and former prime
ministers Margaret Thatcher, Harold Wilson, Edward Heath and James Callaghan
at Spencer House, London, before they hosted a dinner for her, the Duke of
Edinburgh and the Prince and Princess of Wales, July 1992.

TOP: Windsor Castle fire, November 1992.

RIGHT: '*Annus horribilis*': The Queen with firemen inspecting the fire damage at Windsor Castle, November 1992.

BELOW: The Queen and Prince Philip inspecting the tributes left at the gates of Buckingham Palace after the death of Diana, Princess of Wales, 1997.

GB (the author)
welcoming Her Majesty
to a theatre in the 1990s.

GB with the Duke of
Edinburgh at Buckingham
Palace in the 1980s.

GB welcoming the Queen to
a playing field in
Nottingham in 2012.

GB, in attendance, as the Queen goes walkabout in Wiltshire, 2002.

LEFT: The Queen with South Africa's President Nelson Mandela in London, 1996.
RIGHT: The Queen with Russia's President Vladimir Putin in London, 2003.

BELOW: Wedding Day: the Prince of Wales and the Duchess of Cornwall, formerly Camilla Parker Bowles, with the Queen after the blessing of their marriage at St George's Chapel, Windsor Castle, 9 April 2005.

LEFT: Proud grandmother: the Queen smiling at Prince Harry at the passing-out Sovereign's Parade at Sandhurst Military Academy, 12 April 2006. RIGHT: Diamond wedding: to mark their 60th wedding anniversary on 20 November 2007, the Queen and the Duke of Edinburgh visited Broadlands in Hampshire, the home of Earl Mountbatten of Burma, where they began their honeymoon in 1947.

The Sovereign has landed: thanks to James Bond, the Queen appears at London's Olympic Stadium to formally open the 2012 Olympic Games, 27 July 2012.

Elizabeth II shaking hands with former IRA commander, Northern Ireland Deputy First Minister Martin McGuinness, watched by First Minister Peter Robinson, at the Lyric Theatre in Belfast, 27 June 2012.

The Queen with Sophie, Countess of Wessex, at the Royal
Windsor Horse Show, 15 May 2015.

The Queen with Meghan, Duchess of Sussex, at the opening of
the new Mersey Gateway Bridge, 14 June 2018.

RIGHT: The Queen and the Duke of Edinburgh in the quadrangle of Windsor Castle ahead of his 99th birthday, June 2020.

BELOW: The Queen in isolation during the funeral of Prince Philip, Duke of Edinburgh in St George's Chapel at Windsor Castle, 17 April 2021.

The Queen with one of her boxes at Sandringham House, marking
Accession Day, 6 February 2022 and the start of Her Majesty's
Platinum Jubilee.

RIGHT:. GB with the
Prince of Wales during
Platinum Jubilee
celebrations, 5 June 2022.

BELOW: The Platinum
Jubilee: the Queen, the
Duchess and the Duke
of Cambridge, with their
children, Prince George,
Princess Charlotte, and
Prince Louis on the
Buckingham Palace
balcony after the
Trooping the Colour
parade, 2 June 2022.

Two days before her death, Queen Elizabeth II waits in the Drawing Room at Balmoral Castle before receiving Liz Truss, the fifteenth prime minister of her reign, 6 September 2022.

BELOW: The State Funeral of Queen Elizabeth II – King Charles III and William, Prince of Wales follow Her Majesty's coffin as it is carried from Westminster Abbey, 19 September 2022.

A winning smile: the Queen arriving at Epsom Racecourse for Derby Day, 5 June 2010.

Snowdon, and his wife, Serena, separated, too. Marriage is not easy. Nor is parenthood.

The Queen and the Duke of Edinburgh were very different people from Princess Margaret and Tony Snowdon – though, intriguingly, they all seemed to get on. Every Christmas Lord Snowdon proudly displayed the Christmas cards he continued to receive from his former in-laws and I noticed a solo framed picture of the Duke of Edinburgh ever-present on his studio desk. I once asked Snowdon to sum up his marriage to Princess Margaret in a word. He said: 'Fun for five minutes and then hopeless.' How did he rate himself and Princess Margaret as parents? 'Brilliant, the best,' he grinned. 'Seriously,' he said, 'I'm not going to fault her there.' When she died, he wrote me a long letter, remembering their happy times, and saying how the press had led the public to underestimate her. 'She had a good heart,' he said. 'And how she loved the ballet – and understood it.'

I put the same questions about the Queen and Prince Philip's marriage and their role as parents to the Queen's cousin, Margaret Rhodes. Mrs Rhodes was quite shy, a little nervy, but with a sensible head on her shoulders and a countrywoman's values. She had seen all conditions and types of relationship in her long life. She could sense what worked and did not work. Of the Queen and Prince Philip's marriage, she said to me at once, and emphatically, and convincingly: 'On the whole, it ranks as one of the most successful marriages. One of the most successful.'

'And as parents?' I asked.

'I've seen Philip being absolutely sweet with his children's babies,' said Mrs Rhodes, 'absolutely sweet.' She paused and poured out more coffee. She sighed. 'But with their own children it hasn't been easy. There's no use denying it. Things have gone slightly awry with Prince Charles. I've been at Birkhall when he's been there. He's very conscientious, very committed. He'll have dinner and go back to work. He works so hard, but then he's so extravagant.' Another pause. 'The Queen finds Prince Charles very difficult. He is extravagant and she doesn't like that.'

This was twenty years ago. Mrs Rhodes lit one more cigarette and looked at me. 'It's incredibly sad,' she said. 'It's a fractured family. Terribly sad.'

'Why do you think that is?' I asked. 'What's at the root of it?'

'Philip can't bring himself to be close with Charles,' said Mrs Rhodes. 'Perhaps you don't learn to give love if you haven't had love.'

We talked for a while about Prince Philip's childhood and the years when he barely saw – nor heard from – either of his parents.

'But what about the Queen?' I asked. 'Her childhood was very loving, wasn't it?'

Mrs Rhodes pondered for a moment. 'The Queen was always reserved, even as a child. And when she became Queen that did add to her reserve, very definitely. But you're right. The King adored both his daughters. And Queen Elizabeth was brimming with love.' At this point, Margaret Rhodes, who was by nature a woman of restraint, flung her arms wide open to illustrate the warmth and breadth of the Queen Mother's embrace. She smiled and looked again directly at me. 'Perhaps,' she said, 'having married someone who is like Philip, it is difficult to go on expressing emotion to an unemotional person. You find, in time, you can't express love any more. Princess Margaret could. Completely. And her children have been so successful.'

That was not the only view. Gina Kennard, a childhood friend of Lilibet and Philip, who knew them both almost all her life (and was godmother to Prince Andrew), said to me, 'The Queen and Prince Philip were good parents, *really* good parents, *always* interested in their children and *always* actively involved. Whatever Charles says about it now, Philip was a wonderful father. He used to read them stories, play with them, go fishing – the lot. So much nonsense is talked about the Queen and her family. We saw quite a lot of them in the 1950s. They were a young family, full of energy and life, and a very happy one. I remember lots of fun and games, lots of laughter.'

Martin Charteris, a trusted courtier, who was close to Elizabeth from 1949 onwards, told me, 'There's this myth that the Queen cares more about her dogs and her horses than she does about her children. I believe it was fuelled when someone who had written to Her Majesty commiserating on the death of one of her corgis received a six-page hand-written response. Certainly, the Queen is devoted to her animals – absolutely devoted: they're what help keep her sane – but she loves her children deeply, as any mother would. Both she and the Duke of Edinburgh did their level best to give their children a normal family life. Not always easy, under the circumstances.'

Elizabeth II was Queen, after all. In November 1953, Elizabeth and Philip, without their children, embarked on a five-and-a-half-month post-Coronation Commonwealth tour. They took in Bermuda, Jamaica, Fiji, Tonga, the Coco Islands, Aden, Uganda, Malta and Gibraltar. They spent three months in Australia and New Zealand, and ten days in Ceylon. As Ben Pimlott put it in his biography of the Queen, 'Such a marathon of travel, speeches, national anthems, handshakes, troop inspections, Parliament openings, performances, banquets, bouquets and gifts, had never before been undertaken by a British Head of State – or perhaps by anybody.' 'I can't remember much about it,' Prince Philip said to me, laughing, 'but I can tell you the crowds were incredible, the adulation was extraordinary. You wouldn't believe it, you really wouldn't.' It was reckoned that three-quarters of the entire population of Australia turned out to see the Queen in person.

While their parents were away, Charles and Anne, aged five and three, were looked after by their grandmother, the Queen Mother. At the end of the grand tour, the children were to be reunited with their parents in Malta, where their great-uncle, Dickie Mountbatten, was now Commander-in-Chief of the Mediterranean Fleet. The children, sent from England in the newly commissioned Royal Yacht *Britannia*, arrived in Malta ten days ahead of their parents. Mountbatten was not amused to receive a message from 'Boy' Browning – his one-time Chief of Staff who had become Comptroller of the Edinburghs' Household in 1948 – to the effect that Mountbatten should submit a programme of proposed 'excursions for the children' to be laid before Her Majesty for her approval. Understandably indignant, Mountbatten reported the request to his wife, Edwina, telling her he had told Browning that Lady Mountbatten, the children's great-aunt (and, incidentally, mother of Pamela Mountbatten, who was accompanying the Queen on the royal tour as lady-in-waiting), 'would organise the trips, etc, as desirable each day. Really!'

When you become sovereign, nobody treats you quite as they did before. According to Sonia Berry, perhaps Lilibet's closest early childhood friend, 'She would never have chosen to be Queen. She would much rather have lived in the country with horses and dogs and been a normal housewife.'

Lilibet and Sonia's friendship did not end with the Queen's accession, but its nature changed. Suddenly there was a new formality – a sense of strain and distance – in the air. Overnight, the old, easy intimacy disappeared. Letters and invitations were no longer sent to 'you', but to 'Your Majesty'. When Philip was away, the Queen might come to Sonia's for tea or dinner – 'She used to say how nice it was to get out of Buckingham Palace' – but informality and spontaneity were no longer possible. Security was required. Guest lists had to be checked. Curtains had to be drawn so that the sovereign might not be observed. 'Once she arrived, she was completely at ease,' said Sonia Berry. But for everybody else, inevitably, having the Queen in your midst is an honour, maybe exciting, can be exhilarating, but, as experiences go, is rarely wholly comfortable. Sonia Berry reflected, 'Looking back, perhaps the formality was a mistake, but it takes time to change.'

On her accession, Elizabeth II was in no mood for change. Naturally shy, instinctively conservative, she was content to follow in her father's footsteps, to do her duty as he had done his. Her court had much of the character – and personnel – of his. Soon after her Coronation, her private secretary, Sir Alan Lascelles, who had been the late King's private secretary also, was succeeded by Sir Michael Adeane, who had joined the royal household in 1937, aged twenty-seven, as an assistant private secretary to George VI. Adeane, on his mother's side, was a grandson of Lord Stamfordham, assistant private secretary to Queen Victoria and influential private secretary to George V as Prince of Wales and King. Adeane had the traditional courtier's manner: he was effortlessly courteous, he had a nice sense of humour, he understood the ways of the world. Like his father (who was killed in action in 1914), he was an officer in the Coldstream Guards, and, while he was no radical, he was no fool either: he got a First in History at Cambridge. For nineteen years, until 1972, he served the Queen with intelligence, quiet efficiency and complete devotion. He was cautious, he was careful, he was kindly: Her Majesty liked his style. It suited her own.

I was still a teenager when I first met him (with my father: they were the same age) and was much impressed. Sir Michael seemed to me the epitome of courtliness: formal yet easy, and wholly unpatronising. Perhaps he was accustomed to dealing with children. He once said, 'Because you happen to be in Whitehall terms the equivalent of a permanent under-secretary, it is no use thinking you are a mandarin. One moment you may be writing to the prime minister. The next you are carrying a small boy's mac.' The humourist Basil Boothroyd (who was writing an authorised biography of Prince Philip at the time) liked to tell the story of the morning he encountered Adeane crossing the forecourt at Buckingham Palace. Boothroyd was arriving, Adeane was departing. Boothroyd paused to greet the Queen's private secretary. Pleasantries were exchanged. Courtesies were extended. The weather was discussed, the Queen's blooming health was touched on, the vigour and charm of the Queen Mother marvelled at, progress on Boothroyd's book reported – then Adeane threw in gently: 'If you'll forgive me, I must be on my way now. I've just heard that my house is on fire. I wouldn't mind, but as it's part of St James's Palace . . .'

As monarch, the Queen had role models: her father and grandfather. According to Sir Martin Charteris, assistant private secretary to Her Majesty from 1952 and Adeane's successor in 1972, 'She took on the mantle of monarchy as to the manner born – which, of course, she was. Right from the start, she performed all her duties, not only conscientiously – never chafing against her lot – but with a quiet confidence that was moving to behold. Remember, she was not quite twenty-six at the start of her reign.' Dutifully, and thoroughly, she read through her 'boxes', absorbed Cabinet minutes, digested Foreign Office telegrams, signed State papers, met her prime minister, gave audiences to ambassadors, judges, generals, held meetings of the Privy Council, conducted investitures. Her husband was involved in none of this. As consort, the Duke of Edinburgh had no role models (Prince Albert died sixty years before Prince Philip was born) and – in a way – no role. As he put it to me, 'I had to find a way of supporting the Queen, without getting in the way.'

According to Patricia Mountbatten, Philip in the 1950s was 'a dynamo, an absolute dynamo – he was very like my father at the same age'. In her autobiography, Wallis Simpson described Dickie Mountbatten as she found him when they first met and Dickie was in his early thirties: '[He] bubbled with ideas on every conceivable subject – housing, relieving unemployment, new strategies of attack in polo, or how to cure the chronic maladies of the British Exchequer. The more baffling these problems, the more convinced Dickie was that he had a fundamental contribution to make and was determined to make it.' According to Mrs Simpson, the hyperactive Dickie 'bombarded' her lover, then Prince of Wales, 'with pamphlets, books, and clippings, all carefully annotated or underlined and all urgently commended to the Prince's attention.' Philip – equally bubbling with ideas and initiative – might have liked to 'bombard' the Queen, as his uncle had once 'bombarded' hers, but he chose not to. He knew there was no point. It did not occur to the Queen to involve her husband in affairs of state: it would not have been constitutionally appropriate, and Her Majesty, a firm believer in the value of precedent, tradition and continuity, was always one for observing the proprieties.

Besides, as Prince Philip put it to me, her advisers made his position crystal clear. 'Keep out,' they said. 'You mustn't interfere with this.' Lord Brabourne, Patricia Mountbatten's husband, told me that, at the time, Philip found the traditional courtiers' hostility towards him 'intolerable and deeply frustrating'. Fifty years on, the Duke of Edinburgh simply shrugged and said to me: 'I had to fit into the institution. I had to avoid getting at cross-purposes, usurping others' authority. In most cases that was no problem. I did my own thing.' And what he did was extraordinary. The Duke of Edinburgh's Award Scheme, that has spread to 144 countries and touched the lives of *millions* around the world, is just one example. His dogged support for the National Playing Fields Association was another.

Forty years ago, making the smallest of small-talk with the Queen at a drinks reception (where she wasn't drinking, or eating the nibbles, so nor was I), the subject of the National Playing Fields Association came up. The Queen was the charity's patron, the Duke of Edinburgh was its president. 'I don't know very much about the Playing Fields, I'm afraid,' Her Majesty said to me, with a slightly apologetic laugh. 'That's Prince Philip's department. He doesn't tell me much about it. He has his departments, I have mine.'

CHAPTER TWENTY

Private lives

Inevitably, from the time of the Queen's accession, Elizabeth and Philip, to a certain extent, led separate, parallel lives. She was Head of State and did what heads of state must. (She was also Head of the Commonwealth, of course, and Supreme Governor of the Church of England.) He was her consort and, as consort, dutifully, and with some style, did whatever was required. And, when not required, he did his own thing. She had her role, her duties, her enthusiasms, her friends. He had his obligations, his interests, his enthusiasms, his friends. Frequently, they overlapped: often, they did not.

At the start of her reign, the courtiers surrounding the young Queen were of a type, and it was not Philip's type. Mike Parker, Philip's private secretary until 1956, said to me, 'They were old school – Eton, Oxbridge, the Brigade of Guards – which Philip was not, and which I most definitely was not. I think he had the measure of them, but I'm not sure they had the measure of him.' Parker told me that Philip 'understood, sort of' that Elizabeth was required to exclude her husband from affairs of state; in return, said Parker, Philip was left 'in charge of the home-front'. Elizabeth wore the crown, but Philip wore the trousers. The Queen, it seems, was ready – anxious, even – to allow her husband the man's traditional authority in their domestic and private life. Readily, Elizabeth bowed to Philip's wishes in the matter of her children's upbringing and education. (Prince Charles followed in his father's footsteps to Cheam School and to Gordonstoun – and was not at all happy, as we know.) She positively encouraged her husband to take on her late father's role and responsibilities in the active management of the royal estates. 'She was head of state,' said Mike Parker, 'but he was head honcho.'

In public, he walked one step behind her. In private, he treated his wife much as any strong-willed, independent-minded, intelligent, able and energetic naval husband of his temperament and generation might. He questioned her judgement, he called her 'a bloody fool', he swore at her and them when he tripped over a clutch of her corgis. Martin Charteris said to me, 'It sounds worse in the telling than it actually was. He can be grumpy. He is outspoken. He can be argumentative. But it's just his way. If she hadn't been Queen, you wouldn't have noticed.'

But she was Queen and people did notice. Lord Mountbatten liked to tell the story of driving with the Queen and Prince Philip through Cowdray Park. Philip was at the wheel and driving far too fast. The Queen started drawing in her breath and flinching at the way her husband was driving. Philip turned to her and said, 'If you do that once more I shall put you out of the car.' When the hair-raising journey came to an end, Mountbatten asked the Queen why she hadn't protested. 'But you heard what he said,' replied the Queen, 'and he meant it.' Martin Charteris recalled an unhappy half-hour once on the Royal Yacht *Britannia*. 'I'm not going to come out of my cabin until he's in a better temper,' said Her Majesty. 'I'm going to sit here on my bed until he's better.'

Philip could be irascible – even with his wife. 'It means nothing,' Mike Parker insisted when I raised the subject with him. 'Philip is an outspoken kind of a guy. Everyone knows that. He might use colourful language talking privately with the Queen – for all I know, they might have the odd barney, as couples do – but he is devoted to Her Majesty, absolutely devoted, don't be in any doubt about that.' And, according to several reliable witnesses, as the years went by, the Queen got better at holding her own with Prince Philip and, on occasion, giving as good as she got. Martin Charteris smiled impishly when I tackled him on the matter. 'Have I heard Her Majesty say, "Oh, do shut up, Philip, you don't know what you're talking about"?' he asked, tapping his chin with his forefinger. 'Possibly,' he said. 'More than once?' I persisted. 'Perhaps.'

In public and on parade – and the Duke of Edinburgh was on parade with Her Majesty relentlessly: at the State Opening of Parliament, at the Cenotaph on Remembrance Sunday, at the distribution of the Royal Maundy, at the Queen's Birthday Parade, at Royal Ascot, at the Garter Ceremony, at the Thistle Service, at the Braemar Royal Highland Gathering, at garden parties and state banquets: the royal year is nothing if not predictable – towards his sovereign, Prince Philip's manner and his manners were impeccable. Mike Parker said to me, 'From day one, he was clear that his duty was to support the Queen, first, second, third and last. That's what he's there for. That's what he does. And I don't believe he has failed in his duty. Ever.'

Together, the Queen and the Duke undertook thousands of engagements within the United Kingdom, and overseas completed more than 260 visits to 128 different countries. Their travels ranged from the Cocos Islands (5.4 square miles with a population of 655) to the People's Republic of China (3.7 million square miles with a population of 1.25 billion).

At the beginning of 1956, the royal couple spent three weeks in Nigeria, where, shaded from the African sun by an elegant canopy designed in London by Norman Hartnell, their programme included a spectacular Durbar at Kadona and countless cheerful encounters with colourfully clad and broadly beaming tribal chiefs. In Lagos, ten thousand masked 'tribal warriors' danced for them, and a crowd, conservatively estimated at a million-strong, chanted 'Our Queen! Our Queen!' with apparently heartfelt enthusiasm. (Within a decade Nigeria was a republic and soon after embroiled in a devastating civil war: the 'tribal warriors' turned tribal warriors.) In April of the same year, Nikita Kruschev and Nikolai Bulganin, the new leaders of the Soviet Union, visited Britain, took tea with the Queen and Philip at Windsor Castle, and presented Her Majesty with a thoroughbred horse as a thirtieth birthday present. Kruschev, General Secretary of the Soviet Communist Party, and once a farmhand, plumber and locksmith, had expected 'haughtiness' from a Queen, but, to his surprise, found her 'completely unpretentious', 'the sort of woman you would be likely to meet walking along Gorky Street on a balmy summer afternoon.' In June, Queen and Duke paid a state visit to King Gustaf VI Adolf and Queen Louise of Sweden and, in July, received a state visit from King Faisal of Iraq.

The Queen rarely travelled abroad without the Duke. Her solo foreign forays were usually related to her interest in horse breeding, visiting stud farms in Normandy in France and flying to Kentucky in the United States, where her host was William Farish, Texan racehorse owner and breeder and US ambassador to London, 2001–2005. But the Duke undertook frequent overseas assignments without Her Majesty. Between the beginning of 1952 and the end of his life, on behalf of the United Kingdom, the Commonwealth and the range of causes he supported, he took part in more than 620 overseas visits to over 140 different countries.

He set off on his single longest tour in October 1956. He was away for four months – 124 days to be precise. His travels took him to Australia, New Zealand, Ceylon, the Gambia, Antarctica and the Falkland Islands. The tour was controversial. For a start, the timing was unfortunate.

In July 1956, on the fourth anniversary of his overthrow of King Farouk, President Gamal Abdel Nasser of Egypt announced that he was nationalising the Anglo-French-controlled Suez Canal Company, declaring that if the imperialist powers did not like it they could 'choke to death on their fury'. In August, while she was attending a race meeting at Goodwood, the Queen was required to approve a proclamation, to be read out in the House of Commons that very afternoon, ordering 20,000 army reservists to be called up for service in the canal zone. In October, as the Duke of Edinburgh, Mike Parker and their party, in *Britannia*, were sailing east of Trincomalee, on the north-east coast of Ceylon, one of the world's outstanding natural harbours, in the Middle East British and French bombs – and paratroops – were dropping onto Egypt. In the event of war, *Britannia* was designated a hospital ship. There was momentary uncertainty about whether or not the tour could proceed. It did. Within days, international uproar and United States' opposition to the Anglo-French action in Egypt brought about a ceasefire. The crisis was resolved. Anti-British riots in Singapore meant abandoning a proposed stop-over at the south end of the Malay peninsula, but, other than that, the royal itinerary was unaffected. On 22 November, in Melbourne, as planned, the Duke of Edinburgh formally opened the sixteenth Olympic Games, the first to be held south of the equator.

The length of the tour was unusual, but, as Prince Philip pointed out, the scope of the tour was ambitious. 'We were reaching parts of the Commonwealth that, in some cases, had never before been visited by a member of the royal family. And they seemed quite pleased to see us.' To some in 1957 (and, perhaps, to many more today), for a young husband and father to be separated from his wife and family for four months may seem out of the ordinary, but to a naval officer – especially one with experience of war – a sixteen-week tour of duty is not so remarkable. Philip regarded the tour of 1956/57 as a duty to be done and a job worth doing. The Queen agreed and encouraged him to go. As she said in her Christmas message that year: 'If my husband cannot be at home on Christmas Day, I could not wish for a better reason than he should be travelling in other parts of the Commonwealth.'

To the end of their days, it infuriated the Duke of Edinburgh, and to a lesser extent the Queen, that this arduous tour was portrayed perennially as something of a princely 'jolly' and was used as the platform from which to launch a raft of what the Duke's secretary called 'innuendoes about Prince Philip's private life which [are], in my view, overstated and unbalanced.'

Back at the beginning of 1957, what first set the rumour-mill grinding – and allowed 'innuendo' to be translated from a whisper behind the hand to a headline on the front page – was really nothing to do with the Duke of Edinburgh at all. It was a classic case of 'guilt by association'. Mike Parker, Philip's wartime naval friend, his Australian boon companion, and, since 1947, his private secretary, was being sued for divorce by Eileen, his wife of fourteen years. 'We should never have got married in the first place,' Parker said to me. 'It was a wartime romance, exciting at the time, but we weren't suited long-term. And Eileen wasn't suited to royal life either.' She called her memoirs *Step Aside for Royalty*. 'I didn't behave that well,' admitted Parker. 'It was a helluva mess.' And a mess made public when news of Mrs Parker's petition for divorce was published in February 1957, just as *Britannia* – with Parker and his boss on board – was cruising calmly towards Gibraltar on the final leg of the world tour. 'When we reached the Rock,' said Parker, 'the world's press was waiting. It was not a pretty sight.'

Parker told me, 'I decided to get back to London as soon as possible. We had been on this remarkable voyage, testing the newly commissioned *Britannia*, visiting Ascension Island, Tristan da Cunha and goodness knows where, but all that was instantly forgotten. I'd become the story – and a liability to Philip.' Surrounded by rapacious hacks ('Literally – I think they bought every other seat on the plane'), Parker, unusually tight-lipped, and accompanied by his solicitor, flew from Gibraltar to London. At Heathrow Airport he found yet more of the world's press awaiting him – together, surprisingly, with the habitually tight-lipped Commander Richard Colville, the Queen's press secretary, who had motored down from London, not to give the Duke of Edinburgh's friend and secretary a helping hand, but to say to him this, and nothing more: 'Hello, Parker, I've just come to let you know that from now on, you're on your own.'

Colville made this excursion to Heathrow on his own initiative. Parker was not 'on his own' as far as the Queen and the Duke were concerned. 'The Duke saw me off at the airport in Gibraltar and the Queen was wonderful throughout,' Mike Parker told me. 'She regarded a divorce as a sadness, not a hanging offence. Her prime minister at the time [Anthony Eden] was a divorcee, after all. The Queen telephoned me and could not have been more sympathetic.' (From first to last, the Queen was always sympathetic to those for whom things weren't going quite right. Ask Boris Johnson about his last meeting with Her Majesty only two days before she died. 'She could not have been kinder, more sympathetic or personally encouraging,' he said.) Initially, back in the spring of 1957, Parker – and his employer – hoped he might be able to weather the storm. 'But pretty damn quickly I could see it wasn't going to be possible. It was going to take a year for my divorce to come through. I had to resign. I had no choice.' The Queen was sorry to see him go and appointed him a Commander of the Royal Victorian Order in recognition of his years of loyal service to her husband. She often used the private honours at her disposal to make a public point.

Parker flew to London, but Philip remained on board *Britannia*. Since it was now the beginning of February and he had been away from hearth and home since mid-October, the *Sunday Pictorial*, for one, wanted to know why. The royal family, the newspaper reminded its readers, 'is loved and envied throughout the world because it *is* a family.' Why wasn't Philip at home with the kiddies? Anne was six and Charles was eight. 'How can you expect youngsters to understand that Daddy is so near yet cannot come home?'

The reason that Philip remained where he was was simple. It was convenient. And he was not about to dance to the *Sunday Pictorial*'s tune. As planned many months before, the Queen was scheduled to pay a state visit to President Craveiro Lopes of Portugal between 18 and 21 February and Philip was due to join her. He did. But, fairly or unfairly, the collapse of the Parker marriage combined with Philip's prolonged separation from his wife and children created a flood of speculation – and eventually the dam burst. The *Baltimore Sun* – the premier newspaper of Wallis Simpson's home-town – broke 'the story', with the paper's London correspondent reporting that the British capital was awash with rumour that the Duke of Edinburgh was romantically involved with an unnamed woman whom he met on a regular basis in the West End apartment of a society photographer. 'Report Queen, Duke in Rift Over Party Girl' ran the headline.

According to Mike Parker, 'The Duke was incandescent. He

was very, very angry. And deeply hurt. There was no truth in the story whatsoever.' The Queen was equally dismayed, and surprisingly (given her instinct to follow precedent and the unwritten rule that royalty never answers back), authorised the normally uncommunicative Commander Colville to issue an official and complete denial: 'It is quite untrue that there is any rift between the Queen and the Duke.' Having received the Palace's reassurance, *The Times, Daily Telegraph, Mail* and *Sketch* did the decent thing and ignored the story altogether: if it wasn't true it wasn't to be reported. The *Daily Express, Mirror* and *Herald* were less circumspect, however, and splashed the Palace denial on their front pages. On 11 February, from New York, for the *Manchester Guardian*, Alistair Cooke reported to his readers: 'Not since the first rumours of a romance between the former King Edward VIII and the then Mrs Simpson have Americans gobbled up the London dispatches so avidly.' Tongues were wagging, all over the world.

The Queen and the Duke did their best to rise above it. They were reunited at Lisbon's military airport. The scene was a memorable one. During part of the tour, Philip had grown a full set of naval whiskers. Photographs of the bearded Adonis had found their way back to London. When Philip, now clean-shaven in anticipation of the state visit to Portugal, bounded up the steps of the Queen's plane in Lisbon, he was greeted by an extraordinary sight: his wife and her entire entourage, sitting in their seats, all sporting false ginger beards! (As we know, this is a family that is fond of practical jokes.) Minutes later, when the royal couple emerged from the plane, both were beaming, and an eagle-eyed reporter, with a sentimental streak, was sure he spotted a tell-tale smudge of lipstick on the Duke's cheek.

Her Majesty decided to deal with the rumour-mongers' cheek as well. In 1947, when Philip became a naturalised

British subject, he ceased to be a Prince of Greece and, technically at least, a 'prince' of any kind at all. On his wedding day, 20 November 1947, George VI created him Baron Greenwich of Greenwich, Earl of Merioneth and Duke of Edinburgh. The late King had made his son-in-law a Royal Highness, but not a prince. In March 1955, Sir Winston Churchill, a month before his retirement as prime minister, proposed to the Queen, 'in informal conversation', that she might like to consider making her husband 'a prince of the United Kingdom'. She agreed, but, at the time, did nothing about it. Two years later, in February 1957, Harold Macmillan, a month after his appointment as prime minister, put forward the same proposal. Her Majesty warmly welcomed the suggestion and, this time, took action.

On 22 February, the day following their return from the state visit to Portugal, Queen Elizabeth II announced that, henceforward, His Royal Highness the Duke of Edinburgh would carry 'the style and dignity of a prince of the United Kingdom'. This was not merely 'in recognition of the great services which His Royal Highness has provided to the country', but also – and pointedly – 'of his unique contribution to the life of the Commonwealth, culminating in the tour which he has just concluded.'

In 2011, when Prince William married Catherine Middleton, the press talked up the possibility that the Queen might make her grandson's bride a princess on her wedding day. It did not happen – and I was sure it would not happen until William and Catherine had been married for at least ten years. In the event, on the day following the Queen's death, in his first television address as sovereign King Charles said of his eldest son: 'Today, I am proud to create him Prince of Wales, Tywysog Cymru, the country whose title I have been so greatly privileged to bear during so much of my life and duty.' He then went on to speak of the new Prince and Princess of Wales – implying that Catherine is a Princess by virtue of being married to a prince. I do not think that, at present, Catherine is necessarily a princess in her own right – though as my friend Hugo Vickers, constitutional and royal historian, explained to me, 'The monarch can really decide these things as they please. When George V's son, Prince Henry, Duke of Gloucester, died in 1974, his widow should properly have been known as the Dowager Duchess of Gloucester, but that sounded a bit ageing and, naturally, she preferred the idea of being called Princess Alice, Duchess of Gloucester – and the Queen, generous as ever, let it happen.'

The Queen always used the honours at her disposal carefully and to a purpose. On Prince Philip's ninetieth birthday, for example, she found for her husband a unique honour that was singularly appropriate. It was a title she held herself until she transferred it to the Duke of Edinburgh: Lord High Admiral of the United Kingdom. In 2013 Prince Philip spent his ninety-second birthday at the London Clinic, recuperating from an exploratory operation on his abdomen. A few days before, on 6 June, on the morning of his admission to hospital, the Queen presented her husband with yet another honour to add to his collection: the Order of New Zealand. (Well, what else do you give to a man who has everything? On his actual birthday, she arrived at the hospital to see him, carrying his birthday card.)

The Queen gave honours to recognise achievement and service – and to silence critics. In February 2011, Her Majesty gave her second son, Prince Andrew, Duke of York, one of the highest honours at her personal disposal. She made him a Knight Grand Cross of the Royal Victorian Order. The honour was a fifty-first birthday present for the Prince, a 'thank you' from his mother for the support he had given her and an acknowledgement of his work as unpaid United Kingdom trade ambassador. The announcement of the honour coincided both with the Prince's birthday and with a barrage of bad press for 'Airmiles Andy' as the British media chose to dub him.

At the time, Andrew was in the British press because of his association with Jeffrey Epstein, the American billionaire financier sent to jail and placed on the US sex offenders' register after admitting soliciting teenage girls into prostitution. At the end of March 2011, when Prince Andrew called on his mother at Windsor Castle to be invested with his new honour, the *Daily Mail* reported that 'the revelations' about Andrew's 'associations' had led to questions in Parliament about his suitability as a representative of British industry abroad: 'Critics argue that the Prince's public profile has been fatally damaged. Matters have been made worse in recent weeks by further accusations that he has deliberately befriended rich and powerful foreign figureheads – particularly in Eastern Europe and the Middle East – for personal gain. This has always been vehemently denied by Buckingham Palace.'

When the Queen honoured Prince Andrew in February 2011, she was showing her support for her son in as forthright and public a way as she could. It was the same – but only more so – when, in February 1957, she honoured her husband with 'the style and dignity of a prince of the United Kingdom'.

Prince Philip told me that he was aware that 'from the earliest days' of his marriage there were those who were convinced that he was what used to be termed 'a ladies' man', one of those husbands who, publicly, support their wives, while at the same time, albeit discreetly, managing to play the field.

Prince Philip was sensitive to this. I know because he raised the issue with me. I did not bring it up: I would neither have dared nor presumed to do so. He raised it himself and did so repeatedly. You might think that, after all those years in the public eye, and knowing how people love to gossip, and seeing the way the press behaves, he would have simply shrugged his shoulders and laughed it off. To an extent he did. In 1995, for example, when a German newspaper reported that His Royal Highness had twenty-four illegitimate children and that this had been confirmed by Buckingham Palace, he did laugh. It transpired that the newspaper had misinterpreted 'godchildren' for 'love children'. But, as a rule, he did not consider the widespread speculation about his alleged love-life – in print and private – to be any kind of laughing matter. These stories 'damage your reputation,' he said, 'chip away at it insidiously.'

Was there any truth in them? Twenty years ago, for my book, *Philip & Elizabeth Portrait of a Marriage*, and then again, more recently, for *Philip The Final Portrait*, I explored them all exhaustively. 'Exhaustingly', said Dame Anne Griffiths, who had worked for the Duke as a 'Lady Clerk' ('also known as typist and general dogsbody') when she was in her twenties in the 1950s and then, later, in the 1980s, returned to Buckingham Palace to be his Librarian and Archivist. She kindly helped correct the proofs of my first book about the Duke and I got to know her quite well. She was one of many attractive, intelligent women whose company the Queen's husband enjoyed – and there were rumours . . .

Anne first joined the Duke of Edinburgh's office in 1952, when she was only nineteen, originally employed as a 'temp' to help out with the additional workload in the run-up to the Coronation. She was one of the two Lady Clerks who accompanied him on board *Britannia* on the controversial 1956/57 trip to the South Atlantic and the Melbourne Olympic Games. As a consequence, she and her colleague, Ione Eadie, became the first British women to cross the Antarctic Circle. Ione went on to marry the commander of the Royal Yacht and, inevitably, some said that Anne and the Duke became quite sweet on each other during that four months at sea. 'But nothing happened,' she told me, 'nothing at all.' Anne left royal service in 1960 to get married herself, but returned in 1983 and remained part of the Prince's team ever after. I saw him with her family at her memorial service after her death in 2017. On the day of the announcement of her DCVO in 2005, Prince Philip was heard walking along the corridor at Buckingham Palace towards her office cheerily singing, 'There's nothing like a dame . . .'

If you need the detail of what I discovered about the Duke of Edinburgh's alleged extra-marital love-life it's all there in my earlier books – and I will return to the subject briefly in a page or two – but this is a book about Elizabeth, not Philip. The Queen was aware of all the stories about her husband, but after February 1957 and that one official denial of any 'rift' in their marriage, she chose to rise above them.

I think we can take it as read that the Queen herself remained faithful throughout her married life. There are those who persist in believing that Prince Andrew's natural father was the Queen's racing manager, Henry Porchester, 'Porchey', 7th Earl of Carnarvon, suggesting the conception occurred at some point between 20 January and 30 April 1959 when Philip was away on another of his long sea voyages in *Britannia*. Never mind that the dates don't stack up (Andrew was born on 19 February 1960, a happy by-product of the Queen and Philip's post-*Britannia* reunion): the idea of the Queen committing adultery would only occur to someone who did not know her at all.

I asked Geordie, 8th Earl of Carnarvon (and one of the Queen's godchildren), if his father and Her Majesty knew of the rumour and what they made of it. Were they amused?

'They knew all about it,' Geordie told me, 'and were not in the least amused. They were angry. My father was very annoyed by it, and embarrassed. It was dreadful.' The Queen and Porchey were best friends. They had known each other all their adult lives: they shared a passion for racehorses and a sense of humour. They may even have been a little in love – in the nicest possible way – but the idea of a romance between them is risible. 'Both my parents were friends of the Queen and Prince Philip,' Geordie told me. 'Obviously my father saw a lot of the Queen throughout the year, but in October he used to invite them to Highclere [Castle, near Newbury in Berkshire, the Carnarvon family home, now familiar to television viewers around the world as the setting for *Downton Abbey*] for a shooting weekend – partridge shooting. Prince Philip sometimes came, not always. He's an extremely good shot. And the Queen, of course, has always been good at working dogs. On Saturday night, my mother would do dinner, the best of English country house cooking, using old recipes of my great-grandmother's. And on Sunday my father and the Queen might walk round the stables or visit Highclere stud. The Queen adored going on the gallops early in the evening. It was just a perfect, relaxing weekend.' Porchey died in 2001, but two years later the family reinstated the weekend. 'The Queen came again,' said Geordie, 'and Prince Philip, too. Without my father it couldn't be quite the same, but it was very jolly.' In 2012, when I visited Highclere at the height of its *Downton Abbey* celebrity, I was pleased to see from the Visitors' Book that the Queen and Prince Philip were maintaining the tradition.

There are some people, too, who continue to allege that the Queen's youngest child, Prince Edward, born in 1964, was the product of the union between Her Majesty and the Deputy Master of her Household, Patrick, 7th Baron Plunket.

Patrick Plunket was a delightful individual, good-looking and good-humoured, born in 1923, so only three years older than the Queen, and more like a brother than a lover. His parents were 'characters' and great friends of Elizabeth's parents, dating back to the days when they were still the Yorks. In 1938, when Patrick was not yet fifteen, his parents were killed in an aeroplane crash on their way to a party William Randolph Hearst was giving in their honour in California. Educated at Eton and Cambridge, Patrick joined the Irish Guards, rose to the rank of Lieutenant-Colonel and became an equerry to George VI in 1948. He had charm and taste (he was a trustee of the Wallace Collection and the National Art Collections Fund), and, as the Queen's Deputy Master of the Household from 1954 until his early death from cancer in 1975, masterminded the Queen's official entertaining with style and devotion. Martin Charteris told me, 'Patrick Plunket's death was a real loss to the Queen, a personal loss. He was a life-long courtier, but he wasn't a stuffed shirt. He was great fun. He had a wonderful flair for entertaining, of course, but he was also very good at human relations. He was very easy with the Queen and she was very relaxed with him. He treated her almost as an equal, certainly as a friend. If you wanted to say something awkward or difficult to Her Majesty, you could do it through Patrick. When he died a bright light went out in her life.' The Queen mourned the loss of Patrick Plunket: he was a true friend, but he was not the father of Prince Edward. Lord Plunket was a confirmed bachelor: in many ways, that was part of his attraction.

Given her nature and her upbringing, you would expect the Queen to be wholly faithful to her marriage vows. Her role models, after all, were her mother and father and her grandparents, George V and Queen Mary. Yes, there were stories about George V when he was a young Duke of York, but what did they amount to? 'I say, May,' the Duke told his fiancée, Mary of Teck, in the spring of 1893, 'we can't get married after all. I hear I have got a wife and three children...' The alleged 'wife' was an American living in Plymouth. 'Why there I wonder?' pondered the Prince. At first, he found the rumour 'really very amusing', but it rumbled on and gathered momentum. When, eventually, it appeared in print, the year was 1910, the Duke of York was King, and the charge was specific. E. F. Mylius, in an article headed 'Sanctified Bigamy', published in a republican paper in Paris and sent to every British MP, alleged that in 1890, in Malta, the future King had married an admiral's daughter who bore him several children: 'Our very Christian King and Defender of the Faith has a plurality of wives just like any Mohammedan Sultan.' His Majesty found this less amusing and decided to nail the lie. The Crown instigated libel proceedings and Mylius was sentence to twelve months' imprisonment. George V's second son, the eventual George VI, as a young Duke of York, was briefly led astray by his older brother, the Prince of Wales, but, as husbands, George V and George VI were continent and loyal, and, as wives, Queen Mary and Queen Elizabeth were, without doubt, above reproach. Lilibet, as a child and adolescent, had a stable and happy home-life and the example of parents who were as devoted and loving to their children as they were to one another.

The black sheep of the family, of course, was the Duke of Windsor: his love-life as Prince of Wales had been chequered; his married life, living in exile with a double divorcee, was not a bed of roses. Elizabeth II was not judgemental, but she was observant. Her younger sister's love-life may have been more colourful than her own – it was certainly more varied and adventurous – but the Queen saw that Princess Margaret's romantic relationships, and her marriage to Tony Snowdon, while they brought her undoubted 'highs', did not provide her with lasting happiness.

Like the Queen, the Duke of Edinburgh was remarkably self-contained. Unlike the Queen, he might grumble and growl, and occasionally snap, but, like her, as a rule, he kept his true feelings under wraps. And, even with those with whom he was intimate, he was still guarded. Mike Parker told me, 'Philip did not discuss his feelings – at least, not with me. I certainly did not know about him and Princess Elizabeth until virtually the day of the engagement. He's not one to let it all hang out. That's not his style.'

In the public arena, the Prince Philip you would see – the outer man – was accessible (if a little forbidding), confident, bantering, outspoken. The private Prince Philip – the inner man – was infinitely more difficult to reach. He was, from all I saw myself and from what I heard from those who knew him well, more sensitive, more thoughtful, kinder and more tolerant than the well-known caricature would suggest, but he kept these things hidden. His manner appeared open, but his instinct was watchful. Whoever you were, he did not let you get too close. I said as much to him once. He replied briefly, smiling a wintry smile, 'It's safer that way.'

The Duke of Edinburgh was careful of his reputation and conscious of his position, and of the responsibility that came with it. And he had been, from the day he married Princess Elizabeth. That said, he enjoyed the company of attractive, intelligent, interested and interesting women. He never had affairs with models or actresses or personal assistants (the likes of Katie Boyle or Pat Kirkwood or Anne Griffiths), but he did have close female friendships – and they reflected his nature and his interests in the same way that, say, the Queen's friendship with 'Porchey' reflected hers.

I reckon I came as close as we may ever get to understanding the nature of Prince Philip's special relationship with the women who were not his wife when, a few years ago, I went to see the Duchess of Abercorn, the wife of James Hamilton, 5th Duke of Abercorn, and reckoned by some to be one of Philip's mistresses.

Sacha Abercorn was in her fifties at the time, tall, slim and striking, quietly spoken, intelligent, articulate and thoughtful. She was born in 1946 and died in 2018, the daughter of Lt. Col. Harold Pedro Joseph Phillips (known as 'Bunnie', a friend of Dickie Mountbatten, and sometime lover of Edwina) and Georgina Wernher (later, of course, Lady Kennard, known to friends as 'Gina' and to Prince Philip, when they were children, as 'George'). Sacha was christened Alexandra Anastasia – her Russian heritage was important to her. Her mother's mother was Zia Wernher, married to Sir Harold Wernher, but born Countess Anastasia Mikhailovna, elder daughter of His Imperial Highness Grand Duke Mikhail Mikhailovich, the grandson of Tsar Nicholas I.

When I went to see Sacha Abercorn she gave me a copy of *Feather from the Firebird*, a collection of her 'prose poems', published by the Summer Palace Press in County Donegal in 2003. The poems are short, powerfully felt, highly evocative, and beautifully observed. Many of them feel autobiographical, coded tributes to people she had known and loved and lost: her younger brother, Nicholas, who committed suicide in 1991, her father, who died in 1980, her father's friend, Lord Mountbatten, murdered in Ireland by the IRA in 1979. The 'biographical note' in the book reads in full: 'Sacha Abercorn is the founder of the Pushkin Prizes Trust. She received an Honorary Doctorate from the University of Ulster in 2003. She is a descendant of the Romanovs and of Alexander Pushkin, the great Russian poet.' Her husband, the 5th Duke of Abercorn, was twelve years her senior, an officer in the

Grenadier Guards, briefly an Ulster Unionist MP, and for sixty years a force for good and a power to reckon with in the social and economic life of Northern Ireland. In 1999 James Abercorn became a Knight of the Garter. In October 2012, the Queen appointed him Chancellor of the Order of the Garter.

The Abercorns' family home (since 1612) is in Omagh, County Tyrone, but I went to meet Sacha at her London mews house, near Victoria Station, a stone's throw from Buckingham Palace. She was just back from a trip to Russia, in happy form, fielding telephone calls from her mother and her daughter, while making me tea. We moved from the kitchen to the drawing room and sat, facing one another, perched on the edge of sofas. Notebook and pen in hand, I asked her when she first remembered meeting the Queen and Prince Philip.

'When I was a child,' she said. 'I must have been eight or nine. It was in the 1950s. We lived in Leicestershire, at Thorpe Lubenham, and they came to stay. They came with Charles and Anne, who were a bit younger than us. What do I remember best? I think the fun we all had – so much fun. The adults and the children all playing together. I remember dressing up as monsters. I remember huge bonfires and cooking potatoes in the ashes.

'In the evening, indoors, in the dark, after tea, we played a wonderful game called Stone. Do you know it? All the lights are turned out – you are in total darkness. Someone is chosen to be "He" and, in the darkness, when you are touched by "He" you have to stand absolutely still – like stone. There was fear and fun. It was fantastic. The Queen and Prince Philip loved it. They used to play it at Balmoral – all the grown-ups.' Sacha laughed, and covered her mouth with her hand, and said, 'I shouldn't tell you this, but once, my father was "He" and, in the dark, he felt this figure hidden behind the curtains

– and then the Queen giggled and he realised who it was. Can you imagine? The Queen hiding behind the curtains and my father feeling her up and down?'

I asked Sacha how the Queen and Prince Philip seemed to relate to their own children. 'Then?' she asked. 'Yes,' I said. 'Really well. Really, really well. Philip was wonderful. I remember how he used to help Charles with his Go-Kart. And he used to tell them stories that he'd invented. I can't recall any gruff words – ever. Or any tension. I would go with my parents to Balmoral and their children would be there too. It was always fun and jolly. I loved the picnics. They were good times. I remember, once, in the stables, there was a dog fight and the Queen arrived and calmed it immediately. She's intrepid. She doesn't get thrown by things. They were good times for us and, I think, good times for them – human times, filled with good humour. They don't get that much time off, you know. The heavy duty is relentless.'

I asked Sacha how she had got to know Prince Philip, not as a family friend of her parents but as a personal friend of her own. She smiled and sat back and thought for a moment. 'I remember going to Cowes one year,' she said. 'My parents were going to go, but my father had cancer and couldn't come, so I went on my own.'

Cowes, on the north coast of the Isle of Wight, is the headquarters of the Royal Yacht Squadron (founded 1812) and home of the annual 'Cowes Week' yachting regatta, held every August. In 1947, the Island Sailing Club of Cowes gave Philip and Princess Elizabeth a Dragon-class yacht as a wedding present. It was painted dark blue and Philip named it *Bluebottle*. For several years, he sailed her competitively in Cowes Week, with a regular crew that included the larger-than-life local character, yachtsman and boat-builder, Uffa Fox. Fox and Philip became firm friends. While Queen

Victoria's favourite home was at Osborne House in East Cowes, as a rule Queen Elizabeth did not accompany Prince Philip to Cowes Week.

'It was the chaps who did the sailing,' Sacha Abercorn explained. 'I think the girls were there to have fun. It was great fun. All the secretaries from his office were there. And I remember Princess Anne and myself, dressed up as serving wenches. It was hilarious. I remember Uffa Fox telling stories – telling endless, endless stories. I suppose I was seventeen or eighteen, in that funny in-between world.

'And then I got married – at twenty – in 1966. The Queen and Prince Philip came to the wedding. Oh, yes, everyone was there. They all rolled up. It was extraordinary. It was in Westminster Abbey. It really was amazing. And then we would see them, now and again, at weekends, particularly in November, when they came to Luton Hoo [in Bedfordshire, bought by Sacha's great-grandfather, Julius Wernher, in 1903]. My grandparents were there, and uncles and aunts. And the Brabournes. There were ten or twelve in the house-party. There was shooting as usual and then, in the evening, some great entertainment. I remember Victor Borge particularly. And I remember the dinners – my grandmother being bossy, my grandfather bringing his heart and soul with him. The talk was always interesting. I remember my grandfather talking, and Prince Philip. I remember when they spoke, they took it in turns, they gave each other time, and we gave them full-blast attention. It was good.

'But it was later that we became close. I think it was at The Gables – when Nicky was running the shoots – that we particularly got interested in each other. What brought us together? Jung. Yes, Jung. I've always been interested in Jung, his work, his ideas. And Philip is interested in Jung. Prince Philip is always questing, exploring, searching for meaning, testing ideas. We had riveting conversations about Jung. That's where our friendship began.'

The Duke of Edinburgh was not the caricature to which all became accustomed. He was fascinated by Carl Gustav Jung (1875–1961), the great Swiss analyst, who eschewed Freud's obsession with sex and the power of the sexual impulse, and focused instead on what he termed the inherited 'collective unconscious' with its universal ideas or images: the 'archetypes' – coincidentally the name the Duchess of Sussex chose for the series of podcast conversations she launched in 2022: 'From Archewell Audio, *Archetypes with Meghan* – a podcast where we investigate, dissect, and subvert the labels that try to hold women back.' Jung wrote on subjects as diverse as nature, mythology and religion – subjects of deep interest to the Duke of Edinburgh. From the 1950s these interests increasingly intermeshed with his concern for the natural world and the environment.

In the 1950s the Queen wasn't much interested in any of this. She was busy with her 'boxes'. As her right-hand woman, the Mistress of the Robes, the Duchess of Grafton, explained to me, 'She really doesn't have much time for leisure reading. I'm afraid it's duty all the way – and when she does get some time to herself she wants to think about her horses.' Later in life, the Queen came to think more about the environment and to recognise that the Duke of Edinburgh's 'concern for the future of the planet' had been 'ahead of the field'. In 2021, when COP26 came to Glasgow, the Queen was eager to welcome the delegates to the 26th United Nations Climate Change Conference in person. In the event, her health prevented her from being there, so she recorded a video message in which she expressed herself as robustly as her late husband would have done: 'If the world pollution situation is not critical at the moment, it is as certain as anything can be, that the situation will become increasingly intolerable within a very short time . . . If we fail to cope with this challenge, all the other problems will pale into insignificance.'

Liz Truss as prime minister advised Charles III not to attend COP27 in Egypt in 2023 to keep him above the political fray. Elizabeth II endorsed COP26 in 2021, she admitted, in part as a tribute to the memory of her forward-thinking husband.

'Prince Philip cares about the environment,' Sacha Abercorn told me when we had our conversation. 'He has a feeling for nature – in a practical way. He is totally a sentient human being – in a practical way. I saw that at first hand when we travelled with him several times on *Britannia* – James and myself, Aubrey Buxton [television producer and naturalist] and Kay [his second wife]. We went to Borneo, Sarawak, the Galapagos. Philip's feeling for the environment is not sentimental – not sentimental at all. It's emotional and practical.

'He's always asking questions, searching for answers. I think it was at Lubenham, and my mother and he were walking back to the house from church, and she said something like "I don't believe in anything". That made him stop, suddenly, and ask out loud, "What is it? What's behind it all?" He asks the difficult questions and that's what drew me to him. I remember, in the 1980s sometime, we were staying at Windsor for Royal Ascot, and I had just discovered Anthony Stevens' book on *Archetypes* and I told Prince Philip about it and he was riveted. Riveted. We both were.'

Sacha was sitting forward now, smiling, her eyes shining. 'Our friendship was very close. The heart came into it in a big way. There's a hugely potent chemical reaction in him. It's a highly charged chemistry. We were close because we understood one another. He felt he could trust me and I felt I could trust him.'

Silence fell in the little drawing room and the tea had gone cold. 'In Eluthera,' I said – the Abercorns had a beautiful holiday home on the island of Eluthera in the Bahamas where I was lucky enough to stay back in the 1990s – 'In Eluthera, someone told me they had seen you and Prince Philip on the beach holding hands.'

Sacha smiled and said, without any awkwardness, 'It was a passionate friendship, but the passion was in the ideas. It was certainly not a full relationship. I did not go to bed with him. It probably looked like that to the world. I can understand why people might have thought it, but it didn't happen. It wasn't like that. He isn't like that. It's complicated and, at the same time, it's quite simple. He needs a playmate and someone to share his intellectual puruits.'

'Do you think he sleeps with his other playmates?' I asked.

'I doubt it, I doubt it very much.' She paused and thought a moment and said, 'No, I'm sure not. But he's a human being. Who knows? I don't. Unless you are in the room with a lighted candle, who knows?'

'And what about the Queen?' I asked.

Sacha Abercorn smiled and said, 'She gives him a lot of leeway. Her father told her, "Remember, he's a sailor. They come in on the tide."'

The Queen maintained her friendship with the Abercorns to the end of her life, regardless of the stories about Philip and Sacha – just as she accepted her husband's long-standing close friendship with his carriage-driving companion, Penny Romsey, having her to stay, going out to the theatre with her, taking her to church with her, inviting her to attend the Duke of Edinburgh's funeral during the Covid pandemic when only thirty mourners were allowed to be there and all the others were members of the royal family.

But how, I wonder, did the Queen really feel about all this

in the dark watches of the night? She could not say, fully, freely, as Robert Browning said in his poem 'By the Fireside': 'We stood there with never a third.' The answer, I think, is that Robert Browning was a sentimentalist, which the Queen was not. The Queen knew her husband. She knew he had his own interests, passions and enthusiasms – just as she had hers. She missed him when he wasn't there. When he was tucked away in his retirement bolthole on the Sandringham estate, she would say to her page, only half-joking: 'Paul, would you phone Prince Philip at Wood Farm and find out if he's still alive – I haven't seen him for six months.'

She loved her husband from first to last, admired him and accepted him as he was. She looked for the best in everyone. Always. She was Sovereign of the Order of the Garter, after all. *Honi soit qui mal y pense.*

CHAPTER TWENTY-ONE

Family matters

Princess Elizabeth, our future Elizabeth II, was brought up within a family unit that was small, close-knit, loving and giving – 'us four' as George VI put it. Elizabeth was a sweet child, self-contained and well-mannered, with a warm heart and a happy disposition. She was adored by both her grandfathers, and adored them in return. George V died, aged seventy, in 1936, when Elizabeth was ten; 'Grandfather Strathmore', the 14th Earl, died eight years later, in 1944, aged eighty-nine. 'Grandma Strathmore' died suddenly, in the summer of 1938, aged sixty-five. Her daughter, Queen Elizabeth, wrote to the prime minister, Neville Chamberlain:

> *I have been dreading this moment ever since I was a little girl and now that it has come, one can hardly believe it. She was a true 'Rock of Defence' for us, her children, & Thank God, her influence and wonderful example will remain with us all our lives.*
>
> *She had a good perspective of life – everything was given its true importance. She had a young spirit, great courage and unending sympathy whenever and wherever it was needed, & such a heavenly sense of humour. We all used to laugh together and have such fun.*

George VI died in February 1952, aged only fifty-six, followed to the family mausoleum, within fourteen months, by his mother, Queen Mary, aged eighty-five, formidable and for-bidding in appearance, frail and in pain at the end, heartbroken by her second son's early death. In the year of her Coronation, the new young Queen, at the age of twenty-six, was left with just two of her immediate family: her mother, then aged only fifty-two, and her sister, aged twenty-two. Happily, both lived on for almost half a century more. When the Queen died in 2022, she chose to be buried with both her parents and her husband, together beneath the one stone that reads in full:

George VI
1895–1952

Elizabeth
1900–2002

Elizabeth II
1926–2022

Philip
1921–2021

Elizabeth II had a good relationship with her mother – 'loving and normal' is how Margaret Rhodes described it to me. Queen Elizabeth, the Queen Mother was blessed with many of the virtues she recognised in her own mother: a good perspective of life, a young spirit, a heavenly sense of humour. Elizabeth II loved her mother, respected her, liked her. That said, the Queen did occasionally shake her head when contemplating her mother's unruffled extravagance. At the time of her death, the Queen Mother's overdraft at Coutts was reported to be in the region of £4 million. She was supposed to have said at a dinner party once, 'Golly, I could do with £100,000, couldn't you? Had such an awful afternoon today with my bank manager scolding me about my overdraft.' The Queen might, now and again, express envy of her mother's extraordinary capacity for avoiding all unpleasantness, but, fundamentally, mother and daughter were good friends, on the same wavelength, with mutual interests (especially horses), comfortable in each other's company, each looking forward to their regular, easy, uncomplicated chats on the telephone. Prince Philip said to me, eyebrows raised in amazement, 'They're always on the phone!'

The Queen recognised her mother's special star quality and had no desire to compete with her. At times, especially in the early years of her reign, she seemed a little in awe of her. Several of her courtiers and some of her friends said to me they sensed she was 'mindful' of her mother – concerned to secure her mother's approval, anxious not to do anything that she thought might displease her mother. The Queen Mother, in her turn, recognised her daughter as an exemplary sovereign and was always careful to show due deference. On the occasions when she momentarily forgot herself – stepping through a doorway ahead of the Queen, for example – she was always quick to apologise. Margaret Rhodes's description of the Queen coming by to have a drink with Queen Elizabeth on a Sunday morning after church would be the envy of many a mother and daughter. 'There was mutual respect and deep affection,' said Mrs Rhodes, 'but, most of all, they just got on really, really well.'

Mrs Rhodes's description of the Queen's relationship with Princess Margaret was less dewy-eyed. 'The Queen was sometimes infuriated by Margaret, inevitably,' she told me. 'She found her behaviour exasperating at times, of course she did. But Margaret was her sister and she loved her.'

From all the people I have spoken with who were close to the Queen – courtiers, friends and family members – I gained the impression of someone who, though conservative by upbringing and conventional in her own life, was not judgemental when it comes to others. Elizabeth II looked for the best in people and hoped for the best from them and for them. When things went wrong, she prayed (on her knees, with her hands folded together) that they would go better. She was sure of the values, principles and beliefs that guided her own life, but she was neither prescriptive nor dogmatic with regard to the lives of others. She was the Queen, but she did not lay down the law. She was reluctant to interfere in the private lives of members of her family, although she did, now and again, in the case of her children, as we shall see. She was sorry to be depicted, as she felt she was, in a series of articles published in the *Daily Telegraph* in the run-up to her Golden Jubilee[3], as someone who was emotionally inhibited, buttoned-up, psychologically repressed, awkward when it came to being loving and giving. She did not express her emotions in the manner of the Prince William and Prince Harry generation, but that did not mean she was unfeeling.

The Queen was deeply fond of her younger sister, for all Princess Margaret's waywardness. The Queen really loved Margaret's two children, David and Sarah, and sometimes seemed more at ease in their company than she did in the company of one or two of her own offspring. In the 1950s, when Margaret Rose wanted to marry her father's equerry, Peter Townsend, the Queen was not unsympathetic. It was just a very difficult situation. When, in 1960, Princess Margaret married the photographer, Tony Armstrong-Jones, the Queen hoped they would live happily ever after. That they didn't was,

---

3 Articles, based on a wide-ranging series of interviews by Graham Turner, published in book form as *Elizabeth: The Woman and The Queen*, 2002

from the Queen's point of view, a matter for sadness, not recrimination. Again, it was not easy. Divorce is commonplace nowadays (almost routine in the case of the Queen's children), but a generation or two ago, things were different. The Duke of Windsor had married a divorcee in 1937, but it was not until thirty years later that someone in line to the throne (albeit eighteenth in line) was divorced themselves. In 1967, George, the 7th Earl of Harewood, aged forty-four, became the first of George V's direct descendants to be divorced. His wife sued him on the grounds of his adultery with an Australian violinist, which he acknowledged. He wanted to marry his mistress (also a divorcee, and the mother of his son) and to do so, under the terms of the Royal Marriages Act, required the sovereign's consent. The Queen, having taken advice from the Privy Council, granted it. Lord Harewood then slipped discreetly out of the country (to the United States) to marry for the second time. (Lord Harewood's first wife, Marion, was not lucky in love. She went on to marry the Liberal politician, Jeremy Thorpe, later tried and acquitted on a charge of conspiracy to murder.)

As we have seen, the Queen's sister and brother-in-law, the Snowdons, had relationships beyond their marriage and rows within it. By 1976, the position was untenable and separation unavoidable. The Queen was saddened by what had happened, but when her press secretary declared, 'There has been no pressure from the Queen on either Princess Margaret or Lord Snowdon to take any particular course', he was speaking the truth. The Queen would have liked her sister to have had a happier, more fulfilled, less complicated life. In the 1970s and early 1980s, she read in the newspapers – you couldn't not – about her sister's relationship with young Roddy Llewellyn – a sandy-haired charmer (a gentleman gardener and garden designer) eighteen years Princess Margaret's junior – and, no doubt, felt that the publicity was not very good for the royal family and that the romance would, all too probably, end in tears.

It did, after seven years. Roddy moved on and married someone else, very happily; Margaret lived on, but ended her life without a partner – though not without friends. I did not know her, but I know and knew both Roddy Llewellyn and Tony Snowdon, both of them delightful: gifted, engaging, playful, funny. (Kenneth Williams heard Roddy tell a story over dinner at my house and recorded in his diary that he had never heard a story better told.) Princess Margaret did not treat her body as a temple: she smoked and drank and paid the price. She was spoilt; she could be self-indulgent; the stories of her rudeness and bad behaviour are too many not to have had some truth to them. However, from all I have heard of her, from her husband, from her lover, from her friends Angela Huth and Anne Glenconner, among others, it is clear that, at her best, she was great fun: witty, giving, thoughtful, musical and gay. She was loyal to the Queen, proud of her country and did her duty, as and when required. Several said to me that she never quite recovered from the death of her father in 1952.

While the drama of the disintegrating Snowdon marriage unfolded, the Duke of Edinburgh stayed out of the way – figuratively speaking, and, often, literally, too. 'I don't go looking for trouble,' is how he put it to me. And, as a rule, he tried to steer clear of talking about family matters – and not just with me, but within the family, too. He did not talk about his 'feelings' and nor did the Queen. And nor did my parents. They reflected their generation. They would not for a moment have considered the possibility of writing a book telling their own story – with 'the highs and lows, the mistakes, the lessons learnt' as their grandson Harry is promising to do with his book.

I do not think King Charles is looking forward to Harry's book with much relish, either, though he is not in so strong a position to complain about it as his parents would have been, because, in the 1990s, the Prince of Wales, as he then was, cooperated with the broadcaster Jonathan Dimbleby to produce a television film and biography in which he acknowledged his own adultery and made plain how unhappy he had been at times during his childhood. I don't think the King would talk in such terms today, because today he is in a good place, whereas in the 1990s, when his marriage had broken down, he was in a bad one. Then in his forties, going grey and with a pained expression, he let the world know that, as he was growing up, he felt that he was 'emotionally estranged' from both his parents, craving 'the affection and appreciation' from them that they were either 'unable or unwilling' to offer. His stories of small slights that left their scars were many and similar. When, as a little boy, he forgot to call his detective 'Mr' and simply used his surname, as he heard his parents do all the time, he was made to apologise. When he left a door open and a footman went to close it, Philip stopped the footman, barking, 'Leave it alone, man. The boy's got hands.' When, one winter on the Sandringham estate, young Charles was throwing snowballs at a police officer, Philip called to the policeman, 'Don't just stand there, throw some back!' When, again at Sandringham, Charles came back from playing in the grounds one afternoon, having lost a dog lead, his mother sent him straight out again, instructing him not to return until he had found what he had lost, reminding him, 'Dog leads cost money.' When, this time in London, young Charles was seen sticking his tongue out at the crowd watching him drive down the Mall, his father gave him a spanking.

Talking to Jonathan Dimbleby (and, before him, to those of his friends and family who cared to listen), Charles gave the impression that he regarded his father as a bully and a tyrant and his mother as distant and ungiving. As a little boy at Buckingham Palace, he passed his mother's study one day and asked her to come and play with him. Gently closing the door against him, she said, 'If only I could.' When his parents returned from their post-Coronation tour and Charles, aged five, was taken in *Britannia* to the port of Tobruk to greet them, the little boy attempted to join the line of dignitaries waiting to shake Her Majesty by the hand. 'No, not you, dear,' were the mother's first words to her son after five months of separation.

Young Charles felt neglected at home and abandoned at school. The Queen, educated at home, and, though Head of State herself, brought up traditionally to accept the father as the natural head of the family, was content to be led by her husband in the matter of her own children's education. 'The Queen and I,' said Philip in 1956, when Charles was seven, rising eight, 'want Charles to go to school with other boys of his generation and learn to live with other children, and to absorb from childhood the discipline imposed by education with others.' In September 1957, two months before his ninth birthday, Charles was despatched to his first boarding school, Cheam in Hampshire. The school had changed its location since Philip had been a pupil a quarter of a century earlier, but the school's spirit remained the same. Charles later reflected that his first weeks at Cheam had been the loneliest of his life. Five years later, in 1962, again following in his father's footsteps, Charles moved on to Gordonstoun, in Scotland, on the Moray Firth. His new school's spartan regime was not to his taste. 'It's absolute hell,' Charles wrote home. 'It's near Balmoral,' his father told him. 'There's always the Factor there [the agent who managed the estate]. You can go and stay with him. And your grandmother goes up there to fish. You can go and see her.'

Charles did indeed seek comfort and companionship from family retainers. He was close to the nannies of his early childhood, Helen Lightbody and Mabel Anderson, and to his governess, Catherine Peebles, known as 'Mipsy'. She recalled how sensitive and tentative Charles was as a small boy: 'If you raised your voice to him, he would draw back into his shell, and for a time you would be able to do nothing with him.' But, as his father knew, his chief comforter was Queen Elizabeth, the Queen Mother. She was a doting grandmother who always gave her favourite grandson an understanding shoulder to cry on and a warm bosom to embrace.

The Queen Mother was explicitly against Charles being sent to Gordonstoun. 'It is miles & miles away,' she wrote to her daughter in May 1961, '& he might as well be at school abroad . . . He would be terribly cut off and lonely up in the far North.' Prince Charles agreed with Grannie. She wanted her grandson to go to Eton. 'All your friends' sons are at Eton,' Queen Elizabeth told her daughter, '& it is so important to be able to grow up with people you will be with later in life. And so nice, & so important when boys are growing up, that you & Philip can see him during school days & keep him in touch with what is happening.' She apologised for interfering, 'but I have been thinking & worrying about it all'.

In due course, Prince Charles sent his own sons to Eton. He did not consider Gordonstoun for a moment. Prince Philip sent his sons to Gordonstoun. He did not consider Eton for a moment. Charles resented his father because of this, and he adored his grandmother because of the way she championed and cossetted him. In 2002, when she died, he was bereft and did not disguise his anguish. 'She was quite simply the most magical grandmother you could possibly have, and I was utterly devoted to her,' he said. 'For me, she meant everything, and I have dreaded, dreaded this moment.'

Back in 1962, when asked how Prince Charles was getting on at Gordonstoun, Prince Philip replied, 'Well, at least he hasn't run away yet.' In fact, he stayed the course and did rather well. He may have regarded it as 'a prison sentence – like Colditz with kilts', but he ended up as 'Guardian' (the Gordonston equivalent of head boy) as his father had done before him (and Prince Edward would later do) and secured two A levels (Grade B in History, Grade C in French). Later, while recalling the bullying to which he was subjected at the school and the rigours of the spartan Gordonstoun routine, he would come to acknowledge that the school had developed his 'will power' and helped his self-discipline, 'not in the sense of making you bath in cold water, but in the Latin sense, of giving shape and form to your life.' The philosophy of Kurt Hahn that helped form Prince Philip, helped form Prince Charles, too. The values that inspired the Duke of Edinburgh Award scheme and the Outward Bound Trust are not dissimilar from those that underpin the work of the Prince's Trust.

Prince Philip loved his son, even if he did not tell him so, and acknowledged many of his boy's achievements, though not uncritically. He left it to the Queen to sing the Prince of Wales's praises and, over the years, Her Majesty went out of her way to praise her eldest son in public and to thank him – sincerely, and from the heart – both for the support he had given her over the years and for the range of good works he had undertaken, with imagination and dedication, on behalf of the wider community. Privately, she was more critical. As I've mentioned, she used to grumble about her son's extravagance. The Queen kept her breakfast cereals fresher longer by storing them in Tupperware containers. The Prince of Wales did not. He has a style and taste and panache – and way with money – that reflect his maternal grandmother rather than his parents. He entertains, and entertains royally. The Queen is reported to have said, 'The amount of kit and staff he takes about – it's obscene.' I believe he thought that was part of the point of being Prince of Wales. At a party at Highgrove, I thanked him for his superb hospitality and congratulated him on the wonderful way it was all done: the silver, the crystal, the lighting, the flowers – especially the flowers. 'They came from the garden,' he said. 'It's a joy to behold,' I murmured. 'Isn't it?' he said, beaming. 'I'm so glad you like it. I want you to like it. I'm so lucky to have all these lovely things around me. I simply want to share them. I want everyone to love my garden. It is a joy, isn't it? Such a joy.' That simply is not the way his parents ever talked.

The Queen, of course, did not talk to the press. The Duke of Edinburgh did. Indeed, I made the point to him once that he started it all, that he was the first senior member of the royal family to give any kind of extended interview. 'Yes,' he said, 'I made a conscious decision to talk to the media – but not about me, only about what I'm doing, what I'm supporting.' That Prince Charles should voluntarily talk to a broadcaster and journalist about family matters, about his private life, and let the journalist have access to his diaries and private correspondence, seemed to his parents sheer foolishness. Both the Queen and the Duke were appalled by the Dimbleby book. They could not see how their son's indiscretions – or special pleading on his own behalf – could serve his cause, or that of the royal family, in any way. They were also hurt by their son's public complaints about the quality of their parenting. They had meant well, they had done their best, and their recollection of Charles's childhood was rather different from his own. 'Recollections may vary,' was how the Queen felt many years before she used the phrase in relation to Harry and Meghan's television interview with Oprah Winfrey in 2021. In the 1990s, looking back on their older children's childhoods, the Queen recalled fun and games, bath-times, storytelling, picnics and bonfires, laughter, not tears. Prince Philip remembered taking Charles and Anne, regularly during the summer holidays, cruising in his twelve-metre yacht *Bloodhound* and believed that these were 'good times, happy days.'

Gina Kennard said to me of Prince Charles, 'When he was a little boy, there didn't seem to be a problem at all, but, as he was growing up, I think probably the Queen was too tolerant, and Prince Philip too tough.' Countess Mountbatten, Philip's first cousin and one of Charles's godparents, said to me, 'You can see it from both sides, can't you? A resilient character such as Prince Philip, toughened by the slings and arrows of life, who sees being tough as a necessity for survival, wants to toughen up his son – and his son is very sensitive. It hasn't been easy for either of them.' Patricia Mountbatten paused and then added, with a dry laugh, 'Anne, of course, as a natural tomboy, presented no problems.'

Mabel Anderson, who was nanny to both Prince Charles and Princess Anne, said: 'He was never as boisterous and noisy as Princess Anne. She had a much stronger, more extrovert personality. She didn't exactly push him aside, but she was certainly a more forceful child.' Anne is like her father. She will make no complaint of any kind about her upbringing. Father and daughter always got on well. They were alike in many ways: undertaking their public duties in the same brisk, no-nonsense fashion, competing with one another as to which could fulfill the more engagements in the year, vying with one another as to which had the more efficient private office. They had an easy, good-humoured, comfortable relationship. They didn't brood about it: they just got on with it.

Philip was separated from his mother throughout his adolescence but refused – absolutely – to use that as an excuse for anything. He would not find fault with his mother however

424

hard you pressed him. Anne will not find fault with hers, either – whatever Charles may have said in the sad, bad nineties. The idea that, as a mother, the Queen was remote and uncaring is flatly rejected by the Princess Royal. 'I'm not going to speak for anyone else,' she says, 'but I simply don't believe that there is any evidence whatsoever to suggest that she wasn't caring. It just beggars belief. We as children may have not been too demanding, in the sense that we understood what the limitations were in time and the responsibilities placed on her as monarch in the things she had to do and the travels she had to make, but I don't believe that any of us, for a second, thought she didn't care for us in exactly the same way as any other mother did. I just think it's extraordinary that anybody could construe that that might not be true.'

Anne found her father demanding in a way that was encouraging and her mother tolerant in a way that allowed her children to find their own feet. 'If she'd been a disciplinarian,' says Anne, with a wry smile, 'and said "No" to everybody, we'd have all been psycho-analysed out of existence on the basis that we had too controlling a mother. We've all been allowed to find our own way and we were always encouraged to discuss problems, to talk them through. People have to make their own mistakes and I think she's always accepted that.'

'We are a family,' Prince Philip said to me. In much the same way, Princess Anne adds, 'Judging by some families, I think we are all on pretty good speaking terms after all this time, and that's no mean achievement for quite a lot of families. I think we all enjoy each other's company.'

The family grew in the early 1960s. Prince Andrew, now Duke of York, was born on 19 February 1960. Prince Edward, Earl of Wessex, was born on 10 March 1964, weighing in at just 5lbs 7oz. It was the first birth not to involve 'twilight sleep' and the first where Prince Philip was in attendance as his wife's 'birthing partner' – though he snorted derisively when I introduced him to the phrase.

Martin Charteris told me that, when Prince Andrew was conceived, 'the Queen and Prince Philip had been trying for another baby for quite a while.' 'How on earth do you know?' I asked him. 'Because Her Majesty told me so,' he chuckled. 'She wanted me to pass it on to President Nkrumah, you see.' I didn't see, so Lord Charteris, beaming broadly, obligingly explained: 'In late 1959, the Queen was due to visit Ghana. It was going to be a big thing. In May she discovered she was pregnant and realised that the Ghana trip would have to be put off. She knew that Dr Nkrumah was a sensitive chap and might take offence unless he knew the whole story, so I was despatched to Accra to put him in the picture – which I did. At first, he was appalled, then he decided that if the Queen couldn't come to him, he'd go to her – at Balmoral – which he did. I have to say, she has a way with these Commonwealth leaders. They trust her. Absolutely.'

In due course, without any interference from Queen Elizabeth, the Queen Mother, Andrew and Edward followed Charles to Gordonstoun – and survived. In 1979, aged nineteen, exactly forty years after his parents' celebrated encounter there, Andrew enrolled at Dartmouth Royal Naval College. At twenty-one, he qualified as a helicopter pilot and joined 829 Naval Air Squadron, flying Sea Kings from the carrier HMS *Invincible*. In April 1982, *Invincible* sailed for the South Atlantic with the British naval task force sent to recapture the Falkland Islands from the invading Argentines. He put his life on the line: 255 British officers and men died in the conflict – and 652 Argentines. 'Prince Andrew is a serving officer,' said Buckingham Palace in answer to suggestions that the Queen might want to keep her son out of harm's way, 'and there is no question in her mind that he should go.' When Port Stanley was liberated and the conflict over, Andrew telephoned home. 'My mother was in,' he said, 'it was about the right time of evening.' She told him that she was relieved he was safe and how proud his parents were of him, and then, immediately, she asked him 'to pass on how proud she was of everyone and to say how marvellously the troops had done.'

In June 1986, Prince Edward, having graduated from Cambridge (with a respectable degree in modern history), joined the Royal Marines, notoriously the toughest billet in the armed services. Given his slight build and his reported ambition at the time to be an actor, it seemed an odd choice for the twenty-two-year-old to make, but he had signed up before going to university and was determined to make a go of it. He tried, and he failed. It was the psychological as much as the physical demands of the training that overwhelmed him. And, apparently, the attitude of his commanding officer was unsympathetic. In January 1987, with the acquiescence of his parents, Edward resigned his commission. His father (Captain-General of the Royal Marines) was disappointed, but coped. Martin Palmer, a friend of the Duke's, told me how he happened to be having dinner with Prince Philip 'the week after all this'. Prince Edward came into the room and 'Prince Philip got up and gave him the most enormous hug and brought him to the table. Yes, they'd had a humdinger of a row, but it was over.'

Philip, in my experience, spoke of Edward with an ease and warmth that was not in evidence when he talked of the Prince of Wales – who, of course, having secured his own degree from Cambridge (BA Hons, Class II, Division II), went on to serve in Her Majesty's armed services for six not unchallenging years. At the RAF training college at Cranwell, Charles showed immediately that he shared his father's aptitude for flying. He then followed his father to the Royal

Naval College, Dartmouth, and served in a series of war-ships: *Norfolk, Minerva, Jupiter* and *Hermes*. At the time of the Falklands conflict, Charles expressed regret that he had not been 'tested' in action as Andrew had been, but, throughout his years of service (1970–76) – culminating with a stint as a helicopter pilot in the Fleet Air Arm – he was as gung-ho and courageous as any father could wish. There was, how-ever, something perverse about Prince Philip. He liked to be contrary and, perhaps, just because nobody would expect it, he seemed to prefer Edward, who flunked the Royal Marines, to Charles, who served in the services with distinction and pushed himself to the limit. Gradually, Edward took on more and more of his father's commitments, notably as the front-man for the Duke of Edinburgh Award, and then the Queen let it be known that, when Prince Philip died, Prince Edward would succeed his father as the new Duke of Edinburgh. This has not yet happened – the title would have to be 'recreated' for the purpose – but I assume it will, perhaps in the run-up to King Charles's coronation. I know it was the Queen's wish because both she and Prince Edward told me so.

Perhaps inevitably, the youngest of the royal children was the most indulged. In June 1987, a year after he joined the Royal Marines, Edward, aged twenty-three and settled on a new career in entertainment, joined forces with the BBC and John Broome, then owner of the Midlands-based vis-itor attraction, Alton Towers, to present a spectacular royal version of the slapstick-and-games TV show, *It's a Knockout!* According to Edward, 'Both the BBC and John Broome posi-tively drooled at the idea.' Edward persuaded his sister Anne, his brother Andrew and Andrew's new wife, Sarah Ferguson (who needed little persuading), to dress up in mock-Tudor costumes and lead teams of celebrities – Rowan Atkinson, Les Dawson and Barbara Windsor among them – as they competed in a series of silly fun and games loosely disguised as a medieval joust-about. It was well-meant, and useful sums were raised for charity, but *It's a Royal Knockout* did nothing for the dignity of the House of Windsor or the standing of the new generation of young royals. Everyone at Buckingham Palace at the time (from the private secretary to the press office) claims to have been against it, but Edward was determined and the Queen did not have it in her to say 'No'. The embarrassment of the spectacle itself was compounded by Prince Edward's post-show press conference. The attendant hacks, hot and weary after a long day, not satisfied with the access they had been given to the 'royal celebrities', failed to show any enthusiasm for what Edward hoped the world would regard as his finest hour. Faced with the media's indifference, Edward made a couple of sarcastic remarks and stalked out of the press tent. 'Edward Storms Out After Game Show' ran one headline; 'It's a Walkout' ran another.

The press for the young prince did not improve much as the years went by. They were relatively gentle with him when he worked as a backroom boy and production assistant for Andrew Lloyd Webber's Really Useful Group, but when he turned his attention to television film-making, and founded his own production company, Ardent, the gloves were off again. The films were rubbished; he was accused of exploiting his family name to get them made; Ardent was repeatedly reported to be making losses – losses of almost £2 million over seven years, according to the *Guardian*. The knock-out blow came in April 2001 and was delivered by the *News of the World*.

In June 1999, Edward, aged thirty-five, had married Sophie Rhys-Jones, aged thirty-four, a pretty, wholesome, blonde public relations executive who appeared to have a sensible head on resolute shoulders. Appearances can be deceptive – as Sophie, now Countess of Wessex, found to her cost when, in the spring of 2001, on behalf of her PR company, she took a meeting with a potential 'client', an Arab 'sheikh', who turned out to be an under-cover reporter for the *News of the World*. Sophie's small-talk, as recorded by the 'sheikh', was hardly treasonable, but it was unfortunate. She referred to the Queen as 'the old dear' and the Queen Mother as 'the old lady' and described the Prince of Wales and Camilla Parker Bowles as 'number one on the unpopular people list', only likely to be married after the death of 'the old lady'. She was not discreet. She mocked the prime minister, calling him 'President Blair'; she poured scorn on the prime minister's wife, calling her 'horrid, absolutely horrid'; and she desribed the Leader of the Opposition (William Hague) as 'deformed'. Most damagingly, she let slip that, while her company's prestige and royal connections were not officially for hire, 'that is an unspoken benefit.'

When Sophie discovered the truth about the sting, on advice from Buckingham Palace, she sought to bury her indiscretions and buy off the *News of the World* by giving them 'a personal interview' – and promptly fell between two stools. Rival newspapers tumbled over themselves to publish edited highlights of her secretly recorded conversation with the 'sheikh' and the *News of the World* carried a sensational interview that was as personal as anyone could hope for. 'My Edward Is Not Gay' ran the headline, above a story in which the Countess denounced the rumours of her husband's homosexuality and revealed that they were determined to have a baby and were even contemplating in-vitro fertilisation in order to be able to do so. Two years later, in November 2003, their first-born, Louise, arrived and became the first royal child to bear the surname Mountbatten-Windsor. Four years after that, in December 2007, their son, James Alexander Philip Theo Mountbatten-Windsor, Viscount Severn, was born.

Meanwhile, in 2002, Edward and Sophie withdrew from their respective companies, abandoned their business lives and settled on a future as full-time working royals. It has worked out well for both of them: they have done the state much service. And it worked out well for the Queen, too, who was already close to Edward and who, as she grew older, became increasingly fond of Sophie – and dependent on her for company. The Wessexes live in Bagshot Park, just down the road from Windsor Castle. The 'old dear' and her daughter-in-law became good companions, eating together, watching TV together, completely comfortable in one another's company. Sophie felt especially grateful to the Queen for her gentle kindness and sustaining support when she lost her own mother to stomach cancer in 2005. Mary Rhys-Jones was seventy-one when she died and the Queen was seventy-nine. All the Queen's children had sadness etched deep on their faces in those days between her death and her funeral, but none more so than her daughter-in-law, Sophie Wessex, and Sophie's sister-in-law, the Princess Royal – who was the first to reach her mother on the day of her sudden deterioration and who stayed with her to the end, notified the local registrar of her mother's death and accompanied her mother's body on its last journey from Balmoral Castle to Edinburgh and then on to London.

Princess Anne was the first of the royal children to be married, on 14 November 1973 – her brother Charles's twenty-fifth birthday. As far as her parents were concerned, she was free to marry anybody she chose. She chose to marry Lieutenant Mark Phillips, born, like Charles, in 1948, educated at Marlborough College and Sandhurst, a guardsman (The Queen's Dragoons), the soldier son of a soldier, and, more to the point, an achieving equestrian: a key member of the British three-day-eventing team that had triumphed in the

World Championships in 1970, the European Championships in 1971 and the Olympic Games in Munich in 1972. Anne, too, was an achieving equestrian: in 1971 she won the individual European Three-Day-Event at Burghley; in 1976 she would be a member of the British Olympic Team in Montreal. 'I shouldn't wonder if their children are four-legged,' the Queen is supposed to have remarked.

Once upon a time, not so long ago, the only daughter of the Queen of England would have been expected to marry a prince of some kind – or, at least, a high-ranking aristocrat. There were sound reasons for this: he would know the rules, he would know his way around the court, he might even have land and money enough to keep the royal daughter in the style to which she was accustomed. The twentieth century changed all that. Gradually, over several decades, the rigid British class structure – so clear, so certain – began to collapse. The Great War changed much, the Second World War changed more. The 1944 Education Act, the arrival of television, the advent of the Pill, the Angry Young Men of the 1950s, the Beatles, the Rolling Stones, Harold Wilson and 'the white heat of technology' – they all played a part. At the beginning of the Queen's reign, at royal investitures, as Her Majesty passed, everybody bowed or curtsied to the ground. Now, nobody does. Deference isn't what it used to be. Old money has given way to new money. Meritocrats outrank aristocrats, and celebrities outclass them both.

The Queen and the Duke of Edinburgh helped their children adjust to this changing world by sending them away to boarding school. Philip was as royal as they come, but he was nothing like an English aristocrat. He was an outsider; a European; in many ways, an iconoclast. Philip chose Gordonstoun – Kurt Hahn's Gordonstoun – for his sons – not Eton or Harrow. Anne went to Benenden, a girls' school in Kent, because Gordonstoun was not yet coeducational. (Both Anne's children, Peter and Zara, born in 1977 and 1981, went to Gordonstoun and then to Exeter University.) As a child, educated at home, Princess Elizabeth did not mix and mingle – let alone live and play – with the middle classes. At Benenden, Princess Anne did. At Gordonstoun and Benenden, the royal children met middle-class children, with middle-class values, and shared the middle-class experience. William, now Prince of Wales, who went to Eton, met Catherine Middleton, now Princess of Wales, who went to Marlborough, when they were both studying at the University of St Andrews in Scotland. Catherine's parents met when her father was a flight despatcher and her mother was a flight attendant. In the 1980s the Middletons founded a mail order company, Party Pieces, selling decorations and party supplies. By all accounts, they are decent people – discreet, too – and reassuringly middle-class.

Mark Phillips (another Marlburian) also came from middle-class stock. When I met him I liked him. He seemed on the shy side and sparing with the small-talk – but what do I know about dressage? In royal circles, he was reckoned dull and a bit dim, and Prince Charles was credited with giving him the nickname 'Fog'. Four months after their marriage, however, Anne's new husband came into his own. One night, in March 1974, as they were being driven along the Mall on their way back to Buckingham Palace after a charity film show, an armed man yanked open their car door and attempted to abduct the Princess. Shots were fired. The assailant pulled Anne frantically by one arm while she held tight to Mark with the other. Eventually, police arrived in sufficient numbers to subdue the attacker, who turned out to have a history of mental illness. The world was rightly impressed by the Princess's cool under fire. 'Her bravery and superb obstinacy were unbelievable,'

Prince Charles recorded in his diary when he heard about the incident. 'My admiration for such a sister knows no bounds!' Anne was unhurt, but her personal protection officer was shot and wounded during the assault, and later awarded the George Cross for his bravery. Mark Phillips was appointed a Commander of the Royal Victorian Order and Anne was given the Grand Cross.

Mark Phillips was a handsome husband, an outstanding horseman and a good father. He sired two fine bipeds and moved on. The marriage failed, as marriages sometimes do, and, since the passing of the Divorce Reform Act in 1969, nobody needed to take the blame. The couple separated in 1989, the marriage was dissolved in April 1992, and, on 12 December the same year, the Princess Royal married Commander Timothy Laurence, RN, at a private ceremony at Crathie Church, near Balmoral Castle in Scotland.

Tim Laurence, the naval son of a naval father, is also from solidly middle-class stock. When I met him I liked him. He seemed on the shy side and sparing with the small-talk – but what do I know about nautical manoeuvres? He is five years younger than Princess Anne. The couple met when he was the assistant navigating officer in the Royal Yacht *Britannia*. He was an equerry to the Queen, 1986–89, and became an MVO in consequence. In July 2004, promoted to Rear-Admiral, he was appointed Assistant Chief of the Defence Staff, making him the armed services' highest-ranking member of the royal family since Lord Mountbatten was appointed Chief of the Defence Staff in 1959. He went on to even higher things and ended his naval career as a Vice Admiral in charge of the defence estates. The Queen made him a Knight Commander of the Royal Victorian Order in June 2011. I got the impression from Prince Philip that his daughter's second marriage had not been a bed of roses, but what marriage is? There have been ups and downs, and reported rifts and separations, but the couple keep themselves busy (the Princess Royal's commitment to duty is almost obsessive), and the marriage has survived and, with the advent of grandchildren, some say has once again begun to thrive.

Now and then Philip sent Anne letters, offering his daughter support, encouragement and good advice. The Duke of Edinburgh was an assiduous correspondent. While the Queen, in her easy-to-read open hand, wrote shorter, more informal and chatty letters to family and friends, her husband typed his letters himself. While the Queen was most communicative by telephone, written correspondence was her husband's most effective means of personal communication. In conversation he could be hectoring and difficult to read. On paper, he seemed more considered, more considerate. He used letters to show he cared. He used them, too, to think out loud, to explore, to question, to offer ideas and advice, and to say those things that, within a family, are sometimes more comfortably written down than spoken out loud.

At the beginning of 1981, when his eldest son was thirty-two and flirting with the idea of marrying Lady Diana Spencer, then nineteen, Philip wrote to Charles, encouraging him to make up his mind. The girl was young and vulnerable, and the press speculation about a possible match was at fever pitch. The child was in the spotlight and Charles was dithering. He was, he admitted to himself, in 'a confused and anxious state of mind'. Seven years earlier, on Valentine's Day 1974, his great-uncle, Dickie Mountbatten, had written to Charles with his own brand of matrimonial advice:

I believe, in a case like yours, the man should sow his wild oats and have as many affairs as he can before settling down but for a wife he should choose a suitable, attractive and sweet-charactered girl before she met anyone she might fall for. After all Mummy never seriously thought of anyone else after the Dartmouth encounter when she was 13! I think it is disturbing for women to have experiences if they have to remain on a pedestal after marriage.

Throughout his twenties Charles appeared to have been following his great-uncle's advice. He had fallen in love ('whatever love means') a number of times. In the summer of 1971, at Smith's Lawn, the Guards' polo ground at Windsor, he had met Camilla Shand, a year older than him, already the girlfriend of Andrew Parker Bowles, but a game girl, with a reputation as something of a goer, and proud to be the great-granddaughter of Alice Keppel, celebrated mistress to Charles's great-great-grandfather, Edward VII. Charles and Camilla had an affair – Uncle Dickie allowed them to use Broadlands for illicit weekends – but, in March 1973, Camilla announced her engagement to Major Parker Bowles. Charles heard the news while serving in HMS *Fox* somewhere in the Caribbean. He wrote to Uncle Dickie, mourning the end of an idyllic relationship, bleating that now he had 'no one' to return to in England, but concluding, stoically, that 'the feeling of emptiness would eventually pass'. It did and it didn't. Other girls came and went – Mountbatten's granddaughter, Amanda Knatchbull, among them – but the yearning for Camilla never wholly disappeared and, in the aftermath of Uncle Dickie's murder by the IRA, Charles turned to Mrs Parker Bowles for consolation.

Uncle Dickie had indulged Charles at Broadlands, but, before he died, he had also cautioned his great-nephew against selfishness and self-indulgence. In April 1979, five years after sending Charles his Valentine's Day advice, Lord Mountbatten wrote to his great-nephew again, holding out before him this time, not the prospect of wild oats, but the fearful ghost of the black sheep of the family, Charles's other great-uncle, the Duke of Windsor. Uncle Dickie confessed to his great-nephew that his behaviour was the cause of sleepless nights: 'I thought you were beginning on the downward slope which wrecked your Uncle David's life and led to his disgraceful Abdication and his futile life ever after.'

Deep down, Mountbatten knew that Charles would not continue on what he called 'your Uncle David's sad course'. Charles knew it, too. In his diary entry of 29 January 1981, he recognised the absurdity of his own confusion: 'It all seems so ridiculous because I do very much want to do the right thing for this Country and for my family.'

That is all Charles's parents wanted, too. What Mountbatten would have termed 'a suitable, attractive and sweet-charactered girl' was now on the scene. She was innocent and eligible, ready and willing. With the Queen's approval, the Duke of Edinburgh wrote to his son to say it was time for him to put up or shut up. He should either propose to Diana, counselled his father, so 'pleasing his family and the country', or release her. He really should not let her go on dangling in the wind like this.

Mountbatten's daughter, Patricia, Charles's godmother, said to me when I went to see her, 'I take it you've seen the letter? It wasn't a bullying letter at all. It was very reasonable. It was fair. It was sensible.' That is not how it seemed to Charles at the time. Charles said that his father's letter made him feel 'ill-used and impotent'. Faced with what he regarded as a parental 'ultimatum', he felt emasculated, cornered, compelled almost, to do what he did next. He telephoned Diana and suggested they meet. On Friday 6 February, at Windsor Castle, the Prince of Wales, aged thirty-two, asked Lady Diana Spencer, aged nineteen, to marry him. Apparently, she giggled nervously, and said, 'Yes, yes, of course, yes.'

CHAPTER TWENTY-TWO

'Show us you care'

Charles and Diana were married at St Paul's Cathedral on 29 July 1981. Fifteen years later they were divorced. The decree nisi was granted on 15 July 1996, the decree absolute on 28 August – the feast day of St Augustine of Hippo, the fourth-century theologian, famous for his maxim, '*Audi partem alteram*': 'hear the other side'.

There are certainly two sides to the sorry story of the marriage of Charles and Diana, and, having friends who were good friends of each of them, I have heard both sides. Charles, according to Diana's camp, was selfish, self-indulgent, thoughtless, unsympathetic, uncaring and cruel. He made no effort to share her interests and took no trouble to like her friends. He was older than her and more experienced: he had a duty of care which he neglected, almost from the start. Faced with her frailty – her post-natal depression, her mood swings – he was unable to cope. Faced with her cries for help – her bulimia, her attempts at self-injury – he turned away and sought solace in the arms of the one woman he had loved all along, Camilla Parker Bowles.

Diana, according to Charles's friends, was a sad case, almost from the start. She was in love with the position not the prince. She never came close to understanding her man – or trying to. She was self-regarding, self-absorbed, self-obsessed. She resented her husband's range of interests: she demanded a cull of some of his closest friends. She came from a difficult background – a dysfunctional family with a history of marital and mental instability – and it showed. Diana was difficult, deceitful and manipulative. She made up stories, she told lies, she had affairs.

Interestingly, both camps, while unsparing in their attacks on the integrity and character of their villain of choice, offered a guarded truce in the matter of Charles and Diana's children. When it comes to William (born 21 June 1982) and Harry (born 15 September 1984), it seems to be agreed by both sides that both parents, in their different but equally loving ways, meant well and did their best. And Charles's parents meant well and did their best, too. They did not take sides and, at first at least, they tried not to interfere.

Initially, as the marriage began to disintegrate, the Queen did not intervene because, in fairness, what could she do? Unlike Queen Elizabeth, the Queen Mother, the Queen did not avoid unpleasantness by putting her head in the sand, but nor was she an interfering busybody. She was reticent by nature. Time heals so much and 'Least said soonest mended' is a policy that often pays dividends. She believed in prayer and patience and hoping for the best. Philip believed in steering clear of trouble, unless he thought he had something useful to contribute. By the summer of 1992, however, both Philip and Elizabeth reckoned 'something must be done'.

That June, the *Sunday Times* began to serialise Andrew Morton's book, *Diana: Her True Story*. Essentially, the book laid bare the devastation at the heart of her marriage. It portrayed Diana as a wronged woman, locked in a loveless union, psychologically battered by an unfeeling husband who refused to hear or respond to her cries of anguish. It was a gripping read – and everybody read it, or at least got the gist of it from the never-ending reports of what it both said and implied. Morton's sources were acknowledged to be Diana's friends. At Buckingham Palace, they suspected Diana herself. They were right, of course. Diana had not met Morton, but, through an intermediary – James Colthurst, an Old Etonian doctor with an excellent bedside manner and sympathetic ear – she poured her heart out to him, recording tapes in which she told her story her way and answering any supplementary questions that Morton (via Colthurst) fed back to her. Challenged by the Queen's private secretary, her own brother-in-law, Robert Fellowes (who had married her level-headed older sister, Jane, in 1978), Diana flatly denied any involvement in Morton's book. When Prince Philip told her directly that many feared that she had in some way cooperated with the book's author, she told her father-in-law, equally directly, that she had not. She lied.

'Cooperating' with an author to create a book that tells your side of the story is a risky proposition – as Charles found with Jonathan Dimbleby, as Diana found with Andrew Morton. In 2020, Omid Scobie and Carolyn Durand published *Finding Freedom: Harry and Meghan and the Making of a Modern Royal Family*. At first, the Sussexes denied contributing to the book, but later Meghan's legal team admitted that she had permitted a close friend to communicate with Scobie and Durand, 'so the true position . . . could be communicated to the authors to prevent any further misrepresentation,' thus confirming the Duchess's participation in the enterprise.

Back in June 1992, during the week of Royal Ascot, the Queen and Prince Philip sat down with Charles and Diana at Windsor, to listen to their woes and talk about the way ahead. According to Diana, the meeting was frank and, under the circumstances, almost friendly. Charles said very little, but Diana laid her cards on the table. Her husband's behaviour was unreasonable, unjust and unfair. She believed the time had come for a trial separation. The Queen and Prince Philip (again, according to Diana) listened sympathetically, but firmly resisted any suggestion of a formal separation. They counselled the unhappy couple to search for a compromise, to think less of themselves and more of others, to try to work together to make their marriage work, for their own sakes', for the sake of the boys, for the sake of Crown and country. The Queen and the Duke were totally as one. The Prince and the Princess were hopelessly at odds. The Queen hoped that the meeting had done something to clear the air and proposed a second meeting on the following day. Diana apparently agreed, but failed to turn up. The Queen, the Duke and Prince Charles remained at Windsor. Diana returned to Kensington Palace. As Paul Burrell, who began his years of royal service as a page to the Queen and ended it as butler to Diana, put it to me: 'As a person the Queen was always calm and level-headed. She found it difficult to understand Diana's hysteria.'

Diana was a phenomenon. She began her life in the public eye, aged nineteen, as a shy, blushing nursery assistant, sharing a mansion flat in Earl's Court with a bunch of other upper-class Sloane Rangers. She died, sixteen years later, world-famous, iconic: tall, strong, beautiful, compelling. I got to know her because, in the mid-1980s, from a small clothes shop near Kensington Palace, she bought one of the novelty sweaters I had created with my friend, the knitwear designer George Hostler. She loved the sweater because on the front it read, 'I'M A LUXURY . . .', and on the back it said, 'FEW CAN AFFORD'. I loved her because she was photographed wearing the sweater (with little William and Harry in the picture, too) and, as a direct consequence, the sweater (still available from www.gylesandgeorge.com) became the biggest-selling designer sweater in the world.

In 1997, at the start of her last summer, Diana travelled to Washington DC and helped raise millions for the Red Cross; she called on Hillary Clinton at the White House; she went to New York where Christies auctioned seventy-nine of her dresses in aid of five AIDS and cancer charities in Britain and the USA. She did great good works, with style and with feeling. On the world stage, she had presence. One on one, she was special, too. To see her with the very old, and the frail, and the very young, was something lovely. She had a magic touch.

The 'magic touch', of course, is part of the stock-in-trade of royalty. Once upon a time, the sovereign's touch was the one certain cure for the scrofula – tuberculosis of the neck. In 1712, Samuel Johnson, as a sickly child, was taken from Lichfield to London to be 'touched' by Queen Anne. He lived to the age of seventy-five. In the 1920s, Princess Elizabeth's uncle David – Edward, Prince of Wales – recalled 'the touching mania' as 'one of the most remarkable phenomena connected with my travels': 'Whenever I entered a crowd, it closed around me like an octopus. I can still hear the shrill, excited cry, "I touched him!" If I were out of reach, then a blow on my head with a folded newspaper appeared to satisfy the impulse.'

Diana was a star, undoubtedly. From the perspective of the royal family, that was not necessarily a good thing. The Queen and Prince Philip were not, for a moment, envious of Diana's phenomenal popularity with the public (as Charles may well have been), but they were troubled by it. For the Queen and her husband, royalty was not about 'celebrity' or 'star quality', hysterical crowds or newspaper column inches. It was about duty and service and providing a thread of continuity that links the past with the future and helps bind communities together, whether it is a local community or the country or the Commonwealth. In one of his letters to Diana, Philip praised her for her good works, but reminded her that being consort to the Prince of Wales 'involved much more than being a hero with the British people.' More than once, in conversation, the Duke of Edinburgh reminded me that, in the 1950s, he and particularly the Queen were objects of 'adulation – such adulation – you wouldn't believe it, you really wouldn't.' At the time of the Coronation the Queen was repeatedly described – on radio and television, in newspapers and magazines, all across the globe – as 'the world's sweetheart'. In January 1953, Jock Colville recorded the American financier, Bernard Baruch, saying to him that 'England now had three assets: her Queen, "the world's sweetheart", Winston Churchill, and her glorious historical past.'

When Elizabeth II was still in her twenties, hundreds of thousands – no, *millions* – filled the streets to cheer her. But the Queen did not take it personally. She had little sense of 'self'. She was truly quite humble. She took very little interest in the press coverage she got. Diana, by contrast, believed in her own publicity. Needed it. Valued it. Manipulated it. The media used her and she used the media. As the Duke of Edinburgh put it to me, 'Diana played to the gallery. It is a dangerous game.'

Prince Philip also reminded me that while Diana did much that was worthwhile, what she did was not unique. For example, early in 1956, in Nigeria, the Queen and Prince Philip, aged twenty-nine and thirty-four, young and oh-so-glamorous, visited a leper colony. They did so, not simply to visit Commonwealth citizens suffering from leprosy, but, more significantly, to allay the widespread, irrational fear that was attached then to any physical contact with the disease. This was a lifetime before Diana – with the same good intentions – got stuck into AIDS. Diana did much that was wonderful, but the way in which she did it was not necessarily the only way in which it might be done. Princess Anne, a loving mother and pro-active President of the Save the Children Fund since 1970, says pointedly: 'The very idea that all children want to be cuddled by a complete stranger I find utterly amazing.'

The Queen and Prince Philip did not find Diana easy, because she was not easy. They found some of her behaviour frustrating, bewildering and troublesome, because that is what it was. In his book about the Queen, Graham Turner quoted an unnamed courtier who recalled hearing Her Majesty refer to Diana as 'that impossible girl' and 'quite mad'. Those are phrases the Queen could well have used, and with some justification. The 'war of the Waleses' was an unhappy time for all concerned.

On 9 December 1992, Buckingham Palace announced the formal separation of the Prince and Princess of Wales. If the sovereign and her consort hoped for a cessation of hostilities, they were soon disappointed. In the autumn of 1994, Jonathan Dimbleby published his authorised biography of the Prince of Wales. In print, and on television, Charles confessed to his own adultery. In the autumn of 1995, Diana sought her right of reply and gave the now-notorious interview to Martin Bashir for *Panorama*. It may have been secured by deceptive means on Bashir's part, but it remains one of the most watched television programmes in the history of broadcasting. Millions tuned in to see Diana, dewy-eyed, pouring scorn on her husband, confessing to her own adultery, but blaming Charles – and Camilla. She expressed her opinion that Charles would never become King and defined the role she sought for herself. 'I would like to be queen of people's hearts,' she said. Nicholas Soames, a close friend of Prince Charles (and a government minister at the time), said Diana 'seemed on the edge of paranoia'. The Queen said, 'Enough is enough.'

The Queen and the Duke talked it through. Her Majesty consulted the prime minister (John Major), the Archbishop of Canterbury (George Carey), her private secretary (Robert Fellowes). She then wrote concisely, but unequivocally, to both the Prince and the Princess giving it as her decided opinion, supported by her husband, that an early divorce was now desirable. The Queen was never one to rush to judgement, but once her mind was decided she was good at taking action, promptly and with, wherever possible, the minimum of fuss.

In the event, the Waleses' divorce settlement took many months to negotiate. The Duke of Edinburgh was not impressed by reports that his daughter-in-law's demands included the suggestion that any future children she might have by another husband should bear hereditary titles. The Duke's view was that Diana, as well as losing her rank as a Royal Highness, should be downgraded from Princess of Wales to Duchess of Cornwall – on the basis, as he put it, that 'when it's over it's over.' 'I am not vindictive,' the Duke of Edinburgh said to me, emphatically, 'I am not vindictive.' In the end, Diana surrendered her royal status, and agreed to be known as 'Diana, Princess of Wales', in return for a lump-sum sweetener of £17 million and an annual staff and office allowance of £400,000. And that was that.

Except, of course, it wasn't. The worst was yet to be. In the early hours of Sunday 31 August 1997, the chauffeur-driven Mercedes in which Diana and her current lover, Dodi Fayed, were travelling across Paris at speed, pursued by paparazzi on motorbikes, entered the tunnel at the Place de l'Alma and crashed into a concrete pillar. Diana and Dodi and the driver were all killed. The Queen was at Balmoral, on holiday with her family. At 2:00 a.m. she was woken with news of the accident. At 3:30 a.m., the British embassy in Paris confirmed that Diana, Princess of Wales, was dead.

That day the Queen and Prince Philip did exactly what anyone who knew them would have expected them to do.

They comforted their grandsons in private and, in public, went about their business as usual. They took William and Harry to church with them on that fateful Sunday morning because William and Harry wanted to go, and because the Queen believed that, at times of tribulation, there is no better place to be. Her faith was her rock and doing things much as they have always been done was a practice that, on the whole, served her well. There is comfort to be had from familiar hymns and prayers. There is solace to be found in form and custom long-established, and in doing what you have to do in the way that you normally do it.

While Prince Charles flew to Paris to accompany Diana's body back home, the Queen and Prince Philip kept William and Harry at Balmoral, out of harm's way, out of the public eye. The Queen viewed Diana's death as a private tragedy for William and Harry. The public displays of grief – worldwide and extraordinary – caught her by surprise. Her instinct and upbringing had taught her – and her generation – that you kept your tears for the pillow. Crying in public was not something the Queen would allow of herself, or expect of her children and grandchildren. It is not the royal way. It is neither dignified nor necessary – nor helpful. But, on television, in the first week of September 1997, it seemed the whole world was openly weeping and wailing – and baying for Her Majesty to shed some tears, too.

'Show Us You Care' chorused the headline writers. The Queen was at Balmoral, invisible, unhappy and confused. Above Buckingham Palace, the flagpole, traditionally empty except when the sovereign is in residence, remained bare. The people – or, at least, the tabloids on their behalf – demanded a sign from the sovereign: a flag above her principal residence flying at half-mast. By tradition, the only flag to fly above the palace was the Royal Standard and, famously, even at the death

446

of his own father, Edward VII, his son, George V, would not countenance the Royal Standard flying at half-mast. But that was then and this was now. 'Your Majesty, Please Look and Learn' read a hand-written notice left, amid the field of flowers, outside Buckingham Palace. Her Majesty – pressed from all sides: from family, friends and the prime minister, Tony Blair – took notice and, biting the inside of her bottom lip, did as she was counselled. She broke with all precedent and commanded that the Union flag be flown above her palace at half-mast.

She returned to London. On her own initiative, with Philip at her side, she got out of her car and inspected the tributes – the single flowers, the bouquets, the poems, the teddy bears – left, in their thousands, in remembrance of her ex-daughter-in-law. On Friday night, 5 September, on the eve of the funeral, the Queen gave a live broadcast that changed the national mood. She said no more than she meant, that Diana was 'an exceptional and gifted human being' whom she admired 'for her energy and commitment to others, and especially for her commitment to her two boys'. She spoke of the 'extraordinary and moving reaction to her death' and the 'lessons to be learnt' from it. She spoke as a Queen and 'as a grandmother' – and what she said and how she said it, simply and directly, with sincerity but without false sentiment, reminded the people who watched that she wasn't such a bad old stick after all. With dignity, and retaining her integrity, she showed us she cared.

On Saturday morning, before the funeral, the Queen, with her family, stood at the gates of Buckingham Palace, and Her Majesty led by example, bowing her head slowly as Diana's coffin was driven past. The funeral itself was not a comfortable experience. Elton John was never one of Prince Philip's favourite performers. Tony Blair's over-emotional reading of the Lesson was embarrassing. And Charles Spencer's address, while perhaps forgivable under the circumstances, was, from the point of view of the Queen and the Duke, both illogical and insulting. In the course of it, Earl Spencer spoke directly to Diana's sons and, on behalf of his mother and his sisters, with a catch in his throat, solemnly vowed 'that we, your blood family, will do all we can to continue the imaginative way in which you were steering these two exceptional young men so that their souls are not simply immersed by duty and tradition, but can sing openly as you planned.' Outside the Abbey, the listening crowd applauded the Earl's oration. The noise of applause spilt into the Abbey. The congregation began to clap. The applause rumbled down the nave. William and Harry, a little uncertainly, clapped, too. The Queen and the Duke of Edinburgh did not join in. Later, privately, Her Majesty said that what disappointed her about Charles Spencer's address was that it failed to do justice to his sister's memory. He devoted so much of his address to castigating the media and disparaging the royal family that he had left himself no time to pay proper tribute to Diana's many gifts and achievements. The Queen was especially saddened by the fact that her godson (Spencer) failed to acknowledge the importance to Diana of her personal faith.

When I talked to Charles Spencer about his sister's funeral, he told me he had had no intention of upsetting the royal family with his remarks. He had simply spoken as he had felt at the time, from the heart. I asked him how much hands-on involvement the 'blood family' now had with the boys and their upbringing, and he admitted, 'Not a lot', because it was not necessary. He said, 'Prince Charles is obviously a good father and the boys are doing really well. I think Diana would be very happy about the way they have grown up. She'd be very proud of them.' I asked him how he felt about Camilla.

He said, 'It's none of my business. I wish Charles every happiness. He should do whatever he wants to do.'

In due course, he did. On 9 April 2004, Charles and Camilla were married at the Guildhall in Windsor. A few days before, I happened to have lunch at St James's Palace with the Duke of Edinburgh and found him in a mellow mood. He spoke of Prince Charles without the old asperity and seemed content at the prospect of his son's second wedding. 'At least it's settled,' he said, 'and that's good.' When Lord Howard of Rising (a Norfolk neighbour) reminded him of the saying that 'when a man marries his mistress it creates a vacancy', His Royal Highness chuckled obligingly and muttered, 'Don't, please.' I reminded him of one of his best jokes – 'If you see a man opening the car door for his wife, it's either a new car or a new wife' – and asked him if he was planning to use it in his father-of-the-groom's speech. 'I shan't be saying a word,' he replied, firmly.

When the wedding day arrived, all went well. The Queen and Prince Philip did not attend the civil marriage at the Guildhall, but they were there for the blessing in St George's Chapel at Windsor Castle. In the streets of Windsor, the crowds were not vast, but they were sympathetic and good-humoured. As the couple arrived at the Guildhall, I heard one half-hearted 'boo'. It came from a middle-aged man who was quickly hushed by those around him. Inside St George's Chapel, as the guests arrived for the service of blessing and dedication, there was a sense of nervous excitement. 'So far, so good,' said Camilla's father, Major Bruce Shand. 'I'm terribly relieved it's finally happened,' said the actor, Timothy West, who was reading Wordsworth's 'Ode on Intimations of Immortality' during the service.

The day was not easy for Camilla. She was nervous (understandably) and she was suffering from sinusitis, which nobody knew – just as nobody knew she had accidentally broken her toe shortly before the Queen died in September 2022 and had to get her foot into very uncomfortable black shoes every day from the Thursday of the Queen's death until the day after her funeral. On her own wedding day in April 2004, Camilla's head was throbbing, but she looked wonderful – exactly right – and there was something endearing about her moments of awkwardness. Outside the Guildhall, she knocked her hat with her hand. Outside St George's Chapel, she held on to her hat for fear the wind was going to whisk it away. It was touching, too, to see Charles helping her find her place in the order of service, holding her hand to display the ring, whispering to her, 'You're doing so well.'

The reception was a triumph. Everyone was happy – including, it seemed, the Duke of Edinburgh. He was his genial, joshing self, but he did not give much away. Congratulated on the way it was all going, he said, 'Nothing to do with me.' There was a sense of both relief and good humour in the air. When Charles ended his speech with the words, 'Down with the press!' everybody cheered. When William gave Camilla a congratulatory kiss, it was not cursory: it was done with real affection. When Charles thanked 'My darling Camilla who has stood with me through thick and thin, and whose precious optimism and humour have seen me through', there were tears in many eyes. Charles also paid tribute to 'my sons' ('they would be annoyed if I called them my children') and 'my dear mama' for meeting the bill for the occasion. The Duchy champagne flowed freely and the much-mocked 'finger food' went down a treat. (Since you are wondering, the sandwiches included smoked salmon on brown bread, roast venison with Balmoral redcurrant and port jelly on white bread, and egg and cress on granary. There were potted shrimp bridge rolls and mini Cornish pasties; scones with Cornish clotted cream and Duchy strawberry jam; lemon tarts, caramel banana slices and miniature ice-cream cornets.)

True to his word, Prince Philip did not say a word. The Queen spoke and her speech stole the show. This was two years to the week since her mother's death and this was a renewed Queen, wholly her own woman, the fully confident Queen that she would be for the rest of her life. In the 1950s, Elizabeth II was outwardly calm but inwardly uncertain – still subject to heavy guidance from her private secretaries and her prime ministers, and sensitive (as we shall see) to the criticism of her voice and manner that came her way. By the 1990s, when she was in her sixties, she was a wholly seasoned sovereign, but bruised by personal sadnesses – the end of the first marriages of three of her four children, the terrible fire at Windsor Castle – and temporarily knocked off balance by the public response to the death of Diana, which she did not fully understand. Now, in 2004, no longer feeling the need to do things the way her mother would have wanted, and with her Golden Jubilee successfully achieved, she could be herself in a way that she had never been quite able before.

In her speech, she gave her son's second marriage her unqualified seal of approval. She did not speak for long, but what she said was funny, apt and touching. The wedding coincided with the Grand National and the Queen began by saying she had two important announcements to make. The first was that 'Hedgehunter' had won the race at Aintree; the second was that, at Windsor, she was delighted to be welcoming her son and his bride to 'the winners' enclosure'. She said, 'They have overcome Beecher's Brook and The Chair and all kinds of other terrible obstacles. They have come through and I'm very proud and wish them well. My son is home and dry with the woman he loves.'

After years of anxiety and reservation, the Queen accepted

Camilla and did so wholeheartedly. And her reward was to discover quite quickly that Camilla was very much her sort of woman – much more so than Diana could ever have been. Camilla could talk easily (and amusingly) about dogs and horses. She was comfortable with the Queen's view of life (for the most part, she shared it); she was politically incorrect (but like the Queen, in a good way), funny, self-deprecating, realistic; and, like the Queen, too, she was a mother and then a grandmother who had been a bit tempest-tossed but had managed to weather the storms without giving in to self-pity or excessive complaining. In 2012, to mark Charles and Camilla's seventh wedding anniversary, the Queen honoured her daughter-in-law as she had not honoured Diana: she made her a Dame Grand Cross of the Royal Victorian Order.

Prince Philip accepted Camilla into the family because, as he put it to me, 'You can't argue with the inevitable.' And he grew to like her more and more as time went by. He was pleased that his last-ever public duty, aged ninety-nine, was to hand over his role as Colonel-in-Chief of The Rifles to the Duchess of Cornwall in July 2020 – and amused that because of the Covid pandemic and the social distancing rules in force at the time, he was at Windsor Castle for the ceremony while Camilla was a hundred miles away at Highgrove House in Gloucestershire.

Prince Philip told me he was content that for the last decade of his life he did not have to lose any sleep over the matter of his assorted daughters-in-law. Diana was dead. Camilla he accepted. Sophie he could rely on. And Sarah Ferguson he did not think about at all.

'I think Sarah still obsesses about you,' I said.

He snorted derisively. 'You clearly love her daughters,' I persisted. 'You obviously get on well with them. Is their mother completely beyond the pale?'

'Her behaviour was a bit odd,' he said.

When Sarah Ferguson joined the royal family, in the summer of 1986, hopes were high. She was twenty-six and full of fun. I recall being told at the time by Philip's cousin, the exiled King Constantine of Greece, that 'Everybody agrees that Sarah is the best thing to have happened to the royal family in years. She's a breath of fresh air.' She was certainly as lively as they come. She had a past (a live-in relationship with the racing driver, Paddy McNally, twenty-two years her senior), but she also had a pedigree (her maternal grandmother was a first cousin of Princess Alice, Duchess of Gloucester, and, on her father's side, she was a second cousin to Robert Fellowes) and Prince Andrew was head-over-heels in love with her. On their wedding day, he was created Duke of York (the Queen's father's old title), and the wedding itself, at Westminster Abbey on 23 July 1986, was as glamorous and optimistic an occasion as anyone could wish for.

Sadly, the Yorks' honeymoon with the press and public was not prolonged. As the United Kingdom moved into one of its most punishing economic recessions since the war, Andrew and Sarah were building for themselves a £3.5 million mansion on the Sunninghill Estate. Sarah, initially acclaimed by the press as fun and feisty, was soon depicted as freeloading, grasping and ridiculous. She was mocked for her fashion sense, berated for charging *Hello!* magazine £200,000 for a family photoshoot, and accused of bringing out the worst in her sister-in-law and fellow Sloane, Diana. 'Vulgar! Vulgar! Vulgar!' is how the senior courtier Lord Charteris described her.

At first, the Queen and Prince Philip thought she was rather jolly. Philip had known her father, Ronald Ferguson, 'Major Ron', when he had played on Prince Philip's polo team in the 1960s. Philip had been friendly, too, with the Major's first wife, Susie, Sarah's mother, who ran off to Argentina with lover Hector Barrantes when Sarah was twelve – much as Diana's mother had run off with Peter Shand Kydd when Diana was a little girl. The Queen liked Sarah because she was 'outgoing and outdoorsy' and because her son evidently adored her and their two daughters (Beatrice and Eugenie, born 1988 and 1990) were very sweet indeed. When the marriage went wrong, Andrew's parents were disappointed and saddened, but understanding. Through their divorce, Andrew and Sarah remained friends, continuing even to live under the same roof, and Sarah hoped that she would be able to remain on intimate terms with the rest of the royal family, too. She might have managed it, had it not been for press reports of her extramarital behaviour.

On 20 August 1992, while Sarah and Andrew, with their children, were holidaying at Balmoral with the Queen and her family, the *Daily Mirror* published photographs, taken earlier in the month, of the Duchess of York enjoying a rather different kind of summer break. At the beginning of August, Sarah had rented a villa in the South of France and gone there, with her daughters, to soak up some Mediterranean sun. John Bryan, her American 'financial adviser', had come along for the holiday too. Unhappily for Sarah, across the valley from the villa, lurking up in the hillside, was an eagle-eyed jumbo-lensed freelance photographer who managed to take a series of gobsmackingly lurid holiday snaps of Sarah, topless, cavorting with her financial adviser at the poolside, clearly tickling his fancy as – wait for it – he sucked her toes.

The Queen and Prince Philip were, understandably, unamused. Andrew stood by his errant wife, completely and without hesitation, and Sarah, for the sake of form and the children, stayed on at Balmoral for a further three days. The atmosphere was distinctly frosty. At mealtimes, Sarah, as usual, sat next to her husband, but she spent most of the time staring at her plate. She told me later that the Queen had been 'furious, really cross' – something that was very unusual for the Queen. She had 'a session with her' after breakfast on the morning that the photographs appeared and the Queen kept repeating to her 'how dreadfully let down she felt'. Prince Philip's actions spoke louder than words. He decided to steer clear of Sarah altogether. 'It was ridiculous,' Sarah told me. 'As soon as I came in through one door he'd be falling over the corgis to get out of the other. It was very funny. Except, of course, it wasn't.'

After their separations from her sons, the Queen continued to see Sarah and Diana from time to time, to have tea with them to find out how they were. That was the Queen's way: she was always ready to let bygones be bygones and, for her own sake and their sake and the sake of her grandchildren, she wanted to keep in friendly touch with her ex-daughters-in-law. Understandably, Sarah Ferguson was – and is – the Queen's greatest fan. 'She's my icon,' she told me, her eyes glistening. 'I look up to her. I think she's the finest woman I know. HM has got a wonderful sense of humour. She loves to sing. She is the widest-read woman in the world and yet she has this wonderful compassion and total and utter understanding. She is very forgiving. She doesn't poke her nose in. She lets you have free rein, but she doesn't miss a trick.'

When they were small, Sarah made sure that her daughters were on their best behaviour when they went to see the Queen. 'We have three sets of table manners,' Sarah explained to me. 'This is very important. Table Manners C is for at home, when it's just Andrew and me. Anything goes. Table Manners B is for in a restaurant. You can have fun, but always remember people are looking at you. I tell the girls always to smile – because it costs so little and it means so much. Table Manners A is for Granny – their granny – the Boss.'

'And what does that involve?' I asked.

'If we go to tea at Windsor or Balmoral, we do it properly,' Sarah explained to me, acting it out as she described the correct royal tea-time etiquette. 'We have our little napkin. We offer Granny the sandwiches first, before we take the whole lot onto our plate. We don't take the raisins out of the scones halfway through a conversation – or flick them across the table. We don't ask for ketchup when the Duke of Edinburgh is sitting there. We don't say, "Oh, the Ribena tastes old", which it probably is. We don't say, "We don't eat paté sandwiches". We just shut up and eat what we're given. We can have fish fingers when we get home.'

According to Sarah, Duchess of York, 'If we're voting for the best granny in the world, I have to tell you the Boss is the best granny.' All eight of Her late Majesty's grandchildren would doubtless go along with that. They loved their grandmother – and honoured her – and all came to pay their respects to her standing around her coffin at the vigil for her in Westminster Hall on the Saturday before her funeral. It was a touching sight: William and Harry both in uniform, the rest dressed in black. William and Harry, of course, the best known to the public at large, because William is next in line and because Harry is . . . well, Harry – once universally loved and admired (as a bit of a lad when young, as a bit of a hero serving his country in Afghanistan, as a bit of an inspiration creating the Invictus Games) and now, perhaps, more controversially famous for the way in which he is trying, with Meghan, to build a new kind of life for himself and his family in California. Was Harry the Queen's favourite? Yes, she was exceptionally fond of him – and entertained by him – but the Queen was not in the business of having favourites. She loved all her grandchildren equally and when you asked her about them, she usually went down the list in quick succession, by age, so starting with Peter Phillips and Zara Tindall (Princess Anne's two, born in 1977 and 1981), followed by William (1982) and Harry (1984), then the York girls, Beatrice (1988) and Eugenie (1990), and the Wessex children, Louise (2003) and James (2007).

William and Catherine are inevitably in the spotlight as Prince and Princess of Wales. Harry and Meghan have to be in the spotlight because that is how, now, they earn their keep. Peter Phillips keeps below the radar – helped by the fact that his mother did not want him to have a title. He and his Canadian wife, Autumn Kelly, had two daughters, Savannah and Isla, before they divorced in 2021 – another sadness for the Queen. He has a new partner now. His sister, Olympic equestrian silver medallist Zara, is still with her England rugby player husband, Mike Tindall (who the Queen liked a lot) with their three children: Mia Grace, Lena Elizabeth and Lucas Philip. The Philip was in honour of Mike Tindall's father as well as the Duke of Edinburgh. The Queen was delighted that the middle child was named Lena Elizabeth, but was confused about Lena – especially when she was told it is pronounced 'Lay-na'. 'It is short for Elena,' explained Zara. 'What's wrong with Elena?' asked the Queen, 'Elena's a lovely name.' 'Her initials would then have been E.T.,' said Zara. 'I'm afraid you've lost me there,' said the Queen.

Though the Duke of York can no longer use his HRH handle in public, his daughters can – and they are Princesses, too. Beatrice is married to Italian 'property developer and nobleman', Edoardo Mapelli Mozzi, and their first-born was also named in honour of the Queen: Sienna Elizabeth. Eugenie is married to Jack Brooksbank, 'a bar manager and brand manager' and their son, August Philip Hawke, was baptised alongside Lucas Philip Tindall at the Royal Chapel of All Saints in Windsor Great Park. The Queen was intrigued to discover what 'a brand manager' does – and was amused to be told she, the Queen, was actually 'a super brand manager for Brand Britain'. Like the Princess Royal, the Earl and Countess of Wessex decided to spare their two children the burden of royal titles, hoping, in Sophie's words, 'to let them grow up as normally as possible.' Sophie said it came as a bit of a shock to her daughter Louise when she discovered that her granny was also the Queen. 'She couldn't quite get her head around it at first.'

The Queen loved all her grandchildren and wanted them all to find happiness and fulfilment in their own ways. She was occasionally anxious about the press attention some of them received, but accepted that 'unfortunately, these days it rather comes with the territory'. Given her age, nobody could argue with the fact that she really could claim to take the long view. 'One has rather seen it all before,' she said to me – and that was thirty years ago.

Writing and broadcasting about the Queen, I have always been aware that what newspaper editors and TV producers want to know is 'what the Queen really thinks' about whatever happens to be the hot royal topic of the moment. In recent times that has mainly been Harry and his marriage and his move away from Britain. I can tell you, because I know this, that the Queen was always more concerned for Harry's well-being than about 'this television nonsense' – the Oprah interview and the deal with Netflix. I know she liked Meghan, and Meghan's mother, and was sorry the Markle family was 'fractured', and was anxious that Harry should 'find his feet' in California and 'find really useful things to do'. But beyond that, and what else I have shared with you in these pages, there is not much more to say, principally because the Queen did not share the media's obsessive focus on the story (she had eight grandchildren and cared about them all: she took the long view and she was even-handed) and because she wasn't one to gossip about her family – either with me, or with close friends, or indeed with other members of the family. That wasn't her way. As Prince Philip put it to me: 'Very sensibly, she keeps her own counsel.' He added pointedly: 'I wish more people would follow her example.'

When she did talk to me about her family, it was usually because I had said or done something to prompt a response from her. She was amused that at a Playing Fields event in Nottingham, when Prince William had fired the starting pistol to start a children's running race, I promptly took the starting pistol off him and told the Queen that I planned to keep it. 'As a souvenir?' she asked. 'No,' I said, 'because it'll have his DNA on the trigger.' She laughed and waved her hands at me, jazz-hands style: 'That's why I always wear gloves. I'm going to have to warn him about you.'

I asked her that day about her own sporting prowess as a girl. I said I knew that she had learnt to ice-skate on the ice-rink that still exists beneath the floor in the Great Room at Grosvenor House, the large hotel on London's Park Lane. That prompted several happy memories from her – the chief of which was her pride at achieving her life-saving badge when she was fourteen and went for regular lessons at the Bath Club in Mayfair. 'I worked very hard for that. I loved the badge. I sewed it onto the front of my swimming suit. I was very proud of it.'

I think the most surprising discovery I made chatting with the Queen was when I told her that I had just come back from Rome where I had been sent by a newspaper to the Vatican to interview the Papal Exorcist. His name was Father Gabriele Amorth and, intriguingly, Her Majesty seemed to have heard of him. She certainly believed in the value of exorcism. She told me that some of the staff at Sandringham had been anxious about going into one of the rooms in the main house – the room, in fact, in which her father, George VI, had died. She said she had arranged for a small religious service to take place in the room to bless it and calm everyone's fears.

The Queen was good at living in the present, but she was aware of the past – and grateful for the lessons it had taught her. She often drew on them, frequently (according to them) when talking to her prime ministers and, occasionally, when talking to her family. For example, when the Duke of York (who did himself no favours with his now notorious self-justifying interview with Emily Maitlis for *Newsnight* in 2019) was harrumphing about Harry and Meghan's interview with Oprah Winfrey on American television in 2020, the Queen chipped in gently: 'Didn't Sarah do something similar?' She did. In 2011, the Oprah Winfrey Network in the US aired *Finding Sarah*, a six-part TV series, in which the former Duchess of York shared her tears and her heartache with a TV psychiatrist and the viewing millions.

When I say that the Queen loved all her grandchildren equally, and all her great-grandchildren, too ('When I can remember their names!'), I do not say it lightly. The Queen took fairness seriously. All eight of her grandchildren probably thought they were her favourite – and that is what she would have wanted. Being fair, being even-handed, was a matter of policy as far as the Queen was concerned. I know, because in a different context, I discussed it with her.

At the Royal Variety Performance one year, I studied the Queen and Prince Philip's responses to each individual act in turn. Philip laughed at what he found funny, applauded vigorously if something particularly appealed to him (not much did), and sighed tetchily when he realised Elton John was going to start a second song.

By contrast, the Queen greeted every act with almost exactly the same amount of smiling enthusiasm and, almost to the second, the same length of generous applause.

At the interval, I said to her, 'Ma'am, you seem to be enjoying everything equally.'

'I'm glad you say that,' she said.

'But are you enjoying everything equally?' I asked.

'Not really,' she laughed. 'But I like to be seen to be giving everybody the same amount of support. We are on television, after all. Their families might be watching.'

CHAPTER TWENTY-THREE

'What was she really like? What did she actually do?'

If there is one word that sums up Elizabeth II, it is 'dutiful'. When she died, some suggested she be known henceforward as 'Elizabeth the Great'. Others suggested 'Elizabeth the Steadfast'. My choice would be 'Elizabeth the Dutiful'. In her final, formal message to her people, published at the time of her Platinum Jubilee, she signed herself: 'Your Servant, Elizabeth R.' Her life was one of service, driven by duty. She was a dutiful daughter. She became a dutiful queen.

In September 2022, people in their thousands queued for many hours to file past her coffin in Westminster Hall in recognition of that. One young man (an ex-soldier) said to a reporter afterwards, 'I felt I had a duty to come. She did her duty by us.' Twenty years before, on 30 April 2002, in the same Westminster Hall, as a reporter myself, I watched the Queen as she addressed the joint Houses of Parliament on the occasion of her Golden Jubilee. Her speech that day – brief, balanced, well-phrased – reflected both the moderate and modest nature of the monarch, and the decent, enduring values she held dear. As she concluded with her pledge to continue to serve her country in the years to come, the journalists sitting around me twitched with excitement. 'She's staying,' hissed one. 'That's our story,' whispered another. In the newspapers the following morning it was, indeed, everybody's lead story, but it was hardly news.

Anyone who had had five minutes – let alone a lifetime – to consider the Queen should have known that when, as Princess Elizabeth, aged twenty-one, she said, 'I declare before you all that my whole life, whether it be long or short, shall be devoted to your service', she meant it. At her Coronation she made a commitment to God as well as to her people and her faith sustained her in all she did. She was God's anointed monarch. 'Be thou anointed, blessed and consecrated Queen over the Peoples, who the Lord thy God hath given thee to rule and govern . . .' were the words addressed to her by the Archbishop of Canterbury at the most solemn moment of her coronation.

I once asked the Queen what was the most memorable day of her life. She frowned a little. 'I suppose, the Coronation,' she said. She did not call it 'my coronation', though it was – hers and personal. I knew she would not have said 'my accession', which must, inevitably, have been the most significant day of her life, simply because the moment of her accession also marked the moment of her father's death and she mourned his loss all her life. We were having this conversation in London, in the vestry of Holy Trinity, a High Anglican Church at the top of Sloane Street, just off Sloane Square. The occasion was a service to give thanks for the Duke of Edinburgh's years of service to the National Playing Fields Association. I had asked the Queen how we should celebrate her husband's fortieth anniversary as NPFA President, thinking that a party or a dinner or a gala concert might be fun. She suggested a church service. I suggested this particular church because Holy Trinity was conveniently placed halfway between NPFA's headquarters in Knightsbridge and hers at

Buckingham Palace. The Duke of Edinburgh went along with the plan, but had not bargained on the burning incense that was very much a feature of worship at Holy Trinity – properly called The Church of the Holy and Undivided Trinity with Saint Jude. 'I thought this was supposed to be a celebration not a cremation,' he muttered as we processed down the nave.

In the vestry, I asked the Queen if she had visited this church before. 'I don't think so,' said Her Majesty. 'I doubt we'll be coming again,' chuntered the Duke. 'I love the variety of English churches,' continued the Queen, 'Don't you? Victorian, isn't it?' 'Yes,' I replied, 'Arts and Crafts.' 'I imagine it was one of John Betjeman's favourites,' said the Queen. 'We have the most wonderful churches in the world in this country, don't you think?'

Elizabeth II was a global figure, devoted to the Commonwealth, married to a Greek (with Danish and Russian connections), with (given her heritage) a reasonable dash of German blood in her own veins, but she was essentially, profoundly British – and proud of it. When it came to speculation about abdication, yes, Queen Juliana of the Netherlands had abdicated in favour of her daughter, Queen Beatrix (incidentally a fifth cousin of Elizabeth II), just as *her* mother, Queen Wilhelmina, had abdicated in her favour, but the Dutch way is not the British way. Pope Benedict XVI (who the Queen had met and admired) might resign the papacy on grounds of frailty, but Elizabeth II was made of sterner stuff.

Her Majesty never for a moment considered the possibility of abdication, simply because her faith, her sense of duty and her heritage meant that abdication was never a possibility. Her uncle David abdicated and his was not an example she would have wanted to follow. And a commitment made before God was an absolute commitment so far as the Queen was concerned. 'It's a job for life,' she said.

The Queen's was a life of duty, but let's not forget: it was a life of privilege, too. She met everyone and she had been everywhere. She never wanted for anything. Wherever she went she was cosseted. In every car, there was a rug at the ready to keep the royal knees cosy. When she stepped onto a plane and sat down, the plane took off – at once. Air traffic control was ready for her. There was no fuss with passports or landing cards or other passengers clambering over her to stretch their legs or go to the toilet. And wherever she went, when she wanted them, the corgis came, too – flown, if need be, in an Andover of the Queen's Flight.

Her days were sometimes long, and often arduous, but she had solicitous staff ever in attendance and (for her) the comfort of a routine that rarely varied. At 8:00 a.m. Her Majesty's Dresser entered the royal bedroom with the 'calling tray' and a pot of Earl Grey tea. The curtains were drawn, the bath was run (to a depth of seven inches and a temperature of 72° Fahrenheit – tested by thermometer, using Imperial measurements to the last), gently the Palace began to stir. No vacuuming was permitted in the Queen's quarters before 8:00 a.m. Her clothes were laid out for her, her hairdresser was waiting. At 9:00 a.m., as her personal piper played beneath her windows, the Queen would walk from her bedroom, through her sitting room to her dining room, holding her Roberts radio, listening to the news of the day. Breakfast was modest: cereal (from those derided Tupperware containers), a slice of granary toast, a layer of Oxford marmalade.

At 10:00 a.m. the business of the day began: her private secretary appeared; correspondence was considered, state papers noted; if it was a morning for receiving ambassadors or the day of an investiture, Her Majesty studied her briefing material – closely. At 1:00 p.m., before a light lunch (she was not fussy about her food), she might treat herself to a gin and

Dubonnet: equal measures, two lumps of ice and a slice of lemon. (The lemon was sliced for her.) At 2:30 p.m. she liked to walk the corgis. (When the afternoon transmission time of Channel 4's *Countdown* was changed, she stopped watching, she told me. 'I thought you preferred the racing,' I said. 'If I'm honest, I do,' she laughed.) At five she would take tea. At six o'clock the drinks tray reappeared and Her Majesty might allow herself a moderate gin and tonic. At 8:15 p.m. it was dinner time. 8:15 p.m. was always dinner time. The Queen was a creature of habit.

On some days the Queen and Prince Philip would share breakfast, lunch and dinner – but not every day. For example, a few years ago, on a day I happened to be visiting Buckingham Palace to begin the picture research for my book about Prince Philip, I noted that the Queen and the Duke had breakfasted together. At one o'clock, together, they hosted one of their regular, informal Buckingham Palace luncheons for the great, the interesting and the good – an idea instituted by the Duke in 1956. (That day, the party of eight included representatives of the worlds of business, music and sport, the director of the National Maritime Museum and the chairman of the Woking Shah Jahan Mosque – a typical mix.) In the evening, the Duke of Edinburgh, without the Queen, attended a dinner at Draper's Hall in the City of London on behalf of the Royal Academy of Engineering. The Queen was long accustomed to evenings on her own. She watched television, she completed the *Daily Telegraph* crosswords, she gave the corgis their late supper. She telephoned her racing manager – often at 8:45 p.m. When she ate alone, dinner didn't take long. She chatted with her personal page before getting ready for bed.

Because, broadcasting about her, people knew that I had met her, they would sometimes ask me, 'What's the Queen *really* like?' I think my standard answer disappointed them.

'Very nice,' I'd say, 'rather normal, actually; quite straightforward; much as you'd expect, in fact.'

Pressed by a newspaper once, I said, rather boldly, 'I can tell you exactly what the Queen is like. She has the interests, attributes and tastes of an English (or Scottish) countrywoman of her class and generation. Dogs and horses, courtesy, kindliness and community service, count with her. Essentially conservative (with radical flourishes), intelligent (not intellectual), pragmatic (not introspective), "immensely tolerant" (Prince Philip's phrase), even-tempered and utterly reliable, she is what she is and makes no pretence to be what she is not. She may be formally apolitical, but she is definitely not politically correct. If she chooses, she will wear fur, she won't wear a seat-belt, she will go out riding without a hard hat and, in her assorted residences, cigarettes are freely available to her guests.'

That was a few years ago. Eventually, the silver cigarette boxes disappeared from the royal drawing rooms. Times change and the Queen, more or less, went with the flow. She had her own mobile phone and obliging grandchildren ready to show her how it worked. She understood 'texting'. She was rather defeated by 'apps'. And she did not allow her grandchildren to bring their 'devices' to the dining table, under any circumstances.

Believe it or not, I think I once heard her refer to the lavatory as 'the toilet' in a concession to the vocabulary of the younger generation. As a rule, she did not like bad language, but she was by no means a prude – or an innocent. When Lech Walesa was Polish President and came to stay, she told an aide, 'He only knows two English words.' She paused, before adding, '. . .They are quite interesting words.' Famously, at an art gallery, she was confronted by a series of Lucien Freud nudes: heavy, spreading bosoms, weighty blue-veined thighs. Sensing that the photographers present were eager to get a shot of her gazing up at one of them, Her Majesty moved herself adroitly out of range. When her host enquired, 'Haven't you been painted by Lucien Freud, Ma'am?', she smiled and said, *sotto voce*, 'Yes, but not like that.'

Given the weirdness of her life (imprisoned by her fate: destined to be Queen from the age of ten), the Queen seemed to me to be quite remarkably well-balanced, rounded, grounded and at ease with herself, the world and her place in it. Friends who knew her when she was younger tell stories of her sitting on the sofa after dinner, her feet tucked up under her, chatting late into the night. People (even those who knew her well) found it difficult to treat her normally, but she behaved normally nonetheless. She arrived a little late for a supper at a private house in Belgravia. 'Cooee,' she called up the stairwell as she was taking off her coat, 'It's us. Sorry we're late. Terrible traffic.'

One of the Queen's oldest friends was Prudence Penn, who was born in 1926, the same year as the Queen, and who got to know her after the war when she became engaged to Eric Penn – later Lieutenant-Colonel Sir Eric Penn, GCVO, OBE, MC. Eric served Her Majesty with fierce dedication and notable integrity for almost half a century, for twenty-four years in the Grenadier Guards and then, for twenty-one, as Assistant Comptroller and Comptroller of the Lord Chamberlain's Office in the Royal Household. Impressively tall, with pronounced dark eyebrows, he was regularly seen, with ramrod posture, standing behind the Queen at Palace investitures in the 1960s and 1970s. He was brought up by his uncle, Sir Arthur Penn, one of King George VI's advisers, and subsequently the Queen Mother's treasurer and private secretary. He met Princess Elizabeth soon after he returned from Dunkirk in 1940, when she was fourteen and he was twenty-four. The Princess and her mother came to the Penns' wedding on 29 January 1947, the day before the royal family set off in HMS *Vanguard* for the famous trip to South Africa, during which the future Queen made her celebrated twenty-first birthday broadcast.

'Her children and ours were more or less of the same age,' recalls Lady Penn. 'There were tea parties in each other's houses and weekly visits to Buckingham Palace where "Miss Vacani" taught them to dance.' Lady Penn adds pointedly: 'When people say that the Queen didn't have time to be with her children, they are talking nonsense.'

I went to see Prue Penn at her home in Scotland a few days before the Queen died and she showed me, because I asked, the photographs of the Queen and her family at Lady Penn's ninetieth birthday party. They were very old friends. To illustrate the Queen's humility, Prue told me about a dinner she and her husband had given for the Queen and the Duke of Edinburgh and a few friends in their house in London. 'I had made a carefully thought out table plan which I forgot to take with me into the dining room,' she explained. 'Consequently, I got into a serious muddle over the placing of our guests. Seeing my confusion Her Majesty took over and in no time at all had made a very good job of it, sat down and said, "Lucky you weren't giving an important dinner party".'

The Queen added, grinning, 'We don't mind who sits where – but I know a few ambassadors who might.' Prue said to me quickly, 'You mustn't put that last bit in your book,' but I want to risk it because it illustrates the Queen's impish sense of humour. As does another of Lady Penn's stories:

On one occasion when the Queen was staying with us in Suffolk, we went for a walk along the banks of the River Alde. Below the twelfth-century St Botolph Iken Church we met a woman walking her dog which happened to be a corgi. Her Majesty was a magnet to dogs, and it made straight for her. She bent down to stroke and talk to it. Seeing the affinity between them the woman asked if she happened to be a corgi fan too. She said that she was, whereupon the owner said, 'Well, you and I are in good company because the Queen has them too.' 'Wasn't that killing?' she said as we walked away.

Richard Griffin, a former Royal Protection Officer, tells a lovely story in a similar vein of a time when he was out walking with the Queen near Balmoral. 'Whenever we met people on these walks, the Queen would always stop and say hello. One day we met a couple of American tourists and it was clear from the moment we first stopped they hadn't recognised her. After they had been chatting a while, the American said to Her Majesty, "And where do you live?" She said, "Well, I live in London, but I've got a holiday home just the other side of the hills." ' The tourist then asked the Queen how long she had been visiting the area, and she replied: 'For over eighty years, since I was a little girl.' 'Well,' said the American, 'if you've been coming up here for eighty years, you must have met the Queen?' According to Griffin, 'As quick as a flash, she said, "Well, I haven't, but Dickie here meets her regularly." So the American guy said to me, "You've met the Queen? What's she like?" Because I was with her a long time and I knew I could pull her leg, I said, "She can be very cantankerous at times, but she's got a lovely sense of humour."' The American tourist proceeded to put his arm around the protection officer and gave his camera to the Queen, asking if she'd take a picture of them both.

Prue Penn says of the Queen, 'As a friend there was no one better: she was caring and thoughtful but with a degree of remoteness beyond which one didn't trespass.' She adds: 'She will be missed by her subjects too, maybe more than they would ever have envisaged.'

The Queen's essential normality – combined with her fundamental, palpable decency – presented a problem for the media over the years. Where was the story? Where was the drama? Where was the excitement? Princess Margaret's love-life, Charles and Diana, Charles and Camilla, 'Airmiles Andy' and Virginia Giuffre, Harry and Meghan – they got the column inches because they were where the action was. The Queen's life was largely predictable: she walked a straight road with a safe pair of hands and rarely, if ever, said or did anything edgy or out of the ordinary, let alone controversial. It was something of a dilemma for her biographers, too. At the heart of the biographies (and autobiographies) that become best-sellers nowadays is trauma – true 'trauma' from the Greek for 'wound'. The Queen's story encompassed moments of high drama – assassination attempts, strangers in her bedroom, the murder of Lord Mountbatten, the death of Diana – but her own life, her personal life, was neither traumatic nor traumatised.

There was a streak of hysteria in Diana, Princess of Wales: you sensed it even with a brief acquaintance. Some see a streak of narcissism in Meghan, Duchess of Sussex. The Queen was not like that. The Queen was as sane and sensible as they come. She kept her feet on the ground. (Actually, spending time with her, I noticed she stood for long periods, feet slightly apart, moving her weight regularly from one foot to the other.) She was not self-conscious: she applied her lipstick whoever was watching. She was rarely flustered: however hectic the schedule, however many stops on the tour, her own steady pace did not vary. 'Steady as she goes' was her way – but it wasn't all plain sailing. Now and again, she did hit choppy waters.

471

In 1957, for example, a thirty-three-year-old peer, writer and historian, the second Lord Altrincham, became internationally notorious overnight for publishing what many regarded as an unforgivable personal attack on the Queen. In the 1950s, there were others who attacked the monarchy – the playwright John Osborne spoke of it as 'a gold filling in a mouth full of decay', the broadcaster Malcolm Muggeridge called it 'soap opera … ersatz religion' – but Altrincham's strictures caused such a scandal – and really distressed the young queen – because they were so personal and also, perhaps, because there was some truth in them. John Grigg, as Altrincham later became when he was able to renounce his inherited peerage in the 1960s, was denounced as a republican and attacked in the street by outraged royalists. By the time I met him, in the 1990s, the young firebrand had become a genial old buffer. He told me he thought the Queen was 'charming' and chuckled at the recollection of the furore he had caused all those years before.

Altrincham accused the thirty-one-year-old queen of being out of touch, living entirely within the confines of her own class, surrounded by courtiers of 'the "tweedy sort"', making speeches that amounted to 'prim little sermons' in the manner of 'a priggish schoolgirl' and speaking with a voice that was 'a pain in the neck'. 'Like her mother,' wrote Altrincham, the young queen 'appears to be unable to string even a few sentences together without a written text.' He went on:

> When she has lost the bloom of youth, the Queen's reputation will depend, far more than it does now, upon her personality. It will not then be enough for her to go through the motions; she will have to say things which people can remember and do things on her own initiative which will make people sit up and take notice. As yet there is little sign that such a personality is emerging.

At the end of her life, the Queen's reputation did indeed rest upon her personality. With a handful of exceptions, she did not say things which people have remembered, or do things which made people sit up and take notice, but her personality emerged, nonetheless. George V and George VI are remembered as sovereigns because of the visible leadership they provided through two World Wars. Elizabeth will be remembered, not for when she lived or for what happened during her reign, but for who she was – and what she cared about.

Take, for example, her dogged commitment to the Commonwealth. When her reign began, the British Empire was already set on its inevitable decline and the Commonwealth, as we know it, was still in its infancy. In 1952, there were eight members of the Commonwealth. Today, there are fifty-six, of which fourteen are still constitutional monarchies with the British monarch as head of state. Whitehall and Westminster may be more preoccupied with the United Kingdom's relations with Europe and the United States, China and the Middle East, but the Queen's commitment to the Commonwealth never wavered. Indeed, her knowledgeable enthusiasm for what she described as a 'free and voluntary association of equal partners' that 'in all history has no precedent' was a wonder to behold. She was supposed to be above the political fray (and in terms of party politics she was), but she was also a world-class political operator. The Commonwealth contains two and a half billion people. Globally, a third of all young people in the world aged between fifteen and twenty-nine live in Commonwealth countries. The biggest countries in the Commonwealth by population are India, Pakistan, Nigeria and Bangladesh. Most Commonwealth countries are republics, several have no former links to Britain, and five (I bet you did not know this: I did not until the Queen told me) – Lesotho, Swaziland (now known as Eswatini), Brunei Darussalam,

Malaysia and Tonga – have monarchs of their own. By force of personality, and personal diplomacy, and with an authority built up over a lifetime, Elizabeth II, in 2018, aged ninety-two, persuaded the Commonwealth leaders to agree that her successor as Head of the Commonwealth (very much a non-hereditary role) should be her son, King Charles III.

Robin Janvrin, her private secretary from 1999 to 2007, told me about a diary session he was having with the Queen one morning. 'We have got the gathering of Commonwealth Auditors at Buckingham Palace coming up, Ma'am,' he said, 'not the most interesting event in the next two weeks.'

'On the contrary, Robin,' said Her Majesty. 'The auditors are the very people who can help stamp out corruption in their countries. This could be the most significant event of the next two weeks.'

The novelist Daphne du Maurier, when her husband 'Boy' Browning was Comptroller of the Duke of Edinburgh's household, stayed at Balmoral and was struck by the way Prince Philip could talk about anything – literature, art, murder, military manoeuvres – while the Queen's range of interests – and conversation – was much more limited. According to du Maurier, Her Majesty's face only really 'lit up' when the talk was of horses – and world affairs.

The Queen was exceptionally well-informed. This was because she was conscientious. She did her 'boxes' week in, week out, throughout the year. She claimed to be a quick reader, 'though I do rather begrudge some of the hours that I have to do instead of being outdoors.' She knew the presidents and prime ministers of the Commonwealth personally. The way they spoke of her – invariably with respect, often with affection, occasionally with awe – suggests their admiration was genuine.

The Queen had 179 individuals serve as her realms' prime ministers throughout her reign, the first new appointment being Dudley Senanayake as Prime Minister of Ceylon in 1952 and the final one being Liz Truss as Prime Minister of the United Kingdom, appointed two days before she died. Apart from Liz Truss, she got to know her British prime ministers especially well. Queen Victoria had ten in the course of her long reign. Elizabeth II had fifteen in the course of hers. When parliament was sitting, the Queen and her prime minister would meet once a week, usually in person, but occasionally (and especially during the Covid pandemic), by telephone, and, in September, the prime minister plus part-ner would have a short stay at Balmoral. (It is reckoned that the Blairs' youngest son, Leo, born, a tad prematurely, on 20 May 2000, was conceived under the royal roof.) The Queen saw herself as a 'sounding board' for her prime ministers. She said, 'They unburden themselves, or tell me what's going on. If they've got any problems, sometimes one can help in that way, too. I think it's rather nice to feel that one's a sort of sponge. Some things stay there and some things go out the other ear and some things never come out at all. Occasionally you can put one's point of view when perhaps they hadn't seen it from that angle.'

The dynamic between the Queen and her prime ministers changed over the years. In 1952, she came to the throne at the age of twenty-five. Her prime minister then was Winston Churchill, who was seventy-seven, and had first encountered her as a little girl back in the 1920s. He and her first private secretary, Sir Alan Lascelles, sixty-four in 1952, would some-times refer to the Queen as 'the child' – not to her face, of course, but that was how they thought of her. She accepted – and said that she was grateful – that Churchill could advise her from 'a lifetime of experience'. When he retired, she wrote a handwritten note to him, telling him that no one will 'ever for me be able to hold the place of my first prime minister, to whom both my husband and I owe so much and for whose wise guidance during the early years of my reign I shall always be so profoundly grateful.' She broke with royal protocol by arriving first at his funeral in 1965: traditionally, the monarch arrives last, but the Queen wanted Churchill's family to have that honour.

Sir Anthony Eden, born 1897, who succeeded Churchill, and Harold Macmillan, born 1894, who succeeded him, were of a similar vintage and each, in his own way, played the old school charmer with the young queen, entertaining Her Majesty with stories from their palmier days and essentially telling her what was going on rather than seeking to draw any advice from her. Echoing Elizabeth I, Macmillan said (intending it as a compliment) that Elizabeth II had 'the heart and stomach of a man' and 'means to be a queen and not a puppet', but when he became ill in 1963 (with a prostate problem that turned out not to be as serious as first thought) and resigned, the Queen visited him at his hospital bedside and accepted his suggestion that the Earl of Home, then Foreign Secretary, should be his successor. The Marquess of Salisbury, who retired in 1902, the year before Home was born, was the last person to lead a government from the House of Lords. The Queen did not immediately appoint Home to the premiership but, advised by Macmillan and Michael Adeane, invited him to see if he could form a government. Despite divided opinion in Parliament and the press (and the resignation of two senior ministers), he managed it, and though his time at Downing Street was brief (three days short of a year) from the Queen's point of view it was comfortable. Sir Alec Douglas-Home (as he became when he renounced his peerage) was an old friend of the Strathmore family. He had known the Queen Mother since they were children. Elizabeth II probably revered Churchill most among her prime ministers, but Douglas-Home may have been the one most on her personal wavelength.

Everyone will tell you that Home's successor, Harold Wilson, was the Queen's favourite. The avuncular, pipe-smoking, Gannex-wearing Wilson, the country's first Labour prime minister in thirteen years, made it his business to endear himself to his queen and the Queen warmed to him because he was the first of her prime ministers nearer her own age. He was ten years her senior, but treated her as an equal – and she responded in kind, asking him to stay for drinks after their first audience (not the custom previously) and letting him smoke his pipe during their discussions. (His pipe was more of a prop than a habit: he used it for public appearances more frequently than for private pleasure. His Yorkshire accent, however, was authentic – and the Queen could do it, too.) According to Wilson, together they enjoyed a 'relaxed intimacy' – their meetings grew longer and longer: one touched two hours, a prime-ministerial record, and I was intrigued to discover, more than ten years after Wilson had left office, at a dinner where I was sitting on one side of him (and Princess Anne was sitting on the other), that he kept a small photograph of himself and the Queen tucked permanently inside his wallet. The moment he retired, aged sixty, the Queen agreed to have dinner at 10 Downing Street (which she had not done since Winston Churchill's last night as prime minister in 1955) and made him a Knight of the Garter. Tony Blair, by contrast, had to wait fourteen years before receiving his Garter. The Queen kept in touch with the Wilsons as the years went by and the health of Lord Wilson of Rievaulx, as he became, deteriorated as he developed Alzheimer's disease. The Queen told me she admired Lady Wilson's poetry and did not like the way it had been 'belittled in certain quarters' when Mary Wilson had first published a collection of her poems. The Wilsons' son, Robin, told me, 'My mother and the Queen got on well, and around my mother's 100th birthday, in 2016, the Queen invited my mum to tea with her at Buckingham Palace.'

The Conservative Edward Heath and Labour's James Callaghan followed Wilson's two terms as PM. Heath was socially awkward at the best of times (I came to know him quite well) and, unlike Wilson, found it difficult to relax with an attractive, intelligent woman ten years his junior. The reverse was the case with Callaghan, who told me when we were once both guests at a Buckingham Palace Garden Party that Her Majesty 'showed me round the garden here, talking matters of state while we walked around the flower-beds.' Callaghan was a big 6' 1". The Queen was a small 5' 4". He told me she had stopped to carefully pin a flower in his buttonhole. He maintained all his conversations with her were enjoyable. 'One of the great things about her,' he said, 'is that she always seems able to see the funny side of life.' On her Silver Jubilee in 1977, James Callaghan's Cabinet presented the Queen with a silver coffee pot. 'Oh!' the Queen said to Callaghan, apparently delighted, 'I'm so glad you haven't repeated Mr Disraeli's gift to Queen Victoria. He gave her a painting of himself.'

Margaret Thatcher, British prime minister from 1979 to 1990, told me that the talk of her having a strained relationship with the Queen was 'a lot of nonsense'. 'The Queen,' said Lady Thatcher, 'is simply marvellous. And her commitment to the Commonwealth and to our armed services has been especially important.' Mrs Thatcher, throughout her eleven years in office, never failed to show her respect for the Queen. Quoting Louis XVIII of France, 'Punctuality is the politeness of kings,' Mrs Thatcher told me that she was so concerned never to be late for her weekly audience that whenever it was scheduled to take place at Windsor Castle, she would get her driver to arrive on the outskirts of Windsor at least half an hour early for the appointment and they would then sit in a lay-by, with Mrs Thatcher in the rear seat working on her papers and the driver poised to drive through the castle gates at precisely the appointed hour. The equerry who took Mrs Thatcher into the Queen's presence for her very first audience in 1979, sensed how nervous she was. As they were walking down the Buckingham Palace corridor, he said to her, 'Ready with your curtsy, Prime Minister?' 'Oh, yes,' said Mrs Thatcher. When they arrived in the royal presence, he said, 'Your Majesty – the Prime Minister, Your Majesty.' Mrs Thatcher stepped forward and went into the deepest curtsy the equerry had ever seen – so deep that when she had reached the floor, she couldn't get up. 'She simply couldn't,' the equerry told me. 'We had to help her up. I took one side and the Queen took the other. We brought her to her feet and said no more about it. After the audience, when I collected Mrs Thatcher to take her back to her car, I said, "Shall we just pause in this anteroom for a little curtsy practice?" We did.'

Perhaps, privately, the Queen did not always agree with Mrs Thatcher's policies, but there is no evidence she did not like her. Over the years she certainly showed Britain's first woman prime minister considerable respect, dining at Downing Street in 1985, appointing her to the Order of Merit within a fortnight of her resignation in 1990, honouring her with the Order of the Garter in 1995 and attending her seventieth birthday dinner in the same year. She went to her eightieth birthday party celebration as well. The Queen only attended the funeral of two of her prime ministers: one was Winston Churchill, the other was Margaret Thatcher.

Thatcher's successor, John Major, was the first of her prime ministers to be younger than she was. He told me at the time (when I was the most junior member of his government) how much he looked forward to his weekly sessions with her: 'No notes, no formality, no risk of anything leaking, just me, the Queen and the corgis sitting in a semi-circle watching us. I find it quite cathartic. And she's very shrewd. Pity we can't have her in the cabinet.' Major's successor, Tony Blair, prime minister for ten years from 1997, did not find her as relaxed as Major claimed he did from the very start. Blair said he found her an odd mixture at first, 'both shy and quite direct'. I heard the Duke of Edinburgh refer to 'Blairism' with a degree of contempt, and I know that both the Queen and the Duke found New Year's Eve at the start of the new millennium in 2000 'pretty ghastly', as the Windsors and the Blairs stood in a line at midnight in the Millennium Dome, arms raised, holding fingers awkwardly, singing 'Old Lang Syne'.

Gordon Brown, who succeeded Blair, was impressed with Her Majesty. 'She never gave advice in my experience,' he said after her death, 'but she listened intently, she asked questions, and she certainly knew her stuff. I remember being very embarrassed when I arrived at six o'clock for one of our meetings to find that she knew about a Commonwealth prime minister who had just been ousted and I didn't. She was telling me about the new government that had just been formed, when I was supposed to be reporting to her. At Westminster, too, she knew what was going on. She was conscientious and well up on the detail, right to the last.'

Not every prime minister relished the September Balmoral weekend. Margaret Thatcher told me it really wasn't her 'cup of tea'. Mrs Thatcher would rather be working on her papers than walking through the heather and she said she 'dreaded' the charades that she was expected to play after dinner at Balmoral. The Queen, at a gathering of six of her prime ministers, including Mrs Thatcher, joked about 'the party games which some of you have so nobly endured at Balmoral', but nonetheless maintained the tradition.

David Cameron, who followed Gordon Brown into Downing Street, said:

It was an extraordinary treat to be able to go to Balmoral every year for six years, and one of the best parts was when in the evening you'd get into Her Majesty's car, a Range Rover, and she would drive at breakneck speed up the hill and onto the moor. And there at a sort of converted bothy, an old cottage on the hill, would be the Duke of Edinburgh with a barbecue he'd built himself, barbecuing grouse for your dinner. I'm not making this up, you sat down and Prince Philip and Her Majesty The Queen served your dinner and cleared it away and washed it up while you sat talking with the other guests. I remember, I think it was sort of year five, I thought 'Well, I now surely can help' and got up and got on the Marigolds and started doing the washing-up. And I remember Her Majesty saying: 'What on earth is the prime minister doing?' I'd broken with the protocol and rapidly sat back down and did what I was told.

Of course, those of us who have read the wartime diaries of the Queen's childhood friend, Alathea Fitzalan-Howard, will know that Lilibet was always good at domestic chores. In March 1941, when they were having cookery lessons at Windsor, Alathea noted: 'Lilibet actually likes washing up and does more of it than the rest of us put together!'

The point is, the social anxieties of the Balmoral weekend notwithstanding, the Queen's prime ministers valued their time with her. Her thirteenth, Theresa May, said: 'It's a moment in the week when you're away from the hurly burly of politics, and you can actually sit down with somebody with experience and wisdom, knowledge and understanding and have that conversation about the issues of the day.' It was an oasis of calm. It was cathartic. It was therapeutic. According to Boris Johnson, the last prime minister she got to know, it was fun. 'There was a lot of laughter,' he said, 'a lot of laughter.'

As a constitutional monarch, the Queen was not a political animal – and yet she was. She was central to the growth of the Commonwealth during her reign, as we have seen. She made a deliberate contribution to the process of peace and reconciliation in Northern Ireland. In her Christmas Day broadcast in 1987 she denounced IRA terrorism, but to a purpose. Condemning the Remembrance Day bombing in Enniskillen the month before, she made a special mention of a survivor whose twenty-year-old daughter was killed beside him, and of his public forgiveness of the bombers hours later as he called for no reprisals. 'Mr Gordon Wilson,' she said, 'whose daughter Marie lost her life in the horrifying explosion at Enniskillen, impressed the whole world by the depth of his forgiveness. All of us will echo his prayer, that out of the personal tragedies of Enniskillen may come a reconciliation between the communities.' In 2002, she visited the scene of the Omagh bombing and stood on the spot where a Real IRA car bomb exploded, killing twenty-nine. In 2011, she became the first British monarch to make an official State visit to Ireland in a hundred years, and opened her speech in Irish.

She prayed for peace and reconciliation in the world – from Ireland to South Africa – and, both behind the scenes and publicly, worked for them. At home, she did all she could, within the limits of her position, to ensure the continuity of the Union between England and Scotland. In 2014, she openly urged Scots to 'think very carefully' before voting in the referendum on Scottish independence. And after the vote David Cameron had to apologise to her after he was overheard telling the former New York mayor, Michael Bloomberg, that the Queen 'purred down the line' when he informed her that Scotland had voted against independence. In the week of her funeral, Michael Forsyth, the Scottish Secretary in John Major's government, told me that the Queen had been very much in favour of his plan to have the near-mythic Stone of Destiny brought back to Scotland from London after 700 years. Described as 'coarse-grained, pinkish buff sandstone', the Stone of Destiny was originally kept in Scone Palace in Perthshire. In 1296, King Edward I of England took it from Scotland during an invasion and placed it in Westminster Abbey within the coronation chair. Through Forsyth's endeavours, and with Queen's blessing, it was returned to Scotland in 1996 on St Andrew's Day. 'It was a symbolic move,' said Forsyth, 'and Her Majesty understood its significance completely.'

The Queen simply wanted to be a force for good in the world. From Idi Amin to Vladimir Putin, she met whoever she was required to meet and did her level best to treat all her guests with equal diplomatic courtesy. When I told her that (for a film for *The One Show*) I had been to visit Spink's, the London auction house founded in 1666, to view the replicas of all the British orders of chivalry that Idi Amin, when President of Uganda in the 1970s, had ordered for himself to wear – including two Victoria Crosses – she said, simply, 'Goodness,' before adding, diplomatically, 'He was certainly quite a character.'

She told me she was grateful to have had the opportunity to meet 'so many remarkable people' during her lifetime, from Mother Theresa to Barack Obama. Michelle Obama, as First Lady, famously put her arm around the Queen at a reception at Buckingham Palace in 2009. The Queen didn't mind at all and instinctively put her arm around Mrs Obama, who explained later that she and the Queen had just been sympathising with one another after a mutually long day in high heels had left them both with sore feet. They were just 'two tired ladies oppressed by our shoes', she said. The Queen was not so happy when years before, the publisher Robert Maxwell put a bear-like arm around Her Majesty as he escorted her around an event in Scotland. As Queen Elizabeth, the Queen Mother said when on a tour of Australia once, as the crowd drew closer, 'Please don't touch the exhibits.'

The Queen Mother is also supposed to have said that the only man to kiss her on the lips since her husband died was the 39th US President, Jimmy Carter, when he visited the Queen at Buckingham Palace in 1977. With the exception of Lyndon Johnson, from Truman to Biden, the Queen met every American president since the war. Her diplomacy was always very personal. She talked about the Second World War and the Cold War with Dwight Eisenhower – and about drop scones. She wrote to him on 24 January 1960: 'Seeing a picture of you in today's newspaper standing in front of a barbecue grilling quail, reminded me that I had never sent you the recipe of the drop scones which I promised you at Balmoral. I now hasten to do so.' In 1982, she went riding with Ronald Reagan in Windsor Great Park. In 2018 she was amused by Donald Trump striding ahead of her when he visited Windsor and inspected the Guard of Honour, nominally alongside her. That night when she saw herself on television bobbing about behind him, she laughed out loud.

'She really loved a good joke,' according Major-General Sir Sebastian Roberts, Commander of the Household Division in April 1989, when Russia's President Mikhail Gorbachev came on a state visit. The communist leader was due to inspect a Guard of Honour at Windsor and, before the event,

Roberts received a call from Her Majesty. 'What coats will the Coldstreamers be wearing, Sebastian?' asked the Queen. 'Summer coats, Your Majesty, it's almost mid-April,' said Roberts. 'Could they wear their winter coats, Sebastian?' 'By all means, Your Majesty.' 'So,' the Major-General explained to me, 'we scrambled to get the men out of their summer kit into their winter coats. Gorby duly arrived at Windsor and was invited to inspect the Guard of Honour with the Duke of Edinburgh. Inspection done, Gorby said to the Queen – as every visitor always did after any Guard of Honour – "very impressive, marvellous uniforms", to which the Queen replied, with a twinkle in her eye, "Thank you, Mr President. They're the Coldstream Guards. They got their bearskins from Napoleon at Waterloo and their greatcoats from you in the Crimea."'

For seventy years, the Queen did what her country asked of her, travelling the world, meeting everyone, and treating everyone, saints and sinners, Mother Teresa and Richard Nixon, with equal grace and good humour. She broke bread with dictators on a regular basis and even kept a known traitor on her payroll. In 1964, Sir Anthony Blunt, Surveyor of the Royal Pictures, confessed to an MI5 interrogator that he had been a Soviet spy since before the Second World War. In return for his confession, he was offered legal immunity, and, to avoid alerting the KGB, Her Majesty was asked to keep him in royal service until the due date of his retirement. She acquiesced. She had little choice in the matter. Almost invariably, she did her government's bidding. She did manage to resist an attempt by Tony Benn (when Postmaster-General in the mid-1960s) to have the sovereign's profile removed from British postage stamps, but, in the 1990s, she failed to secure a successor to the Royal Yacht *Britannia*.

The Queen told me she had a soft spot for spies. I think she probably meant fictional spies like James Bond, though she regularly met with the heads of MI5 and MI6 and, in 2014, appointed the former intelligence officer and head of MI5, Eliza Mannigham-Buller, to the Order of the Garter. When she was at Oxford in 1968, Eliza appeared as the Fairy Queen in my student production of *Cinderella,* making her and Her Majesty (given those wartime productions at Windsor) the only two Ladies of the Garter to appear in panto.

Spies, soldiers, countrymen, members of the racing community, fellow dog lovers, pigeon fanciers – these were among the Queen's favourite people. She told me she enjoyed the 'brief encounters' that came her way when she was having her portrait painted. Incredibly, during her long life, she sat for more than 960 photographic and painted portraits. She told me she had especially enjoyed being painted by Andrew Festing, because he had been a soldier before he became a painter, and she had known his father, Field Marshal Sir Frankie Festing, so 'We had plenty to chat about.' Andrew Festing told me that chatting with the Queen was 'always fun, but it sometime got in the way of the painting – you do rather need your subject to sit still – and it's a bit difficult to tell them to shut up when it's the Queen.' Michael Noakes, who painted her several times, told me about the sitting he had with her in the 1970s, when because of the light he had to move where she was sitting closer to the window. This was at Buckingham Palace and the room overlooked the Mall and Birdcage Walk. 'Looking out of the window,' Michael said, 'the Queen kept up a running commentary of what was going on outside. There was a taxi that was hit by a car. She got quite excited by that. "Oh, he's got out now," she said, "I think there's going to be a fight!"'

Robbie Elvin, the Norfolk artist, who painted the Queen at Sandringham, revealed to my cousin, picture-framer George Brandreth, who framed Elvin's portrait of the Queen, that Elvin and Her Majesty spent much of their time together chatting about racing pigeons – after horse racing, the Queen's favourite sport. Elvin discovered that the Queen would quite often go discreetly from Sandringham to King's Lynn to meet up with a pigeon breeder in his council flat there. They would happily spend the afternoon together discussing their birds. The Queen kept her own racing pigeon lofts at Wolferton, near Sandringham, and her pigeons were the descendants of birds first given to the royal family in 1886.

Of course, as well as being Head of the Commonwealth, the Queen was also the Supreme Governor of the Church of England, so she made it her business to entertain each of her bishops in turn. They all have their stories to tell, but I am sharing that of Richard Harries, former Bishop of Oxford, now Lord Harries of Pentregarth, because you may be familiar with his voice from 'Thought for the Day' on Radio 4's *Today* programme, and because he did not start out as a monarchist:

> I was a teenage republican. In those days the National Anthem was played at the end of every theatre and cinema performance. I had furious rows with my mother when I refused to stand as she did. Later I underwent a genuine intellectual conversion to monarchy. I can remember the exact spot and occasion. It was when I was chaplain of Westfield College at a reception held in summer on the lawn. I was in conversation with Norman St John Stevas, an ardent monarchist, and he convinced me that the monarchy was the great unifying symbol in our society now. I have never been emotional or sentimental about royalty, but I

believe that what Norman St John Stevas said then is still true and I have the utmost respect for the way the Queen has carried out her duties so faithfully over so many years. One of her acts of hospitality is to invite every Diocesan bishop once in their time to spend a weekend with her at Sandringham. You arrive on Saturday afternoon and after a briefing and a cup of tea go to your room where your clothes have been laid out and your bath run. Then there are drinks and dinner at which you sit next to the Queen. I was advised to choose either horses or the Commonwealth, about which the Queen knows a great deal, as subjects of conversation. After dinner there was the choice of going into the sitting room with the Duke of Edinburgh and members of staff to watch a film. As keeping up conversation in a royal context is something of a strain, I chose this as the easier option. It was I think the worst film I have ever seen. It was also a black mark. For when I emerged from this terrible film there was the Queen and the Queen Mother busy doing a jigsaw puzzle. I realised that this was the option I should have chosen.

Sunday morning at breakfast was bizarre. I sat next to Princess Diana, gorgeously arrayed in a white trouser suit, for it was at a time before the split, and all the family were there. On a nearby table were all the Sunday papers with the usual salacious gossip about the royal family. The bishop has to preach at the 11 a.m. service of morning prayer in Sandringham Church, which is one of the reasons he is invited for the weekend. After the service various people gathered round a local lady who had read the lesson rather well, including the Queen. 'You weren't listening, Bishop,' she said. Second black mark. I had indeed been having a surreptitious glance at my notes before going up to preach, which the Queen had noticed and remarked on. 'I was doing both, Ma'am,' I replied. After lunch and various activities in the afternoon, including some shooting for those who wanted it, I left with a pair of unplucked grouse.

I am trying to give you a flavour of what the Queen was like in private because in public she revealed so little of herself. If you asked her, 'How are you?' she would invariably reply, 'Very well, thank you.' She would never say, as Meghan famously did, 'Thank you for asking, because not many people have asked if I'm okay.'

The Queen did not talk about herself. That was her rule and she rarely broke it, though she did, most famously, on 24 November 1992, at a lunch at London's Guildhall marking her fortieth year as Queen: her Ruby Jubilee. My wife and I were there as guests of the Queen and Prince Philip and we heard her give what was perhaps the most personal and memorable speech of her reign. She had a cold and a sore throat on the day, but she had some things she wanted to say and she hoped to be heard and was not sure how long her voice would last, so she decided to speak before we all tucked into the turbot, partridge and soufflé, rather than after. The speech – wry, reflective, personal – was made all the more moving by being spoken in a husky voice. The Queen talked of her *annus horribilis,* 'not a year I shall look back on with undiluted pleasure'. (The phrase was suggested by her former assistant private secretary, Sir Edward Ford, and the next day brilliantly translated by the *Sun* newspaper's headline writer as 'One's Bum Year'.) She did not mention Princess Anne's divorce, Prince Andrew's separation or Prince Charles's marriage on the rocks, but they were in her mind, clearly – and in ours. She talked, poignantly, about the fire that had done so much damage to Windsor Castle the weekend before and – because the lunch was to mark the fortieth anniversary of her accession – reflected on lessons learnt over four decades. She said, rather wistfully, that, of course, any institution – monarchy included – must accept scrutiny and criticism, but asked, 'Couldn't it be done with a touch of humour, gentleness and understanding?' She commended loyalty and 'moderation in all things'.

'*Annus horribilis*' is one of just a few of the Queen's turns of phrase that will not be forgotten. 'My husband and I . . .' is another. It was a phrase that the Queen used in almost every public utterance in the early years of her reign. She used it to such an extent that it became a joke and she was forced to drop it. Her last significant speech contained another memorable phrase – an echo of a song sung by 'the Forces' sweetheart', Vera Lynn, during the Second World War. On 5 April 2020, in the early days of lockdown during the Covid pandemic, she gave a rare broadcast from within her own 'Covid bubble' at Windsor Castle. She began:

> I am speaking to you at what I know is an increasingly challenging time. A time of disruption in the life of our country: a disruption that has brought grief to some, financial difficulties to many, and enormous changes to the daily lives of us all.

She saluted the NHS, she encouraged those facing self-isolation to go through it with good-humoured resolve, she evoked the wartime spirit that she remembered well, and ended on a note of measured encouragement:

> We should take comfort that while we may have more still to endure, better days will return: we will be with our friends again; we will be with our families again; we will meet again.

'We will meet again' – that is what she felt almost exactly a year later, on 9 April 2021, when the Duke of Edinburgh died.

On 3 December 1947, the Duke of Edinburgh, aged twenty-six and just married, wrote to his mother-in-law and outlined for her the course he had set himself: 'Lilibet is the only "thing" in the world which is absolutely real to me and my ambition is to weld the two of us into a new combined existence that will not only be able to withstand the shocks directed at us but will also have a positive existence for good.'

I believe that Lilibet would tell you that he achieved his ambition. Their marriage was not a fairytale: it was 'absolutely real' to them both. Welded together, they withstood all the shocks and, between them, theirs was indeed 'a positive existence for good'.

The Duke of Edinburgh formally 'retired' in the summer of 2017, a couple of months after his ninety-sixth birthday. He retired because his wife encouraged him to do so. She wanted to stop him 'pushing himself all the time'. She had become anxious about him. A senior courtier told me he had found the Queen in the corridor at Buckingham Palace one day looking for her husband. 'Where's he got to?' she asked. 'Where is he? I can't find him.'

Inevitably, as he moved through his mid-nineties, the Duke was beginning to look his age: his eyes were increasingly red-rimmed, his nose grew beakier, he became more stooped, he shrank a bit. 'I'll soon be dead,' he kept saying. Increasingly, of course, there were reminders of mortality all around him – and her, too. With advancing years, the Queen, also, began to lose more of her closest friends. Her cousin, Margaret Rhodes, died aged ninety-one, in November 2016 and, two weeks later, Elizabeth Longman, another of her childhood friends and bridesmaids at her wedding, died, aged ninety-two. In January 2017, Shirley, the Marchioness of Anglesey died. Until the death of the Marquess in 2013, the Angleseys were the only surviving couple to have both attended the Coronation, other than the Queen and Prince Philip. A generation was disappearing: an era was drawing to a close.

Happily, relations between Prince Philip and his son mellowed with the passing years. In 2016, for the Queen's ninetieth birthday, Charles organised a private celebration for his mother at Windsor Castle and invited the theatre director Christopher Luscombe to provide the post-dinner entertainment. Knowing the Queen's fondness for the songs of George Formby, I suggested to Christopher that the Ukulele Orchestra of Great Britain might amuse Her Majesty. It did, along with magic (involving Prince Harry) and a ventriloquist (the brilliant Nina Conti). It was not a show that Prince Charles would have chosen for himself (which would have included Shakespeare and an operatic aria): it was a show entirely designed to please his mother. The day after the party Prince Philip called his son to congratulate him on organising a perfect family evening. Charles was touched and delighted to receive the call.

How did the Duke of Edinburgh spend his retirement? He divided his time principally between Wood Farm on the Sandringham estate and Windsor Castle – his two favourite homes – where he read, wrote letters, dabbled with watercolours, harrumphed now and again at stories in the *Daily Telegraph* and invited friends to stay. He continued to make occasional public appearances alongside the Queen – at the Cenotaph on Remembrance Sunday, going to church at Sandringham on Christmas Day – but their 70th wedding anniversary on 20 November 2017 was a low-key affair. In the morning, the Duke took two of his nephews – Ludwig and Max of Baden

– out for a carriage drive in Windsor Great Park; in the evening, there was a family dinner at Windsor Castle.

The Queen wanted to honour her husband on their wedding anniversary. On his ninetieth birthday the Queen had made the Duke Lord High Admiral, the titular head of the Royal Navy. It was a title she had held and she handed it over to him, both because it seemed appropriate and because she had already bestowed on him almost every other available honour. In 2015, to mark ANZAC Day and the centenary of the Gallipoli landings, the Queen invested the Duke of Edinburgh with the Insignia of a Knight of the Order of Australia. In 2016, as her anniversary present, she appointed him a Knight Grand Cross of the Royal Victorian Order. Prince Philip wasn't entirely sure about this – most of the recipients of honours within this order are long-serving members of staff who have given personal service to the sovereign and, in any event, he already had the Royal Victorian Chain (given to him in 2007) – but he accepted it with a slightly grudging grace and was amused (and pleased) because it meant that he was the first person to be able to wear four orders of chivalry breast stars – alongside the Order of the Garter, the Order of the Thistle and the Order of the British Empire – since his uncle, Earl Mountbatten of Burma.

In her Christmas broadcast that year, the Queen said she was 'grateful for the blessings of home and family, and in particular for seventy years of marriage'. She went on:

I don't know that anyone had invented the term 'platinum' for a 70th wedding anniversary when I was born. You weren't expected to be around that long. Even Prince Philip has decided it's time to slow down a little – having, as he economically put it, 'done his bit'. But I know his support and unique sense of humour will remain as strong as ever, as we

493

enjoy spending time this Christmas with our family and look forward to welcoming new members into it next year.

The Queen did not retire when her husband did, but she did reduce her workload. She maintained her interests, of course. She continued to ride up until the year she died, and to walk her corgis after lunch; she continued to phone her racing manager in the evening. (From 1988 onwards, her racehorses were reckoned to have won her £8.7 million in prize money, including £557,650 in a record-breaking 2016.) She and Prince Philip went out for dinner with friends and enjoyed weekends away together. She was often alone in the evenings (she was accustomed to that), watching television and having supper in her rooms, but frequently she saw friends and family – grandchildren and great-grandchildren – for afternoon tea. Her faith remained her abiding comforter and her solace in times of sadness. (On a Sunday morning, she would often attend church twice – first, privately, for Holy Communion, and then, later, dressed in an outfit in which to be photographed, for Matins with other members of the family. The press, as a rule, respected her privacy and photographs and footage were rarely taken of her first church visit of the day.)

There was some turbulence at court in the summer of 2017 when Sir Christopher Geidt, for ten years the Queen's private secretary, took early retirement and Samantha Cohen, number three in the Palace hierarchy, stepped down in support of her boss. The feeling was that Sir Christopher was man-oeuvred out by Prince Charles (abetted by Prince Andrew) to improve relations between the secretariats at Buckingham Palace and Clarence House. The Queen, usually averse to unnecessary change, accepted it in this case because it was what her sons wanted – though apparently her grandson, Prince William, didn't. Prince Andrew felt that Sir Christopher was side-lining him when it came to public duties and pre-venting him from appearing on the Palace balcony when the Prince felt he had a right to be there. Andrew also reckoned Geidt had not supported him sufficiently when he had been under media attack for his role as a UK 'trade ambassador'. Sir Christopher's departure (sweetened by the award of the GCVO – the honour Prince Philip received as an anniversary gift but rather felt was the preserve of staff – and a peerage and then another knighthood in the Order of the Bath a few months later) caused some fluttering in the court dovecotes. Prince Philip told me he had 'kept out of all that'. From the time of the Queen's accession in 1952 onward, he had always found internal Palace politics 'frustrating and infuriating'. He was proud of the straightforward, streamlined way in which he and his small team ran his office and suggested that, had he been given the opportunity (as Prince Albert had been), he would have been able to 'run the show with half the staff'.

By the time the obituaries of Prince Philip appeared in 2021 the caricature of him had been replaced by a fuller, fairer portrait. At the end, he was recognised as a remarkable man: as an individual, progressive, challenging, thoughtful, pragmatic, unexpected; as the Queen's consort, uniquely supportive from start to finish. In 1997, at the time of her 50th wedding anniver-sary and in the aftermath of the death of Diana, Princess of Wales, in a speech at the Banqueting House in Whitehall the Queen acknowledged that it was sometimes difficult to fully understand 'the message' of the people, 'obscured as it can be by deference, rhetoric or the conflicting currents of public opinion'. She said, 'I have done my best, with Prince Philip's constant love and help, to interpret it correctly through the years of our marriage and of my reign.' Theirs was an extra-ordinary partnership and the worldwide coverage of the Duke's death acknowledged the fact.

Some myths, of course, were hard to put to rest. Most of obituaries repeated the line that Princess Elizabeth first met Prince Philip when she was thirteen and, from that moment on, had eyes only for him. Not so, as you will recall. From the letters she sent to her cousin, Diana, in 1943, we know she regretted that Andrew Elphinstone was also her first cousin because he was 'just the sort of husband any girl would love to have'. In 1945, when Lilibet was nineteen, she wrote to Diana about another young man who took her fancy, describing him as 'a devastatingly attractive young giant (with fair hair and blue eyes, of course) from Skye called Roddy Macleod!' The twenty-six-year-old 6' 4" tall Eton-educated Cameroon Highlander, assigned to the royal guard at Balmoral, danced with the young princess and took her out to the theatre, but the fun evenings did not develop into a full-blown romance.

When I tackled Prince Philip about how and when he came to woo his future wife, he was not particularly forthcoming. He and Princess Elizabeth were cousins; they became friends; they got to know one another better; they became closer; in due course, they became engaged. 'That's about it, really,' he said to me, with a shrug.

Interestingly, the Queen's own account of her engagement to Prince Philip tallies very much with his own – and I can share it with you. In 1947, in the run-up to the royal wedding in November, an author by the name of Betty Shrew contacted the twenty-one-year-old princess with a request for accurate background information for a souvenir book about the royal wedding. Princess Elizabeth was happy to oblige. She said the first time she remembered meeting Philip was at the Royal Naval College in Dartmouth in July 1939.

I was thirteen years of age, and he was eighteen and a cadet just due for leave. He joined the Navy at the outbreak of war, and I only saw him very occasionally when he was on leave – I suppose about twice in three years. We first started seeing more of each other when Philip went for a two-year job to the RN Petty Officer School at Corsham [after the war] – before that we hardly knew each other. He'd spend weekends with us, and when the school was closed he spent six weeks at Balmoral.

The young princess was ready to supply the enquiring author with details of her engagement and wedding rings: 'The wedding ring will be made of Welsh gold, but not from the Craigwen mine. The engagement ring was made by Antrobus [jewellers of Bond Street]. Princess Alice took it in as Philip obviously couldn't, but he designed the ring.'

Elizabeth told her correspondent:

We both love dancing – we have danced at Ciro's and Quaglino's as well as at parties. Philip enjoys driving and does it fast! He has his own tiny MG which he is very proud of – he has taken me about in it, once up to London, which was great fun, only it was like sitting in the road, and the wheels are almost as high as one's head. On that one and only occasion we were chased by a photographer which was disappointing.

The behaviour of photographers continued to be a disappointment to the royal couple as the years went by. Prince Philip did his best to protect the Queen from their excesses, barking ferociously at them when necessary. He always did what he could to safeguard her person and her dignity. He hated to see her taken advantage of in any way. One year, at the Royal Variety Performance, one of the stars performed a routine directly aimed at the Queen. Prince Philip was

497

incandescent and descended on the producer in the interval: 'I've been coming to this for fifty years. It never ends on time. The jokes are lavatorial. And now you insult the Queen!'

He was her 'liege man of life and limb' for more than seventy years, but when he retired, very deliberately, she left him to it. She carried on with her royal duties at Buckingham Palace or at Windsor Castle while he lived out his days at Wood Farm on the Sandringham Estate. They would speak regularly on the phone, but weeks could go by without them seeing one another. That shocked some people, though not those who knew them and who appreciated how well the Queen understood her husband – understood his wish to be left to his own devices, 'not to be fussed over', to be allowed, after more than seventy years of duty, to see out his days in his own way.

The Duke was bowing out, but the royal story was carrying on, and the Queen was carrying on, too, doing her duty, as assiduously as ever. The year 2019 proved a busy one: she said goodbye to her thirteenth prime minister (Theresa May) and hello to her fourteenth (Boris Johnson); she opened parliament and read the Queen's Speech, twice; she did all the things she had been doing since 1952, year in, year out, opening this, unveiling that, hosting receptions for ambassadors and diplomats – and the rest.

As the end drew nearer for him, Prince Philip, always his own man, even in crowds always something of a loner, retreated from the world. He still saw friends and he still turned up for family occasions. At the wedding of his grandson Prince Harry with Meghan Markle in May 2018, he appeared, aged ninety-six, still upright, still without a stick, despite having had a hip operation only a few weeks before and having cracked a rib in a fall in the shower a few days before. At the wedding of his granddaughter, Princess Eugenie in October 2018, he appeared, now aged ninety-seven, still upright, still without a stick, impeccably dressed but looking gaunt and cadaverous. In the official wedding photograph he was seated immediately in front of his former daughter-in-law, Sarah, Duchess of York. In May 2019, at Windsor Castle, the Duke joined the Queen for a rare official appearance together when they hosted a lunch for members of the Order of Merit. It was the week of the arrival of Harry and Meghan's firstborn and Philip was photographed admiring his eighth great-grandchild, Archie Harrison Mountbatten-Windsor, alongside the Queen and Meghan's mother, Doria Ragland. In the same month he was on parade again for another family wedding at St George's Chapel, Windsor, when Lady Gabriela Windsor, daughter of the Queen's first cousin, Prince Michael of Kent, married her longtime boyfriend, Thomas Kingston. 'I don't know who half these people are,' said the Duke of Edinburgh, laughing.

There was no laughter later in the year when the Queen, having consulted both her husband and the Prince of Wales, decided that the time had come for her second son, Prince Andrew, to give up all his royal duties and step back from public life. The Duke of York had given that disastrous *Newsnight* interview about his friendship with the convicted paedophile, Jeffrey Epstein, and the accusation that he, Andrew, had slept with an American girl, 'trafficked' by Epstein, when she was just seventeen. In the interview, Andrew protested his innocence, but appeared to show no empathy for Epstein's victims nor to regret his friendship with the man.

The backlash that followed forced the Queen's hand. On 20 November 2019, HRH The Duke of York KG issued a statement:

It has become clear to me over the last few days that the circumstances relating to my former association with Jeffrey

Epstein has become a major disruption to my family's work and the valuable work going on in the many organisations and charities that I am proud to support.

Therefore, I have asked Her Majesty if I may step back from public duties for the foreseeable future, and she has given her permission.

The Queen essentially fired her own son, but the following day showed us how much she loved him by taking him riding with her through Windsor Great Park in the rain and ensuring that there were photographers on hand to capture the shot. A senior courtier said to me, 'There was a lot of nonsense talked about no one being at the helm, but the Queen took a firm grip of things. To use the military jargon, there was only a few days between flash and bang. Action was called for and the Queen took it.'

The Queen took further firm action in January 2020, when Harry and Meghan, the Duke and Duchess of Sussex, announced their desire to 'step back' from their lives as 'senior Royals'. They planned to divide their time between the United Kingdom and North America; they wanted financial independence; they hoped to be able to continue to serve Queen and Commonwealth, but on their own terms. It was a naïve hope and not to be. The Queen convened a family meeting at Sandringham – attended by her immediate heirs, the Prince of Wales and the Duke of Cambridge, as well as the Duke of Sussex – and a way forward was agreed. Harry and Meghan could do as they pleased, but they could not represent the Queen while doing so. Their HRH titles would be put in abeyance and Harry, to his dismay, was required to give up his royal patronages and military appointments. Harry was distressed, as he put it, 'that it should come to this'. So was his grandmother. In a personal statement, she made it clear that

Harry and Meghan would always be close members of her family, and she went out of her way to praise her American granddaughter-in-law, but, so far as the Crown was concerned, she was equally clear: she wasn't going to have a couple of freelance royals roaming the world doing their own thing in any sense in her name.

The Duke of Edinburgh was equally sorry 'that it should come to this'. Harry had only succeeded his grandfather as Captain General of the Royal Marines in 2017. Philip had done the job for sixty-four years. Harry had barely managed thirty months. The Duke of Edinburgh was not pleased, nor did he believe that Harry and Meghan were doing the right thing, either for the country or for themselves. 'It's a big mistake to think about yourself,' he told me, more than once. 'No one is interested in you in the long run. Don't court popularity. It doesn't last. Remember that the attention comes because of the position you are privileged to hold, not because of who you are. If you think it's all about you, you'll never be happy.'

Prince Philip regretted Harry's decision but did not get involved in its aftermath. On the day the Queen held her Sandringham 'summit' with Charles, William and Harry, he made himself scarce, deliberately leaving the main house and retreating to Wood Farm. 'I'll soon be out of it,' he said, 'and not before time.'

Prince Philip of Greece was born in the aftermath of the influenza pandemic that swept the world between 1918 and 1920, infecting around 500 million people – about a third of the world's population at the time – in four successive waves. As Prince Philip, Duke of Edinburgh, he was still alive a century later, as the Covid-19 pandemic swept the world in 2020. He spent 'lockdown' with the Queen, and a small retinue of staff, at Windsor Castle.

When lockdown was lifted, Philip and Elizabeth, having spent more time close together than they had done in years, decided it rather suited them. They left Windsor together and travelled up to Balmoral together for their traditional summer break. When that was over, they went back to Sandringham – but not the big house. Instead, together they went to live at Wood Farm, Philip's bolt hole, the ungrand, unpretentious place he regarded as his home on the Sandringham estate. It's where he wanted to end his days and she wanted to be with him to the end.

On 16 February 2021, the Duke was admitted to hospital in London as a precautionary measure after feeling unwell. On 3 March 2021, he underwent a successful procedure for an existing heart condition. On 16 March, he was discharged and returned to Windsor Castle. Three weeks later, his death was announced at noon on 9 April 2021, with the release of a statement saying he had 'died peacefully' that morning at Windsor Castle. His daughter-in-law, Sophie, Countess of Wessex, described his death as ' . . . so gentle. It was just like somebody took him by the hand and off he went.' The Queen was reportedly at her husband's bedside when he died.

In fact, I don't believe the Queen was with him at the end.

He was in a hospital bed set up in his dressing room. In the morning he went to the bathroom, helped by the nurse. When he came back he said he felt a little faint and wanted help getting back into bed. The nurse called the Duke's valet and the Queen's page, Paul Whybrew, to help – and he died before the Queen could be called.

The Queen wasn't yet up. The doctor came and pronounced him dead, then the Queen was called.

He was being laid out when the Prince of Wales arrived. He waited with a cup of tea and went away without seeing his father. Prince Edward did see him and then, gradually, the rest of the family began to arrive, and, as they tried to comfort the Queen, the Queen comforted them.

Grief is the price we pay for love.

CHAPTER TWENTY-FOUR

Diary days

What was she really like?

Above all, she was kind. And kind at so many levels. Patricia Mountbatten told me that when her father and her fourteen-year-old son, Nicholas, and her mother-in-law were all killed by an IRA bomb in 1979, 'the Queen's kindness and love were all-enveloping'. Nicholas's twin brother, Tim, remembers how the Queen invited him and his sister Amanda to Balmoral after the murder and was in 'almost unstoppable mothering mode', plying them with soup and sandwiches when they arrived, unpacking their bags for them, being 'like a second mother, completely wonderful'. James Mackay, Lord Mackay of Clashfern, Lord Chancellor under Margaret Thatcher and John Major, told me how he had been an elder of the Free Presbyterian Church of Scotland, but had been suspended for attending two Catholic funeral masses and so breaking the church's prohibition of showing 'support for the doctrine of Catholicism'. In the world of Free Presbyterians it was a big story, deeply painful at the time for Mackay, if barely noticed in the wider world. While he was having these problems with his church, he was at a gathering and the Queen arrived. He had positioned himself in the third row to be inconspicuous. The Queen sought him out and said, 'I hope you are managing to rise above your recent troubles, Lord Chancellor.' Lord Mackay said, 'That small act of kindness made all the difference.' Better known is the story of the surgeon, Dr David Knott, who volunteered with *Médecins Sans Frontières* and the International Committee of the Red Cross, working in war zones and major humanitarian crises. He had performed life-saving surgery in Afghanistan, Bosnia, Iraq, Libya, Pakistan and Syria. In 2014, at one of the Queen's lunches at Buckingham Palace, when it was his turn to speak he found he couldn't. Having suffered from Post-Traumatic Stress Disorder, 'I didn't know what to say. It wasn't that I didn't want to speak to her – I just couldn't. I just could not say anything. She picked all this up and said, "Well, shall I help you?" I thought, "How on earth can the Queen help me?" All of a sudden the courtiers brought the corgis and the corgis went underneath the table.' Dr Nott said the Queen then opened a tin of biscuits and invited him to feed and stroke the dogs. 'And so for twenty minutes during this lunch, the Queen and I fed the dogs. She did it because she knew that I was so seriously traumatised. You know the humanity of what she was doing was unbelievable.'

And what did she actually do?

Throughout her reign, she did her best to be a force for good at home, within the Commonwealth, and across the world. In almost her last broadcast, a documentary about her life made for the Platinum Jubilee, she said: 'We sometimes think that the world's problems are so big we can do little to help. On our own we cannot end wars or wipe out injustice, but the cumulative impact of thousands of small acts of goodness can be bigger than we imagine.' She believed in small acts of goodness, in the satisfaction of duty done and in the value of service.

But on a day-to-day basis, what did she actually do? Inevitably, less as she grew older. In the days before her funeral, walking across Green Park towards Buckingham Palace, I was struck by how many young people there were coming to pay their respects and to feel they were playing their part in a moment of history. They had only known the Queen as an old lady.

Her reign was such a long one, begun when she was barely more than a girl in her mid-twenties. She was so busy, year in, year out, right from the start. Take 1957, for example, five years into her reign. Ghana and Malaya joined the Commonwealth that year. She went to Canada to open the new Canadian Parliament in Ottawa, the first time any sovereign had done so. She said, 'I was overwhelmed by the loyalty and enthusiasm of my Canadian people.' That same year she and the Duke of Edinburgh travelled to every part of the United Kingdom and paid visits to Portugal, France, Denmark and the United States. 'In each case,' she reported in her Christmas Day broadcast, the first one to be shown on television, 'the arrangements and formalities were managed with great skill, but no one could have "managed" the welcome we received from the people. In each country I was welcomed as Head of the Commonwealth and as your representative. These nations are our friends largely because we have always tried to do our best to be honest and kindly and because we have tried to stand up for what we believe to be right.'

Seasoned observers of her trajectory (long-standing private secretaries and other royal biographers) reckon that she did not begin to become her own woman and escape the long (if, to her, comforting) shadow of her father's reign and the 'old school' way of doing things, until the 1970s. Later, the *annus horribilis* was debilitating and the aftermath of Diana's death was bruising, but she soldiered on and, with a new century, came renewed energy and fresh confidence. As one of the best-informed of her many biographers, Robert Hardman, put it: 'By that Golden Jubilee of 2002, she knew she had turned a corner.'

To give you a flavour of what she was doing then, on a day-to-day basis, to give you an idea of the royal routine when the Queen was at her busiest and completely in her stride, here is my diary of the time I spent with her in 2001–2002, watching her, walking with her, talking with her, as she went about her duties, in the aftermath of the September 11 al-Qaeda terrorist attacks in the United States and in the run-up to that Golden Jubilee.

Wednesday 7 November 2001

Last night the Queen hosted a state banquet at Windsor for the King of Jordan. Today she has come to open St Luke's Hospice in Harrow. Last night she was decked out in a dazzling diamond tiara and the sash and badge of the Order of Qeladet El-Hussein Ibn Ali. Today she is wearing a powder-blue suit with a straw boater.

She arrives seven minutes behind schedule. As she steps from her car, I fall in behind her. I have been in attendance at sufficient royal visits to hospitals/factories/civic centres to know that the feel of them never varies. Before the royal arrival, there is a heightened sense of expectation: nervous laughter from those due to be presented, repeated checking of watches, self-conscious straightening of ties, last-minute visits to the loo. When the royal party appears, a sudden hush descends, the atmosphere is a mixture of excitement and awkwardness, interrupted by sudden bursts of laughter. When the Queen says to a hospital orderly, 'You work here full-time? Really?', for no good reason we all fall about with merriment. In the presence of Her Majesty, nobody behaves naturally. And the moment the royal visit is over, the relief is intense. 'When royalty leaves the room,' said Joyce Grenfell's mother, 'it's like getting a seed out of your tooth.'

Wherever the Queen officially goes within the United Kingdom, she is greeted on arrival by her local Lord-Lieutenant, usually an amiable buffer, good-hearted, well-connected, and sharper than he looks, often a local grandee with a military background, excellent with the other ranks and a fount of sound advice for those less accustomed to meeting royalty: 'It's "Ma'am" to rhyme with "ham" and, ladies, if the wind blows, skirts gripped between the knees.' Today it is Sir Neil Thorne (thirty years in the Territorial Army, former MP), Deputy-Lieutenant of Greater London, who smartly salutes Her Majesty and presents the local dignitaries (the mayors of Harrow and Brent: 'Two mayors,' says the Queen. 'How nice') followed by the chairman of the trustees and his wife (who steals the millinery honours in a purple, feathery, flowerpot hat) and the chief executive who leads us on the tour. (The route and timing have been agreed several months in advance: at least two members of the Palace team, in addition to the police, will have walked the course before the event. There is a Buckingham Palace adage that 'a minute of visit requires three hours of planning'.)

As we tour the hospice, meeting patients, workers, volunteers, the Queen takes her time. She listens, she nods, occasionally she smiles (and her smile quite transforms her appearance), but she does not say a great deal. In a conversation in 1991 (which I recorded) Lord Charteris (who worked for her, as her assistant private secretary and private secretary, from 1950 to 1977) told me, 'The Queen combines her mother's charm with her father's shyness.' On visits like this, other members of the royal family (Prince Philip, Prince Charles, the Princess Royal, the Duke of York) are more chatty, asking questions, initiating the conversation, forcing the pace. The Queen is much more passive.

*

In the last ward we meet three patients who are gravely ill. The first appears too frail to notice Her Majesty; the second tells the Queen, almost chirpily, 'I am going to die in about two weeks' time', and shows her the football-based board game he has developed. He believes it also has potential as a television series. Her Majesty nods attentively, murmurs 'Yes, I see', and moves on. The third patient is a distinguished-looking Asian from Kenya who is propped up in bed and who, as the Queen approaches, sweeps his arm in front of his chest and bows his head. The Queen smiles. The man cannot speak and scribbles a message for Her Majesty on his notepad. The Queen fumbles with her handbag – she is never without her handbag. 'Oh dear,' she says, 'I don't seem to have my glasses.' The courtly patient's elegant wife (in a shimmering sari) takes a snapshot of the scene and tells the Queen, 'We come from Nairobi. We were there when you came in 1952. We were waving flags. Do you remember?' 'Yes, indeed,' says the Queen. 'The visit was cut short, sadly.' (This, of course, was the tour during which the Queen's father died of cancer. She does not mention this, but it is part of the subtext of today's visit to St Luke's Hospice. On the fortieth anniversary of her accession, 6 February 1992, she began the day at a church service at Sandringham and then went to visit cancer patients at a local hospital. Lord Charteris told me, 'The Queen feels things very deeply, but she doesn't put her emotions on display. On 6 February 1952, when word reached us in Kenya that the King had died, I went in to see the new Queen and found her seated at her desk, erect, no tears, fully accepting her destiny. On the long flight back to London, she gazed out of the window. She loved her father dearly. She may have cried in private, but, if she did, she did not let it show.')

Back in the hospice Main Reception the Queen is invited to sign a huge photograph of herself. She removes her gloves and writes 'Elizabeth R' in a large and practised hand. 'Shall I put the date?' she asks. 'What is it?' Nobody else responds, so I volunteer: 'The seventh, Your Majesty.' 'And where is the picture to go?' No one seems to know, so I choose a large empty wall and announce, 'Here, Your Majesty.' This news is greeted with a smattering of applause. The visit is reaching its climax.

As the Queen moves across to the tea-tent in the garden, one of the hospice helpers, assuming I am some extra equerry-in-waiting, whispers to me, 'Is Her Majesty comfortable? We've set a room aside.' I say, breezily, 'She's fine, thank you.'

In the marquee the Queen is mingling with the hospice volunteers and fundraisers: 'Do you live nearby?' 'Have you been involved for long?' 'Community work is so important.' Gradually she is steered towards a commemorative plaque which she unveils with almost no ceremony. She says not a word. She merely pulls the string. She does not make 'an event' out of anything. She does not need to: she is the event.

And suddenly, she's gone. She has stepped out of the marquee, into the car and she's away. The whole visit has lasted fifty-five minutes. It seems to have been much longer. Back on the ward, the dignified gentleman from Nairobi shows me his notepad with the message the Queen had not been able to read: 'Thank you for coming to see me, Your Majesty. This has been the happiest and proudest day of my life.'

Wednesday 14 November 2001

I am waiting for Her Majesty in the company of Denis MacShane, MP, junior Foreign Office Minister, a friend of mine from university days. Denis says, 'The Queen has lovely legs for a woman of her age.' He is still recovering from the excitement of hosting Queen Elizabeth, the Queen Mother at the Foreign Office window for the Remembrance Day service at the Cenotaph last Sunday. 'When the Queen arrived,' he reports, 'she said, "Hello, Mummy", and when the Prince of Wales arrived, he said, "Hello, Granny" and when Sophie Wessex arrived, she curtsied all the way to the ground.'

Denis and I are standing in the quadrangle at Goodenough College, Mecklenburgh Square, London WC1. The College houses 670 post-graduate students from seventy countries. I had never heard of it, but the Commonwealth is well represented at the College and, consequently, the Queen is an enthusiastic supporter: this will be the seventh visit of her reign.

She arrives ten minutes late (again), in a lilac coat plus boater, and, as we fall in behind her, makes her customary, steady progress, nodding appreciatively, commenting occasionally, reviewing stands representing Africa, the Caribbean and Asia, meeting groups involved in the aftermath of the Gujerat earthquake and a project for helping Romanian gypsy children. In the Large Common Room she meets representatives of the College's assorted social clubs. Helpfully, they are dressed in the appropriate kit. A young Australian in a rubber wetsuit is holding a gigantic oar. 'Ah,' says the Queen, 'Rowing.' Chiara Crisculo from Italy and Mehreen Zaki from Pakistan (working on PhDs in economics and molecular parasitology) tell Her Majesty about the biscuits they bake at the College's Sunday morning cookery club. They hope Her Majesty might be tempted to try one. She isn't, but she says, 'They look very nice.' Today I time each of the Queen's encounters: none lasts more than a minute, most last around ten seconds.

In form and content, I imagine this visit (which is a huge success and overruns by three-quarters of an hour) is very much like the Queen's previous six visits to Goodenough (there is even a seventh identical commemorative plaque to go alongside the earlier six) – except for two features in the programme. As she arrives, the Queen is greeted by a fanfare, an original and impressive 'Vivat Regina' composed for the occasion by a six-foot six-inch Icelandic lad and performed by a massed choir on the Library balcony: it appears to make no impact on Her Majesty whatsoever. As she leaves, she is introduced to Lieutenant Frank Dwyer of the New York City Police Department, one of the heroes of Ground Zero and a former resident of Goodenough College. Dwyer's brother, also a New York police officer, was killed in the collapse of the World Trade Center towers. The young policeman has light red hair, clear blue eyes, a soft Brooklyn accent and a very gentle way with him. He tells the Queen his story and then, from his back pocket, produces his brother's NYPD badge and presents it to Her Majesty, explaining that his mother would like her to have it.

The Queen is moved by the lieutenant. She says almost nothing, but I see her eyes are pricked by tears. The moment takes me back to Westminster Abbey on Friday 14 September when I watched her emerge from the special service in the immediate aftermath of the terrorist attacks in New York and Washington, DC. She had tears in her eyes then and said, very simply, to the relatives of the British victims of the tragedy, 'I hope the service was of some help.'

The Earl of Snowdon (a vocal admirer of his former sister-in-law and a friend of mine) told me, 'After 11 September I watched the service on television. I was on my own at home. During the National Anthem, alone in my kitchen, I stood up facing the TV. I wanted to. Was that silly or was it the right thing to do?'

The Queen, in powder pink, has gone off to Northern Ireland, for her first visit to Londonderry since 1953. I have come to Salisbury to see Sir Edward Heath, Knight of the Garter and sixth of Her Majesty's ten prime ministers to date. The Queen has a playful streak. She likes to tease Sir Edward. Famously, in 1992, she was caught on camera, at a gathering of foreign heads of government, telling her former premier, 'You're expendable now.' Some commentators interpreted the remark as a deliberate put-down. She was simply being playful. On another occasion, as he came aboard the Royal Yacht *Britannia*, the sovereign greeted Heath, mimicking a conductor, with the words, 'Are you still waving your stick about?'

'The Queen hates music,' says Sir Edward, grinning and heaving his shoulders. 'I saw her on Monday of this week, at a concert for the Musicians' Benevolent Fund at the Festival Hall. I said to her, "Good evening, Your Majesty – if that's the word for it."'

The Queen has around twenty-five audiences a year with her prime minister (usually early on a Tuesday evening when parliament is sitting[4]) and also entertains them for the weekend at Balmoral in September. What do they discuss at their weekly sessions? According to Sir Winston Churchill, it was 'Racing, mostly.' Heath's approach was more po-faced. He

---

4   Changed to Wednesdays to accommodate Tony Blair. The Prime
    Minister answers questions in the House of Commons on a
    Wednesday morning. When Michael Howard became the Leader
    of the Opposition, Mr Blair decided that he needed more time
    to prepare for his weekly joust at the despatch box and asked
    Buckingham Palace if he might meet Her Majesty immediately after
    Prime Minister's Questions rather than the evening before.

always went to the audience with an agenda agreed earlier in the day between No. 10 and the Palace. At his first audience, in June 1970, the topics were 'Northern Ireland, our approach to Europe and our planned legislative programme.' Heath says, 'The Queen is undoubtedly one of the best-informed people in the world.' She has always read all her briefing papers; she is unfailingly up-to-speed, and her concentration never wavers. 'I enjoyed my audiences with the Queen chiefly because it was a relief to be able to discuss everything with someone knowing full well there was not the slightest danger of any information leaking. I could confide in Her Majesty absolutely.'

Sir Edward tells a funny story about his first ever lunch at Buckingham Palace. He was seated next to Princess Margaret and, searching for something to say, enquired, 'Have you been busy lately, Ma'am?' 'That,' said Princess Margaret, 'is the sort of question Lord Mayors ask when I visit cities.' 'Oh,' said poor Ted, quite thrown, 'and what do you reply?' 'In the first four months,' said Princess Margaret, 'they're so green it's not worth talking to them. In the last four months, they're so tired they can't answer any question at all, and, in the middle four months, I am on holiday.'

Wednesday 21 November 2001

Yesterday, the Queen held an investiture in the morning, visited the Blue Cross Animal Hospital in the afternoon, and gave an audience to Tony Blair in the evening.

This morning, when I arrive at Buckingham Palace, I sense a touch of resentment that it is the Prince of Wales (sporting a black eye patch, with the comedian Jim Davidson in attendance) who has scooped today's press coverage, with nary a mention of the Queen at the Blue Cross Animal Hospital. 'It's a shame,' says Major James Duckworth-Chad (twenty-nine, blond, boyish, nice manners, nice manner, good shot), equerry-in-waiting to Her Majesty. 'There were some lovely pictures of the Queen with the dogs, but I suppose you can't trump an eye patch.' The resentment springs not just from the well-known rivalry between the Prince's court and the monarch's, but also from a feeling at Buckingham Palace that, these days, the Queen's tireless endeavours go mostly unregarded. The Queen's press secretary, Penny Russell-Smith (thirty-something, spiky-haired, boyish, modern: when she is in her trouser suit she bows to Her Majesty, she doesn't curtsy), says to me, plaintively, 'The public probably think the Queen's spent the morning reading the *Racing Post* and playing with the corgis. In fact, she's been doing her boxes and mugging up for the credentials.'

'The credentials' is what I have come to witness: at twelve noon the Queen will receive His Excellency the Ambassador of Burkina-Faso, Monsieur Kadré Desiré Ouedraogo, who will present his Letter of Credence to Her Majesty. The Queen gives an individual audience to every incoming ambassador, and similar audiences to British diplomats going abroad, to judges, bishops, service personnel, privy counsellors – a total last year of 224 separate audiences. This morning we are getting through just four.

This is what happens. At 11:55, the Queen, accompanied by her piper (of whom more anon), proceeds from her apartments along the Palace corridors to the 1844 Room. She slips in by a side door, checks her notes, presses a discreet bell to indicate that she is ready for her first caller and then positions herself in the centre of the room facing the main doors. She is standing alone, handbag on arm[5], spectacles on nose, chewing her lower lip. Four beats after her Majesty has rung her bell, her page and a footman open the main doors (from the outside) and the ambassador, flanked by the Marshal of the Diplomatic Corps (Sir Anthony Figgis in full court dress) and the equerry-in-waiting, enter the room. They bow once, take two steps forward, and bow again. The Marshal announces the ambassador who now moves towards Her Majesty as the Marshal and equerry step backwards out of the room.

'*Bonjour Monsieur l'Ambassadeur,*' says the Queen, with an engaging smile. She takes his Letter of Credence from him, invites him to take one of the four fairly formal chairs positioned around the fireplace and proceeds to engage him in fairly informal, but wonderfully informed, small talk – in French. Her French is competent and she seems to know where Burkina-Faso is, what it was (Upper Volta), what its problems are (considerable) and why M. Ouedraogo and his wife are actually living in Brussels rather than London. The ambassador is impressed. So am I.

When Burkina-Faso's time is up (about twelve minutes: the Queen does not check her watch: in fifty years she has given upward of ten thousand audiences: her instinct is good) she discreetly presses her bell and the ambassador retreats. The door closes, the Queen checks her notes, presses the bell again and the process is repeated.

This morning's line-up includes three British ambassadors and two High Commissioners on their way to new postings

---

5   I once asked one of her ladies-in-waiting what Her Majesty kept in her handbag. The answer: a hankie, lipstick and a powder compact, plus, sometimes but not always, a little bunch of keys, the keys to unlock her red boxes, and a small gold St Christopher medallion that her father gave her to keep her safe on her travels.

(the Queen's small talk ranges from the weather in Paraguay, through the divisions in Cyprus to her forthcoming trip to New Zealand), two senior soldiers (the outgoing and incoming colonels of The Queen's Lancashire Regiment: the Queen is very good with soldiers) and a High Court judge (the Queen is less comfortable with judges). The judge is to be knighted. An extra equerry is on hand to brief him on the correct kneeling posture and to remind him to bow as he meets Her Majesty. The reminder is necessary because, apparently, one senior justice was so overwhelmed by the occasion that he curtsied right to the floor. I am not altogether surprised: when the door of the 1844 Room opens to admit the judge, the Queen is standing alone in the middle of the room brandishing a hefty sword. It belonged to her father. Concentrating fiercely, she sweeps it in a mighty arc before her. It is a startling sight.

Thursday 22 November 2001

'I'm really pleased.' The Queen is beaming. She turns to me happily, 'I've just seen a Pembrokeshire corgi. They're very special. And aren't these daffodils lovely?' She hands them to me. I pass them to a police officer who in turn gives them to the Countess of Airlie, Lady of the Bedchamber, and today's attendant lady-in-waiting.

We are on 'walkabout' in Haverfordwest. Last night, it was a reception at Windsor Castle for the Diplomatic Corps; today, it's meet-the-people in West Wales. Her Majesty got from there to here by Royal Train: she spent the early hours asleep in a siding outside Carmarthen. The turnout isn't bad: on a cold and cloudy Thursday morning, about three hundred souls (assorted ages), with Union flags and Welsh ones, are here to salute the Queen in the new County Hall car park.

Even Rohdri Morgan (First Minister of the Welsh Assembly, in a crumpled suit) is on parade. The sovereign is looking rather chirpy. 'Wales is important,' she says to me, out of the blue.

Today's programme is wholly predictable: opening County Hall, visiting St David's Cathedral (and signing the visitors' book with the same Parker pen she used here in 1955), touring a primary school, mingling with the local worthies at a garden party at Pembroke Castle, joshing with the Lord-Lieutenant. 'You're my longest-servicing Lord-Lieutenant, Sir David,' says the Queen. 'So I am, Your Majesty,' purrs Sir David Mansel Lewis, seventy-four, moustache twitching, spurs clicking.

At Pembroke Dock Community School, I am told (*sotto voce*) that the Vice-Chairman of Governors has absented himself because he is not in favour of the monarchy, and the same mole whispers to me that the throng outside County Hall was not entirely what it seemed. First, an e-mail was despatched inviting Council staff to join the crowd: later, a second e-mail was sent *instructing* them to do so.

But there was nothing forced about the children's reaction to Her Majesty. As she proceeds around the school, they gaze at her in amazement. 'Are you the real Queen, miss?' asks one boy. 'I hope so,' says Her Majesty. Tracey Lewis, just three years into teaching, has had a bright idea. She has been teaching her nine-year-olds about the Tudors. She has timed her lessons so that this afternoon she can point to the screen in her classroom and say, 'This is Elizabeth I', and a moment later the door opens, and the headmaster announces, 'This is Elizabeth II.' The *coup de théâtre* works. The Queen looks at the picture of her predecessor and says to the children 'She's dressed very grandly there, isn't she? That dress is not very practical. I don't think she could have got through many doors, do you?'

When she meets a little group of autistic children several of them call out excitedly, 'Queen, Queen! Kiss! Kiss!' The Queen smiles and says, 'I'm pleased to meet you.' She does not hug them, as Diana, Princess of Wales, would have done. That is not her style. The headmaster says to me, 'It's exactly like showing an interested grandmother round the school. She is completely at ease with small children, but at the same time she reflects her generation.'

As she clambers back into the royal Rolls-Royce and the Countess of Airlie spreads a tartan rug over the monarch's knees, the Queen says, 'That was really nice, very special.'

Monday 26 November 2001

Today I could do with a royal Rolls and a tartan rug across my knees. Instead I make do with the London Underground, Northern Line. The Queen and I are making our separate ways to the Dominion Theatre, Tottenham Court Road, for the 73rd Royal Variety Performance. We meet up outside the Royal Box where I am to join the party. 'You'll enjoy the show,' I say cheerily, 'I've seen the rehearsal. It's fun.' The Queen and Prince Philip look distinctly doubtful. 'At least I know when to laugh,' I say. 'Yes,' says Prince Philip, 'but will we?'

The tone of the evening is set by the camp comedian, Julian Clary, who comes on 'in the Queen's colours', accompanied by a posse of 'stout-hearted men' – genuine Chelsea pensioners. Prince Philip squints at their medals. 'God,' he mutters, 'none of them served in the war. It comes to something when I'm older than the Chelsea Pensioners.' The Duke is eighty, the Queen is seventy-five: this is not their kind of show – but they take what they are given. As the Duchess of Grafton, Mistress of the Robes, and the Queen's longest-serving lady-in-waiting, explains to me, 'Go with the flow. That's the policy.' The first act closes with the finale of *The Full Monty*, the Broadway musical version of the hit film. The Royal Box affords a clear and uninterrupted view of the male dancers as they complete their striptease. In the Royal Box there is not a flicker of reaction from the royal couple. They have been to Papua New Guinea. They have seen it all before.

When the interval comes, Philip takes a whisky gratefully. He says to the Queen, 'Dear, do you want a gin and tonic?' (They get on together: they are allies, engaged in a mutual conspiracy that has sustained them over fifty-four years. If you press Prince Philip on the secret of the success of his marriage, he says, simply, 'The Queen has the quality of tolerance in abundance.') Her Majesty already has her drink in hand. She is positively chatty. It turns out she knows all about Tottenham Court Road tube station. She and her sister, aged thirteen and nine, were taken there on a secret 'underground adventure' by their governess, Marion Crawford, in 1939. She is surprised to hear from me that the trains are so crowded. 'I'd heard that everyone was staying at home watching television,' she says. 'People tell me the sales of take-away pizzas have rocketed.'

The bar is filling up with show-business royalty. The Queen is mingling happily. A generation ago this would not have happened. For the first twenty years of her reign, divorcees were not presented to Her Majesty. Now, here I am saying to the Queen, 'Do you know the Lloyd-Webbers?' and here is Her Majesty shaking hands with Andrew's third wife and trilling, 'Of course. It's so lovely to hear those tunes.'

I introduce Julian Clary's agent to Prince Philip. 'How are you enjoying the show?' she asks. 'How do you think I'm enjoying the show?' he replies, left eyebrow raised. 'You laughed at Jackie Mason,' I protest. The Prince shakes his head: 'I didn't understand a word he said.' 'But you laughed,' I say. 'Did I?' chunters Prince Philip, 'I'm not sure why.'

The bell goes, summoning the audience back to their seats. The Queen is applying her lipstick: she does this quite frequently. She is looking rather impish, as if someone has just told her something quite preposterous. It turns out she has been speaking to the head of ITV. 'He said there are going to be some good things on ITV in the New Year and the spring.' She can barely conceal her amusement. 'Did he name any?' asks Prince Philip. 'No,' says the Queen, suppressing a laugh, 'he just said there are going to be good things coming in the spring.'

The advantage of the Royal Box is that from it Prince Philip can read the autocue supplied for the performers (and so anticipate the next dire turn) and the Queen can see into the wings. 'It's rather fun watching them waiting to come on and wondering which gap they'll pop out of next,' she says. As we troop back in I say, 'You'll find plenty of honest vulgarity in part two.' 'Oh dear,' mutters Philip. The Queen sucks in her lower lip. They have not come to be entertained: they have come to support the Entertainment Artistes' Benevolent Fund and they are pleased (genuinely) that the evening will raise half a million pounds for a worthy cause. Sir Elton John is top of the bill tonight. He sits at the piano and sings three songs. He has his back to the Royal Box. 'I wish he'd turn the microphone to one side,' says the Queen. 'I wish he'd turn the microphone off,' says Prince Philip.

Tuesday 27 November 2001

Last night I told the Queen that Jennifer Lopez (with whom her equerry-in-waiting was rather hoping he might have his photograph taken) had reportedly come to the Royal Variety

Performance with an entourage five times the size of Her Majesty's. The Queen was amused (I think). Today the newspapers are full of pictures of two of the stars of last night's show, Cilla Black and Barbara Windsor, in basques and fishnet tights, strutting their stuff for their sovereign. Her Majesty, however, has already moved on.

It is an Investiture Day at Buckingham Palace and the court of Elizabeth II is bustling. Her Majesty's Piper (only the tenth since the tradition was established by John Brown for Queen Victoria in 1843) has been up since the wee hours. In his striking kilt of Ancient Hunting Stuart and warmed by coffee and a nip of brandy ('You need it in this weather,' he tells me) he plays his pipes beneath Her Majesty's window for fifteen minutes at 9.00 a.m. each morning. He does it with one finger missing: 'I lost it to the IRA in 1992,' he explains. He plays for Her Majesty again before dinner and, in between, he says, 'I help out around the place, escorting guests in and out, accompanying Her Majesty around the Palace.'

The equerry-in-waiting (looking very fresh and pink: his blond flop of hair is especially bouncy this morning) is a key player at investitures. He stands at Her Majesty's side while she is handing out the gongs, telling her who's who. 'The citation might say "For services to the Foreign Office",' he explains, 'but I can whisper to Her Majesty, "Spy in Afghanistan."' Does the Queen go through the list beforehand? 'Oh, yes, line by line. She's doing it now. There are just a hundred and forty-three this morning, but she'll read each citation. She marks up the list and then gives her copy to me so that, when the moment comes, I can remind her of the bits she's underlined.'

In the ballroom, Lord Luce (one-time Tory MP and Arts Minister, now Lord Chamberlain) is checking the dais. In the Picture Gallery, Colonel Sir Malcolm Ross, Comptroller of the Lord Chamberlain's Office, is giving those about to be honoured a pep talk: 'Relax. If you do, you'll enjoy it and, more important, you'll remember it. When you hear your surname, ladies, curtsy, if you will. Gentlemen, bow. When the Queen has invested you with the insignia of your award, she will shake your hand. It is a firm and positive handshake. You will not miss it. It is the indication that your time is up.'

At 11:03 a.m. the Queen, in peacock blue, sporting a dazzling diamond brooch and pearls, makes her way on to the dais and, for what one courtier reckons will be the fifty thousandth time in her life, hears the National Anthem played. Then without further ado, we're off. The Lord Chamberlain reads the citation, the equerry whispers in the royal ear, the sovereign dispenses gongs, congratulations and handshakes. Amazingly when some chap comes up to get a CBE for 'services to the New Deal in Derbyshire', Her Majesty does not have a fit of the giggles. Less surprisingly, when a lady receives an MBE for 'services to trampolining and the homeless in North-West England', the Queen rewards her with extra time. The average length of each encounter is twenty seconds.

By 12:20 p.m. it's over. The National Anthem is played once more, Her Majesty steps down from the dais and passes along the central aisle and out of the ballroom. She does this twenty times a year – she takes investitures seriously: she is particularly interested in rewarding voluntary work, believes the system uncovers unsung heroes, thinks that 'people deserve pats on the back sometimes, otherwise it's a very dingy world' – and has been doing it consistently for half a century. 'In all that time,' one of the attendant gentleman Ushers tells me, 'there's really only been one noticeable change. At the beginning of her reign, as Her Majesty passed, everyone would have bowed or curtsied. Now nobody does.'

A long day, one of the 'themed days', where the Palace (in order to maximise impact) picks a specific area of national life (farming, manufacturing, publishing) and despatches the Queen and Prince Philip on a round of related visits. Today it's been 'broadcasting' and the Queen's itinerary has included banter with Barbara Windsor on the set of *EastEnders* ('You've got more clothes on today, haven't you?' says Her Majesty, drily), trips to the studios of ITN and *Blue Peter*, and the official opening of CNN's new London bureau.

At 6:00 p.m. we're back at BP, as the inmates call it (it's never 'Buck House') for a reception for industry worthies. Her Majesty passes along the initial line-up of luminaries (Michael Parkinson, Terry Wogan, Rowan Atkinson, David Attenborough, Floella Benjamin, Greg Dyke, etc.) with barely a murmur, though Cilla Black gets, word for word, 'You've got more clothes on today, haven't you?'

As the Queen makes her progress through the throng, she appears unattended. In fact, the equerry and the Mistress of the Robes are keeping an eye on her from a discreet distance. 'I keep my eye on the ball,' says the Duchess of Grafton. 'Once you lose sight of it, you're sunk.' (Like many before me, I have fallen for the Duchess. She doesn't give her age in *Who's Who*, but she must be eighty, the archetypal game old bird, decent, devoted, of her class, of her kind, but, like her boss, both amused and amusing.) The Queen thrills two senior executives from CNN. She recalls meeting them earlier in the day. 'It's always a problem remembering who you've met,' she says to me. 'Sometimes I think it's the worst thing about this life. You meet someone and then ten minutes later you meet them again and you can't quite place them.' The Queen laughs (her smile is dazzling) and the guys from CNN, quite bowled over, tell me, 'This is a moment we'll never forget – never.'

The Queen is now extolling the virtues of the royal website (www.royal.gov.uk) and telling another group of guests how keen Andrew and Edward are on surfing the Net.

It's a jolly bash, plenty to drink, nice nibbles, an all-star cast. The chaps from British Forces Broadcasting are beaming because they know the Queen is very keen on them. Elinor Goodman (from Channel Four) and the Duke of Kent are shaking their heads sadly as they contemplate the death of hunting. An elderly broadcaster keels over behind us and hits the deck with a clatter. A footman says, 'The parquet's bloody murder here.'

As the Duke of York bounds cheerily between female newscasters and Prince Philip throws himself into group after group (invariably with a wry remark on arrival), I watch the Queen move steadily through the crowd, always friendly, never familiar. I have now spent many days in her company. Her pace never varies. Ronald Allison, once her press secretary, who is here, tells me, 'Whatever the climate, wherever she is, however hot it is, she never sweats. The rest of us could be drenched, but not the Queen. She's a phenomenon.'

Friday 7 December 2001

Another day, another outing. The Queen's routine is relentless: unending and unchanging. Flick through the cuttings file for the past fifty years and you will find her programme, week by week, barely alters from year to year.

There is a touch of novelty today, however. We're touring Wiltshire and the Queen is coming by train – not the Royal Train (average cost, £30,000 per journey) but the 9:45

a.m. Paddington–Chippenham First Great Western express (Apex awayday fare, £39.70). 'We might have come by helicopter,' explains Sir Robin Janvrin, her private secretary, 'but we weren't sure about the weather. It's all a matter of balancing cost, convenience and reliability.'

En route, Her Majesty and Sir Robin discuss the Queen's Christmas Day broadcast and the Duke of Edinburgh reads the newspaper. Today's stories include the suspended sentence (for rowdy behaviour) imposed on Prince Ernst August von Hanover (a distant kinsman of the Queen), much ballyhoo about Prince Charles's efforts to improve the public image of Mrs Parker Bowles, and page after page on the Countess of Wessex's emergency operation for an ectopic pregnancy. The tabloids (which the Queen does not see, as a rule) are urging Her Majesty to show herself at her daughter-in-law's bedside. 'Don't snub Sophie,' they plead.

The Queen has no intention of snubbing Sophie, but nor would she dream of modifying today's agreed programme for sentimental reasons. That's not her style and never has been.

Today turns out to be a marvellous day for the monarch. Wherever she goes, her subjects are ready and waiting, eager to wave and cheer her on her way. Outside the village of Calne the inhabitants of an old people's home have lined the road. An ancient lady in a wheelchair has tears in her eyes and a Union flag in her fist. At Calne's new public library even the *Guardian*-reading librarians seem pleased to see Her Majesty. (The Queen squints at a copy of a Mills & Boon classic, *A Ruthless Passion*, and purses her lips. The Duchess of Grafton tells me the boss hasn't much time for reading books: 'Those boxes,' she sighs.) At the John Bentley School there is an extraordinary turnout: 1,200 children applauding with enthusiasm. I am amazed. So is the Lord Chamberlain: 'We keep being told there's indifference. There's no evidence of that here.' It is cold and the Queen is stamping her feet to keep them warm.

By the time we reach Malmesbury Abbey, Her Majesty has unveiled three plaques, signed four visitors' books and shaken upwards of two hundred hands. 'I'm getting on,' says an old man in the crowd. 'Aren't we all?' says the Queen. 'Another year gone,' I mutter. 'Isn't it terrifying?' says the Queen.

In the Abbey there is a Service of Celebration and a moment of pause. I watch the Queen closely as she prays. She concentrates: her eyes tight shut. I imagine no one (other than someone in religious orders) goes to church more frequently than the Queen. She is Head of the Church of England in more than name.

Everywhere we go there are people and, without exception, they are cheering. In Chippenham High Street it is quite amazing: there are many *thousands* in the crowd. The Queen moves along at her steady pace, nodding, smiling, shaking hands, accepting bouquets by the score. Having been in similar circumstances, on different occasions, with Princess Diana, with David Beckham, with the Beatles in their prime, I observe a distinct difference between each of them and the Queen: the Queen does not play the crowd. She is on show (her clothes are designed to make her stand out in the crowd) but she is not 'performing' in any way, shape or form. It is gripping to behold. She is what she is and what she is is the Queen.

By 5:00 p.m. darkness has fallen and the day is done. Prince Philip says, 'Come on, dear' and the Queen gives a final wave and follows her husband into the back of the royal Jaguar.

I climb into the front of the royal people carrier. Squashed behind me are the Mistress of the Robes, the Lord Chamberlain and the Queen's private secretary. The equerry-in-waiting and the assistant press secretary bring up the rear. The day has been a triumph and they know it. 'The response was extraordinary,' says the Duchess of Grafton, contentedly, 'it bodes rather well for the Golden Jubilee.' 'At the Abbey,' asks the equerry, 'did we all know the surprise second verse of the National Anthem?' We did – and to prove it, we sing it now. Trundling towards Swindon, the Queen's courtiers are singing her song. As the Mistress of the Robes nods off, Sir Robin murmurs happily to Lord Luce, 'We had a ten-year planning meeting the other day. There's some good stuff coming up. We're going to have some fun in 2005 with the anniversary of the Battle of Trafalgar.' 'Good-o,' says the Lord Chamberlain. 'That's not for publication, Gyles,' says Sir Robin. Why not? I think the people should be told: this one will run and run. And they plan ahead.

Thursday 14 February 2002

Princess Margaret has died, aged seventy-one. The funeral is tomorrow, but today duty calls. This morning, in mourning, at BP, the Queen received the Governor of Victoria, gave audience to the new Bolivian ambassador and received the new Bishop of Lincoln 'who did homage upon his appointment'. (A survey of 1,300 Anglican clergy published today suggests that more than half of them have reservations about the Queen's role as Supreme Governor of the Church of England. They do not realise how lucky they are. The Queen is a formidable ally. The Church of England's hold on the British people is slipping inexorably, but the Church – and church-going – remain central to the Queen's life.)

This afternoon, clad in black but smiling, Her Majesty visited the Great Ormond Street Hospital for Sick Children on its 150th anniversary. On parade was Miss Gwendolyn Kirby, now in her eighties, who was matron when the Queen came to the hospital fifty years ago to mark its centenary. 'It seems like yesterday,' said Miss Kirby. 'Yes,' said the Queen. She has spent half a century visiting the same places in the same way, showing the same interest, saying the same things, sometimes to the same people. She is completely reliable, utterly consistent.

Princess Margaret was rather different. A final formal portrait of her is being issued tonight. The photograph was taken last October, in the dining room of her apartment at Kensington Palace, by candlelight to protect the Princess's eyes. It is a poignant picture: you can see she has suffered a stroke, yet she looks both handsome and dignified. She is wearing the insignia of a Lady of the Imperial Order of the Crown of India. The insignia consists of Queen Victoria's cipher, with the V for Victoria picked out in diamonds, the R for Regina in pearls, and the I for Imperatrix in turquoises. Margaret's father, George VI, gave both his daughters the insignia in 1947, just months before India achieved her independence from the British Empire. As Margaret was only seventeen at the time, the statutes of the Order had to be altered to admit somebody so young. (The Queen and her family take these orders, honours and appointments in deadly earnest. When once I asked a senior courtier why it was that the Queen's relations had so many decorations bestowed on them, he replied, without smiling, 'Her Majesty is the fount of honour, so it is hardly surprising that those closest to the fount get splashed the most.') George VI believed he was giving his daughter something precious with her appointment as a Lady of the Imperial Order of the Crown. Margaret believed it too. Tomorrow, her funeral takes place fifty years to the day after that of her father. Today, Queen Elizabeth, the Queen Mother, who is one hundred and one and had a fall on Wednesday, flew from Sandringham to Windsor for the funeral. Prince Philip, who is eighty-one himself, helped his mother-in-law up the steps into the Sikorsky helicopter. He has spent time with Queen Elizabeth every day since Princess Margaret's death last Saturday.

Monday 18 February 2002

The Queen and the Duke of Edinburgh attended Princess Margaret's funeral on Friday. Today – barely seventy-two hours later – they are in Jamaica, at the start of Her Majesty's golden jubilee tour. The funeral – a private service at St George's Chapel, Windsor, attended by four hundred mourners, followed by a cremation at Slough Crematorium attended by nobody – passed off without incident. The press coverage has been sympathetic and proportionate. The Queen Mother, in a wheelchair, managed a brave smile for the cameras. The Queen, calm and collected throughout the service, appeared to wipe away a tear as she emerged from the Chapel with her sister's two children. That, of course, is the picture that appeared on Saturday's front pages. It seems we want to see the Queen crying. She would rather we did not, but the world has changed this past half-century: a stiff upper lip is not considered the virtue it once was.

In Jamaica Her Majesty is much admired. She is an elderly English white woman, who remains true to the values of her upbringing and her class, who has paid just six visits to the Caribbean island during her reign, but opinion polls show that the majority of Jamaicans – fifty-seven percent – consider that her presence here is important. According to the Jamaican polling organisation, Stone: 'Over the years local social scientists have been confounded by the fascination that Jamaicans have for Queen Elizabeth.' In Jamaica, Her Majesty is known affectionately as 'Mrs Queen'.

The Jamaican visit has been a knock-out success. Thousands – old and young – have turned out, cheering, waving, singing, dancing, blowing kisses. So warm was the welcome in Montego Bay – where crowds in their thousands filled Sam Sharpe Square and the Queen opened a new civic centre – that an impromptu walkabout was added to the itinerary.

The only wobbly moments came at the farewell banquet at King's House, the official residence of the Governor-General, Sir Howard Cooke. The lights failed – and kept on failing. The first black-out came while the Queen was dressing for dinner. 'I was just putting on my tiara when the lights failed,' she reported to Sir Howard. The lights went out again as the royal couple were descending the steep steps into the banqueting hall. Prince Philip stumbled in the gloom, blinded by the flashes from the cameras covering the event. 'No flash, no photographs,' snapped the Queen, 'I can't see. I don't know where my table is.' Armed with a candle, her lady-in-waiting managed to lead Her Majesty to her place. Grace was said in darkness, as waiters were sent scurrying for candles and kerosene lamps and cars with headlights on full beam were driven up to the doors. An hour later, power was restored. What was the Queen's verdict on the evening? 'Memorable.'

Sunday 3 March 2002

What is going on? One day soon Australia and New Zealand will be republics. The politicians and the opinion polls suggest it will be any minute now.[6] And yet, today, more than

---

6   Twenty years on, they aren't yet.

thirty thousand people gathered in the rain to hear the Queen address Queensland's 'People's Day' fair in Brisbane. In fact, the rain stopped as Her Majesty appeared. Perhaps the people knew it would. Perhaps there is some peculiar magic going on here. Why else should crowds – in their tens of thousands – turn out to cheer a head of state who is essentially a foreigner and lives twelve thousand miles away? Carpets of petals have been thrown down for her, hundreds of individual flowers have been presented to her, everyone is smiling. Queensland – named after the Queen's great-great-grandmother, Queen Victoria, 142 years ago – is the last stop on a tour that the Palace hoped might go quite well but has turned out to be a total triumph. It is bizarre, because, despite the hoopla, on a royal visit nothing much happens. The Queen and the Duke appear, smile, wave, shake hands, accept bouquets, murmur pleasantries, and move on. The people stand and stare: many cheer, many wave flags, everybody looks happy. Perhaps that's what the royal couple provide: a focus for celebration, an excuse to cheer.

Easter Sunday, 31 March 2002

Queen Elizabeth, the Queen Mother died yesterday at 3:15 p.m. The formal announcement was not posted on the gates at Buckingham Palace until 5:45 p.m. but the news began to break mid-afternoon in the ski resort of Klosters where Prince Charles is on holiday with his sons. (The Duke of York is on holiday with his daughters, and his ex-wife, in Barbados. There are perks to the royal life.) At 5:53 p.m. BBC1 interrupted *Auntie's Bloomers* (an 'outtakes' show presented by Terry Wogan) with the news of the royal death, brought to us by Peter Sissons, dressed not in black, but in an everyday suit and sporting a burgundy-coloured tie. It seems that the BBC guidelines on these matters stipulate that a black tie and jacket are only to be worn in the event of the death of the sovereign. Sissons appeared uneasy with his role and conducted a particularly cack-handed telephone interview with Margaret Rhodes, Queen Elizabeth's niece and lady-in-waiting, who was with her when she died.

At Buckingham Palace, the response to the royal death is more sure-footed. The Palace cinema is converted into the control centre for 'Operation Tay Bridge', under the command of Lieutenant Colonel Sir Malcolm Ross, Comptroller of the Lord Chamberlain's Office. The billiard room becomes a computerised ticketing hall. The guest list for the Royal Ceremonial Funeral – scheduled for 9 April at Westminster Abbey – has been constantly updated over the years as Queen Elizabeth has outlived her friends and contemporaries. (And, yes, Mrs Parker Bowles is invited.) There will be a lying-in-state in Westminster Hall on Friday afternoon and all day on the Saturday, Sunday and Monday before the funeral.

Thursday 4 April 2002

The *Guardian* appears to have taken its tone from the BBC. 'Uncertain farewell reveals a nation divided' is the headline to Jonathan Freedland's front-page report. Inside the paper, Christopher Hitchens urges 'contained mourning' for a woman who 'symbolised reaction and philistinism'. Courtesy of ITN, Prince Charles, returned from Klosters, gives a huskily spoken, deeply felt and endearingly personal tribute to his 'magical grandmother'. Prince Andrew, back from Barbados, comes up with the idea that Queen Elizabeth's four grandsons should stand vigil during the lying-in-state, echoing the tribute paid to George V by his four sons in 1936. At Windsor, Prince Philip narrows his eyes and shakes his head at reports of Prince Charles's public displays of grief. Whenever the Prince of Wales is photographed he looks ashen, utterly bereft and close to tears. The Queen, by contrast, smiles when she makes her first public appearance, thanks well-wishers for their thoughtfulness and condolences, and says (because it's true), 'My mother had a wonderful life.'

This morning, in Windsor Great Park, the Queen, seventy-five, went riding and I called at Garden House to have coffee with the Hon. Margaret Rhodes, seventy-six, whose mother was the Queen Mother's sister and who has been a friend of the Queen since they were both little girls. In a grey top and black skirt, trim and upright, Benson & Hedges to hand, Mrs Rhodes sits at a kitchen table littered with letters of condolence, bills, invitations and old newspapers. 'The Queen will be wonderful at the funeral,' she tells me. 'She always is. I'm a frightful old crier. I only have to hear "God Save the Queen" and I start to cry. I'm going to be in an awful state.'

As I clamber past the ironing board to make myself another mug of coffee at the Aga and Mrs Rhodes goes in search of another packet of cigarettes, she tells me how her father, as Captain General of the Royal Company of Archers, marched behind the coffin at the funeral of King George V in 1936. 'There was a dreadful wind and my father thought the long eagles' feathers in his cap were going to blow away. He lifted his arms to hang on to the feathers and his braces snapped. He had to walk four and a half miles in the funeral procession desperately holding his trousers up with his elbows.'

I laugh. 'That's the kind of story Queen Elizabeth loved,' she says. 'If something could go wrong on some fairly formal occasion, it made the day. She and Prince Charles shared this wonderful sense of the ridiculous and could go into hysterical laughs. She got wonderful giggles. And, of course, she had impeccable manners. For instance, every Sunday, after the Queen has attended the service here, in the little chapel in the park, she would pop in to have a drink with her mother. When it was time to go, Queen Elizabeth, however frail she was, would always accompany her daughter to the door to see her off. She'd never say goodbye in the drawing room and let her go alone. She was properly brought up. Duty was the guiding light in her life.'

Mrs Rhodes tells me about the day the Queen Mother died without my prompting her. 'It was very simple. I went in as usual. She was weaker. The doctors were called. It was clear she was going to die. The Queen was out riding. She was called. She came at once. In the morning I rang up our local clergyman, from the chapel here in the park. He's one of the canons from St George's Chapel. He's very nice. He came before she died and said some prayers and signed the cross on her forehead. It was wonderfully peaceful because Queen Elizabeth became unconscious. It was just rather agonising waiting. The Queen went away to get out of her riding clothes. She came back. There were two doctors. Also there were Sarah Chatto and David Linley (Princess Margaret's children). Sarah is a super girl and Queen Elizabeth simply adored David. The moment of death was peaceful. She just slipped away. There is an element of relief, isn't there? One is glad for them. It's over. It was lovely that the Queen was there at the end. Death is not horrific. It's very reassuring that. It's something you'll never forget.'

Sunday 7 April 2002

Two thousand bouquets are counted on the lawn of St George's Chapel, Windsor. At Westminster, the queue for the lying-in-state stretches for more than three miles: the doors of Westminster Hall are left open through the night. The people in the line are young and old, black and white. On my way to Westminster I happen to meet Alan Titchmarsh, gardener and television presenter (and, incidentally, currently the most popular waxwork at Madame Tussaud's), who says, 'The BBC got it completely wrong. People care about the royal family. People loved and respected the Queen Mother, just as they love and respect the Queen.' In the evening, I have supper with two actors: Eileen Atkins and Neil Stacey. Eileen is playing Queen Mary in a film about the Queen Mother when she was a young Duchess of York. She says that the film is making the Yorks 'too sympathetic' and the Windsors (the abdicating Edward VIII and Mrs Simpson) 'too evil'. Neil Stacey interrupts her and says, with passion: 'Sympathetic or evil, good or bad, it's irrelevant. That's not what it's about. The royals *are* England. They are what make me British. They are our soul.' (I believe that is how they see it at Buckingham Palace, too. 'The Queen represents the country's soul' is a line I have heard Robin Janvrin use.)

Friday 12 April 2002

On the day of the funeral, one million people lined the route, and, around the world, an estimated one billion watched the event on TV. In the *Guardian* Jonathan Freedland admits he misread the public mood. 'These are days for republicans to walk humbly,' he writes. At the Palace, as Operation Tay Bridge disbands, the Lord Chamberlain's men are careful to avoid triumphalism. 'Quiet satisfaction,' is the order of the day.

Thursday 30 April 2002

Three weeks later and Her Majesty is back at Westminster Hall, no longer in black, no longer mourning, but now celebrating her Golden Jubilee in dazzling peacock blue. She is here to address the joint Houses of Parliament. She is not a natural orator. She reads her speech with clarity, but without expression. Michael Martin, Speaker of the House of Commons, responds. 'Parliament salutes its sovereign,' he says. 'May God save Your Majesty and give you His blessing for many years to come.' David Dimbleby, commentating on the occasion for the BBC, supplies the broadcasters' response. As the Queen and the Duke of Edinburgh enter William Rufus's magnificent hammer-beamed hall, and the Band of the Grenadier Guards play Holst's Second Suite in F, Dimbleby gives his troops their starter's orders. 'Remember,' he chuckles, 'no arse-licking.'

Wednesday 22 May 2002

Tonight, at Burlington House in Piccadilly, I stood next to the Queen as she made the smallest of small talk with assorted luminaries from the world of the arts. David Hockney, J. K. Rowling, Simon Rattle, Victoria Wood beamed and purred as Her Majesty smiled at them and said little more than 'How do you do?' The beautiful ballerina Darcey Bussell and three actresses, Joanna Lumley, Penelope Keith and Patricia Hodge, stood in a semi-circle around the diminutive monarch, towering over her, grinning happily. The content of their conversation was desultory, but nobody seemed to mind. The Queen recognised only a smattering of the famous faces that surrounded her. Dame Vera Lynn and Dame Edna Everage were two she knew. Introduced to the Simply Red singer Mick Hucknall for the second time, she asked him, for the second time, 'What do you do?' He took it in his stride. 'She meets a lot of people,' he said, adding, as Prince Philip, scowling, wandered past, 'I've presented the Duke of Edinburgh Awards for two years now and the old fellow still doesn't have a clue who I am.'

The Duke was looking particularly grumpy tonight. Asked which bit of the jubilee celebrations he was most looking forward to, he answered, 'August' – when it will all be over. It's been a long haul, but there have been occasional days off. At the weekend, the Duke took part in the Royal Windsor Horse Show, winning the dressage heat in the carriage-driving competition. The Queen, headscarf on, camera in hand, watched him, with rapt attention and real excitement. As he put his horses through their paces, she bit her lip with anxiety and, when he came through victorious, she laughed and cheered and clapped. She revealed an energy and sense of enthusiasm she never displays when going about her official duties. Clearly, she still loves her man. Watching her at Windsor last Friday, I would say she adores him. She stood in the stand alongside Lord and Lady Romsey. Penny Romsey, forty-eight, is Philip's regular carriage driving companion – and rather more than that, if the rumour-mongers are to be believed. I wonder.

Tuesday 4 June 2002

In her speech at Guildhall today, the Queen paid a touching tribute to her family. 'The Duke of Edinburgh has made an invaluable contribution to my life over these past fifty years,' she said. 'We both of us have a special place in our hearts for our children. I want to express my admiration for the Prince of Wales and for all he has achieved for this country. Our children, and all my family, have given me such love and unstinting help over the years and especially in recent months.' Earlier, at St Paul's Cathedral, the Archbishop of Canterbury quoted a line from Elizabeth I's famous 'Golden Speech': 'Though God hath raised me high, I count the glory of my Crown that I have reigned with your loves.' He told Elizabeth II that she, too, reigns 'with our loves'. The streets of London have been filled with *millions* of happy, cheering, chanting people. They sang 'God Save the Queen' and 'Rule, Britannia!' again and again. And again. The Queen said she was 'overwhelmed'. The Duke conceded it was 'pretty amazing'. Shabaka Thompson, director of the Notting Hill Carnival and something of an expert on street parties, said, 'It is love, man, pure love.'

Forty-nine years ago, on Tuesday 2 June 1953, millions turned out to cheer the Queen on her Coronation Day. I am reading Ben Pimlott's fine biography of the Queen[7] and he asks, of those crowds then, 'What were they cheering? A twenty-seven-year-old woman who had no chance in her life to do anything except make polite conversation and launch ships? The Monarchy? The nation, the Commonwealth, the system of Government – or themselves?' Pimlott also quotes the then Archbishop of Canterbury, Geoffrey Fisher, who argued at the time that diminution of the temporal power of the monarchy in the twentieth century, far from reducing the institution's importance, had enhanced it – giving the sovereign 'the possibility of a spiritual power far more exalted and far more searching in its demands: the power to lead, to inspire, to unite, by the sovereign's personal character, personal convictions, personal example'. Such power might be

---

7   *The Queen: Elizabeth II and the Monarchy*, Golden Jubilee Edition, 2001.

inoperable in the wrong hands. Fortunately, said Fisher, the Queen was well equipped, through upbringing and Christian faith, to uphold 'the pillars of true society', whose goals included 'domestic fidelity' and 'united homes'.

For the Queen today's service was the most significant of all the jubilee celebrations. The Queen is quite clear about the centrality of Christianity to her life. She says, uncompromisingly, 'The teachings of Christ and my own personal accountability before God provide a framework in which I try to live my life.'

Tuesday 9 July 2002

Today I went to Buckingham Palace for a lovely event, the brainchild of Andrew Motion, the Poet Laureate. Children in schools throughout the United Kingdom were asked to write poems inspired by the Queen's Golden Jubilee. Andrew selected what he judged to be the best of them and the authors of the winning poems – and their families – were invited to the Palace to meet the Queen and receive a medal and a royal handshake. James Duckworth-Chad, equerry-in-waiting, introduced the proceedings, explained what was going to happen, and suggested that the presentations be made without applause. Needless to say, as each presentation was made, the Duke of Edinburgh led the applause! As the Queen handed out the medals, bending forward and talking quietly to each child in turn, I looked around and saw that almost every adult in the room had tears in their eyes. Afterwards I said to Philippa de Pass, the Queen's lady-in-waiting, 'It was rather moving, wasn't it?' She said, 'It's all been rather moving. I've spent most of the jubilee in floods of tears. We all have.' I know Prince Philip occasionally reads poetry. His personal library contains more than two hundred volumes of verse. I asked Philippa de Pass if the Queen ever read a poem. 'I don't really know what the Queen reads,' she said. 'Apparently, Queen Mary expected her ladies-in-waiting to read to her. Fortunately, the boss does not require us to read to her. Of course, she has had thousands of letters sent to her during the jubilee, lots with poems in them. She reads those.'

Andrew Motion had not met the Duke of Edinburgh before. 'I think he'll surprise you,' I said. 'He reads poetry.' 'The Queen has already surprised me,' said Andrew. 'She's really interested. She really cares.' We stood by the Palace window and watched as the Queen and the Duke, together, in step and side by side, nodding and smiling, went on their way. 'What makes them tick, I wonder?' mused Andrew, brow furrowed. 'I'm thinking of writing a book about them,' I said. 'Goodness,' said Andrew, suddenly laughing. 'I find writing a short poem about them difficult enough. A whole book? Good luck.'

EPILOGUE

September 2022

Wednesday 14 September 2022

She was alive a week ago. Last night, I stood in the drizzle outside Buckingham Palace and watched as the royal hearse brought her body back to the London headquarters of the Family Firm for the last time. Her oak coffin was draped in the Royal Standard and topped with white flowers. The interior of the hearse was a blaze of light. It was almost shocking how brightly lit it was. Even in death, she was on show. As she passed through the Palace gates, I took a photograph on my iPhone; the police officers bowed their heads in unison; the crowd applauded to make their feelings heard. Inside the quadrangle, a guard of honour from the 1st Battalion Coldstream Guards gave the royal salute as the hearse came to a halt. At the steps of the Grand Entrance the new King and the Queen Consort were waiting.

When I watched Charles arriving earlier – the inside of his car lit up, too – he was sitting with his hands on his knees, staring blankly, bleakly ahead, puffy-eyed, visibly bereft. Camilla, seated on his right, was looking out of the car window and gently waving.

I was watching with one of Charles's godchildren, India Hicks – we were standing opposite the Victoria memorial, sheltering under the same umbrella. 'You've got to keep waving,' she said. 'You must keep waving. My mother taught me that.' Her mother is Pamela Hicks, who, as Pamela Mountbatten, was with the Queen in Kenya on 6 February 1952 when George VI died. 'You know, the Queen was so calm when she heard the news. She simply said, "I am so sorry, this means we all have to go home." She was extraordinary. She was always thinking of other people.'

I said to India how strange it was that this naturally private person – inherently quite reticent and shy – had, by accident of fate, been obliged to live her life in public, on constant show. 'Even now,' I said, 'when she is dead.' 'On constant show,' repeated India – and then she told me a hilarious story about the time her mother had been accompanying the Queen on her post-Coronation Commonwealth tour. They were in Tonga, in the South Pacific, and it was late at night, and Pamela bumped into the Queen when they were both stumbling around the Governor's house, or whatever it was, looking for the bathroom. When they found it, they turned on the light – only to discover that on the other side of the bathroom a second door was wide open and looking out onto the garden where 400 men were sitting by their campfires staring at them. The next morning was a Sunday and the royal party had been hoping for a lie-in. Instead, the Queen and Prince Philip were woken at dawn by four men at their bedroom door blowing nose flutes in their honour.

One day, I hope, we will be able to read the Queen's own account of that trip to Tonga. She kept a diary. She wrote it up every night, in pencil, sitting up in bed after she had said her prayers. The pencil usually had a rubber attached so she could erase anything if she had second thoughts.

Last night at Westminster Hall I watched as the Queen's four children stood in silence, heads bowed, keeping their vigil at the four sides of their mother's coffin. Strange to witness this private grieving in a public place. As they stood there, totally still, members of the public continued to file past – silently, steadily, some stopping briefly to salute or bow or curtsy, some genuflecting or making a sign of the cross. David Beckham wiped away a tear as he paid his respects to the Queen after queueing for more than twelve hours. When he reached the coffin, the footballer slowly bowed his head and stared at the ground. He told a reporter afterwards that the atmosphere in the queue had been 'really friendly, really lovely'. That seems to be the general verdict.

I was watching with Valerie Amos – Baroness Amos, Labour peer and the first Black member of the Order of the Garter since its foundation in the 1340s. She was only installed a matter of months ago, on 13 June. The Queen was not well enough to walk in the traditional Garter Day procession, but she helped Lady Amos into her robes. 'Lord Butler was trying to help, but the Queen said, "I'm not sure he knows what he's doing" and came to the rescue. She was extraordinary.'

She was extraordinary. And her position was extraordinary, too – bizarre, if you stop to think about. Being a queen, wearing a crown, sitting on a throne, having people address you as 'Your Majesty' – how weird is that in 2022? Especially for your children and grandchildren. I have talked with several of her grandchildren and they were all conscious of her being as much their Queen as their grandmother.

Tonight, it is their turn to stand vigil in Westminster Hall. Earlier Prince William, the new Prince of Wales, told someone in the crowd that walking behind the Queen's coffin had taken him back to 1997 when, aged fifteen, he had walked behind his mother's coffin at her funeral. When someone else in the crowd told him she was close to tears, he said: 'Please don't cry – you'll get me started.'

Monday 19 September 2022

The world has come to London to honour the Queen. Heads of state, presidents, prime ministers, princes – more than 250 of them in all. I had to leave home at 5:00 a.m. to get to Westminster Abbey, walking the last mile on foot, because the police closed all the surrounding streets an hour earlier than planned at the behest of the American security people. While the kings and queens of Jordan and Sweden and Denmark, the prime ministers of Australia and Canada and the president of France, all arrived at the Abbey by bus – ferried in on what was dubbed 'the royal park-and-ride service' – President Biden and his wife were given special dispensation to drive up to the Abbey door in the presidential limousine: the $1.3 million Cadillac nicknamed 'the Beast'. Once inside the Abbey, the 46th US President had to make do with an aisle seat in the fourteenth row of the south transept. Organising the seating plan had been 'a complete nightmare', according to my mole in the Foreign Office. It was not just a matter of giving precedence to the fifty-six countries of the Commonwealth, there were tricky issues when it came to seating the President of Israel, Isaac Herzog, and the Palestinian prime minister, Mohammad Shtayyeh, to say nothing of the current King of Spain, Felipe VI, and the ex-King, his father, Juan Carlos, who had flown in unexpectedly from his self-imposed exile in Abu Dhabi. Apparently, father and son are not on speaking terms. (This can happen.) On the plus side, it was considered a diplomatic coup that the Emperor of Japan was there. Emperor Naruhito and Empress Masako had not been outside their own country for three years and their presence was not expected because the Japanese imperial family traditionally avoids funerals on account of a cultural belief, rooted in Shintoism, about the impurity of death. For Elizabeth II, they came.

There were around two thousand guests in all. The service itself was magnificent – moving – and traditional. It reflected the Queen's Anglicanism to the full, though, of course, the Churches of Wales and Scotland and Northern Ireland were there as well. And in procession, too, came representatives of other faiths, from Baháí to Buddhist, from Sikh to Hindu, from a Muslim scholar to the Chief Rabbi. The music before the service was all English (almost): Orlando Gibbons, Ralph Vaughan Williams, Peter Maxwell Davies, Herbert Howells, Malcolm Williamson (Australian), and Elgar, Elgar, Elgar. (I am guessing it was chosen by the new King rather than the late Queen – and, of course, selected when this service was first planned, several years ago.) The hymns were some of Her late Majesty's favourites: 'The day thou gavest, Lord, is ended'; 'The Lord's my shepherd, I'll not want' (she had that at her wedding); 'Love divine, all loves excelling'; and, after the Last Post and the Reveille, two verses of the National Anthem, opening with an unfamiliar line: 'God save our gracious King'.

I am the resurrection and the life, saith the Lord: he that believeth in me, though he were dead, yet shall he live: and whosoever liveth and believeth in me shall never die.

The liturgy for the service was taken from the Book of Common Prayer, and the Lessons, reflecting the Queen's core beliefs, came from the New Testament: 1 Corinthians ('Now is Christ risen from the dead') and John 14 ('Let not your heart be troubled'). It was a service with which either her father or her grandfather would have been comfortably familiar, though they would have been startled to find each of the Lessons being read by a woman: one Black, one white, one Baroness Scotland KC, Secretary-General of the Commonwealth, the other Elizabeth Truss MP, Prime Minister of the United Kingdom.

George VI's funeral took place in St George's Chapel at Windsor Castle in 1952 and film and television cameras were not admitted. Elizabeth II's funeral was watched by a worldwide television audience estimated at four billion. It was beautifully done, and the pageantry that went with it – involving more than four thousand service personnel – was impressive in the way that our pageantry always is. For me, though, perhaps more moving than the Abbey funeral was the smaller Committal Service at St George's Chapel at Windsor in the afternoon. There was more fine music (including Bach this time, and the lone female composer of the day, Dame Ethel Smyth), psalms and hymns, a motet and 'The Russian Contakion of the Departed' (Prince Philip's idea?), readings and responses, and The Lord's Prayer. 'Sometimes,' I remember the Queen saying, 'the Lord's Prayer is all you need.'

The congregation at Windsor was smaller (800 in all) and more personal to Her Majesty. The Officers of Arms were on parade – Portcullis Pursuivant, Bluemantle Pursuivant, Rouge Dragon Pursuivant, Maltravers Herald Extraordinary, Clarenceaux King of Arms, and the rest – but behind them came the members of her Household: the Master of the Horse, the Keeper of the Privy Purse and more, with, bringing up the rear, the ones who really counted, the Queen's Pages and the Palace Steward.

At the end of the service, before the Queen's coffin was lowered into its final resting place in the memorial chapel in the Royal Vault below, the Instruments of State – the Imperial State Crown and the Orb and Sceptre – were removed from the top of her coffin by the Queen's Bargemaster and a Serjeant of Arms and received by the Dean of Windsor who placed them on the High Altar. Then, at the close of the final hymn, the King placed 'The Queen's Company Camp Colour' – the banner of the Queen's Company of the Grenadier Guards, carefully folded – at the foot of her coffin and the Lord Chamberlain broke his Wand – his Staff of Office – and laid it in two pieces on the coffin alongside the King's wreath of flowers – taken from the gardens at Buckingham Palace, Clarence House and Highgrove House – which bore a handwritten card that simply read: 'In loving and devoted memory. Charles R.'

The recessional voluntary was Bach's Prelude and Fugue in C minor. The new King, who will be seventy-four in November, has been a long-standing and active patron of the Bach Choir. In 1952, at the committal of George VI, after the twenty-five-year-old Elizabeth II had placed the King's Colour of the Grenadier Guards on his coffin at the end of the service, the recessional voluntary was Hubert Parry's prelude to 'Ye boundless realms of joy', which the young Queen particularly requested so that the service would end on a hopeful rather than a mournful note.

She was a committed optimist. 'My father expressed undiminished hope and trust in the future,' she said in her last broadcast, only four months ago. And only a matter of weeks ago, on the eve of her Platinum Jubilee celebrations, she wrote, 'I continue to be inspired by the goodwill shown to me, and hope that the coming days will provide an opportunity to reflect on all that has been achieved during the last seventy years, as we look to the future with confidence and enthusiasm.'

It is exactly two weeks since I sat in the Royal Library at Windsor Castle leafing through the little book of psalms that belonged to Elizabeth I and wondering if and how, in painting my small portrait of Elizabeth II, I could reach beyond what Elizabeth I called 'the outward shadow of the body' to reveal her 'inward mind'.

Elizabeth I died on 24 March 1603 at the age of sixty-nine after a reign of forty-five years. The cause of her death remains unknown. Some speculate that she may have died of blood poisoning, brought on by her use of a lead-based make-up known as 'Venetian Ceruse'. Others suggest it could have been pneumonia, or a bacterial infection, or cancer. No one knows.

Elizabeth II died on 8 September 2022 at the age of ninety-six after a reign of seventy years. I had heard that she had a form of myeloma – bone marrow cancer – which would explain her tiredness and weight loss and those 'mobility issues' we were often told about during the last year or so of her life. The most common symptom of myeloma is bone pain, especially in the pelvis and lower back, and multiple myeloma is a disease that often affects the elderly. Currently, there is no known cure, but treatment – including medicines to help regulate the immune system and drugs that help prevent the weakening of the bones – can reduce the severity of its symptoms and extend the patient's survival by months or two to three years. Was the Queen given steroids to help get her through that important final day of duty two weeks ago? Was that bruise on the back of her hand that we saw in the photographs of her with Liz Truss the mark left by an intravenous cannula – or simply the kind of accidental bruise that comes with old age? I do not know. All I do know is that

'Cause of death' on her death certificate will be given simply as 'Old age' – as it was for the Duke of Edinburgh last year. 'Old age' is a quite commonly listed cause of death when a patient is over eighty and their doctor has cared for them over time and seen their gradual decline.

Prince Philip endured a variety of health problems in his last ten years. It irritated him when his health became 'the story'. By dying as she did, when she did, where she did, the Queen managed to avoid months of speculation about her health (and the future of the Crown) and ensured a sudden, seamless succession. Dying in Scotland was politically astute, too, given her lifelong commitment to the Union. Even at the end, she seemed to get everything right.

The Right Reverend Dr Iain Greenshields, a Kirk minister and moderator of the General Assembly of the Church of Scotland, stayed with the Queen at Balmoral the weekend before she died. He was giving the sermon at Braemar and Crathie Parish Church on the Sunday morning and had dinner with Her Majesty on Saturday evening and lunch with her on Sunday afternoon. He found her in 'fantastic form'. They talked about her childhood and her horses – and church affairs (she was 'well up to speed') and her sadness at what was happening in Ukraine. 'She was so alive and so engaging, and this was only days before she died. Her faith was everything to her. She told me she had no regrets.'

'And now abideth faith, hope, charity, these three; but the greatest of these is charity.' They have a King James Bible in the Royal Library at Windsor – one that belonged to King James himself, of course. One of the more modern treasures the royal librarians had brought out for me to see on my visit a fortnight ago was the manuscript of a poem that the Poet Laureate, Ted Hughes, had presented personally to Elizabeth

II on the fortieth anniversary of her accession, on 6 February 1992. Hughes had become a friend of Queen Elizabeth, the Queen Mother (they went fishing together in Scotland), and Elizabeth II – though admitting to not fully understanding Hughes' poem – very much liked and respected him. Towards the end of his life, in 1998, when he was only sixty-eight but seriously ill with cancer, he was awarded the Order of Merit and went to Buckingham Palace to receive it from the Queen. 'The conversation that ensued seemed for the most part a strange monologue from Ted,' recalled his wife, Carol, who went with him. 'The monologue allowed little space for the Queen to participate or respond, but she listened intently and courteously throughout. Her sensitivity to his situation was very apparent, and for that I will be forever grateful. Ted died twelve days later.'

Faith, hope, charity – belief, optimism, love – they were central to Elizabeth II's life. What formed her inward mind? In the main, I believe, the lessons she learnt from her parents and her grandparents (on both sides of the family) – from the good example of her father, George VI, from the poor example of her uncle, Edward VIII, and, from a very early age, from the companionship of her dogs and her horses and her observation and instinctive understanding of their natures.

I sang the beginnings of a duet with the Queen once. It was a fragment of a song from the 1950s musical, *Salad Days*:

If I start looking behind me and begin retracing my track,
I'll remind you to remind me we said we wouldn't look back.

And if you should happen to find me with an outlook dreary and black,
I'll remind you to remind me we said we wouldn't look back.

In fact, towards the end of her life, the Queen did not mind looking back.

'To look back is not necessarily to be nostalgic,' she said. 'Winston Churchill, my first prime minister, said that the further backward you look the further forward you can see.'

She took time to look back in a personal way earlier this year, sitting looking at reels of old 'home movies' that she and her parents had shot over the years. 'Like many families my parents wanted to keep a record of our precious moments together,' she explained. 'Cameras have always been a part of our lives. I think there's a difference to watching a home movie when you know who it is on the other side of the lens holding the camera. It adds to the sense of intimacy.' Her public life was filmed by strangers constantly. 'Private photos show the fun behind the formality,' she said. She hoped that her grandchildren's generation might find the home movies interesting – 'and perhaps be surprised that you, too, were young once.'

She recorded the commentary to go with the home movies on 19 May 2022, just a month after her ninety-sixth birthday. Was she aware it might be her last broadcast? I know she thought carefully about what she wanted to say, and I think that what she said shines an even clearer light onto the workings of her inward mind.

'One of the joys of living a long life,' she said, 'is watching one's children, then grandchildren. We can't be certain what lies ahead for them, but we should know enough to put them on the right path. We can do this if we have the good sense to learn from the experience of those who have gone before us.'

She learnt from her grandfather, George V, 'Grandpa England', and his unshakeable 'faith in the future'. She learnt from her own parents. She recalled her mother's 'infectious zest for living' and her 'extraordinary capacity to bring happiness into other people's lives'. She recalled her father and his service in the Royal Navy during the First World War: 'He was a midshipman in HMS *Collingwood* at the Battle of Jutland in 1917. The British Fleet lost fourteen ships and 6,000 men in that engagement. He wrote in a letter, "How and why we were not hit, beats me."' She recalled her father's courage then and his leadership and fortitude during and after the Second World War: 'He was the living symbol of our steadfastness.'

George VI had only just turned fifty-six when he died. Elizabeth came to the throne aged twenty-five. 'In a way I didn't have an apprenticeship, my father died far too young. It was all a very sudden taking on and making the best job you can.' But she accepted what she came to call her 'fate', just as she accepted all that life threw at her.

At ninety-six, she acknowledged 'the years have slipped by so quickly.' She said, 'There is no point in regretting the passage of time,' and talked instead about the benefits of taking 'the long view': 'Some cultures believe that a long life brings wisdom. I'd like to think so. Perhaps part of that wisdom is to recognise some of life's baffling paradoxes, such as the way human beings have a huge propensity for good and yet a capacity for evil.'

She said: 'I have lived long enough to know that things never remain quite the same for very long.' Change is inevitable. 'No one can make history stand still. Events change with startling speed.' But – and this was important: 'In my experience the positive value of a happy family is one of the factors of human existence that has not changed . . . Faith, family and friendship have not only been a constant for me, but a source of personal comfort and reassurance.'

It is clear: it always comes back to her three fundamental values:

FAITH

'I rely on my own faith to guide me through the good times and the bad.

'Each day is a new beginning. I know that the only way to live my life is to try to do what is right, to take the long view, to give of my best in all that the day brings, to put my trust in God.'

HOPE

'There is a traditional proverb that says, "He who has health has hope and he who has hope has everything."'

LOVE

'People matter and it is our relationship with one another that is most important.'

Monday 26 September 2022

Thinking about my book, with me banging on about faith, hope and charity, service, duty and kindness – is it all getting a bit po-faced? One of the reasons I wanted to write this book was to show what fun she was, how funny she could be. It wasn't just her fondness for practical jokes and those spot-on impressions she did (from the light entertainment stars of the 1940s to an alarmingly accurate vocal recreation of Concorde coming in to land over Windsor Castle), it was her wry, dry, humorous way of looking at things.

I write for the *Oldie* magazine and chair 'The Oldie of the Year Awards' where we honour people of a certain age who still have what might be described as 'snap in their celery'. In the past Queen Elizabeth, the Queen Mother and HRH The Duke of Edinburgh both accepted the award, so last year, post the pandemic lockdown, I wrote to the Queen's private secretary to ask whether Her Majesty might consider accepting the Oldie of the Year Award. A witty reply was sent to me from Balmoral Castle on 21 August 2021:

> *Her Majesty believes you are only as old as you feel. As such The Queen does not believe she meets the relevant criteria to be able to accept and hopes you will find a more worthy recipient. This message comes to you with Her Majesty's warmest best wishes.*

We had the judges' lunch today to choose this year's Oldie of the Year. Someone (me) suggested honouring all the Queen's living ladies-in-waiting with a group award. Someone else suggested honouring Terry Pendry, the Queen's groom, but, looking him up, we found that he is only seventy-two, which feels a bit young for an Oldie award. Eventually, unanimously, we settled on Paddington Bear as our Oldie of the Year. Michael Bond found the original Paddington in a shop near Paddington Station on Christmas Eve in 1956, but the bear meets our age requirement because Paddington, like the Queen (who had her actual birthday on 21 April followed by an official one in June), has two birthdays every year, one on 25 June and the second on 25 December, which makes him twice the age you think he is.

The Queen was born in the same year as Michael Bond, 1926. Sir David Attenborough OM was born in that year, too. For the service of thanksgiving at St Paul's Cathedral to mark the Queen's ninetieth birthday, Michael Bond wrote a short piece celebrating their shared vintage and Sir David read it to the congregation. The Queen was pleased – and amused.

1926, of course, was also the year when Winnie the Pooh made his first appearance. The Queen was very fond of Pooh and Paddington, as we know. She also, she told me, had a soft spot for Rupert Bear. She remembered reading the Rupert annuals when she was a girl. She said that Prince Charles loved Rupert, too. I told her that Rupert aficionados claim that Rupert isn't a bear at all: he is a boy with a bear's head. 'That can't be right,' she said. 'Surely not.' 'Well,' I said, 'if you look at the pictures, you'll see he's got fingers on his hands and very human-looking feet.' 'I'm sorry you told me that,' she said. 'Some things are best left unknown, don't you think?'

Thursday 29 September 2022

The Queen's death certificate has just been published, confirming that she died at Balmoral Castle, Ballater, Aberdeenshire, AB35 5TB, on 8 September 2022 at 3:10 p.m. Forenames: Elizabeth Alexandra Mary. Surname: Windsor. Occupation: Her Majesty The Queen. Cause of death: Old age.

The death was registered by her daughter, Princess Anne, the Princess Royal, and the death itself was certified by Dr Douglas James Allan Glass, a local GP and official apothecary to the Queen who had been looking after her in Scotland for more than thirty years and who was with her when she died. Dr Glass said: 'We have been concerned about the Queen's health for several months. It was expected and we were quite aware of what was going to happen.'

This morning, outside Clarence House, I bumped into Peter Rosslyn (also known as Peter St Clair-Erskine, 7th Earl of Rosslyn, CVO, QPM, sixty-four, former police officer, and, since 2014, Master of the Household here). He is a lovely man, tall, handsome, intelligent, good-humoured, calm. I told him how well the transition is going. He knows that, of course. He gave his impish smile. 'Early days,' he said. I wonder what will happen to his counterpart, the late Queen's Master of the Household, Vice-Admiral Sir Tony Johnstone-Burt, also sixty-four, also a lovely man, not so tall but more obviously extrovert than Peter, and a good companion to the Queen, making her laugh when they shared their lockdown 'bubble' and he was her *Line of Duty* 'explainer'. I think the new King will stay on at Clarence House for as long as possible, eating and sleeping here, and using Buckingham Palace as his workplace. (That's what Prince Philip hoped could happen when Elizabeth II became Queen in 1952.) I noticed the Royal Standard flying above both buildings simultaneously this week, so that must be the plan. There will be many changes in the months ahead. As the Queen observed: 'things never remain quite the same for very long.'

I went into York House, part of St James's Palace, to see HRH The Duke of Kent, eighty-seven next month, now the oldest surviving grandchild of George V and Queen Mary, one of the last living links with the people who made the Queen who she was. His father, the Queen's uncle, 'poor Uncle George', who was killed in that air accident in 1942, lived at York House for a while, sharing it briefly with his older brother, Prince Edward, when he was Prince of Wales. The dark Chinese wallpaper from their day still hangs on the wall.

The Duke of Kent is another good man: tall, undeniably old, a bit unsteady on his feet, alarmingly thin, thoroughly decent, devoted to the Queen's memory and endearingly modest about his years of unsung service as an ever-dutiful second-rank royal. Because his father died when he was just a boy, he has been Duke of Kent for more than eighty years. As a child, because of his title he was bullied mercilessly at school. He loved his twenty-one years in the army and still walks and salutes like a soldier. He stood alone with the Queen on the Buckingham Palace balcony to take the salute after this year's Trooping the Colour. And ten days ago, he marched in procession behind her coffin as he had marched behind her father's coffin in 1952 – the only person to have walked in two sovereigns' state funerals seventy years apart.

He told me he was feeling the Queen's death very much. He had gone to Westminster Hall to watch the new King and his siblings during their vigil around the Queen's coffin. 'It didn't really get to me until then,' he said. 'Watching the lying-in-state – I found it quite overwhelming.'

I told him about my book and asked him for his happiest, most vivid recollection of the Queen. He didn't hesitate. 'She was just the best company,' he said, now smiling. 'So easy, so relaxed, so much fun. When you were alone with her, when she was just being herself, she was simply the best company in the world.'

I walked from York House, around St James's Palace, down Marlborough Road, past the statues of George VI and Queen Elizabeth on the Mall, and on into Trafalgar Square. Thirty years ago, when I was an MP and Parliamentary Private Secretary to the Secretary of State for National Heritage, the department was based in Trafalgar Square and every day, walking in to work, I passed the empty fourth plinth in the north-west corner of the square. One day I asked the Permanent Secretary at the department if he knew why it was empty. He did. It was originally intended to hold an equestrian statue of William IV, but remained bare due to lack of funds. 'We must do something about that,' I said and proposed (only half-joking) a statue of a group of characters created by British children's authors – including Rupert, Winnie the Pooh and Paddington Bear. That idea was summarily dismissed. 'It's Trafalgar Square,' said the

Permanent Secretary, reasonably enough, 'the statue should have a martial theme.' I said blithely, 'How about Margaret Thatcher in her tank in the Falklands?' That is when he mentioned that there had been talk of earmarking the plinth as a place for a future statue of the Queen, in her Grenadier Guards uniform riding her horse, Burmese. Two such statues have since been unveiled: one in Saskatchewan in 2005, the other at the Royal Military College, Sandhurst, this year. We then set in motion the rolling programme of changing modern works of art that adorn the fourth plinth to this day. The current Mayor of London, Sadiq Khan, does not feel Trafalgar Square is the right place for a statue of Her Majesty.

I walked on, down Whitehall, past the Banqueting House, where a scaffold was erected in 1649 for the execution of King Charles I, past the gates of Downing Street, past the Cenotaph, where last year the Duke of Kent had stood on the Foreign Office balcony on Remembrance Sunday in place of the Queen. As I crossed Parliament Square, I paused by the statue of Winston Churchill, one of Elizabeth II's heroes and her first prime minister. Her Majesty declined to unveil the statue in 1973, saying that honour should be given to Churchill's widow, but the Queen came to the unveiling and gave a speech in Churchill's praise, in which she revealed that he had turned down her offer of a dukedom because he had wanted to spend his remaining years as a member of the House of Commons.

Finally, I reached my destination, Westminster Abbey, where her funeral took place just ten days ago, where she was crowned on 6 June 1953. In her Coronation Day message, she said: 'I have in sincerity pledged myself to your service. Throughout all my life and with all my heart, I shall strive to be worthy of your trust.' And she was, for seventy years.

Since the coronation of William the Conqueror in 1066, all coronations of English and British monarchs have taken place in Westminster Abbey. Elizabeth II knew that her reign would not be like those of most of her predecessors. 'In the old days, the monarch led his soldiers on the battlefield,' she reflected in 1957, in her first televised Christmas broadcast. 'I cannot lead you into battle,' she said. 'I do not give you laws or administer justice, but I can do something else. I can give you my heart and my devotion to these old islands and all the peoples of our brotherhood of nations.'

In a way, Westminster Abbey tells our national story. Chaucer is buried here. Shakespeare and P. G. Wodehouse are honoured here. It is the final resting place of thirty of our Kings and Queens. The first king to be buried in the Abbey was Edward the Confessor in 1066. The last was George II in 1760. Richard II, Henry V, Elizabeth I, they all lie in Westminster Abbey.

Westminster Abbey is the church where the Queen came most often to distribute the Maundy money on Maundy Thursday – for her, one of the most important days in her calendar, the day commemorating Christ's *novum mandatum*: 'A new commandment I give you, that you love one another; even as I have loved you, that you also love one another.'

Westminster Abbey was important to Elizabeth II as an historic place of public worship, and it was important to her for private, personal reasons, too. Since 1100, sixteen royal weddings have taken place at the Abbey – including the Queen's parents' marriage in 1923 and her own to the Duke of Edinburgh in 1947.

You will recall that on her wedding day, the King, her father, George VI, had walked his Lilibet down the aisle, and had written a touching letter to her a few days later, while she was on her honeymoon:

I was so proud of you & thrilled at having you so close to me on our long walk in Westminster Abbey, but when I handed your hand to the Archbishop I felt that I had lost something very precious. You were so calm and composed during the Service & said your words with such conviction, that I knew everything was all right.

She was calm, she was composed, she said her words with such conviction. She was happy.

All these years later, we can see now that we, too, have lost something very precious, but please believe this: she would want you to know that everything is all right.

SOURCES & ACKNOWLEDGEMENTS

This book is based on the conversations I have had over many years with the multiplicity of people mentioned in the text, notably, of course, Her Majesty The Queen and His Royal Highness The Duke of Edinburgh, but scores of others, too: members of their families, members of their staff, their friends, biographers, historians, and others. Without them, there would have been no book. I am indebted to them all.

In the book I quote extensively from assorted diaries – briefly from those of 'Chips' Channon, 'Jock' Colville, Noël Coward, Harold Nicolson, Kenneth Rose, Roy Strong and Virginia Woolf – and, more extensively, from my own and, by kind permission, from those of Cecil Beaton and Alathea Fitzalan-Howard. I am especially grateful to my friend Merlin Holland for the use of the extracts from the unpublished diaries of his father, Vyvyan Holland, and for the extracts from his mother Thelma Besant's unpublished memoir. I am also indebted to the memoirs of Paul Burrell, Marion Crawford, Robin Dalton, John Dean, Anne Glenconner, Pamela Hicks and Ian Ogilvy, as detailed below, as well as William Shawcross's wonderful edition of the selected letters of Queen Elizabeth, the Queen Mother. My special thanks, too, to my friend Richard Harries, Lord Harries of Pentregarth, for the extract from his memoir set for publication in 2023. I also gratefully acknowledge the use of the lines from the song 'We Said We Wouldn't Look Back' from *Salad Days*, the 1954 musical by Dorothy Reynolds and Julian Slade.

I hope everything in the book is accurate and based on primary sources, but the blame for any errors of commission or omission should be laid at my door and no one else's.

Alice: Princess Andrew of Greece by Hugo Vickers, 2000

An Appreciation of Kurt Hahn, with a foreword by HRH The Duke of Edinburgh, 1975

The Asquiths by Colin Clifford, 2002

Charles by Anthony Holden, 1998

Charles, Prince of Wales by Anthony Holden, 1979

Cheam School from 1645 by Edward Peel, with a foreword by HRH The Duke of Edinburgh, 1974

Chips: The Diaries of Sir Henry Channon, edited by Robert Rhodes James, 1967

Counting One's Blessings: The Selected Letters of Queen Elizabeth, The Queen Mother, edited by William Shawcross, 2012

The Crown in Focus by Claudia Acott Williams, 2020

Daily Mirror interview with Norman Barson, 1996

Daily Telegraph interview with Sonia Berry by Cassandra Jardine, 2002

Daughter of Empire by Pamela Hicks, 2012

Dearest Child: Private Correspondence of Queen Victoria and the Crown Princess of Prussia, 1858–61, edited by Roger Fulford, 1964

The Duke: a portrait of Prince Philip by Tim Heald, 1991

Edward VII by Christopher Hibbert, 1976

Elizabeth by Sarah Bradford, 1996

Elizabeth R by Elizabeth Longford, 1983

Elizabeth: The Unseen Queen, BBC Studios documentary, produced and directed by Simon Finch, 2022

Elizabeth, The Woman and The Queen by Graham Turner, 2002

Elizabeth The Queen Mother by Grania Forbes, 2002

Elizabeth The Queen Mother by Hugo Vickers, 2005

Elizabeth Taylor's Kiss by David Wood, 2022

Feather from the Firebird by Sacha Abercorn, 2003

The Final Curtsey by Margaret Rhodes, 2012

Footprints in Time by John Colville, 1976

Friends, Enemies and Sovereigns by Sir John Wheeler-Bennett, 1976

The Fringes of Power: Downing Street Diaries 1939–1955 by John Colville, 1985

George V by Kenneth Rose, 1984

George V: Never a Dull Moment by Jane Ridley, 2021

George VI by Sarah Bradford, 1989

George VI: His Life and Reign by John Wheeler-Bennett, 1958

Harold Nicolson Diaries and Letters 1930–39, edited by Nigel Nicolson, 1966

The Heart Has Its Reasons by The Duchess of Windsor, 1956

A Horseman through Six Reigns: Reminiscences of a Royal Riding Master by Horace Smith, 1955

HRH Prince Philip, Duke of Edinburgh: A Portrait by John Dean, 1954

An Incidental Memoir by Robin Dalton, 1998

It Wasn't All Mayhem by Harry Hargreaves, 2004

Kings, Queens and Courtiers by Kenneth Rose, 1986

A King's Story by The Duke of Windsor, 1951

Kruschev Remembers, edited by Edward Crankshaw, 1971

Lady in Waiting by Anne Glenconner, 2019

Letters from a Prince: Edward Prince of Wales to Mrs Freda Dudley Ward, March 1918 – January 1921, edited by Rupert Godfrey, 1999

The Little Princesses by Marion Crawford, 1950

The Macmillan Diaries, 1950–57, edited by Peter Catterall, 2004

A Moment's Liberty: The Shorter Diary of Virginia Woolf, edited by Anne Olivier Bell, 1990

The Noël Coward Diaries, edited by Graham Payn and Sheridan Morley, 1982

Once a Saint by Ian Ogilvy, 2016

The Other Side of the Coin: The Queen, the Dresser and the Wardrobe by Angela Kelly, 2019

Our Queen by Robert Hardman, 2011

Philip & Elizabeth Portrait of a Marriage by Gyles Brandreth, 2004

Philip The Final Portrait by Gyles Brandreth, 2021

The Prince of Wales by Jonathan Dimbleby, 1995

The Queen by Ben Pimlott, 2001

The Queen: 50 Years – a celebration by Ronald Allison, 2001

A Queen for All Seasons by Joanna Lumley, 2021

Queen Mary and Others by Osbert Sitwell, 1974

Queen of Our Times by Robert Hardman, 2022

Queen of Tomorrow by Luis Wulff, 1949

The Queen's Speech by Ingrid Seward, 2012

The Real Elizabeth by Andrew Marr, 2012

Recollections of Three Reigns by Frederick Ponsonby, 1951

A Royal Duty by Paul Burrell, 2003

Royal: Her Majesty Queen Elizabeth II by Robert Lacey, 2002

A Royal Life by HRH The Duke of Kent and Hugo Vickers, 2022

Royal Orders: The Honours and the Honoured by Hugo Vickers, 1994

Royal Secrets by Stephen Barry, 1985

Royal Yacht Britannia: The Official History by Richard Johnstone-Bryden, 2003

The Shaping of a Soul: a life taken by surprise, Richard Harries, 2023

Silver and Gold by Norman Hartnell, 1955

Splendours and Miseries: The Roy Strong Diaries 1967–1987 by Roy Strong, 1997

Step Aside for Royalty by Eileen Parker, 1982

Thatched with Gold by Mabell, Countess of Airlie, 1962

Time and Chance by Peter Townsend, 1978

To Be a King: A Biography of HRH Prince Charles by Dermot Morrah, 1989

The Tongs and the Bones by The Earl of Harewood, 1981

Types and Shadows: The Roy Strong Diaries 2004–2015 by Roy Strong, 2020

The Unexpurgated Cecil Beaton Diaries by Cecil Beaton, 2003

Victoria R.I. by Elizabeth Longford, 1964

Wallis & Edward, Letters 1931–37, edited by Michael Bloch, 1986

The Wheel of Life, The Diary of Beatrice Webb, Vol. 4, 1924–43, edited by B. and J. Mackenzie, 1985

The Windsor Diaries by Alathea Fitzalan-Howard, 2021

Many people have been involved in the making of this book. My then agent, the late, great Ed Victor first suggested to me that I write *Philip & Elizabeth Portrait of a Marriage* more than twenty years ago. I am grateful to him and to Mark Booth, the original publisher of that book and its successor, *Philip The Final Portrait*, for their guidance and support. I am equally grateful (literally so: they take the same percentage) to my present agent, my friend Jonathan Lloyd, and to his colleagues at Curtis Brown.

I am also hugely grateful to my present publisher and friend Dan Bunyard and to his team at Penguin Michael Joseph for the skill, speed and care they have shown with the publication of this book in the aftermath of the Queen's death on 8 September 2022. The book would not have happened without the commitment and encouragement of Dan Bunyard and that of Beatrix McIntyre, Senior Editorial Manager at Michael Joseph, whose dedication, kindness and attention to detail have been appreciated by the author in equal measure.

It takes a village to publish a book and the Michael Joseph village is an especially inspiring one, led by Louise Moore, whose colleagues involved in this project have also included Ella-Aliisa Kurki, Paula Flanagan, Francisca Monteiro (who designed the picture plates), Lee Motley (who designed the cover), Alice Chandler (picture researcher), Nicola Evans and Nathalie Coupland (the in-house legal team), Deirdre O'Connell and Katie Corcoran (the principal sales directors for the book), Olivia Thomas, Gaby Young and Ciara Berry (Publicity), Sophie Shaw (Marketing), and Rachael Sharples and Jane Kirby (Rights). I am also grateful to Jill Cole, Sarah Bance and Eugenie Woodhouse for reading the proofs, and to my friend of many years, Rebecca Croft, for typing up the extracts from my diaries.

PICTURE CREDITS

1. Hughes & Mullins / Hulton Royals Collection via Getty Images
2. Hulton Archive / Hulton Royals Collection via Getty Images
3. Central Press / Hulton Royals Collection via Getty Images
4. PA Images / Alamy Stock Photo
5. Laing / Hulton Royals Collection via Getty Images
6. Classic Image / Alamy Stock Photo
7. Lisa Sheridan / Hulton Royals Collection via Getty Images
8. Lisa Sheridan / Hulton Royals Collection via Getty Images
9. Lisa Sheridan / Hulton Royals Collection via Getty Images
10. Central Press / Hulton Royals Collection via Getty Images
11. Pictorial Press Ltd / Alamy Stock Photo
12. Lisa Sheridan / Hulton Royals Collection via Getty Images
13. Popperfoto via Getty Images
14. Imperial War Museums via Getty Images
15. Bettmann via Getty Images
16. Granger - Historical Picture Archive / Alamy Stock Photo
17. SuperStock / Alamy Stock Photo
18. Topical Press Agency / Hulton Royals Collection via Getty Images
19. PA Images / Alamy Stock Photo
20. Hulton Deutsch / Corbis Historical via Getty Images
21. Keystone-France / Gamma-Keystone via Getty Images
22. Paul Popper / Popperfoto via Getty Images
23. Topical Press Agency / Hulton Royals Collection via Getty Images
24. Keystone / Hulton Archive via Getty Images
25. Fox Photos / Hulton Royals Collection via Getty Images
26. PA Images / Alamy Stock Photo
27. Pictorial Press Ltd / Alamy Stock Photo
28. Keystone / Hulton Royals Collection via Getty Images
29. Hulton Archive / Hulton Royals Collection via Getty Images
30. Fox Photos / Hulton Royals Collection via Getty Images
31. Keystone / Hulton Royals Collection via Getty Images
32. Hulton Archive / Hulton Royals Collection via Getty Images

33. Roger Jackson / Hulton Royals Collection via Getty Images
34. Trinity Mirror / Mirrorpix / Alamy Stock Photo
35. Lichfield / Lichfield Archive via Getty Images
36. Lichfield / Lichfield Archive via Getty Images
37. PA Images / Alamy Stock Photo
38. PA Images / Alamy Stock Photo
39. Trinity Mirror / Mirrorpix / Alamy Stock Photo
40. Anwar Hussein / Hulton Archive, via Getty Images
41. Bob Thomas / Popperfoto via Getty Images
42. Ron Bell, PA Images / Alamy Stock Photo
43. Tim Graham / Tim Graham Photo Library via Getty Images
44. PA Images / Alamy Stock Photo
45. Tim Graham / Tim Graham Photo Library via Getty Images
46. Tim Graham / Tim Graham Photo Library via Getty Images
47. John Stillwell / AFP via Getty Images
48. John Holborn, National Playing Fields Association
49. John Holborn, National Playing Fields Association
50. National Playing Fields Association
51. Wiltshire Herald & Gazette
52. Simon Kreitem, Reuters / Alamy Stock Photo
53. Tim Graham / Tim Graham Photo Library via Getty Images
54. Odd Andersen / AFP via Getty Images
55. Tim Graham / Tim Graham Photo Library via Getty Images
56. Tim Graham, PA Images / Alamy Stock Photo
57. WENN Rights Ltd / Alamy Stock Photo
58. John Stillwell / AFP via Getty Images
59. Mark Cuthbert / UK Press via Getty Images
60. Samir Hussein / WireImage via Getty Images
61. WPA Pool / Getty Images Entertainment via Getty Images
62. Chris Jackson / Chris Jackson Collection via Getty Images
63. Jamie Lorriman / AFP via Getty Images
64. Chris Jackson / Chris Jackson Collection via Getty Images
65. Jane Barlow / Contributor, AFP via Getty Images
66. Karwai Tang / WireImage via Getty Images
67. Paul Marriott / Alamy Stock Photo